REPARATIONS FOR CHILD VICTIMS OF ARMED CONFLICT

SERIES ON TRANSITIONAL JUSTICE

The Series on *Transitional Justice* offers a platform for high-quality research within the rapidly growing field of transitional justice. The research is, of necessity inter-disciplinary in nature, drawing from disciplines such as law, political science, history, sociology, criminology, anthropology and psychology, as well as from various specialised fields of study such as human rights, victimology and peace studies. Furthermore, the research is international in outlook, drawing on the knowledge and experience of academics and other specialists in many different regions of the world.

The series is aimed at a variety of audiences who are either working or interested in fields such as crime and justice; human rights; humanitarian law and human security; conflict resolution and peace building. These audiences include academics, researchers, students, policy makers, practitioners, non-governmental organisations and the media.

All books published within the series are subject to a double-blind peer review by recognised authorities in the field.

The General Editors of the Series are:
- Prof. Stephan Parmentier (Catholic University of Leuven, Belgium)
- Prof. Jeremy Sarkin (University of South Africa)
- Prof. Elmar Weitekamp (University of Tübingen, Germany)
- Mina Rauschenbach (Université de Lausanne and University of Leuven) (Assistant Editor)

The general editors receive the support from an Editorial Committee and an Advisory Board, consisting of internationally renowned academics and practitioners.

Published titles within this Series:

8. Nicola Palmer, Phil Clark and Danielle Granville (chief editors), *Critical Perspectives in Transitional Justice* (2011), 978-1-78068-035-4
9. Edda Kristjánsdóttir, André Nollkaemper and Cedric Ryngaert (eds.), *International Law in Domestic Courts: Rule of Law Reform in Post-conflict States* (2012), 978-1-78068-041-5
10. Bas van Stokkom, Neelke Doorn and Paul van Tongeren (eds.), *Public Forgiveness in Post-Conflict Contexts* (2012), 978-1-78068-044-6
11. Ilse Derluyn, Cindy Mels, Stephan Parmentier and Wouter Vandenhole (eds.), *Re-Member. Rehabilitation, Reintegration and Reconciliation of War-Affected Children* (2012), 97894-000-0027-4
12. Anne-Marie de Brouwer, Charlotte Ku, Renée Römkens and Larissa van den Herik (eds.), *Sexual Violence as an International Crime: Interdisciplinary Approaches* (2012), 978-1-78068-002-6
13. Estelle Zinsstag and Martha Albertson Fineman (eds.), *Feminist Perspectives on Transitional Justice: From International and Criminal to Alternative Forms of Justice* (2013), 978-1-78068-142-9
14. Josep M. Tamarit Sumalla, *Historical Memory and Criminal Justice in Spain. A Case of Late Transitional Justice* (2013), 978-1-78068-143-6
15. Catherine Jenkins (ed.), Max du Plessis (ed.), *Law, Nation building and Transformation The South African experience in perspective* (2014), 978-1-78068-184-9
16. Susanne Buckley-Zistel and Stefanie Schäfer (eds.), *Memorials in Times of Transition* (2014), 978-1-78068-211-2
17. Nico Wouters (ed.), *Transitional Justice and Memory in Europe (1945–2013)*, 978-1-78068-214-3
18. Agata Fijalkowski and Raluca Grosescu (eds.), *Transitional Criminal Justice in Post- Dictatorial and Post-Conflict Societies*, 978-1-78068-260-0
19. S. Elizabeth Bird and Fraser M. Ottanelli (eds.), *The Performance of Memory as Transitional Justice* 978-1-78068-262-4
20. Bo Viktor Nylund, *Child Soldiers and Transitional Justice*, 978-1-78068-394-2
21. Peter Malcontent (ed.), *Facing the Past: Amending Historical Injustices through Instruments of Transitional Justice*, 978-1-78068-403-1

For previous volume in the series, please visit http://tj.intersentia.com

Series on Transitional Justice, Volume 22

REPARATIONS FOR CHILD VICTIMS OF ARMED CONFLICT

State of the Field and Current Challenges

Francesca Capone

intersentia

Cambridge – Antwerp – Portland

Intersentia Ltd
Sheraton House | Castle Park
Cambridge | CB3 0AX | United Kingdom
Tel.: +44 1223 370 170 | Fax: +44 1223 370 169
Email: mail@intersentia.co.uk
www.intersentia.com | www.intersentia.co.uk

Distribution for the UK and Ireland:
NBN International
Airport Business Centre, 10 Thornbury Road
Plymouth, PL6 7 PP
United Kingdom
Tel.: +44 1752 202 301 | Fax: +44 1752 202 331
Email: orders@nbninternational.com

Distribution for Europe and all other countries:
Intersentia Publishing nv
Groenstraat 31
2640 Mortsel
Belgium
Tel.: +32 3 680 15 50 | Fax: +32 3 658 71 21
Email: mail@intersentia.be

Distribution for the USA and Canada:
International Specialized Book Services
920 NE 58th Ave. Suite 300
Portland, OR 97213
USA
Tel.: +1 800 944 6190 (toll free) | Fax: +1 503 280 8832
Email: info@isbs.com

Artwork on cover: Author Jan Jordaan, title 'Hurt', medium Linocut, 1999. From the *Universal Declaration of Human Rights – International Print Portfolio*, Article 5, published by Art for Humanity, South Africa, 1999.

ISBN 978-1-78068-438-3
D/2017/7849/20
NUR 828

British Library Cataloguing in Publication Data. A catalogue record for this book is available from the British Library.

To my beloved grandmothers, Rosaria and Iole

FOREWORD

As properly noted in this scholarly work, in situations of armed conflict, children are not merely bystanders but targets and direct victims. In fact, children are disproportionally affected by war. It is against this background that Francesca Capone applied her research capacity by exploring a broad range of issues relating to reparations for child victims of armed conflict. This book follows the perception, already asserted in the Universal Declaration of Human Rights and affirmed in the United Nations Convention on the Rights of the Child, that childhood is entitled to special care and assistance, including legal protection. A special feature requiring full attention and also covered in this book is the intricate question of recruitment of children into armed forces and armed groups, raising issues of the victim-perpetrator dichotomy and the reintegration of child soldiers into national and local society.

A core element obvious from the title is the victim's right to remedies which includes – as spelled out in the UN Basic Principles and Guidelines on the Right to a Remedy and Reparation for Victims of Gross Violations of International Human Rights Law and Serious Violations of International Humanitarian Law – equal and effective access to justice, adequate, effective and prompt reparation for harm suffered, and access to relevant information concerning violations and reparation mechanisms. The Basic Principles and Guidelines have been playing, in the ten years since their adoption by the UN General Assembly, an important role in setting into motion a better understanding of the right to reparation and in providing guidance in this area, as evident in the increasing reference made to this document in the jurisprudence of judicial and quasi-judicial bodies such as those functioning in the Inter-American human rights protection system, the International Criminal Court and its Trust Fund for Victims. At the same time the law and practice of reparations faces intricate challenges requiring new and innovative responses. This applies in particular to means and methods of repairing harm suffered by juvenile victims in terms of their past, present and future life situations in their communities. One such issue discussed in depth in this book relates to the transformative potential of reparations so as to broaden the effective reach of reparations to encounter not only the consequences of violations but also their structural causes. In this perspective as correctly analyzed in this book, reparations should not necessarily aim at serving traditional patterns of restoration or return to the *status quo ante* but rather other reparational designs which fall in the categories of rehabilitation, satisfaction or guarantee of non-repetition. For instance, education and training may have a welcome transformative impact on the lives of child victims. Another important issue brought to the fore by Francesca Capone is the question of the relationship between reparation compared with assistance or development. It may be expeditious to make a shift from reparation to development because such an approach avoids complex issues of accountability as well as troublesome classifications of people into victims and perpetrators. But as argued in this book a distinction has to be made between the entitlement to reparation for harm suffered by victims and more generally the entitlement to basic rights and relief of citizens. Assistance and development measures should not serve as a substitute for reparations.

Civilian populations, notably women and children as particularly vulnerable people in situations of armed conflict, are to a greater extent affected in intra-state or non-international armed conflicts than in traditional inter-state conflicts. In the latter type state dimensions and interests tend to prevail. For long international law was not victim-oriented anyway. A leading motive of this study carried out with precision and persuasion is the design of transitional justice processes in law and practice. In many situations the plight of victims and for that matter the plight of child victims in armed conflicts happens to be ignored as inopportune and inconvenient. While relevant international legal framework and applicable mechanisms are developing as part of the process of an assumed humanization of international law, major complexities and shortcomings still abound. One such complex issue of a legal nature concerns the status of non-state actors, in particular armed non-state entities. Recent and current monitoring and reporting mechanisms progressively work on the assumption that fundamental human rights and humanitarian law standards apply to all actors in all circumstances. Reports of the UN Independent International Commission of Inquiry on the Syrian Arab Republic follow this line and confirm this principle in keeping with various other monitoring mechanisms on armed conflict situations.

This book with its focus on reparations for child victims of armed conflict is timely and pertinent. Building on innovative jurisprudence and conclusions of international judicial and quasi-judicial organs and monitoring bodies, but also clearly indicating major shortcomings in law and practice, this study presents challenges and offers perspectives and ouvertures for the rehabilitation and social reintegration of child victims of armed conflict. This work is highly commended as a valid source of reference and an effective tool of orientation, inspiration and guidance.

Theo van Boven

Former UN Special Rapporteur on the Right to Reparation for Victims of Gross Violations of Human Rights and Professor Emeritus of International Law at the University of Maastricht.

ABOUT THE AUTHOR

Francesca Capone is a Research Fellow in public international law at the Scuola Superiore Sant'Anna and the Coordinator of the Masters Programme in Human Rights and Conflict Management. She is also a lecturer, both at undergraduate and postgraduate level, in human rights law, international criminal law, children's rights and transitional justice.

Francesca Capone gained her law degree from the University of Naples Federico II in 2008 and a joint Ph.D. from the Scuola Superiore Sant'Anna and Tilburg University in 2013.

From June 2012 to October 2013 Francesca Capone was a Research Fellow at the British Institute of International and Comparative Law, where she worked on a project on reparations for education-related violations of international law. She has been a visiting fellow at several academic institutions, including Tilburg University, Leiden University and the Max Planck Institute for Comparative Public Law and International Law. She is the author of several articles and book chapters and in 2016 she co-edited, with Professor Andrea de Guttry and Dr Christophe Paulussen, a volume entitled *Foreign Fighters under International Law and Beyond* (Asser Press/Springer).

ACKNOWLEDGEMENTS

This book is the final outcome of a Joint Ph.D. degree earned from the Scuola Superiore Sant'Anna and Tilburg University. I was lucky enough to be supervised by two brilliant scholars, Professor Rianne Letschert and Professor Andrea de Guttry, who supported me throughout the whole process, from the selection of the topic to the completion of the thesis and its defence. I am most grateful to both of them for their professionalism and kindness, I could not have hoped for a better combination of personalities and competences.

I wish to thank the members of the Ph.D. Committee in Tilburg, in particular Professor Theo van Boven whose work has had a profound impact on my understanding of victims' rights and needs, for their constructive feedback and challenging questions, I will always remember the day of my Ph.D. defence as one of the most beautiful and happy moments of my life.

My gratitude goes to the editors of the Intersentia Series on Transitional Justice, Professor Stephan Parmentier, Professor Jeremy Sarkin and Professor Elmar Weitekamp for their valuable comments and the guidance provided. I also wish to thank the two anonymous reviewers who helped me transform my thesis into a book, it was a very stimulating process and I could not have done it without them. I am also grateful to Ms Anna Riddell for her help with the linguistic review of this book and for agreeing to lend a hand to a friend on such short notice!

My passion for international law started back in 2006 at the University of Naples Federico II and I am profoundly indebted to Professor Massimo Iovane, Professor Fulvio Palombino and Professor Daniele Amoroso for their friendship and guidance throughout all these years.

I wish to thank my mom, my dad and my two incredibly talented brothers for their support and endless care. I was raised in the most amazing family and my love for all of them continues to grow with each passing day. Finally, my utmost gratitude goes to Filippo for his patience, love and encouragement when I was tired, sad and incapable of concentrating; thank you for always standing by my side and for pushing me to follow my dreams wherever they may lead.

CONTENTS

TABLE OF CASES

International Criminal Court

International Court of Justice

International Criminal Tribunal for Rwanda

International Criminal Tribunal for the Former Yugoslavia

Permanent Court of International Justice

Special Court for Sierra Leone

TABLE OF INTERNATIONAL INSTRUMENTS

INTERNATIONAL TREATIES

HUMAN RIGHTS TREATY BODIES

UN GENERAL ASSEMBLY

UN SECURITY COUNCIL

OTHERS

LIST OF ABBREVIATIONS

ACHR	American Convention on Human Rights
ACHPR	African Charter on Human and Peoples' Rights
ACJHR	African Court of Justice and Human Rights
ACRWC	African Charter on the Rights and Welfare of the Child
ACtHPR	African Court on Human and Peoples' Rights
ANSA	Armed Non-State Actor
AOG	Armed Organised Group
AP ACHR	Additional Protocol to American Convention
AU	African Union
AUC	Autodefensas Unidas de Colombia
CABAC	Children Affected by Armed Conflict
CAFF	Children Associated with Fighting Forces
CAP	Conflict-Affected Person
CAT	Convention against Torture and Other Cruel, Inhuman or Degrading Treatment or Punishment
CAVR	Commission for Reception, Truth and Reconciliation in Timor-Leste
CDF	Civil Defence Force
CEDAW	United Nations Convention on the Elimination of All Forms of Discrimination Against Women
CEJIL	Centre for Justice and International Law
CERD	Committee on the Elimination of All Forms of Racial Discrimination
CESCR	Committee on International Economic, Social and Cultural Rights
CoID	Commission of Inquiry on the Disappearances
CPA	Comprehensive Peace Agreement
CRC	Convention on the Rights of the Child
CRC-OP3	Convention on the Rights of the Child-Optional Protocol 3
CRPD	Convention on the Rights of Persons with Disabilities
CVR	Comisión de la Verdad y Reconciliación
DDR	Disarmament Demobilization and Reintegration
DDRR	Disarmament Demobilization Reintegration and Rehabilitation
DRC	Democratic Republic of the Congo
EAC	East Africa Community

ECCC	Extraordinary Chambers in the Courts of Cambodia
ECHR	European Convention on Human Rights
ECOMOG	Economic Community of West African States Military Observer Group
ECOSOC	United Nations Economic and Social Council
ECOWAS	Economic Community Of West African States
ECtHR	European Court of Human Rights
EECC	Eritrea-Ethiopia Claims Commission
EU	European Union
FARC-EP	Fuerzas Armadas Revolucionarias de Colombia-Ejército del Pueblo
FSA	Free Syrian Army
GLB	Girls Left Behind
HRC	United Nations Human Rights Committee
HRW	Human Rights Watch
IAC	International armed conflict
IACHR	Inter-American Commission on Human Rights
IACtHR	Inter-American Court of Human Rights
ICC	International Criminal Court
ICCPR	International Covenant on Civil and Political Rights
ICCs	Interim Care Centres
ICESCR	International Covenant on Economic, Social and Cultural Rights
ICJ	International Court of Justice
ICL	International Criminal Law
ICRC	International Committee of the Red Cross
ICTJ	International Centre for Transitional Justice
ICTR	International Criminal Tribunal for Rwanda
ICTY	International Criminal Tribunal for the Former Yugoslavia
IDPs	Internally Displaced Persons
IHL	International Humanitarian Law
IHRL	International Human Rights Law
ILA	International Law Association
ILC	International Law Commission
ILO	International Labour Organization
IRP	Interim Relief Program
ISIL	Islamic State of Iraq and the Levant
ISIS	Islamic State of Iraq and Syria
JA	Jewish Agency
JDC	Joint Distribution Committee
JPL	Justice and Peace Law
JRSO	Jewish Relief Survivor Organisation
LRA	Lord's Resistance Army

MACR	Minimum Age of Criminal Responsibility
MoPR	Ministry of Peace and Reconstruction
MRM	Monitoring and Reporting Mechanism
NaCSA	National Commission for Social Action
NGO	Non-Governmental Organisation
NIAC	Non-international armed conflict
NSAG	Non-State Armed Group
OAS	Organisation of American States
OAU	Organisation of African Unity
OHCHR	Office of the United Nations High Commissioner for Human Rights
OPCV	Office of Public Council for Victims
OSRSG-CAAC	Office of the Special Representative of the Secretary-General on Children and Armed Conflict
PCIJ	Permanent Court of International Justice
PIR	Plan Integral de Reparaciones
POW	Prisoner of War
ROP	Reintegration Opportunity Programme
RPE	Rules of Procedure and Evidence
SADC	Southern African Development Community
SCSL	Special Court for Sierra Leone
SBU	Small Boys Unit
SGBV	Sexual and gender-based violence
SGU	Small Girls Unit
STL	Special Tribunal for Lebanon
TC	Truth Commission
TFV	Trust Fund for Victims
TJRC	Truth, Justice and Reconciliation Commission
TRC	Truth and Reconciliation Commission
TSA	Transition Support Allowance
UDHR	Universal Declaration of Human Rights
UN	United Nations
UNAMI	United Nations Assistance Mission for Iraq
UNAMSIL	United Nations Mission in Sierra Leone
UNBPG	United Nations Basic Principles and Guidelines on the Right to a Remedy and Reparations for Victims of Gross Violations of International Human Rights and Serious Violations of International Humanitarian Law
UNCC	United Nations Compensation Commission
UNESCO	United Nations Educational, Scientific and Cultural Organization
UNGA	General Assembly of the United Nations
UNGA Res	United Nations General Assembly Resolution

UNHCR	United Nations High Commission for Refugees
UNICEF	United Nations International Children's Economic Foundation
UNMIL	United Nations Mission in Liberia
UNSC	United Nations Security Council
UNSG	United Nations Secretary-General
VPRS	Victims Participation and Reparation Section
VWU	Victims and Witnesses Unit
WHO	World Health Organization
WVSU	Witnesses and Victims Services Unit

CHAPTER 1
SETTING THE SCENE

1.1. CHILDREN AND REPARATIONS: TOGETHER UNDER THE SPOTLIGHT

According to Tomuschat few would argue that persons suffering a grave breach of their human rights should not have a right to full reparation;[1] even fewer would affirm that children should not be awarded adequate, prompt and effective reparations for the harm suffered, especially as a result of violations perpetrated during or in the aftermath of armed conflict, when children are particularly vulnerable and, thus, overexposed to victimisation. Since the approval, in 2005, by the UN General Assembly ('General Assembly') of the Basic Principles and Guidelines on the Right to a Remedy and Reparation for Victims of Gross Violations of International Human Rights and Serious Violations of International Humanitarian Law ('Basic Principles and Guidelines' or 'UNBPG') much emphasis has been placed on the existence of individuals' reparation claims under international law. Moreover, thanks to the innovative character of the Basic Principles and Guidelines, collective and symbolic reparations have finally also been given proper consideration.[2] Reparation has been accepted as a term with a well-established legal meaning, which refers both to the obligation to repair and the right to claim and obtain redress. According to Redress, 'reparation' comprises 'the wide range of measures that may be taken in response to an actual or threatened violation, including the substance of the relief as well as the procedure to attain it'.[3] Under international law the forms of reparation identified are restitution, compensation and satisfaction. Within the human rights framework rehabilitation and guarantees of non-repetition are also included among the kinds of reparation available for the victims.[4]

---

1 C. Tomuschat, 'Reparation for Victims of Grave Human Rights Violations', (2002) 10 *Tulane Journal of International and Comparative Law* 157, at 157–159.

2 UN General Assembly, Basic Principles and Guidelines on the Right to a Remedy and Reparation for Victims of Gross Violations of International Human Rights Law and Serious Violations of International Humanitarian Law, 21 March 2006, UN doc. A/RES/60/147.

3 See Redress, 'A Sourcebook for Victims of Torture and Other Violations of Human Rights and International Humanitarian Law', 2003, available at: http://www.redress.org/downloads/publications/SourceBook.pdf.

4 See the UNBPG above note 2.

Thus far international institutions, such as the Inter-American Court of Human Rights ('IACtHR'), have mostly focused on reparations awarded in the aftermath of gross human rights violations.[5] The role played by regional human rights bodies, in particular by the IACtHR, has been essential for the development of an innovative and forward-looking approach to reparation, especially in the aftermath of mass-scale violations of human rights.[6] The legal consequences arising from gross violations of international human rights law ('IHRL') and serious violations of international humanitarian law ('IHL'), which, under certain circumstances,[7] may constitute crimes under international law, are very specific: universal jurisdiction, the non-applicability of statutes of limitations, and, in particular, the right to a judicial remedy.[8] From the mid-twentieth century to the present, wars,[9] insurgencies, ethnic unrest and the repressive actions of authoritarian regimes have produced enormous human suffering and the deaths of tens of millions, the majority of whom have been

---

5 In its judgments the IACtHR refers to 'reparations'. The recourse to the plural, which is often used to allude to national administrative programmes, highlights the Court's tendency to award many forms of redress, ranging from material to symbolic reparation.

6 On the IACtHR jurisprudence in general, see L. Burgorgue-Larsen and A. Ubeda de Torres, *The Inter American Court of Human Rights: Case Law and Commentary*, Oxford University Press, Oxford, 2011. With regard to violations against children, see M. Feria Tinta, *The Landmark Rulings of the Inter American Court of Human Rights on the Rights of the Child*, Martinus Nijhoff Publishers, Leiden, 2008.

7 As stated in the Report of the International Commission of Inquiry on Darfur to the United Nations Secretary-General 'serious violations of human rights law and humanitarian law may amount to international crimes, subject to the conditions set out by the ICTY in *Tadić* and largely codified in the ICC Statute'. The conditions identified by the ICTY in the *Tadić case* are four, namely the violation must constitute an infringement of a rule of international humanitarian law; the rule must be customary in nature or, if it belongs to treaty law, the treaty must be applicable to the concrete case; the violation must be 'serious' in the sense that it must constitute a breach of a rule protecting important values and the breach must involve grave consequences for the victim; the violation of the rule must entail, under customary or conventional law, the individual criminal responsibility of the person breaching the rule. Judgment of 2 October 1995 (Decision on the Defence Motion for Interlocutory Appeal on Jurisdiction), (1995) ICTY, Case No. IT-94-1-AR72, §94. See also *Report of the International Commission of Inquiry on Darfur to the United Nations Secretary-General Pursuant to Security Council Resolution 1564 of 18 September 2004*, §175.

8 See C.J. Tams, *Enforcing Obligations Erga Omnes in International Law*, Cambridge University Press, Cambridge, 2005; see also M.C. Bassiouni (ed.), *International Criminal Law* 3rd edn., Martinus Nijhoff Publishers, Leiden, 2008. See also Redress, 'A Handbook on the Basic Principles and Guidelines on the Right to a Remedy and Reparation', March 2006, available at: http://www.redress.org/downloads/publications/Reparation%20Principles.pdf.

9 L. Harbom, E. Melander and P. Wallensteen, 'Dyadic Dimensions of Armed Conflict, 1946–2007', (2008) 45 *Journal of Peace Research* 697, at 700–710. According to the authors there has not been a single war since 1945, although there have been more than 232 armed conflicts. The difference between 'war' and 'armed conflict' lies in the fact that the state and condition of 'war' is created by means of a formal declaration, whereas the State and condition of 'armed conflict' is created by means of an informal declaration. Bearing in mind the distinction, in the course of the present work the terms may be used interchangeably.

civilians.[10] A consistent proportion of those civilians killed or injured are children. According to the United Nations Children's Fund ('UNICEF') in 2014 as many as 15 million children have been caught up in violent conflicts in the Central African Republic, Iraq, South Sudan, the State of Palestine, Syria and Ukraine, including those internally displaced or living as refugees. Globally, an estimated 230 million children currently live in countries and areas affected by armed conflicts.[11]

This large group of children can be defined as 'children affected by armed conflict'.[12] An important caveat is needed from the outset: in the case of armed conflict the whole population is potentially affected, however, from a legal point of view, there is a difference between those who have been affected and those who have experienced IHL and IHRL violations.[13] Only those who have suffered direct or indirect harm as a result of acts or omissions that amount to a violation of international law can be recognised as victims and are consequently entitled to claim for reparation. In a background report prepared by the International Law Association ('ILA') Committee on Compensation for Victims of War[14] it has been highlighted that, according to some authors,[15] the requirement of a violation of humanitarian law or human rights law in the definition of the victim, as presupposed by the term 'reparation', might lead to injustices in practice. Gillard suggested the possibility of avoiding these problems 'by having recourse to a wide definition of victims so as to include all persons adversely affected by a conflict or another wide test such as the violation of *jus ad bellum*'.[16] The point

---

10 M.C. Bassiouni, 'Facing Atrocity: The Importance of Guiding Principles on Post-conflict Justice', *Introduction to the Chicago Principles on Post-conflict Justice*, International Human Rights Institute, Chicago, 2007.

11 UNICEF, 'Children and Emergencies in 2014, Facts and Figures', available at http://www.unicef.org/media/files/UNICEF_Children_and_Emergencies_2014_fact_sheet.pdf. See the Annual Report of the Secretary-General on Children and Armed Conflict, 5 June 2015, UN doc. A/69/926–S/2015/409.

12 Children affected by armed conflict ('CABAC') is a very broad category referring to the various groups of children that are adversely affected by armed conflict. There is no single universally agreed upon definition of the term, which has been used in various ways. See International Committee of the Red Cross, Workshop Report, 'Children Affected by Armed Conflict and other Situations of Violence', Geneva, March 2011, available at: https://www.icrc.org/eng/assets/files/publications/icrc-002-4082.pdf.

13 In a judgment issued on 29 November 2002 the Dutch Supreme Court decided that rules of IHL do not protect persons against stresses and tensions that are consequences of air strikes as such and do not protect persons with regard to whom the rules and norms have not been violated *in concreto*. The right to invoke the rules of IHL is therefore confined to those who personally were the victims of violations of IHL. See L. Zegveld, 'Remedies for Victims of Violations of International Humanitarian Law', (2003) 85 *International Review of the Red Cross* 497, at 501–502.

14 ILA Committee on Compensation for Victims of War, Background Report prepared by R. Hofmann and F. Riemann, 17 March 2004, at 6.

15 See E.C. Gillard, 'Reparations for Violations of International Humanitarian Law', (2003) 85 International Review of the Red Cross 529, at 551.

16 Ibidem.

raised is certainly valid, but it contradicts some fundamental legal principles that cannot be ignored while determining who is a 'victim' in a judicial context. However, as this book will argue, the concept of 'victims' is much broader in non-judicial settings, where the terms 'child victims' and 'children affected by armed conflict' tend to overlap. In fact, as stressed by the ILC in the Commentary to its Articles on State Responsibility 'the requirement of a causal link *is not necessarily the same* in relation to every breach of an international obligation'.[17] The degree of connection thus may vary depending upon the nature of the claim and other circumstances, including the setting where the reparation claim is brought.[18]

As the 'new wars'[19] or 'dirty wars' have gradually subverted the traditional understanding of armed conflicts as inter-State conflicts, the current warfare 'arises from the political failure of the State and the disintegration of state institutional structures'.[20] Since new wars take place within States instead of between States the result is that children are no longer the passive bystanders of armed conflicts: they have become the target of atrocities or have been forced to turn themselves into perpetrators. More and more children on a daily basis experience gross human rights violations and/or serious violations of humanitarian law. Being victims of such violations entails three different remedies in the aftermath of conflicts, namely the right to know, the right to access justice and the right to reparation, the latter representing the focus of the present work.[21]

The study of those remedies, provided by public international law, involves different actors. On the one side stand the victims, individuals or groups entitled to reparation; on the other side stand the subjects in charge of providing redress; these are perpetrators, individuals and members of non-State entities, States and their agents, alternative mechanisms such as Truth Commissions ('TCs'), trust funds and administrative reparations programmes.[22] Reparations can

---

17 See Articles on Responsibility of States for Internationally Wrongful Acts (with commentaries), *Yearbook of the International Law Commission*, 2001, vol. II, Part II, at 93 (emphasis added).

18 Declaration of International Law Principles for Victims of Armed Conflict at the 74th ILA Conference, The Hague, Resolution 2/2010, at 11.

19 See in general M. Kaldor, *New and Old Wars: Organised Violence in a Global Era*, Polity Press, Cambridge, 2006.

20 See M. Drumbl, *Reimagining Child Soldiers in International Law and Policy*, Oxford University Press, Oxford, 2012, 41.

21 These are the remedies traditionally identified for violations of international human rights law. See in general D. Shelton, *Remedies in International Human Rights Law*, 2nd edn., Oxford University Press, New York, 2005.

22 On States as subjects responsible for awarding reparations, see D. Shelton, 'The UN Principles and Guidelines on Reparation: Contest and Contents', in K. De Feyter, S. Parmentier, M. Bossuyt and P. Lemmens (eds.), *Out of the Ashes: Reparations for Victims of Gross and Systematic Human Rights Violations*, Intersentia, Antwerp, 2005, 11, at 22: 'The State is responsible for providing reparation for its acts or omissions constituting violations within the scope of the Basic Principles and Guidelines. In cases where a non-State actor is responsible for the violation, liability should be imposed if possible and the State should

be awarded as the outcome of a criminal proceeding, or they can be part of a broader strategy within a State to acknowledge the victimisation and encourage reconciliation and peace in the aftermath of a conflict. The latter presupposes the involvement of the victims in the decision-making process and in all the stages of the reparation programme adopted.[23]

While both the theory and practice of the right to reparation have been steadily developing, there has been limited concern about children's access to and enjoyment of the redress measures awarded by the relevant actors involved in the reparations discourse. Bearing in mind that children, in particular child victims of war, are not adults in miniature, but human beings with specific needs, it is necessary to investigate the extent to which the current international law framework governing the right to reparation is able to provide child victims of armed conflict with measures that are adequate, prompt and effective.

1.2. GENERAL OVERVIEW OF THE KEY ISSUES AT STAKE

It is a truism that the issue of reparation for individual victims has finally gained momentum and important milestones have marked this long pattern, including the decision on reparations in the *Lubanga* case, issued by the International Criminal Court's ('ICC') Trial Chamber I in 2012 and amended by the Appeals Chamber on 3 March 2015, which has singled out the principles that will be applied by the Court to provide redress to the victims of the crimes committed by Mr Thomas Lubanga Dyilo.[24] In the past years the right to reparation has been periodically commented on and scrutinised, both at the domestic and at the international level,[25] especially since its enhancement can be instrumental in

---

enforce any judgment for reparation against individuals or entities held responsible'. As for the TCs, commonly their role is to provide States with recommendations, which also include reparations policy, but, as will be further explained and discussed, some TCs, e.g. the South African TC, have an *ad hoc* Reparation Committee explicitly charged with restoring victims' dignity. On this point see Chapter 7 of this book. See also R. Falk, 'Reparations, International Law, and Global Justice: A New Frontier', in P. de Greiff (ed.), *The Handbook of Reparations*, Oxford University Press, New York, 2006, 478, at 478–504.

23 P. de Greiff, *The UN Rule of Law Tools for Post-Conflict States*, OHCHR, 2008, at 3. De Greiff underlines the difference between 'reparation efforts' and 'reparation programmes' by stating that 'This publication distinguishes between reparations "efforts" and "programs". The latter should be reserved to designate initiatives that are designed from the outset as a systematically interlinked set of reparations measures. Most countries do not have reparations programs in this sense. Reparations benefits are most often the result of discrete initiatives that come about incrementally rather than from a deliberately designed plan.'

24 Decision of 7 August 2012, (Decision Establishing the Principles and Procedures to be Applied to Reparations), (2012) ICC (Trial Chamber I), Case No. ICC-01/04-01/06-2904.

25 The adoption by the UN General Assembly of the UNBPG is the result of a growing interest in victims' rights.

the promotion of a victim-oriented approach before courts and within the States' decision-making processes concerning the transition from conflict to peace. At this point in time it is quite trivial to affirm that the right to a remedy and reparation constitutes part of international law, as it is embedded in regional and global human rights treaties, in humanitarian law, international criminal law and the law of State responsibility.[26] Nevertheless, the efforts made to concretely apply these provisions are still far from being satisfactory. There is a significant lacuna between the normative framework and the concrete assessment of victims' needs, and a consistent gap between the needs' assessment and the efforts put into practice by the actors responsible for awarding reparations to the victims.[27]

The situation becomes even more complicated when it comes to children. As human beings, they are entitled to the fundamental rights embodied in the Universal Declaration of Human Rights ('UDHR'), the International Covenant on Civil and Political Rights ('ICCPR') and the International Covenant on Economic, Social and Cultural Rights ('ICESCR'). In particular Article 2(3) of the ICCPR sets forth States' obligations to provide each person whose rights have been violated with an effective remedy, promptly enforced by the authorities when awarded.[28] Children first and foremost benefit from the protection granted to them by the Convention on the Rights of the Child ('CRC'), the most comprehensive and exhaustive body of children's rights, which has been universally ratified with the exception of only one country.[29] Within the African human rights system a specific instrument focusing on children's rights was adopted in 1990, i.e. the African Charter on the Rights and Welfare of the Child ('ACRWC').[30] The ACRWC post-dates the adoption of the CRC. The two documents share a number of elements, including a wide range of civil, political, economic, social and cultural rights, the principles of non-discrimination and best interests, an emphasis on the right to the life, survival

26 See Shelton, above note 22.

27 On this point see Falk above note 22, at 491, 'As the 2004 Advisory Opinion on the legal status of the Israeli security wall clearly reaffirmed, there does exist in international law a well-established entitlement for the victim of legal wrongs to appropriate reparations. But between the affirmation of the legal right/duty and its satisfaction there exists a huge conceptual gap'. See also J. Sarkin, 'Reparations for Gross Human Rights Violations as an Outcome of Criminal versus Civil Court Proceedings', in De Feyter et al., above note 22, at 151.

28 See Art. 2(3) of the ICCPR, 16 December 1966, entered into force on 23 March 1976, UNTS, vol. 999, p. 171.

29 CRC, 20 November 1989, entered into force on 2 September 1990, UNTS, vol. 1577, p. 3. The only country worldwide that has not ratified the CRC is the USA. Somalia and South Sudan were the last two countries to ratify the Convention, on 20 January and 4 May 2015 respectively.

30 ACRWC, 11 July 1990, entered into force on 29 November 1999, CAB/LEG/24.9/49. For a discussion about the ACRWC see D. Chirwa, 'The Merits and Demerits of the African Charter', (2002) 10 *International Journal of Children's Rights* 157.

and development of the child, and participation rights.[31] Moreover, both the CRC and the ACRWC contain a specific provision on children in armed conflicts.[32] Children 'in war' also enjoy the safeguards provided by IHL, either as civilians or as persons taking part in the hostilities.[33] Furthermore, in international law there are specific treaties which recognise children's particular vulnerability as girls or children affected by disabilities.[34] What is missing in the existing legal framework is a substantial effort to guarantee and provide effective reparations to child victims, who have specific characteristics and needs. It feels, indeed, as if these two 'worlds' – child victims of armed conflict and reparations – albeit recently objects of extensive discussions and debates, have not yet 'met'. Despite the widespread recognition of the impact that reparations, if adequately awarded to the youngest members of a war-torn community, can have, especially in terms of prevention, recovery and the achievement of long-term peace, the study of this topic has been, quite surprisingly, neglected. Several issues deserve to be duly and exhaustively taken into account when it comes to reparations for child victims of armed conflict. Events which happened in the past, which never gave rise to remedies for the victims, are still difficult to cope with and exacerbate frustration and hatred in those who have been directly or indirectly affected. As stressed by Boyden and Mann, 'modern policy has clearly embraced the ethical and moral view that children have a right to special consideration and that children exposed to exceptionally harsh situations merit the greatest concern'.[35] Armed conflicts, either international or internal, obviously fall within the definition of 'exceptionally harsh situations'. Nonetheless, until the launch of the ground-breaking report by Graça Machel on the impact of armed conflict on children in 1996, scant attention had been devoted to one of the most shocking

---

31 A. Nolan and U. Kilkelly, 'Children's Rights Under Regional Human Rights Law – A Tale of Harmonisation?' (pre-edit version 19 May 2015, on file with author).

32 See Art. 38 of the CRC and Art. 22 of the ACRWC.

33 See F. Kalshoven and L. Zegveld, *Constraints on the Waging of War: An Introduction to International Humanitarian Law*, 4th edn., Cambridge University Press, Cambridge, 2011, 87.

34 Namely, the Convention on the Elimination of all Forms of Discrimination Against Women, 18 December 1979, entered into force on 3 September 1981, UNTS, vol. 1249, p. 13; and the Convention on the Rights of Persons with Disabilities: resolution adopted by the General Assembly, 24 January 2007, A/RES/61/106. Several other legal tools have the scope to guarantee and trigger children's rights under every circumstance, and particularly in conflicts. See also the Nairobi Declaration on Women's and Girl's Right to a Remedy and Reparation, International Meeting on Women's and Girl's Right to a Remedy and Reparation, Nairobi, 2007, available at: http://www.fidh.org/IMG/pdf/NAIROBI_DECLARATIONeng.pdf. For an exhaustive collection of children's rights in international law, see E.M. Belser, K. Hanson and A. Hirt, *Sourcebook of International Children's Rights*, Staempfli Publishers, Berne, 2009.

35 J. Boyden and G. Mann, 'Children's Risk, Resilience, and Coping in Extreme Situations', in M. Ungar (ed.), *Handbook for Working with Children and Youth: Pathways to Resilience Across Cultures and Contexts*, Sage Publications, Thousand Oaks, CA, 2005, 3.

outcomes of war: the annihilation of children's rights.[36] As a result, despite being entitled to special care and protective measures, children are often the targets of violations committed by the parties to an armed conflict. The term 'parties' refers to both State armed forces and Non-State Armed Groups ('NSAGs'),[37] which, given the changing nature of warfare and the increasing number of civil wars fought all over the world, have become prominent actors, expected to abide by IHL[38] and IHRL.[39] The extent and the limits of such abidance, however, still pose plenty of unanswered questions that also affect the victims of the violations committed by these non-State entities. The difficulties range from the lack of existing mechanisms to deal with breaches of IHL and IHRL perpetrated by NSAGs to the reluctance of States to engage with, and hence recognise, their counterparts. Children victimised by the unlawful acts committed by NSAGs, including illegal recruitment and use in the hostilities, have little opportunity to obtain redress for the harm suffered. This concern has been raised, but not fully addressed yet.

Another transversal issue that emerges with regard to the right to reparation for child victims of armed conflict and the effectiveness of the existing remedies pertains to the scope of such a right in those instances where blatant structural inequalities have led to the commission of the violations in the first place. The transformative potential of reparations in cases of wrongful acts perpetrated against particularly vulnerable groups or individuals has been grasped by the doctrine and the case law of a few judicial bodies, but it has not been sufficiently analysed and discussed in relation to child victims and their peculiarities.

The variety and complexity of the issues that need to be tackled when dealing with reparations for child victims of armed conflict will be better highlighted in the coming paragraphs, which introduce the rationale, the goal and the limitations of this study.

---

36 UN General Assembly, Impact of Armed Conflict on Children: Note by the Secretary-General, 26 August 1996, UN doc. A/51/306.

37 This book uses the terms NSAGs, armed groups and armed opposition groups interchangeably and as opposed to armed forces, which refers to the combined military, naval and air forces of a State.

38 S. Sivakumaran, 'Re-envisaging the International Law of Internal Armed Conflict', (2011) 22 *European Journal of International Law* 219, at 220–234.

39 International lawyers have long been grappling with the question relating to the existence of human rights obligations of NSAGs. Currently the issue at stake seems to be not 'whether' but rather 'to what extent' armed opposition groups are bound by human rights obligations. See D. Amoroso, 'Armed Opposition Groups' (and Foreign Fighters') Abidance by International Human Rights Law: The Issue of Compliance in Syria and Iraq', in A. de Guttry, F. Capone and C. Paulussen (eds.), *Foreign Fighters under International Law and Beyond*, Springer/ Asser Press, The Hague, 2016, 205, at 215–218. See also A. Clapham, 'Focusing on Armed Non-State Actors', in A. Clapham and P. Gaeta (eds.), *The Oxford Handbook of International Law in Armed Conflict*, Oxford University Press, Oxford, 2014, 766, at 770–780.

1.3. WHY FOCUS ON CHILD VICTIMS OF ARMED CONFLICT?

Atrocities against children have been, and still are, committed in every region of the world and in different contexts, i.e. peacetime, situations of insecurity[40] and armed conflict. Breaches of fundamental rights occur in every context, during peacetime and armed conflict, within and outside the family or the community of origin. In order to prevent the violations and cope with their consequences, campaigns and monitoring mechanisms have been set up by relevant stakeholders.[41] Children's victimisation has been the subject of thorough studies[42] and considerable efforts have been made during recent years to encourage children and their families to report victimisation to the authorities. Nonetheless, concern persists that most crimes against children remain hidden, hampering the victims' possibility of obtaining redress. If this is true with regard to 'normal crimes' that affect children in every society and setting, it is legitimate to argue that the difficulties are exacerbated in the case of armed conflict. The 'state of silence and disregard' that van Boven associated with the fate of victims of IHL and IHRL violations[43] is a widespread phenomenon that both the 'humanisation of international law'[44] and the growing recognition of victims' rights have not been able to thwart.

In situations of armed conflict, children, one of the most vulnerable segments of the civilian population, are disproportionately affected in various ways. Children are victims of serious violations of IHL, including recruitment into armed forces and armed groups, and they are particularly harmed by widespread and systematic attacks against the civilian population. They suffer from the indirect consequences of armed conflict and violence, which strike them both physically and mentally. For example, as a result of an armed conflict children

---

40 K. Hausler, N. Urban and R. McCorquodale, *Protecting Education in Insecurity and Armed Conflict: an International Law Handbook*, BIICL/PEIC, London, 2012, 7. According to the authors '"insecurity" is a non-legal term. It is used to describe situations of disturbance and tension within a State that disrupt the normal functioning of key political, social and legal institutions, including those that are used to facilitate education. Insecurity may refer to "national insecurity", which is a territorial concept, or to "human insecurity", which is a people-centred concept.'

41 An example is the global campaign 'Make the Invisible Visible' launched by UNICEF in 2013 to end violence against children.

42 See D. Finkelhor and J. Dziuba-Leatherman, 'Children as Victims of Violence: A National Survey', (1994) 4 *Pediatrics* 413, at 416–420. K. Kracke and H. Hahn, 'The Nature and Extent of Childhood Exposure to Violence: What We Know, Why We Don't Know more, and Why it Matters', (2008) 8 *Journal of Emotional Abuse* 29, at 35–49.

43 T. van Boven, 'Victim-Oriented Perspectives: Rights and Realities', in T. Bonacker and C. Safferling (eds.), *Victims of International Crimes: An Interdisciplinary Discourse*, T.M.C Asser Press, The Hague, 2013, 16, at 18–20.

44 T. Meron, *The Humanization of International Law*, The Hague Academy of International Law Monographs, Martinus Nijhoff Publishers, Leiden, 2006.

are at high risk of either losing their loved ones through death or being separated from them. Moreover, children and their families are often forced to relocate or move from place to place to escape conflict. Many children witness violence, in addition to suffering violence or abuse themselves.[45] Significantly, armed conflicts have the greatest impact on the poorest communities in the poorest countries, and children and adolescents under the age of 18 years are among the most severely affected in these communities. As a result children's educational development is also often interrupted, putting at risk the possibility to study and, consequently, exacerbating factors that lead to discrimination, such as poverty, inequality and economic stagnation.[46]

Often forgotten and unsupported by governmental agencies and non-governmental organisations ('NGOs'), children victimised by violations occurring during an armed conflict are left to run households, take care of younger siblings or wander the streets of larger towns. Those associated with the 'enemy', possibly due to the military or political involvement of parents or other relatives or due to their own participation in the hostilities, are likely to experience stigmatisation and abandonment. In addition to the scant attention devoted to their situation one should consider also the fear of discovery by government authorities, which can act as a strong deterrent for these children to claim justice and reparations. The issue of reparations for victims of armed conflict in general has already been the subject of a thorough analysis,[47] and specific focus has been placed on the integration of a gender perspective in the design and implementation of reparations for victims of human rights violations.[48] Child victims have been included in the broader studies, but without duly taking into account their special short- and long-term post-conflict needs, especially with regard to redress measures and social reintegration, which are essential to overcome the enduring effects of victimisation. In addition to those immediately affected, it is important to consider also that the impact of armed conflict on

---

45 In a survey of 3,030 children conducted by UNICEF in Rwanda in 1995, nearly 80 per cent of the children had lost immediate family members, and more than one-third of these had actually witnessed their murders. These atrocities indicate the extremes to which children have been exposed during conflicts. L. Gupta, UNICEF, 'Rwanda: Follow-up Survey of Rwandan Children's Reactions to War Related Violence from the 1994 Genocide', 1998, available at: http://www.unicef.org/evaldatabase/index_14242.html. See also R. Neugebauer, P.W. Fisher, J.B. Turner, S. Yamabe, J.A. Sarsfield and T. Stehling-Ariza, 'Post-traumatic Stress Reactions among Rwandan Children and Adolescents in the Early Aftermath of Genocide', (2009) 38 *International Journal of Epidemiology* 1033, at 1040–1045.

46 UNESCO, EFA Global Monitoring Report, 'The Hidden Crisis: Armed Conflict and Education', 2011, available at: http://unesdoc.unesco.org/images/0019/001907/190743e.pdf.

47 See the work of the ILA Committee on the Right to Reparation for Victims of Armed Conflict, whose Reports are available at: http://www.ila-hq.org/en/committees/index.cfm/cid/1018. See also C. Evans, *The Right to Reparation in International Law for Victims of Armed Conflict*, Cambridge University Press, Cambridge, 2012.

48 See generally R. Rubio-Marin (ed.), *The Gender of Reparations Unsettling Sexual Hierarchies while Redressing Human Rights Violations*, Cambridge University Press, Cambridge, 2011.

future generations may sow the seeds for conflicts to continue or to re-emerge. Therefore the award and implementation of reparative measures that are able to redress, to the maximum extent possible, the consequences of the violations that have occurred is remarkably important with regard to child victims, who have a twofold role, representing at the same time one of the most vulnerable segments of the population and its future pillar.

1.4. DEFINITION OF THE KEY TERMS

The study of the right to reparation for child victims of armed conflict entails the adoption of concepts that need to be clarified from the outset. Those include in particular the notions of 'reparation', 'victim' and 'children'.

The term 'reparation', from the Latin term *reparare*, 'to dispose again', refers to the process, as well as the result, of remedying the harm caused by a wrongful act. The purpose of reparation is generally understood to be to re-establish the situation that existed before the harm occurred.[49] Within the international criminal law ('ICL') framework 'reparations fulfil two main purposes … they oblige those responsible for serious crimes to repair the harm they caused to the victims and they enable the Court to ensure that offenders account for their acts'.[50]

Nonetheless, awarding reparations can also pursue the twofold aim of ending ongoing breaches and deterring future ones. Reparations can help rehabilitate physical and psychological integrity and dignity; they can act as a vehicle for reconciliation as well as a measure to establish a new relationship between the violator and the victim. Although the ultimate goal of reparation is traditionally reckoned to be the restoration of the *status quo ante*, in the form of restitution, the current focus on individuals rather than States has led to the adoption of a different approach in the field of remedies, which entails efforts to design reparations as a tool to adequately, effectively and promptly redress the harm suffered by the victims.[51] As stated in Principle 18 of the UNBPG:

> In accordance with domestic and international law, *and taking account of individual circumstances*, victims of gross violations of international human rights law and serious violations of international humanitarian law should, as appropriate and proportional

---

49 See generally M. Evans and K. Stratos (eds.), *Remedies in International Law: The Institutional Dilemma*, Hart Publishing, Oxford, 1998; see also C. Gray, *Judicial Remedies in International Law*, Clarendon Press, Oxford, 1987; Shelton, above note 21.

50 Judgment of 3 March 2015 (Judgment on the appeals against the 'Decision establishing the principles and procedures to be applied to reparations' of 7 August 2012 with amended order for reparations (Annex A) and public annexes 1 and 2), (2015) ICC (Appeals Chamber), ICC-01/04-01/06-3129-AnxA 03-03-2015, §2.

51 See UNBPG above note 2, §9.

> to the gravity of the violation and the circumstances of each case, be provided with full and effective reparation.[52]

'Adequate', in particular, refers to reparations that are acceptable in quality and/or quantity,[53] and thus both appropriate and proportional to the harm suffered. In other words, the forms and modalities of reparation should be suitable, taking into account the harm, the victims, the violations, and the broader society.[54] 'Effectiveness' describes reparations' ability to produce a desired or intended result, meaning that, for example, the scarce resources of countries in transition should be used in an optimised manner.[55] 'Prompt', finally, indicates the importance of providing timely redress to the victims, taking into due account those instances when, as stressed by the ICC, priority may need to be given to certain victims who are in a particularly vulnerable situation or who require urgent assistance.[56] The requirement to award reparations that match these characteristics is embedded in the UNBPG and it refers to all victims of gross IHRL and serious IHL violations. There is thus no indication of what these criteria exactly mean in relation to child victims. The right to reparation for child victims is not spelled out in any binding instruments, including the CRC, which enshrines only a general provision concerning children's reintegration and social recovery.[57] Nonetheless some direction in this area is provided by the Guidelines on Justice in Matters involving Child Victims and Witnesses of Crime adopted by the United Nations Economic and Social Council ('ECOSOC') in 2005 ('ECOSOC Guidelines').[58] According to the ECOSOC Guidelines:

> Child victims should, wherever possible, receive reparation in order to achieve full redress, reintegration and recovery. Procedures for obtaining and enforcing reparation should be readily accessible and child-sensitive. Provided the proceedings are child-sensitive and respect these Guidelines, combined criminal and reparations proceedings should be encouraged, together with informal and community justice procedures such as restorative justice. Reparation may include restitution from the offender ordered in the criminal court, aid from victim compensation programmes administered by the State and damages ordered to be paid in civil proceedings. Where possible, costs of social and educational reintegration, medical treatment, mental health care and legal

52 Ibidem.

53 'Adequate', OED online, Oxford University Press, 29 June 2015, available at: http://www.oxforddictionaries.com/definition/english/adequate.

54 See H. Rombouts, P. Sardaro and S. Vandeginste, 'The Right to Reparation for Victims of Gross and Systematic Violations of Human Rights', in De Feyter et al. above note 22, at 345–500.

55 Ibidem, at 459.

56 Judgment of 3 March 2015, ICC, Order for Reparations, Annex A, above note 50, §19.

57 Art. 39 of the CRC.

58 ECOSOC Resolution 2005/20, 'Guidelines on Justice in Matters involving Child Victims and Witnesses of Crime', available at: http://www.un.org/en/ecosoc/docs/2005/resolution%202005-20.pdf.

services should be addressed. Procedures should be instituted to ensure enforcement of reparation orders and payment of reparation before fines.[59]

The ECOSOC Guidelines summarises the key elements that reparations for child victims should encompass in order to be truly meaningful, and therefore adequate, effective and prompt. However, the ECOSOC Guidelines consider reparations for children in general, i.e. most likely in the context of ordinary crimes, but do not address the peculiarities of IHRL and IHL breaches that are 'particularly serious in nature because of their cruelty or depravity'.[60] When dealing with violations that have a severe impact on the enjoyment of victims' fundamental rights, an attempt to apply the concept of restitution would generate what has been defined by Roht-Arriaza as the 'basic paradox at the heart of reparation', namely the tension between a promised return to the *status quo ante* and the knowledge that such a status could not, in any case, be restored.[61] Moreover, in cases in which the victims have been targeted due to a discriminatory practice or policy that has exacerbated their vulnerability the restoration of the *status quo* seems not only impossible, but also not desirable. On the contrary reparative measures that also take into account the factors that led to the violation in the first place and that invest in children's resilience are more likely to have a positive impact on child victims' lives.

The caveats presented above in relation to reparations and victims will be applied in this study to a specific group, i.e. children who suffer as a consequence of severe violations of IHRL and IHL perpetrated during an armed conflict of international or non-international character.[62] International armed conflict ('IACs') encompasses both the use of force between States and situations of belligerent occupation.[63] Non-international armed conflict ('NIACs') refers to protracted armed violence between a State and a non-State armed group; as well as protracted armed violence between NSAGs on the territory of a State.[64] As for

59 Ibidem, §§35–37.

60 Shelton, above note 21, at 390.

61 N. Roht-Arriaza, 'Reparations in the Aftermath of Repression and Mass Violence', in E. Stover and H.M. Weinstein (eds.), *My Neighbor, My Enemy: Justice and Community in the Aftermath of Mass Atrocity*, Cambridge University Press, Cambridge, 2004, 121, at 122.

62 On the distinction between international and non-international armed conflicts see generally D. Fleck, 'The Law of Non-International Armed Conflict', in D. Fleck (ed.), *The Handbook of International Humanitarian Law*, Oxford University Press, Oxford, 2013, 605, at 620–629.

63 Common Art. 2 to the Geneva Conventions of 1949.

64 This definition is the customary international legal definition of non-international armed conflict as recognised by the Appeals Chamber of the ICTY in the *Tadić* case. See Judgment of 2 October 1995 (Decision on the Defence Motion for Interlocutory Appeal on Jurisdiction), (1995) ICTY (Appeals Chamber), Case No IT-94-1-AR72, §70. Both situations of non-international armed conflict require a minimum level of intensity of violence (protracted) and a minimum level of organisation of the non-State armed group involved. It is these two factors which distinguish non-international armed conflicts from situations of violence amounting to only internal disturbances and tensions such as riots, isolated and sporadic acts of violence and other acts of a similar nature.

the definition of children, Article 1 of the CRC establishes that 'a child means every human being below the age of 18 years unless under the law applicable to the child, majority is attained earlier'. This definition has also been embraced at the regional level. In the Inter-American arena, there is no standard definition of the child for legal purposes, therefore both the IACtHR and the Inter-American Commission have stipulated that the definition of child is based on the provisions of Article 1 of the CRC.[65] The same criterion has been applied within the European and the African human rights systems: in particular Article 1 of the European Convention on the Exercise of Children's Rights states that it targets everyone who has not yet attained the age of 18 years and also the ACRWC, adopted in July 1990, defines as a child every human being less than 18 years of age. For the purpose of this study, therefore, child victims of armed conflict are human beings under the age of 18 years, who have been, individually or collectively, affected by violations of IHRL and IHL committed by any of the parties involved in an armed conflict. As a result of those violations child victims are entitled to reparations awarded and implemented either through judicial or non-judicial mechanisms.

1.5. AIM OF THE STUDY

The study stems from the need to fill a gap in the current literature on transitional justice, in particular on the right to reparation. Even though reparations are well-established legal measures in several domestic judicial systems all over the world, in transitional periods reparations are not just a means to redress the harm suffered by the victims of wrongful acts, but they also seek to contribute to the reconstitution or the constitution of a new political community in the aftermath of an armed conflict.[66] This double role and scope makes it very difficult to determine how to effectively and adequately repair damages that arguably affect large segments of the population and/or individuals and groups that are most in need of protection. Children clearly fall within this category and they are very often the target of violations, especially in situations of insecurity and war. It should be noted that this study does not suggest that violation of the rights of minors is worse than the violation of the same rights of others, but simply that children's victimhood, alongside its causes and consequences, needs to be better understood in order to identify the best and most suitable ways to redress the harm suffered. This is a very important step towards the design of

65 Advisory Opinion of 28 August 2002 (Juridical Condition and Human Rights of the Child), (2002) IACtHR, Series A No. 17, Chapter V. Of course, reparations can also be the outcome of administrative proceedings, which for the purpose of this book fall within the reparations awarded by the State through national plans and strategies.

66 P. de Greiff, 'Justice and Reparations', in P. de Greiff, above note 22, 451, at 458.

transitional justice processes able to encompass meaningful reparative measures and to promote the inclusion of child victims. The overview of the relevant cases and materials provided in this book will, hopefully, contribute to paving the way for reparations that are effective, adequate, prompt, *and* in line with the international standards set forth by the CRC and other instruments. This book ultimately strives to highlight the shortcomings of the existing mechanisms and it points out the main issues that need to be improved and/or overcome in pursuance of child victims' redress.

While extensive, but not exhaustive, analysis has been devoted to the recognition of an individual right to access justice and claim for reparation in the wake of armed conflict or widespread human rights violations,[67] several issues concerning the most recent developments and their impact on the design and award of reparations for child victims have not been investigated yet. Approaches to post-conflict analysis have tended to be short sighted with regard to the perspective of the victims.[68] This is especially true in relation to vulnerable groups, above all children, who face additional hurdles and challenges to report the violations suffered and demand redress. The present study argues that reparations must necessarily be included in every transitional justice process in order to cope with the legacy of widespread abuses as well as to prevent future victimisation.[69] Moving from this basic assumption, the research undertaken has focused on child victims of war to determine whether (i) the existing international law framework is sufficiently developed to provide child victims of IHRL and IHL violations occurring in conjunction with an armed conflict with adequate, effective and prompt reparations for the harm suffered; (ii) the judicial and non-judicial mechanisms in place have been established taking into due account child victims' rights and specific needs; (iii) the reparations awarded and implemented by regional and international bodies fully reflect child victims' peculiarities, both individually and as members of a given subgroup, and are able to thwart the short-term consequences of the harm suffered as well as the most enduring ones.

The outcomes of this study reveal that, in spite of an overall growing interest in victims both internationally and domestically,[70] the degree of neglect with

67 See Shelton, above note 21; see also C. McCarthy, *Reparations and Victim Support in the International Criminal Court*, Cambridge University Press, Cambridge, 2013; Rubio-Marin above note 48; and Evans above note 47.

68 Evans, above note 47, at 9.

69 On this point see generally L. Moffett, 'Transitional Justice and Reparations: Remedying the Past', in D. Jacobs (ed.), *Research Handbook on Transitional Justice*, Edward Elgar, Cheltenham, forthcoming 2016. See also the Report of the Secretary-General, 'The Rule of Law and Transitional Justice in Conflict and Post Conflict Societies', UN doc. S/2004/616, 23 August 2004, §8.

70 On the complex status of victims in transitional justice processes see K. McEvoy and K. McConnachie, 'Victims and Transitional Justice: Voice, Agency and Blame', (2013) 22 *Social & Legal Studies* 489, at 500–513.

respect to child victims shows no signs of abating and many challenges remain unaddressed. With regard to the first point raised, i.e. the development of the norms regulating how reparations are claimed and implemented, it has emerged that children's right to reparation is embedded in the existing general international law framework, but there is a lack of specific provisions able to cope with children's peculiar victimhood, and this ultimately undermines children's meaningful inclusion in the reparations discourse. Furthermore, the current set of norms fails to engage all the actors involved, leading to the inference that, with regard to the many violations against children committed by non-State entities, victims' rights to reparation tend to remain unsatisfied.

Concerning the mechanisms, either judicial or non-judicial, the research carried out shows that most of them fall short of measures and provisions to guarantee that children's participation is sufficiently promoted and strengthened. A dearth of information about reparations, lack of qualified and trained personnel, widespread inability to strike a balance between a fair trial standard and equitable access to remedies for children represent some of the shortcomings common to many of the bodies analysed in the course of this study.

Finally, the reparations awarded so far accurately echo the deficiencies of the existing normative framework and of the mechanisms created to enforce it. In this regard the book asserts that the implementation of adequate, prompt and effective reparations for child victims of armed conflict will remain a mirage unless (i) specific provisions on children are enshrined in a binding instrument that crystallises the right to reparation for victims of IHRL and IHL violations; (ii) the existing mechanisms and tools envisage child-friendly proceedings in accordance with the CRC key principles; (iii) the consequences of the violations committed against children in conjunction with an armed conflict are redressed keeping in mind also the long-term impact of the harm suffered, i.e. by favouring forms of reparation that empower the victims and promote resilience and by considering the residual effects of children's victimhood when designing and implementing remedial strategies for adults who have experienced violations as minors.

1.6. STRUCTURE OF THE BOOK

This book begins with the perspective of child victims, providing a critical appraisal of the limitations that still characterise the current framework, explaining children's particular characteristics and needs, and analysing how and to what extent those have been taken into account within the mechanisms for awarding reparations. The main body of the book, which consists of six chapters, is divided in two main parts, followed by a concluding section. The first part introduces the key issues and concepts analysed in this study and it provides an overview of the existing legal framework. In more detail the second chapter explores and discusses the victimhood of children affected by violations of

IHRL and IHL perpetrated during an international or non-international armed conflict. In particular the chapter tackles various relevant aspects, including the international law provisions that enshrine children's rights relevant to reparations, the vulnerability of child victims, the relationship between children and women as vulnerable groups, whose fate is often entwined, and finally the question of child soldiers and their complex status as victims.

The third chapter scrutinises the current general framework governing reparations and how its developments impact on child victims. The chapter sheds light on the principal dichotomies within the realm of reparations and it addresses the issue of accountability in relation to all the actors, i.e. States, individual perpetrators and NSAGs, which commit violations against children in armed conflict.

The fourth chapter completes the overview of the normative and theoretical framework. The chapter unpacks the different forms that reparation for child victims of armed conflict can take, presenting a number of examples in relation to each of them. The chapter further deals with the distinction between individual and collective reparations, as well as between material and symbolic ones. Chapter 4 also discusses the scope of reparation for violations of IHRL and IHL that stem from rooted inequality and discrimination, highlighting the transformative potential that all forms of reparations can convey.

The second part of the book assesses the current application of the principles and norms described in the first part. The fifth chapter narrows down the focus on quasi-judicial and judicial international mechanisms, i.e. the complaint procedures of the UN treaty bodies, the international and hybrid courts, and tribunals. The chapter presents the approaches followed by the various bodies, pointing out the implementation of the procedural and substantive dimensions of the right to reparation and assessing the extent to which these mechanisms have been able to provide adequate, prompt and effective reparations to child victims of armed conflict. The same structure, aim and methodology apply to the sixth chapter, which presents an analysis of the way quasi-judicial and judicial regional bodies have performed in light of the research question identified by this study. Consistently with the focus of this book, the chapter analyses solely the African and the Inter-American human rights system. Chapter 7, which marks the end of the second part, provides an overview of non-judicial mechanisms that have dealt with reparations for child victims of armed conflict. These include national reparations programmes, TCs, Disarmament, Demobilisation and Reintegration ('DDR') processes and the projects implemented by the ICC Trust Fund for Victims ('TFV') through its assistance mandate.

Chapter 8 concludes the monograph. The chapter summarises the findings and the ideas developed in the other parts of the book and it paves the way for future possibilities to enhance child victims' right to reparation. This study has been undertaken in the hope that it will make a contribution to understanding child victims' needs and promoting their rights.

PART I

THE NORMATIVE AND THEORETICAL FRAMEWORK

CHAPTER 2

CHILDREN AS VICTIMS OF ARMED CONFLICT

2.1. INTRODUCTION

During its forty-eighth session, the General Assembly adopted Resolution 48/157, entitled 'Protection of Children Affected by Armed Conflicts', in which it requested the Secretary-General to appoint an expert to undertake a comprehensive study with the support of the Centre for Human Rights and UNICEF. The expert, Ms Graça Machel, was asked to make recommendations in five areas: the participation of children in armed conflict; the reinforcement of preventive measures; the relevance and adequacy of existing standards; the measures required to improve the protection of children affected by armed conflict; and the actions needed to promote the physical and psychological recovery and social reintegration of children affected by armed conflict.[71] The Machel' study underlined with deep concern how 'new' war tactics had evolved, resulting in civilians, including children, increasingly becoming the targets of violence and the victims of atrocities.[72] This trend continues as armed conflicts nowadays have an even more horrific impact on children, and on civilians generally. In today's wars, the strategies adopted by armed groups 'seek to bring the battle more immediately, more systematically, and more massively to the core of the civilian population', and into the lives of millions of children.[73] As a result, the notion of armed conflict itself has become more blurred and less easily defined. The Stockholm International Peace Research Institute has stressed the fact that armed conflicts are moving towards 'further fragmentation of violence'.[74] According to this analysis, such trend has been accompanied by

71 See 'Impact of Armed Conflict on Children: note by the Secretary-General', above note 36.

72 UNICEF, 'Machel Study 10-Year Strategic Review: Children and Conflict in a Changing World', April 2009, available at: http://www.unicef.org/publications/files/Machel_Study_10_Year_Strategic_Review_EN_030909.pdf.

73 Programme on Humanitarian Policy and Conflict Research, Transnationality, 'War and the Law: A Report on a Roundtable on the Transformation of Warfare, International Law, and the Role of Transnational Armed Groups', Programme on Humanitarian Policy and Conflict Research, Harvard University, Cambridge, MA, April 2006, at 6.

74 See Stockholm International Peace Research Institute, 'Trends in Armed Conflicts', SIPRI Yearbook 2008, SIPRI, Stockholm, 2008, at 43–54.

the diversification of armed groups and the further erosion of the boundaries between different forms of violence. Consequently much of this 'fragmented' violence is difficult to assess and categorise.

The alarming situation of children in armed conflict has become a thematic issue on the UN agenda after the submission of Machel's ground-breaking report. As a result more initiatives and resolutions have been adopted and implemented.[75] In the first place Machel's study led to the adoption by the General Assembly of Resolution 51/77 (1996) establishing the mandate of the Special Representative of the Secretary-General for Children and Armed Conflict for a period of three years. The General Assembly has since extended this mandate five times. In line with the recommendations enshrined in the report, through the UN Security Council ('UNSC') Resolution 1539/2004, six grave violations against children have been identified due to their ability to be monitored and quantified, their egregious nature and the severity of their consequences on the lives of children. Such violations are killing or maiming of children, recruitment or use of child soldiers, rape and other forms of sexual violence against children, abduction of children, attacks against schools and hospitals, and denial of humanitarian access to children.[76] Although forced labour and all forms of slavery were mentioned in UNSC Resolution 1539/2004, they are not retained in the Annual Report of the Secretary-General on Children and Armed Conflict, the document that sets out the parameters of the Monitoring and Reporting Mechanism ('MRM').[77] Through UNSC Resolution 1612/2005, a Working Group on Children and Armed Conflict and a MRM have been established with the purpose of systematically monitoring, documenting and reporting on children's situations in war-torn countries. In 2009, with the adoption of UNSC Resolution 1882, the scope of the MRM was further expanded and enforced.[78]

---

75 All the documents on children and armed conflict issued by the UN are available at: http://www.securitycouncilreport.org/children-and-armed-conflict/.

76 See Office of the Special Representative of the Secretary-General for Children and Armed Conflict, Working Paper 1, 'The Six Grave Violations against Children During Armed Conflict: The Legal Foundation', October 2009, available at: https://childrenandarmedconflict.un.org/publications/WorkingPaper-1_SixGraveViolationsLegalFoundation.pdf.

77 K. Barnett and A. Jefferys, 'Full of Promise: How the UN's Monitoring and Reporting Mechanism Can Better Protect Children', commissioned and published by the Humanitarian Practice Network at ODI, Network Paper 62, 2008, at 3.

78 This resolution in fact related to killing and maiming of children and sexual violence against children as an additional trigger for listing parties to conflict in the Annual Report of the Secretary-General on Children and Armed Conflict, 4 August 2009, UN doc. S/RES/1882, §3 '... requests the Secretary-General also to include in the annexes to his reports on children and armed conflict those parties to armed conflict that engage, in contravention of applicable international law, in patterns of killing and maiming of children and/or rape and other sexual violence against children, in situations of armed conflict, bearing in mind all other violations and abuses against children, and notes that the present paragraph will apply to situations in accordance with the conditions set out in paragraph 16 of its Resolution 1379 (2001)'.

A MRM is formally established when parties in country-situations are listed in the annexes of the Annual Report of the Secretary-General on Children and Armed Conflict. While at first the recruitment and use of children by armed forces and groups was the only criterion for inclusion in the annexes, nowadays four more grave violations trigger the listing, namely killing or maiming children, committing rape and other forms of sexual violence against children, engaging in attacks on schools and/or hospitals in situations of armed conflict, or abducting children.[79] The legal basis for the six grave violations lies in the relevant international law, which in turn encompasses IHL, IHRL and ICL. These violations reflect the specificity of the harm suffered by the children most affected by armed conflicts and therefore the most vulnerable: child soldiers, unaccompanied children, refugees and internally displaced children, children sexually abused or exploited, and children injured by landmines and unexploded ordnance. All these categories of children have experienced a severe breach of their fundamental rights and are entitled to receive reparations. The question remains as to who is responsible for providing reparations and what kind of reparations ought to be implemented in order to promote physical and psychological recovery and social reintegration of child victims. The solution to these issues is not straightforward. As noted above the growing involvement of non-State actors and the use of non-traditional forms of warfare add to the difficulty of understanding the impact of war on children and, therefore, finding adequate measures to redress the harm suffered.

The UN mechanisms set up following the first report on the impact of armed conflict on children provide some useful insight on the violations perpetrated against child victims and their specific victimhood. All the six grave violations committed against children amount to crimes under ICL. Crimes perpetrated against children in armed conflict can be divided into three sub-categories: child-specific crimes, in which children are a material element of the crime (e.g. forced transfer of children and imposition of measures intended to prevent births in order to perpetrate genocide, enlistment, conscription and use of children to participate in hostilities); crimes which target children in such a way that they are disproportionally victimised in comparison to the adult population (e.g. destruction of schools and hospitals, attacks on humanitarian missions); crimes with particularly serious effects on children, where children, due to their age and development, face more difficulties in rehabilitation than adult victims (e.g. rape and sexual violence).[80] The discussion about how children's victimhood and

79 O/SRSG-CAAC,UNICEF, DPKO, 'MRM Field Manual Monitoring and Reporting Mechanism on Grave Violations Against Children in Situations of Armed Conflict', April 2010, available at: http://www.unrol.org/files/39.%20MRM%20Field%20Manual%2016-04-10-1.pdf.

80 C. Chamberlein, Legal Adviser of the International Criminal Court, Paper presented at Leiden University on 12 November 2010, on the occasion of the seminar on children's rights before the ICC, organised within the course on 'Children's Rights in International Law'.

vulnerability in armed conflict should be defined highlights *in primis* the fact that child victimisation differs from adult victimisation. As a result children's victimisation poses a number of questions and challenges, which also impact the design and award of reparative measures able to address these peculiarities and duly take them into account. In order to understand the framework governing the right to reparation for child victims of war and its implementation in different settings a number of preliminary caveats are needed, in particular with regard to some important concepts and principles that will often surface in the course of the present study.

2.2. 'VICTIM' WITHIN THE INTERNATIONAL LAW FRAMEWORK

After noting the importance of understanding children's victimhood and analysing its peculiarities in order to better grasp the crucial role of adequate, prompt and effective reparations for child victims of armed conflict, it is worth further elaborating on the concept of 'victim' as defined under the current international law framework.[81] Each of the branches of international law that is relevant to the present study, namely IHRL, IHL and ICL, has a different approach to victims. Within the human rights law framework victims are mainly acknowledged when the State is the author of the breach of an international obligation, when the breach is attributable to the State or when it is the result of the State's failure to act with due diligence.[82] Traditionally this branch of international law does not consider breaches of international obligations perpetrated by non-State actors that cannot be linked to the conduct of States. Under ICL and IHL, on the other hand, it is easier to single out the responsibility of non-State actors for wrongful acts committed against individuals or groups. However, the international responsibility rests only with the individual agents[83] as currently there is no international court to hear complaints against

81 See generally C. Fernández de Casadevante Romani, 'International Law of Victims', in A. von Bogdandy and R. Wolfrum, (eds.), (2010) 14 *Max Planck Yearbook of United Nations Law* 219, at 219–272.

82 R. McCorquodale, 'Non-State Actors and International Human Rights Law', in S. Joseph and A. McBeth (eds.), *Research Handbook on International Human Rights Law*, Edward Elgar, Cheltenham, 2010, 97, at 100–104. See J. Wouters, E. Brems, S. Smis and P. Schmitt 'Accountability for Human Rights Violations by International Organisations: Introductory Remarks', in J. Wouters, E. Brems, S. Smis and P. Schmitt (eds.), *Accountability for Human Rights Violations by International Organisations*, Intersentia, Antwerp, 2010, 1, at 5–13.

83 G. Werle, 'Individual Criminal Responsibility in Article 25 ICC Statute', (2007) 5 *Journal of International Criminal Justice* 953, at 953–958. See also E. van Sliedregt, *The Criminal Responsibility of Individuals for Violations of International Humanitarian Law*, TMC Asser Press, The Hague, 2003, at 41–115.

entities.[84] Despite the different approaches which emerge in relation to the specific areas of international law under consideration, it is useful to elaborate on the various definitions of 'victim' as they will have a significant impact on the reparative measures that stem from the recognition of such status. The word 'victim' has a broad meaning, for example, according to the *Oxford English Dictionary* it derives from the Latin word *victima*, i.e. a living creature killed as a religious sacrifice. The term 'crime victim' instead generally refers to any person, group or entity that has suffered injury or loss due to illegal activity; the harm can be physical, psychological or economic. For the purpose of the present study 'victim' is used in the sense of 'crime victim'.

The term 'victim' appears in almost all the core human rights treaties,[85] however only one convention defines what constitutes a victim for its purposes.[86] In relation to the regional human rights systems it should be noted that there is a lack of homogeneity with regard to the possibility for individuals or groups of victims to access the different courts. Within the inter-American human rights system the concept of 'victim' has been developed in the jurisprudence of the IACtHR, whereas in the American Convention on Human Rights ('ACHR') the word 'victim' does not appear and those who suffer from the violation of any right embodied in it are defined as the 'injured party'.[87] A definition of 'victim' was included in the IACtHR Rules of Procedure in 2001, which states that a victim is 'the person whose rights have been violated, according to a judgment pronounced by the Court'.[88] Despite this definition, the IACtHR jurisprudence has adopted a broader approach, considering a 'victim' to be any natural person or victim group whose rights were directly or indirectly violated, or could potentially be violated.[89] The IACtHR over the years has steadily interpreted the notion of victim so as to include in some instances not only the victim's

---

84 On this point see A. Clapham, 'Extending International Criminal Law beyond the Individual to Corporations and Armed Opposition Groups', (2008) 6 *Journal of International Criminal Justice* 899, at 907–912.

85 There are nine core international human rights instruments; all the texts are available at: http://www.ohchr.org/EN/ProfessionalInterest/Pages/CoreInstruments.aspx.

86 Art. 24 of the International Convention for the Protection of All Persons from Enforced Disappearance, resolution adopted by the General Assembly, 12 January 2007, A/RES/61/177.

87 Art. 63 of the ACHR, 22 November 1969, entered into force on 18 July 1978, OAS Treaty Series No. 36, 1144 UNTS 123, OEA/Ser.L.V/II.82 doc.6 rev.1 at 25, 1992. See J.M. Pasqualucci, *The Practice and Procedure of the Inter-American Court of Human Rights*, 2nd edn., Cambridge University Press, Cambridge, 2013, 193.

88 See Rule 2(3) of the Rules of Procedure and Evidence (RPE) of the IACtHR.

89 See D. Contreras-Garduño and J. Fraser, 'The Identification of Victims Before the Inter-American Court of Human Rights and the International Criminal Court and its Impact on Participation and Reparations: A Domino Effect?', (2015) 7 *Inter-American and European Human Rights Journal* 174, at 174–203.

direct family members, but also those who suffered as a result of the violation occurring, even if they were unrelated through blood or marriage.[90]

Concerning the European human rights system, Article 34 of the European Convention on Human Rights ('ECHR') states that 'the Court may receive applications from any person, non-governmental organisation or group of individuals claiming to be the victim of a violation by one of the High Contracting Parties of the rights set forth in the Convention or the Protocols thereto'.[91] The word 'victim' in the context of Article 34 of the ECHR refers to the person or persons affected by the alleged violation. Hence, Article 34 concerns not just the direct victim or victims of the alleged breach, but also any indirect victims to whom the violation has caused harm or who would have a valid and personal interest in seeing it brought to an end. For example, if the alleged victim of a violation has died before the introduction of the application, it may be possible for the person with requisite legal interest as next of kin to introduce an application raising complaints related to the death or disappearance. In several cases,[92] the Court has accepted that close family members, such as parents of a person whose death or disappearance is alleged, can engage the responsibility of the State, claiming themselves to be indirect victims of the supposed violation of Article 2.[93] With regard to the African human rights system, the youngest of the three regional human rights systems currently in place,[94] it should be noted that, similarly to the Inter-American human rights system, victims cannot bring a complaint directly before the African Court on Human and Peoples' Rights ('ACtHPR'). In fact the African Commission on Human and Peoples' Rights is the body in charge of receiving complaints ('communications') from individuals, groups of individuals, NGOs, and States concerning alleged violations of the African Charter on Human and Peoples' Rights ('ACHPR').[95] Remarkably the word 'victim' is not used either in the African Charter or in the Protocol on the Establishment of an African Court on Human and Peoples' Rights; it appears

---

90 Judgment of 3 April 2009 (Merits, Reparations, and Costs), (2009) IACtHR, Series C No. 196, §128. See also Judgment of 27 November 2008 (Merits, Reparations, and Costs), (2008) IACtHR, Series C, No. 192, §119.

91 Art. 34 of the ECHR, as amended by Protocols Nos. 11 and 14, 4 November 1950, entered into force on 3 September 1953, ETS 5.

92 See for instance Judgment of 18 September 2009, ECtHR (Grand Chamber), Application No. 16064/90.

93 Art. 2 of the ECHR.

94 The African Commission on Human and Peoples' Rights ('African Commission') was established in 1987 as the body responsible for the implementation of the ACHPR. Protocol to the African Charter on Human and Peoples' Rights on the Establishment of an African Court on Human and Peoples' Rights, adopted by the Assembly of Heads of State and Government of the Organisation of African Unity on 10 June 1998. The Protocol came into force, following the ratifications of 15 Member States, on 25 January 2004.

95 Art. 55 of the ACHPR.

only in the Rules of Procedure of the African Commission.[96] In the Rules there is a reference to the way the African human rights system interprets the concept of victim; in fact Rule 109, which deals with the amicable settlement of disputes, states that the successors of the victim also have the power to consent to the terms of a settlement.

Concerning the definition of victim within the IHL framework it is important to bear in mind the caveat submitted in the introductory chapter. The wider category of war victims, which potentially refers to an entire population that has been caught up in an armed conflict, is to be distinguished from what is, hopefully, a smaller category: victims of violations of IHL, i.e. those who are actually injured by such violations.[97] With regard to the first group of victims it should be noted that they are the primary concern of IHL, although the word 'victim' does not appear in the Geneva Conventions or in other humanitarian law treaties.[98] In fact, the overall goal of IHL is to safeguard those persons who are not, or are no longer, taking part in hostilities and who shall be respected, protected and treated humanely. In other words the IHL regime focuses solely on persons to be protected against the dangers of war, leaving open the question of the actions required when such protection fails. Indeed, as with the 1949 Geneva Conventions, no general rights or legal status are conferred upon victims of IHL violations.[99]

Under ICL the idea that international criminal proceedings are, and should be, focused upon the punishment of individual perpetrators has been prevalent since the inception of this field of international law.[100] The legal framework created by the Rome Statute of the International Criminal Court amended this traditional approach. Alongside procedures for the trial and punishment of individuals, the Statute provides for victims' participation and for the possibility

96 Rules of Procedure of the African Commission on Human and Peoples' Rights Approved by the African Commission on Human and Peoples' Rights during its 47th ordinary session held in Banjul (The Gambia) from May 12 to 26, 2010.

97 On this point see C. McCarthy, 'Victim Redress and International Criminal Justice: Competing Paradigms, or Compatible Forms of Justice?', (2012) 10 *Journal of International Criminal Justice* 353, at 356. According to the author 'although the two 1977 Additional Protocols to the Geneva Conventions of 1949 do refer, on a number of occasions, to 'war victims', this terminology is generally used to denote those affected by conflict in general, rather than to refer to those persons injured by violations of the laws of war as such'. See also Zegveld, above note 13, at 501.

98 Zegveld, above note 13, at footnote 17.

99 Ibidem. As noted by the author the word victim does appear in the title of the two Protocols Additional to the Geneva Conventions of 1949: Protocol Additional to the Geneva Conventions of 12 August 1949, and relating to the Protection of Victims of International Armed Conflicts, 8 June 1977, entered into force on 7 December 1978, 1125 UNTS 3; and Protocol Additional to the Geneva Conventions of 12 August 1949, and relating to the Protection of Victims of Non-International Armed Conflicts, 8 June 1977, entered into force on 7 December 1978, 1125 UNTS 609.

100 See McCarthy, above note 97, at 352.

to obtain reparation. In order for an individual to be recognised as a victim in a trial before the ICC, he or she must meet the criteria set out in the Rome Statute and in the Court's Rules of Procedure and Evidence ('RPE'). The definition of who is considered a victim is outlined in Rule 85 of the RPE. According to this Rule:

> a) 'Victims' means natural persons who have suffered harm as a result of the commission of any crime within the jurisdiction of the Court;
>
> b) Victims may include organisations or institutions that have sustained direct harm to any of their property which is dedicated to religion, education, art or science or charitable purposes and to their historic monuments, hospitals and other places and objects for humanitarian purposes.[101]

As noted by some authors, the term 'victim' is presented as a wide-ranging concept since Rule 85(a) does not demand that the victim becomes the direct object of the criminal offence.[102] The provision seems in fact to cover all natural persons who have, directly or indirectly, suffered harm as a result of the commission of any crime within the jurisdiction of the ICC.[103] Crucial to shedding light on this important point has been the judgment on victims' participation issued by the Appeals Chamber in the *Lubanga* case. Previously the Trial Chamber in its analysis of the link between 'the harm allegedly suffered and the crime' juxtaposed Rule 85(a) and Rule 85(b) of the Rules, finding significance in the omission of the word 'direct' in Rule 85(a) and concluding that on a purposive interpretation of Rule 85(a) 'people can be the direct or indirect victims of a crime within the jurisdiction of the Court'.[104]

The Appeals Chamber has subsequently clarified that the harm suffered by a natural person is harm to that person, i.e. personal harm. Material, physical and psychological harm are all forms of harm that fall within Rule 85(a) if they are suffered personally by the victim. Harm suffered by one victim as a result of the commission of a crime within the jurisdiction of the Court can give rise to harm suffered by other victims.[105] This is evident, for instance, when there is a

---

101 Rule 85 of the Rules of Procedure and Evidence of the International Criminal Court, ICC-ASP/1/3.

102 M.H. Gozzi and J.P. Laborde, 'Les Nations Unies et le Droit des Victimes du Terrorisme', (2005) 76 *Revue Internationale de Droit Pénal* 297.

103 Judgment of 11 July 2009 (Judgment on Victims' Participation), (2009) ICC (Appeals Chamber), ICC-01/04–01/06, §32.

104 Judgment of 11 July 2008 (Judgment on the appeals of The Prosecutor and The Defence against Trial Chamber I's Decision on Victims' Participation of 18 January 2008), (2008) ICC (Appeals Chamber), ICC-01/01/01/06-1119, §91.

105 According to the judges 'the harm suffered by indirect victims must arise out of the harm suffered by direct victims'. See Judgment of 8 April 2009 (Redacted Version of Decision 'Indirect Victims'), ICC (Trial Chamber I), ICC-01/04–01/06–1813, §49.

close personal relationship between the victims such as the relationship between a child soldier and the parents of that child. The recruitment of a child soldier may result in personal suffering of both the child concerned and his/her parents. It is in this sense that the Appeals Chamber understands the Trial Chamber's statement that 'people can be the direct or indirect victims of a crime within the jurisdiction of the Court'.[106] The breadth of the concept of 'victim' within the ICC framework depends, thus, on whether the harm suffered is personal to the individual. If it is, it can attach to both direct and indirect victims.

As has emerged from this brief overview, there is a gap, or at least a lack of homogeneity, with regard to the definition of 'victim' in use within the different international law regimes covered by the present analysis. This problem has, to some extent, been solved by two soft law instruments adopted by the UN General Assembly. The first document is the Declaration of Basic Principles of Justice for Victims of Crime and Abuse of Power, according to which:

> 'Victims' means persons who, individually or collectively, have suffered harm, including physical or mental injury, emotional suffering, economic loss or substantial impairment of their fundamental rights, through acts or omissions that are in violation of criminal laws operative within Member States, including those laws proscribing criminal abuse of power ... The term 'victim' also includes, where appropriate, the immediate family or dependants of the direct victim and persons who have suffered harm in intervening to assist victims in distress or to prevent victimization.[107]

The same definition was included 20 years later in the UNBPG and will be used throughout this study.[108] In 2010 the ILA Committee on the Right to Reparation for Victims of Armed Conflict also relied on the key elements of this definition while drafting the Hague Declaration, which is dedicated to the substantive dimension of the right to reparation. According to Article 4 of the Declaration, the term 'victim' means natural or legal persons who have suffered harm as a result of a violation of the rules of international law applicable in armed conflict. The provision is without prejudice to the right of other persons, in particular those in a family or civil law relationship to the victims, to submit a claim on

106 Ibidem.

107 Declaration of Basic Principles of Justice for Victims of Crime and Abuse of Power, 29 November 1985, UN General Assembly, UN doc. A/RES/40/34.

108 See UNBPG, above note 2, §5: 'For purposes of the present document, victims are persons who individually or collectively suffered harm, including physical or mental injury, emotional suffering, economic loss or substantial impairment of their fundamental rights, through acts or omissions that constitute gross violations of international human rights law, or serious violations of international humanitarian law. Where appropriate, and in accordance with domestic law, the term 'victim' also includes the immediate family or dependants of the direct victim and persons who have suffered harm in intervening to assist victims in distress or to prevent victimization.'

behalf of victims provided that there is a legal interest therein. This may be the case where the victim is a minor child, incapacitated or otherwise unable to claim reparation.[109]

2.3. CHILDREN'S RIGHTS

Before the entry into force of the CRC, discussion of children's rights mainly referred to moral rights, understood as 'ideal rights' or 'conscientious rights', rather than legal or institutional rights.[110] The long path towards the eventual affirmation of children's rights, which used to be portrayed as 'a slogan in need of a definition',[111] has been especially marked by the rapid spread of various theories that defended, or denied, the legitimacy of children as bearers of moral and legal rights. The slow establishment of children's rights within the international legal framework represents a milestone in the struggle to foster the dignity and protection of children worldwide, although the mere enactment of legal rights risks remaining an abstract and general concept that does not improve children's lives until it is put into practice. As noted by Van Bueren, 'the definition of childhood in international law is critical because it determines which specific rights attach to the status of childhood and which legal remedies are available to children as a class', meaning that, in order to identify the kind of remedies and therefore the kind of reparations that a person can claim, it is necessary to have in mind which rights he/she is entitled to.[112] Historians traditionally define childhood as a 'social construction',[113] referring mainly to the fact that in Western countries until the Renaissance, children worked side by side with adults, wearing the same clothes and often depicted as 'men on a smaller scale'.[114] The notion of childhood came into existence quite recently and according to Freeman it is only since the Middle Ages that children have been perceived as different from adults and labelled as 'weak, innocent and in need of

109 'Declaration of International Law Principles for Victims of Armed Conflict' at the 74th ILA Conference, The Hague, Resolution 2/2010.

110 M. Freeman, *The Rights and Wrongs of Children*, F. Pinter Publishers, Dover, 1983, 33.

111 See H. Rodham, 'Children Under the Law', (1973) 43 *Harvard Education Review* 487; and by the same author 'Children's Policies: Abandonment and Neglect', (1977) 86 *Yale Law Journal* 1522, at 1529–1531.

112 See G. Van Bueren, *The International Law on the Rights of the Child*, Martinus Nijhoff Publishers, The Hague, 1998, 32.

113 'In medieval society the idea of childhood did not exist … It corresponds to an awareness of the particular nature which distinguishes the child from the adult … in medieval society this awareness was lacking'. P. Ariès, *Centuries of Childhood*, Jonathan Cape, London, 1962, 128.

114 According to Freeman, above note 110, at 9: 'One can only speculate as to why the idea of childhood did not exist in the medieval society. It may in part have been the result of fear of the infant's bestiality, itself the product of ignorance of, and pain associated with, child birth. In part too there is an element of indifference, since infant mortality rates were so high.'

special treatment'.[115] The change emerged first among the upper ranks of society, due to their better education and prosperity, and it slowly spread to the whole community.[116] Nevertheless, children were not considered individuals with an independent will as they were under the control of their parents. Only in the latter part of the twentieth century did the idea that rights may directly pertain to children finally emerge, generating debates and conflicting theories on the status of children within the international and national normative frameworks.

Prior to the drafting of the CRC the international community questioned itself about the possibility of enshrining the rights of children in a proper document.[117] To a certain degree the 'sudden' interest in children's rights and freedoms can be ascribed to the growing recognition of the existence of human rights pertaining to all human beings and to the urge to identify within mankind different sub-groups, or clusters, of individuals in need of extra safeguards and *ad hoc* provisions. The core human rights treaties laid the groundwork for a comprehensive set of rights from which each and every man in the world should benefit. Nonetheless, some categories of people required the international community to deploy special efforts. With regard to children the unprecedented degree of harm suffered during the 'Great War' and WWII, and their respective aftermaths, contributed to raising awareness of the fact they were no longer bystanders, but victims of grave violations and as such in need of extensive and specific protection.[118]

2.3.1. THE TWO DECLARATIONS OF THE RIGHTS OF THE CHILD

The first global attempt to draft a document entirely devoted to children dates back to 1924, when the Fifth Assembly of the League of Nations adopted the Declaration of the Rights of the Child, better known as the Geneva Declaration.[119] The Geneva Declaration was brief and aspirational, since its aim was to invite the

---

115 Ibidem. See also L. de Mause, *The History of Childhood*, Souvenir Press, London, 1974; and H. Cunningham, *Children and Childhood in Western Society since 1500*, Addison Wesley, London, 2005.

116 The controversial theory about childhood as 'an artefact of modernity' was first developed by the French historian Philippe Ariès. See Ariès above note 113.

117 'The earliest instruments focused on the protection of children, but providing only a piecemeal protection from specific forms of economic and sexual exploitation. In 1919 the International Labour Conference adopted the Minimum Age Industry Convention followed two years later by the adoption by the League of Nations of the International Convention for the Suppression of Traffic in Women and Children.' See G. Van Bueren, *International Documents on Children*, Martinus Nijhoff Publishers, The Hague, 1993.

118 See Freeman, above note 110, at 19.

119 Geneva Declaration of the Rights of the Child of 1924, adopted on 26 September 1924, League of Nations OJ Spec. Supp. 21, at 43 (1924).

States parties to follow its principles to promote children's welfare. It contained only five principles focused on the urge to guarantee children's well-being by feeding them, encouraging by all means their normal development and stressing the need to relieve them in times of distress.[120] Moreover, the Geneva Declaration was not concerned with States' obligations, but rather placed duties upon the men and women of all nations, underlining that the Assembly's intention was not to create a binding instrument, but rather to shed light on children's special needs. The 1924 Geneva Declaration was followed by a second one, adopted by the Temporary Social Commission of the Economic and Social Council of the United Nations ('Social Commission') in 1959.[121] Instead of writing a brand new charter, the Social Commission decided to maintain the form, the structure and the contents of the previous declaration, but adding the amendments needed to transform it into a more comprehensive text.[122] The preparatory work for the new Declaration started in 1949 and it took ten years before the draft Declaration was finally submitted to the General Assembly. Again, the Declaration contained no binding obligations towards States parties and there were a number of additional rights proposed by both States and international organisations which failed to be incorporated.[123]

In particular, during the drafting stage a number of States, above all Poland, did express their preference for the adoption of a convention rather than of a second declaration. As an alternative they supported the idea that the Declaration should contain at least an appeal to the governments, requesting them to adjust their domestic legislation to the principles enshrined therein.[124] The majority of States, however, opposed these requests mostly because 'the time had not yet come for the conclusion of a convention' nor to oblige States parties to translate their abstract commitment to the cause of children's rights into practice.[125] On 29 November 1959 the Declaration was adopted by the General Assembly without abstentions, unlike the UDHR. Although the Declaration of the Rights of the Child was not a binding legal instrument, its unanimous adoption accords it a greater weight than other General Assembly resolutions as it suggests that

---

120 The Declaration's preamble states that 'by the present Declaration ..., men and women of all the nations, recognising that mankind owes to the child the best it has to give, declare and accept it as their duty that, beyond and above all considerations of race, nationality or creed ... '.

121 UN General Assembly, Declaration of the Rights of the Child, 20 November 1959, UN doc. A/RES/1386(XIV).

122 See ECOSOC, 3rd year, 7th Session, Supplement no 7, at 31.

123 See Van Bueren above note 112, at 11.

124 Ibidem, at 10.

125 Ibidem, at 15. According to the author 'the great economic, social and cultural differences and the greatly divergent view on morality and religion prevailing in the various member States would give rise to many problems which must, at least for the time being, be considered to be insoluble'.

it was characterised by a strong moral force and that its principles were widely accepted and recognised by the international community. Notwithstanding its status of 'manifest rights' the 1959 Declaration represented a step towards the enhancement of children's rights, especially if compared to its predecessor. Within the 'new' Declaration children eventually began to be perceived as subjects of international law and not as only mere recipients, in particular since they were finally recognised as being capable of enjoying the benefits of specific rights and freedoms.

The United Nations established that 1979, which marked the 20th anniversary of the Declaration of the Rights of the Child, was to become the International Year of the Child.[126] Such a designation, according to Van Bueren, acted as 'an emotional magnet', which drew States towards the idea that the time was ripe to draft a convention on the rights of the child.[127] Poland was probably the most motivated upholder of the Convention, in fact it submitted a first draft to the Commission on Human Rights in 1978 in the hope of seeing the treaty concluded in 1979 to properly celebrate the International Year of the Child. The text proposed by Poland did not match the wishes either of the Commission or of the other Member States, who did not share Poland's desire to expand the contents of the Convention and its impact. The preparatory works started when the Convention against Torture and other Cruel, Inhuman or Degrading Treatment or Punishment ('CAT') was still in the negotiation phase. The CRC at the beginning of its drafting stage was 'pushed into the background' since States' delegates were required to attend both treaty working groups and priority was given to the CAT.[128] Notwithstanding its initial impasse the Convention developed far beyond the original expectations as it did not just focus on economic, social and cultural rights as was originally foreseen in the first draft.

2.3.2. CHILDREN'S RIGHTS WITHIN THE CONVENTION ON THE RIGHTS OF THE CHILD

Since its adoption in 1989, the Articles embodied in the CRC have been classified in several ways. One possible approach is to identify 'welfare rights'

126 'The International Year of the Child does not belong to the tradition of child liberation. Its values, its whole ethos, harked back to an earlier era of concern for children ... Almost every country in the world took part in the International Year of the Child in some way or other. Lip-service at least was paid to the ideal entrenched in the United Nations Declaration.' On this point see Freeman above note 110, at 24. See also J. Harris, 'The Political Status of Children' in K. Graham (ed.), *Contemporary Political Philosophy: Radical Studies*, Cambridge University Press, Cambridge, 1982, 45, at 46–50.

127 See Van Bueren, above note 112, at 14.

128 See in general S. Detrick (ed.), *The United Nations Convention on the Rights of the Child: A Guide to the Travaux Préparatoires*, Martinus Nijhoff Publishers, Dordrecht, 1992.

and 'agency rights' as the main clusters of rights within the Convention. The former guarantee to children certain forms of treatment such as the minimum standard of health care, education and protection from violence and cruelty; while the latter require children to take action and choose whether to exercise them or not, such as the right to participation.[129] For other authors, *in primis* Archard, the 'summa division' within the CRC has to be drawn between 'participation rights' and 'protection rights'. The former assume that children are independent agents capable of making their own choices, while the latter cluster of rights qualifies children as vulnerable and dependent beings in need of protection against harms.[130] This distinction, compared with the previous one, probably has the merit of offering a wider understanding of what 'participation' means since it directly connects the principle embodied in Article 12 to other provisions of the CRC, such as Articles 5, 13, 14 and 15.[131]

Hammarberg proposed a classification based on the so-called four 'P's', namely participation of children in decisions involving their own destiny; protection of children against discrimination and all forms of neglect; prevention of harm to children; and provision of assistance for their basic needs.[132] LeBlanc divided the rights into survival rights, membership rights, protection rights and empowerment rights.[133] The survival rights include not only the right to life, but also the right to all those rights which sustain life, e.g. the rights to an adequate standard of living and to health care. Membership rights are those that regulate the role of the child within his/her community and family. Protection rights are in charge of safeguarding the child against abuses perpetrated by the State or individuals. Empowerment rights secure respect for children as effective members of the communities they live in, fostering their freedom of thought and conscience and encouraging their capacity for self-determination. All the classifications proposed thus emphasise the existence and the relevance within the CRC of provisions which trigger and protect children's direct involvement in

---

129 On this point see J. Hart, 'Children's Participation and International Development: Attending to the Political', (2008) 16 *International Journal of Children's Rights* 407. According to the author 'For some, participation is a means either to ensure the greater relevance, efficiency and impact of development projects or to achieve democratic and inclusive processes of governance. For others, it is an end in itself: through the processes understood as participatory practice, the poor and marginalised acquire influence, skills, knowledge, networks and experience that they can use to improve their lives. Overall, participation is conceptualised as "empowering", oriented towards the transformation of lives and societies.'

130 D. Archard, *Children, Rights and Childhood*, Routledge, London, 2004, 70–84.

131 Ibidem, at 10, 'If participation is interpreted more broadly, meaning any involvement in activities, other rights such as those to physical integrity (articles 19 and 37) and to a name and identity (article 7) might belong to this cluster as well.'

132 T. Hammarberg, 'The UN Convention on the Rights of the Child and How to Make it Work', (1990) 25 *Human Rights Quarterly* 97, at 97–100.

133 L.J. LeBlanc, *The Convention on the Rights of the Child: UN Law-making on Human Rights*, University of Nebraska Press, Lincoln, 1995, 28.

every social dynamic that might affect them, including also those which take place during armed conflicts and within transitional justice contexts. Significantly, with the purpose of addressing growing abuse and exploitation of children worldwide, the United Nations General Assembly in 2000 adopted two Optional Protocols to the CRC, which increase the protection of children from involvement in armed conflicts and from sexual exploitation.[134] On 14 April 2014, a third Optional Protocol ('CRC-OP3') entered into force, allowing children to bring complaints directly to the Committee on the Rights of the Child.[135]

2.3.3. ARTICLES IN THE CONVENTION ON THE RIGHTS OF THE CHILD RELEVANT TO CHILDREN'S RIGHT TO REPARATION

The provisions enshrined in the CRC pursue mainly a twofold aim; on the one hand they set a higher standard of protection for human beings under the age of 18 years, and on the other hand they promote children's recognition as active stakeholders. There are a number of Articles that are relevant to children's right to reparation, for example Article 19, which protects children from all forms of physical or mental violence, injury or abuse, neglect or negligent treatment, and maltreatment or exploitation, including sexual abuse. As stressed by the Committee on the Rights of the Child in General Comment No. 13, Article 19 is strongly linked to a broad range of provisions in the Convention beyond those relating directly to violence,[136] for example children's rights to respect for their human dignity, physical and psychological integrity and to equal protection under the law. Furthermore the Committee specifies the obligations pertaining to States parties in relation to violence against children. Such obligations encompass the duty to act with due diligence and to prevent violence or violations of human rights, the obligation to protect child victims and witnesses from human rights violations, the obligation to investigate and to punish those responsible, and the obligation to provide access to redress.[137] In many instances children affected by violence will need to take part in a judicial proceeding to obtain justice and reparations. Remarkably, the first consideration in relation to children who

---

134 UN General Assembly, Optional Protocol to the Convention on the Rights of the Child on the Sale of Children, Child Prostitution and Child Pornography, 16 March 2001, entered into force on 18 January 2002, UN doc. A/RES/54/263. UN General Assembly, Optional Protocol to the Convention on the Rights of the Child on the Involvement of Children in Armed Conflict, 25 May 2000, entered into force on 12 February 2002, UN doc. A/RES/54/263.

135 UN Human Rights Council, Optional Protocol to the Convention on the Rights of the Child on a Communications Procedure: resolution adopted by the Human Rights Council, 19 December 2011, UN doc. A/RES/66/138.

136 Committee on the Rights of the Child, General Comment No. 13 (2011), The Right of the Child to Freedom from all Forms of Violence, UN doc. CRC/C/GC/13.

137 Ibidem, §5.

come into contact with such procedures is what is in their best interests.[138] Article 3, paragraph 1, of the CRC gives the child the right to have his/her best interests assessed and taken into account as a primary concern in all actions or decisions that affect him/her, in both the public and the private sphere. The concept of the 'child's best interests' is not a new one, in fact it pre-dates the CRC and was already enshrined in the 1959 Declaration of the Rights of the Child[139] and the Convention on the Elimination of All Forms of Discrimination against Women ('CEDAW'),[140] as well as in regional instruments, much national legislation and international law.[141] Despite the wide use of this concept, the 'child's best interests' was only properly defined through the adoption of General Comment No. 14, in 2013. According to the Committee the 'best interests of the child' is a dynamic concept that encompasses various issues which are constantly evolving. It should be read as a threefold concept, which entails a substantive right, a fundamental interpretative legal principle and a rule of procedure. With regard to the first, the Committee explains that Article 3(1) creates an intrinsic obligation for States, is directly applicable ('self-executing') and can be invoked before a court. Moreover, as a substantive right it should be guaranteed that it will be implemented whenever a decision is to be made concerning a child, a group of identified or unidentified children or children in general. Secondly, the 'best interests of the child' as a fundamental, interpretative legal principle implies that if a legal provision is open to more than one interpretation, the interpretation which most effectively serves the child's best interests should always prevail. Thirdly, as a rule of procedure, the 'best interests of the child' requires that whenever a decision is to be made that will affect a specific child, an identified group of children or children in general, the decision-making process must include an evaluation of the possible impact (positive or negative) of the decision on the child or children concerned. In other words, the decision must be the result of the assessment and determination of what is in the best interests of the child in the specific circumstances. Assessment and determination of the child's best interests are two fundamental steps. The 'best-interests assessment' consists in evaluating and balancing all the elements and factors necessary to make a decision in a specific situation for a specific individual child or group of children. It is carried out by the decision maker and his/her staff – if possible a

---

138 See Art. 3(1) of the CRC. According to this provision: 'In all actions concerning children, whether undertaken by public or private social welfare institutions, courts of law, administrative authorities or legislative bodies, the best interests of the child shall be a primary consideration.'

139 UN General Assembly, Declaration of the Rights of the Child, 20 November 1959, UN doc. A/RES/1386(XIV), §2.

140 See Arts. 5(b) and 16(1)(d) of the CEDAW.

141 See Committee on the Rights of the Child, General Comment No. 14 (2013) On the Right of the Child to have his or her Best Interests Taken as a Primary Consideration (Art. 3, para. 1), UN doc. CRC/C/GC/14.

multidisciplinary team – and requires the participation of the child. The 'best-interests determination' describes the formal process with strict procedural safeguards designed to determine the child's best interests on the basis of the best-interests assessment.[142] In cases where a child finds him/herself in what the Committee defines as a 'situation of vulnerability' (e.g. children affected by armed conflict, disability, gender violence, children belonging to a minority group, refugees or asylum seekers, victims of abuse, street children, etc. …) authorities and decision makers need to take into account the different kinds and degrees of vulnerability of each child, as each child is unique and each situation must be assessed according to the child's uniqueness.[143]

The notion of the 'child's best interests' is aimed at ensuring both the full and effective enjoyment of all the rights recognised in the CRC and the holistic maturation of the child, which shall embrace the child's physical, mental, spiritual, moral, psychological and social development.[144] In one of its General Comments, the Committee on the Rights of the Child has explained that 'an adult's judgment of a child's best interests cannot override the obligation to respect all the child's rights under the Convention'.[145] As within the provisions enshrined in the CRC there is no hierarchy of rights, all the rights provided for therein are in the 'child's best interests' and no right could be compromised by a negative interpretation of this concept.[146] Significantly the Committee clarifies that the assessment of the child's best interests must include respect for the child's right to express his or her views as stated in Article 12 of the CRC. These two Articles, 3 and 12, appear to be intimately entwined and mutually reinforcing. In particular Article 3(1) cannot be correctly applied if the requirements of Article 12 are not met. Similarly, by facilitating the essential role of children in all decisions affecting their lives, Article 3(1) is crucial for the implementation of Article 12.

Article 12 of the CRC is represented as one of the most innovative of the Convention and it is considered as a unique provision in human rights treaty law.[147] Its scope is to address the legal and social status of children, who, on

---

142 Ibidem, §47. See also UNHCR, 'Guidelines on Determining the Best Interests of the Child', May 2008, available at: http://www.unhcr.org/4566b16b2.pdf.

143 Committee on the Rights of the Child, General Comment No. 14, §76.

144 See Committee on the Rights of the Child, General Comment No. 5 (2003), General Measures of Implementation of the Convention on the Rights of the Child, UN doc. CRC/GC/2003/5.

145 See Committee on the Rights of the Child, General Comment No. 13 (2011), The Right of the Child to Freedom from all Forms of Violence, UN doc. CRC/C/GC/13, §61. See also Rodham, above note 111, at 487.

146 See Committee on the Rights of the Child, General Comment No. 14, §4.

147 Art. 12 of the CRC states that: '1. States Parties shall assure to the child who is capable of forming his or her own views the right to express those views freely in all matters affecting the child, the views of the child being given due weight in accordance with the age and maturity of the child. 2. For this purpose the child shall in particular be provided the opportunity to be heard in any judicial and administrative proceedings affecting the child, either directly, or through a representative or an appropriate body, in a manner consistent with the procedural Rules of the national law.'

the one hand, lack adults' full autonomy but, on the other hand, are recognised by the CRC as subjects of rights. Paragraph 1 assures to every child capable of forming his/her own views the right to express those views freely. Paragraph 2 states, in particular, that the child shall be afforded the right to be heard in any judicial or administrative proceedings affecting him/her.[148] As explained above, Article 12 of the Convention establishes the right of every child to freely express his/her views, in all matters affecting him/her, and the subsequent right for those views to be given due weight, according to the child's age and maturity. Article 12 attributes the right to be heard not only to an individual child, but also to a group of children (e.g. the children in a neighbourhood, the children of a given country, children with disabilities, girls, children associated with armed forces or groups). In both cases, i.e. views expressed individually or as a group, due weight should be given in accordance with age and maturity. Article 12 states very clearly that age alone cannot determine the significance of a child's views. In fact children's levels of understanding are not uniformly linked to their biological age. Research has shown that many factors, such as information, experience, environment, social and cultural expectations, and levels of support, contribute in different ways to the development of the child's capacities to form his/her view.[149] For this reason, the views of the child have to be assessed on a case-by-case examination. Maturity is mentioned in Article 12 as one of the factors that shall be taken into account when determining the individual capacity of a child. Generally speaking, maturity refers to the ability to understand and assess the implications of a particular matter; in the context of Article 12 it can be defined as the capacity of a child to express, in a reasonable and independent manner, his/her views on various issues. As pointed out by the Committee, in evaluating the views expressed by the child the impact of the matter on the child cannot be disregarded. In particular it shall be borne in mind that 'a child cannot be heard effectively where the environment is intimidating, hostile, insensitive or inappropriate for her or his age'.[150]

According to the principles embedded in the CRC, proceedings must be both accessible and child appropriate. In particular it is necessary to pay attention to the provision and delivery of child-friendly information, adequate support for self-advocacy, appropriately trained staff, design of court rooms, clothing of judges and lawyers, sight screens, and separate waiting rooms.[151] As stressed by the Committee, children are free to decide whether or not they wish to exercise the

---

148 Committee on the Rights of the Child, General Comment No. 12 (2009), The Right of the Child to be Heard, UN doc. CRC/C/GC/12, §3.

149 See generally UNICEF, 'Inequities in Early Childhood Development: What the Data Say, Evidence from the Multiple Indicator Cluster Surveys', February 2012, available at: http://www.unhcr.org/4566b16b2.pdf. See also R.H. Bradley, and R.F. Corwyn, 'Socioeconomic Status and Child Development', (2002) 53 *Annual Review of Psychology* 371, at 380–391.

150 See Committee on the Rights of the Child, General Comment No. 12, §34.

151 Ibidem.

right embedded in Article 12. Expressing views, in fact, is a choice for the child, not an obligation, and this is true in all kinds of proceedings – administrative, civil or criminal. In line with the provisions enshrined in Articles 3(1) and 12 of the CRC, judicial and non-judicial mechanisms, both at the national and at the international level, must take all possible steps to minimise the risk of harm to the child and ensure that his/her rights, including the right to reparation, are fully respected and duly implemented. Despite the standard set forth in the CRC, according to the Office of the Special Representative of the Secretary-General for Children and Armed conflict:

> at the present time, all the international and hybrid courts require children to give evidence during the trial and to be subject to cross-examination. It is not possible for the child to give pre-recorded testimony, although many western legal systems now permit this. Neither does the ICC permit the use of intermediaries to rephrase questions in simpler language, enabling the child to give a clear and unambiguous response.[152]

The issue of children's participation in proceedings affecting them will be further analysed and discussed in later chapters. What has emerged so far is that the CRC provides a number of provisions aimed at fostering child victims' rights in the aftermath of any type of violation. Moreover, the CRC applies also during an armed conflict, as IHRL and IHL are mutually reinforcing,[153] and extraterritorially, meaning that it covers all people within a State party's jurisdiction.[154] The relevance of children's rights in armed conflict is also highlighted in the text of the CRC. Two provisions, namely Article 38 and Article 39, specifically refer to the situation of children affected by war. The first Article prohibits the recruitment of children under the age of 15 years and their use in the hostilities. Furthermore Article 38 requests States parties to take all feasible measures to ensure protection and care of children who are affected by an armed

---

152 See Office of the Special Representative of the Secretary-General for Children and Armed conflict, Working Paper No 3 'Children and Justice During and in the Aftermath of Armed Conflict', September 2011, at 16, available at: http://childrenandarmedconflict.un.org/publications/WorkingPaper-3_Children-and-Justice.pdf. See also S. Beresford, 'Child Witnesses and the International Criminal Justice System: Does the International Criminal Court Protect the Most Vulnerable?', (2005) 3 *Journal of International Criminal Justice* 721, at 730–735.

153 On this point see C. Tomuschat, 'Human Rights and International Humanitarian Law', (2010) 21 *The European Journal of International Law* 15, at 18–23. See also Advisory Opinion of 9 July 2004 (Legal Consequences of the Construction of a Wall on the Occupied Palestinian Territory), (2004) ICJ Reports p. 136, §106, where the ICJ found that the Convention applied within the occupied Palestinian territory.

154 Committee on the Rights of the Child, Concluding Observations on the second to fourth Periodic Reports of Israel, adopted by the Committee at its sixty-third session (27 May–14 June 2013), UN doc. CRC/C/ISR/CO/2-4.

conflict.[155] Article 39 is deemed as the key provision for the analysis of children's right to reparation. According to it:

> State parties shall take all appropriate measures to promote physical and psychological recovery and social reintegration of a child victim of: any form of neglect, exploitation, or abuse; torture or any other form of cruel, inhuman or degrading treatment or punishment; or armed conflicts. Such recovery and reintegration shall take place in an environment which fosters the health, self-respect and dignity of the child.

Article 39 does not refer explicitly to reparation, however it places on States parties the obligation to restore children's well-being in the aftermath of any wrongful act, including those perpetrated during an armed conflict. In General Comment No 5, the Committee on the Rights of the Child stressed that

> [f]or rights to have meaning, effective remedies must be available to redress violations. This requirement is *implicit* in the Convention and consistently referred to in the other six major international human rights treaties. Children's special and dependent status creates real difficulties for them in pursuing remedies for breaches of their rights. So States need to give particular attention to ensuring that there are effective, child-sensitive procedures available to children and their representatives. These should include the provision of child-friendly information, advice, advocacy, including support for self-advocacy, and [effective] access to independent complaints procedures and to the courts with necessary legal and other assistance. Where rights are found to have been breached, there should be *appropriate reparation*, including compensation, and, where needed, measures to promote physical and psychological recovery, rehabilitation and reintegration, as required by Article 39.[156]

Significantly, individual complaints about violations of the rights enshrined in the CRC and its Optional Protocols can, as of April 2014, be heard by the Committee on the Rights of the Child, finally filling the gap in the enforcement provisions of the CRC in comparison to other human rights treaties.[157] The issue remains as to whether this procedure can truly be deemed 'child friendly' and in line with the approach taken by the Committee. This question will be addressed in Chapter 5 when the international quasi-judicial and judicial mechanisms are discussed.

---

155 Art. 38(4) of the CRC.

156 Committee on the Rights of the Child General Comment No. 5 (2003), General Measure of Implementation of the Convention on the Rights of the Child, UN doc. CRC/GC/2003/5, at 7 (emphasis added).

157 Optional Protocol to the Convention on the Rights of the Child on a Communications Procedure, above note 135.

2.4. CHILDREN'S VULNERABILITY AND RESILIENCE

The need to provide child victims with specific measures of protection and redress stems from the assumption that children constitute a particularly vulnerable group of victims. Vulnerability can be generally defined as 'the exposure to uninsured risks leading to a socially unacceptable level of well-being' and it is measured according to 'physical and emotional development, ability to communicate needs, mobility, size and dependence'.[158] From a legal point of view, even though the notion of vulnerability has not been clearly defined at either the national or international level, the necessity of special treatment of certain categories of victims is well established and acknowledged.[159] According to the Recommendation on Assistance to Crime Victims of the Council of Europe, '[S]tates should ensure that victims who are particularly vulnerable, either *through their personal characteristics or through circumstances of the crime*, can benefit from special measures best suited to their situation'.[160] Thus, 'vulnerable victims' are those victims who find it especially difficult to fully exercise their recognised rights due to cultural, physical or psychological reasons.[161] Children's experiences of vulnerability have been described as 'multidimensional and different from those of adults'.[162] Besides child-specific factors, some authors have also recognised 'child-intensified' vulnerabilities, which may affect the whole population, but have a stronger impact on children,[163] i.e. physical/biological vulnerabilities, dependency-related vulnerabilities and institutionalised disadvantages.[164] Furthermore, it has been argued that child-specific sources of vulnerability are related to (a) their multi-dimensionality;

---

158 J. Hoogeveen, E. Tesliuc and R. Vakis, *A Guide to the Analysis of Risk, Vulnerability and Vulnerable Groups*, World Bank, 2005, available at: http://siteresources.worldbank.org/INTSRM/Publications/20316319/RVA.pdf.

159 See the Report 'Victims in Europe: Implementation of the EU Framework Decision on the standing of victims in the criminal proceedings in the Member States of the European Union', July 2009, at 39, available at: http://www.bkb.cz/files/uploaded/UserFiles/File/Project_Victims_Europe_Final_Report.pdf.

160 Art. 3.4 of Recommendation 8 of the Committee of Ministers to Member States on Assistance to Crime Victims, adopted 14 June 2006, available at: https://wcd.coe.int/ViewDoc.jsp?id=1011109&Site=CM&BackColorInternet=9999CC&BackColorIntranet=FFBB55&BackColorLogged=FFAC75.

161 See F. Capone., K. Hausler, D. Fairgrieve and C. McCarthy, *Education and the Law of Reparations in Insecurity and Armed Conflict*, BIICL/PEIC, London, 2013.

162 DFID, HelpAge International, Hope & Homes for Children, Institute of Development Studies, International Labour Organization, Overseas Development Institute, Save the Children UK, UNDP, UNICEF and the World Bank (2009), 'Joint Statement on Advancing Child-Sensitive Social Protection', available at: https://www.unicef.org/aids/files/CSSP_joint_statement_10.16.09.pdf.

163 R. Sabates-Wheeler, S. Devereux and A. Hodges, 'Taking the Long View: What Does a Child Focus Add to Social Protection?', (2009) 40 *IDS Bulletin* 109, at 115–119.

164 K. Roetten and R. Sabates-Wheeler, 'A Child Sensitive Approach to Social Protection: Serving Practical and Strategic Needs', paper presented at the conference 'Social Protection for Social Justice', London, Institute of Development Studies, 13–15 April 2011.

(b) their changing pattern over the life-cycle; (c) the relationship with their caregivers; and, (d) their 'voicelessness', a category including the lack of proper legislative frameworks to allow children to participate in societal settings, including judicial proceedings.[165]

With regard to children affected by armed conflict, Machel has pointed out that children in war-torn countries face higher risk than their peers of experiencing

> infant, child and adolescent mortality, low immunization, low access to health services, high malnutrition, high burden of disease, low school enrollment rates, high repetition rates, poor school performance and/or high drop-out rates; intra-household neglect; family and community abuse and maltreatment, in particular harassment and violence; economic and sexual exploitation, due to lack of care and protection.[166]

Moreover, Machel explains that armed conflicts across and between communities result in massive levels of destruction – physical, human, moral and cultural. Not only are large numbers of children killed and injured, but countless others grow up deprived of their material and emotional needs, including the structures that give meaning to social and cultural life. The entire fabric of their societies, their homes, schools, health systems and religious institutions are torn to pieces.[167]

When an armed conflict occurs children suffer from all the victimisations that adults do, however, as noted by Finkelhor, one salient difference is that children also suffer from offences that are *particular to their status.*[168] Generally speaking the main status characteristic of childhood is its condition of dependency, which is a function, at least in part, of social and psychological immaturity. The violation of this dependency status results in forms of daily victimisation that are not suffered by most adults.[169] In relation to situations of armed conflict, the dependency status is a key characteristic, which, however, does not alone explain the exacerbated vulnerability and the disproportionate suffering of children. What makes their victimhood 'unique' is the likely exposure to multiple forms of victimisation, which may result in what some authors have described as polyvictimisation.[170] Only a few studies have applied the notion of

---

165 N. Jones, 'Promoting Synergies between Child Protection and Social Protection: West and Central Africa', Regional Thematic Report 5 Study, UNICEF WCARO and Overseas Development Institute, 2009, Dakar. Cited in M. Sanfilippo, C. de Neubourg and B. Martorano, 'The Impact of Social Protection on Children: A Review of the Literature', Working Paper 2012-06, UNICEF Innocenti Research, Centre, 2012, Florence.

166 See 'Impact of Armed Conflict on Children: note by the Secretary-General', above note 36.

167 Ibidem.

168 See D. Finkelhor, *Childhood Victimisation: Violence, Crime, and Abuse in the Lives of Young People*, Oxford University Press, New York, 2008, 13.

169 Ibidem.

170 The term 'polyvictimsation' describes the multiple and interrelated nature of child victimisation, to distinguish it from traditional child victimisation studies that customarily focus on only one type of victimisation, such as sexual abuse. K. Cyr, C. Chamberlandb, M.E. Clément, G. Lessard, J. Wemmers, D. Collin-Vézina, M.H. Gagné and D. Damant,

polyvictimisation to war-torn settings so far,[171] while a larger body of research has looked at the entire spectrum of children's exposure to violence, crime, abuse across all ages, settings, and time frames in peacetime.[172] In particular with regard to children who suffered as a result of an armed conflict, Ms Schauer, a psychologist who served as an expert witness in the *Lubanga* case, noted that

> [a]mong a number of at risk populations, children of war and child soldiers are a particularly vulnerable group and often suffer from devastating long-term consequences of experienced or witnessed acts of violence. Child war survivors have to cope with repeated traumatic life events, exposure to combat, shelling and other life threatening events, acts of abuse such as torture or rape, violent death of a parent or friend, witnessing loved ones being tortured or injured, separation from family, being abducted or held in detention, insufficient adult care, lack of safe drinking water and food, inadequate shelter, explosive devices and dangerous building ruins in proximity, marching or being transported in crowded vehicles over long distances and spending months in transit camps.[173]

Moreover, the expert witness highlighted the fact that these experiences can hamper children's healthy development and their ability to 'fully function' even once the violence has ceased. In fact, children's experiences during armed conflict affect their recovery and also their capacity to participate in transitional justice processes, including criminal proceedings. As stated above, all children are affected by an armed conflict, remarkably though, not all of them suffer in the same way and to the same degree. For example, children who are direct victims of violence associated with armed forces or groups or victims of sexual violence or who have very little support to rely on are particularly exposed to stigma and discrimination, which significantly increases the difficulties of achieving rehabilitation and reintegration. UNICEF, in its submission on the principles to

'Polyvictimization and Victimization of Children and Youth: Results from a Population Survey', (2013) 37 *Child Abuse and Neglect* 814, at 816–820. D. Finkelhor, R.K. Omrod, and H.A. Turner, 'Poly-victimization. A Neglected Component in Child Victimisation', (2007) 31 *Child Abuse and Neglect* 7, at 10–16.

171 B. Cole, M. Maxwell and A. Chipaca, 'Surviving in the Shadows of War: Polyvictimised Children in Post-conflict Angola', (2014) 16 *Crime Prevention and Community Safety* 87, at 94–104.

172 See Cyr et al. above note 170, at 816. J.D. Ford, D. J. Grasso, J. Hawke and J.F. Chapman, 'Poly-victimization among Juvenile Justice-Involved Youths', (2013) 37 *Child Abuse and Neglect* 788, at 796–800. See also H.A. Turner, D. Finkelhor and R. Omrod, 'Poly-victimisation in a National Sample of Children and Youth', (2010) 38 *American Journal of Preventative Medicine* 323, at 325–329.

173 Expert Report of Ms Schauer (CHM-00001), 'The Psychological Impact of Child Soldiering', ICC-01/04-01/06-1729-Anxl (EVD-CHM-00001).

be applied and the procedures to be followed with regard to reparations in the *Lubanga* case, stressed that

> [t]he fact the victims were children at the time of the commission of the offence should be given great weight by the Court in assessing the harm they endured because of their vulnerability as children. The physical and psychological effects of crimes on children are extensively long lasting and harmful. The victims, in addition to suffering from violations of their fundamental rights, were also denied basic needs. The denial of their rights and needs can have enduring and sometimes lifelong repercussions, for example where children have lost access to education.[174]

Besides affecting the victims, it has been scientifically assessed that psychological exposure and suffering from trauma can cripple individuals and families even into subsequent generations. For example, after having experienced organised violence, affected parents can leave an imprint in their grandchildren's generation.[175] In particular, violence and trauma at the time of the parents' childhood may result in problematic attachment relationships that have long-term consequences for mental health and interpersonal relationships on the side of their children, meaning that an intergenerational cycle of dysfunction is set in motion.[176] Within the broader group of child victims of armed conflict it is possible to identify several sub-groups that present specific characteristics, including the types of violations to which they may be exposed. The Committee on the Rights of the Child in its General Comment No. 6 on the Treatment of Unaccompanied and Separated Children Outside their Country of Origin has stressed that

> ... States must assess and address the particular plight and vulnerabilities of such children. They should take into account the fact that unaccompanied children have undergone separation from family members and have also, to varying degrees, experienced loss, trauma, disruption and violence. Many of such children, in particular, those who are refugees, have further experienced pervasive violence and the stress associated with a country afflicted by war. This may have created deep-rooted feelings of helplessness and undermined a child's trust in others.[177]

---

174 See UNICEF, 'Submission on the Principles to be Applied and the Procedures to be followed by the Chamber with regard to Reparations', ICC-01/04-01/06-2878 11-05-2012, §2.

175 Expert Report of Ms Schauer, above note 173, at 25.

176 See R. Yehuda, S.L. Halligan and L.M. Bierer, 'Relationship of Parental Trauma Exposure and PTSD to PTSD, Depressive and Anxiety Disorders in Offspring', (2001) 35 *Journal of Psychiatric Research* 261, at 263–270.

177 Committee on the Rights of the Child, General Comment No. 6 (2005), Treatment of Unaccompanied and Separated Children outside their Country of Origin, UN doc. CRC/GC/2005/6, at 14.

The Committee thus underlined how the vulnerability of unaccompanied and separated children can be exacerbated by the confluence of an array of events, factors and negative experiences also connected to the absence of a caring adult/guardian. Similarly with regard to girls the Committee highlighted that they are 'particularly susceptible to marginalization, poverty and suffering during armed conflict, and many may have experienced gender based violence in the context of armed conflict'.[178] In the case of child soldiers the Criminal Chamber of Colombia's Constitutional Court stated that 'the recruitment of boys, girls and teenagers [for the purpose of participating in] the armed confrontations inter alia violates their rights to personal integrity, life, liberty, free development of their personality, freedom of expression, education, health, family and recreation'.[179] What emerges quite strongly is that traumatic events leave children with deep wounds that heal slowly, especially when the violations occur in conjunction with an armed conflict, when the risk of being affected by multiple violations is maximised.

Despite the undisputed vulnerability of child victims of armed conflict and the exposure to multiple forms of victimisation, children and youth can demonstrate remarkable resilience in the face of war experiences. This aspect, which is largely overlooked, especially when it comes to reparations awarded through judicial mechanisms, is, however, extremely important to determine the kind of intervention and the redress measures that can minimise the effects of war and the consequences of IHL and IHRL violations. The umbrella term 'resilience' encompasses a number of phenomena, namely (1) beating the odds in situations of high cumulative risk for developing mental problems, (2) coping well under difficult circumstances, (3) bouncing back after some catastrophe or severe deprivation and (4) post-traumatic growth following adversity, through transformational reorganisation of developing systems.[180] In other, and simpler, words resilience can be understood as the capacity to adapt and function reasonably well despite exposure to adversity.[181] As stressed by Werner, who has reviewed and reflected on studies that have explored the effects of war on children around the world,[182] a number of protective factors appear to moderate

178 Ibidem.

179 Judgment of 2 March 2004, Colombian Constitutional Court, Criminal Chamber, Case No. C-172/04.

180 A.S. Masten, 'Resilience in Children Threatened by Extreme Adversity: Frameworks for Research, Practice, and Translational Synergy', (2001) 23 *Development and Psychopathology* 493, cited in C. Fernando and M. Ferrari (eds.) *Handbook of Resilience in Children of War*, Springer-Verlag, New York, 2013, 3.

181 See A.S. Masten, K.M. Best, and N. Garmezy, 'Resilience and Development: Contributions from the Study of Children who Overcome Adversity', (1990) 2 *Development and Psychopathology* 425, at 426.

182 See E.E. Werner, 'Children and War: Risk, Resilience, and Recovery', (2012) 24 *Development and Psychopathology* 553, at 555–558.

the impact of war-related adversities on children. Among them, Werner particularly emphasised

> a strong bond between the primary caregiver and the child; the mother's mental health; the availability of additional caregivers, such as grandparents and older siblings; the social support of members in the community who are exposed to the same hardships, especially teachers and peers, a shared sense of values; a religious belief that finds meaning in suffering; the assumption of responsibility for the protection and welfare of others; an internal locus of control, and the use of humour and altruism as defence mechanisms.[183]

Whereas many studies have been conducted on the traumas suffered by children affected by war,[184] only recently has attention been focused on the resilience of these children and the pathways to social reintegration.[185] Stark and Wessells, in fact, suggested replacing the trauma approach, which focuses on the deficits and thus underestimates children's abilities to cope with distress and to function, with a resilience paradigm that is based instead on strengthening empowerment, young people's agency, and voice.[186] Without digging too much into the psychological and psychosocial aspects relevant to assess the impact of war on child and adolescent mental health, this book argues that vulnerability and resilience are two sides of the same coin as both play a crucial role in the determination of the forms of reparation that can better serve the purpose of redressing children who, individually or collectively, have been affected by violations of international law committed during an armed conflict.

---

[183] Ibidem, at 555.

[184] See for example J. Barenbaum, V. Ruchkin and M.C. Schwab-Stone, 'The Psychosocial Aspects of Children Exposed to War: Practice and Policy Initiatives', (2004) 45 *Journal of Child Psychology and Psychiatry* 41, at 50–62; V. Attanayake, R. McKay, M. Joffres, S. Singh, F. Jr Burkle and E. Mills, 'Prevalence of Mental Disorders among Children Exposed to War: A Systematic Review of 7,920 Children', (2009) 25 *Medicine Conflict and Survival* 4, at 10–19; W.H. Sack, C. Him and D. Dickson, 'Twelve-year Follow-up Study of Khmer Youths who Suffered Massive War Trauma as Children', (1999) 38 *Journal of the American Academy of Child & Adolescent Psychiatry* 1173, at 1174–1179.

[185] T.S. Betancourt and K.T. Khan, 'The Mental Health of Children Affected by Armed Conflict: Protective Processes and Pathways to Resilience', (2008) 20 *International Review of Psychiatry* 317, at 320–328; A.S. Masten and A.J. Narayan, 'Child Development in the Context of Disaster, War, and Terrorism: Pathways of Risk and Resilience', (2012) 63 *Annual Review of Psychology* 1, at 11–15.

[186] See L. Stark and M. Wessells, 'The Fallacy of the Ticking Time Bomb: Resilience of Children Formerly Recruited into Armed Forces and Groups', in Fernando and Ferrari, above note 180, at 95.

2.5. CHILDREN AND WOMEN AS TWO DISTINCT GROUPS OF VULNERABLE VICTIMS

The recognition of women and children as particularly vulnerable groups was strongly supported by the social movements that got a foothold in the early 1970s. Such movements identified children as one of the major oppressed groups in Western society, alongside women, black people and the proletariat.[187] Several authors highlighted in particular the link between the liberation of women and the liberation of children, as they considered their respective oppressions as 'intertwined and mutually reinforcing'.[188] This correlation continues to emerge since children's destiny, especially during or after an armed conflict, is often associated with that of women'. The main difference though is that women over the course of time have gained a stronger position, which has empowered them to demand specific reparations and ask for effective and adequate measures. Most of the projects submitted to the ICC's TFV, for instance, have incorporated gender-specific interventions in order to support the special vulnerability of women and girls. These efforts are far from being a peculiarity of the ICC alone.[189] In fact many reparations programmes aim to prioritise women's redress, especially in post-conflict countries where the female population usually constitutes the main resource left.[190]

Nowadays it is also widely accepted that the many forms of violence that target or affect women's reproductive function or capacity, in particular rape or other sexual abuses, must be properly conceptualised in reparation debates.[191] As the outcome of the International Meeting on Women and Girls' Right to a Remedy and Reparation, held in Nairobi from 19 to 21 March 2007, the Nairobi Declaration was adopted aiming to 'enlighten the debate on the issue

---

187 See ARCHARD, above note 130, at 70–84.

188 S. FIRESTONE, *The Dialectic of Sex: The Case for Feminist Revolution*, Farrar, Strauss and Giroux, New York, 2003.

189 See Guidance Note of The Secretary-General, 'Reparations for Conflict-Related Sexual Violence', June 2014, available at: http://www.ohchr.org/Documents/Press/GuidanceNoteReparationsJune-2014.pdf.

190 For instance in Rwanda after the 1994 genocide there were twice as many women as men and while the gap has since narrowed, more than a third of households are still headed by women. According to the Rwandan Commerce Minister Monique Nsanzabaganwa, actually women make up 55 per cent of the workforce and own about 40 per cent of businesses. On this point see also C. FERSTMAN, M. GOETZ and A. STEPHENS, 'Introduction', in C. FERSTMAN, M. Goetz and A. STEPHENS (eds.), *Reparations for Victims of Genocide, War Crimes and Crimes against Humanity*, Martinus Nijhoff Publishers, Leiden, 2009, 7, at 10.

191 On this point please see RUBIO-MARIN, above note 48, at 39, and by the same author, *What Happened to the Women? Gender and Reparations for Human Rights Violations* Social Science Research Council, New York, 2006.

of reparations, most specifically in cases of sexual violence'. The Declaration is intended to give voice to women who have survived such atrocities:

> In this respect, the Nairobi Declaration builds on the Basic Principles and Guidelines on the Right to a Remedy and Reparation for Victims of Gross Violations of International Human Rights Law and Serious Violations of International Humanitarian Law. However, it adds to the debate in that it seeks to redefine reparation from a gendered perspective.[192]

These efforts may be considered as a legacy of the International Criminal Tribunal for the Former Yugoslavia ('ICTY') and the International Criminal Tribunal for Rwanda ('ICTR'), since, through the issuing of some almost revolutionary judgments, crimes of sexual violence were recognised as war crimes, crimes against humanity and genocide.[193] The *Akayesu case* and others held before the *ad hoc* tribunals created a new awareness that women had been used as a means of war.[194] They became visible, personalised and recognised in the international criminal justice framework as a specific group of vulnerable victims. The same thing is happening nowadays with child soldiers as the crime of recruiting or using children to participate actively in hostilities has been brought to world prominence through a number of ground-breaking cases.[195] Not surprisingly, the attention placed on specific crimes has had a ripple effect of increasing interest in the victims, their needs and their vulnerability. Of course as in the case of women, who are affected by SGBV in greater numbers than men and boys[196] but should not be confined solely within that victimological pattern, children can be victims of enlistment, conscription and use in hostilities *as well as* the target of many other kinds of violations that trigger exposure to different consequences and the urge to identify appropriate reparative measures and resilience pathways. The exploitation of girls and their sexuality through marked gender disparity certainly makes them more exposed than their male

---

192 V. Couillard, 'The Nairobi Declaration: Redefining Reparations for Women Victims of Sexual Violence', (2007) 1 *International Journal of Transitional Justice* 444, at 445–450.

193 See A.L.M. de Brouwer, *Supranational Criminal Prosecution of Sexual Violence*, Intersentia, Antwerp, 2006, 9–23.

194 See, for instance, Judgment of 2 September 1998, (1998) ICTR, ICTR-96-4, §416 et seq.; and also Judgment of 22 February 2001, (2001) ICTY, IT-96-23 and IT-96-23/1.

195 For an overview of the relevant case law see J. McBride, *The War Crime of Child Soldier Recruitment*, TMC Asser Press, The Hague, 2014.

196 As reported by Denov in 2002, Physicians for Human Rights conducted a survey of female heads of households in communities of displaced persons. The organisation calculated that as many as 215,000 to 257,000 Sierra Leonean women and girls may have been subjected to sexual violence during the conflict period. See M.S. Denov, 'Wartime Sexual Violence: Assessing a Human Security Response to War-Affected Girls in Sierra Leone', (2006) 37 *Security Dialogue*, 319, at 320.

peers to certain types of violence.[197] However, it is also quite obvious to stress that a girl, due to the above-mentioned child-intensified vulnerabilities, is likely to face more difficulties than an adult woman in overcoming sexual violence and its consequences.[198] In 2000 the UNSC acknowledged the particular situation of girls in armed conflict, stressing

> the importance of giving consideration to the special needs and particular vulnerabilities of girls affected by armed conflict, including, inter alia, those heading households, orphaned, sexually exploited and used as combatants, and urges that their human rights, protection and welfare be incorporated in the development of policies and programmes, including those for prevention, disarmament, demobilization and reintegration.[199]

More specifically the Paris Principles highlight the importance of addressing the peculiar situation of girls associated with armed forces and groups, explaining that

> [p]ro-active measures must be taken to ensure the full involvement and inclusion of girls in all aspects of prevention of recruitment, release and reintegration, and services should always respond to their specific needs for protection and assistance. Extreme sensitivity is required when seeking to identify and assist girls in order not to increase the stigma attached to their involvement and make their situation worse. It is central to programming interventions that attention be paid to the particular needs for protection and support both of girl mothers and of children born to girls as a result of their recruitment by an armed force or armed group.[200]

Without denying the intimate correlation between children and women, in peacetime as well as during and in the wake of war, this book considers children as a distinct vulnerable group and girls as a subgroup that is very often disproportionately affected by gendered harm.

---

197 The threat or use of sexual violence as a form of ill-treatment in detention settings against men and boys is common in several contexts, as stressed by the UN Secretary-General in his Report on Conflict-related Sexual Violence, 23 March 2015, UN doc. S/2015/203. According to the Report the practice of subjecting boys to sexual exploitation also remains widespread: in Afghanistan there is a specific term to describe it, i.e. *bacha bazi*.

198 The consequences of sexual violence could be even worse than the violence itself according to Denov 'In its aftermath, sexual violence brings forth a profound and long-term sense of insecurity, whether physical, psychological or socio-economic in nature', above note 196, at 327.

199 UNSC, Resolution 1314 (2000), UN doc. S/RES/1314, §13.

200 UNICEF, The Paris Principles: 'Principles and Guidelines on Children Associated With Armed Forces or Armed Groups', February 2007, principle 3.2.

2.6. CHILD SOLDIERS

Graça Machel has emphasised how 'war undermines the very foundations of children's lives, destroying their homes, splintering their communities and shattering their trust in adults'.[201] This is true for all the children affected by an armed conflict, especially those who have experienced IHRL and IHL violations, such as child soldiers illegally recruited and used to actively participate in hostilities.

According to a working paper released by the Office of the UN Special Representative of the Secretary-General for Children and Armed Conflict, 'while many children are affected by armed conflicts and some of them are direct victims of war crimes, a very small minority of children are also involved in committing crimes'.[202] The number of children unlawfully recruited to participate in armed conflicts is certainly low if compared to the number of children affected by them, in particular those injured, sexually abused, orphaned and so on. Nevertheless, in the past two decades the use of children as soldiers, or more generally as active stakeholders in war, has increased, generating a widespread phenomenon, endemic in almost every context where an armed conflict arises.[203] It is well established that socio-economic conditions including poverty and other forms of deprivation contribute to the recruitment of children, as can cultural attitudes towards children and circumstances such as displacement and family separation.[204]

According to Drumbl, minors associated with armed forces or armed groups largely get there in one of three ways: (1) they are abducted or conscripted through force or serious threats; (2) they present themselves, whether independently or through recruitment programmes and become enlisted/enrolled; or (3) they are born into forces or groups.[205] With regard to the latter option, it should be noted that comparatively fewer children enter military life through birth than through the first two paths.[206] Often these children's mothers are very young themselves

---

201 See G. Machel, *The Impact of War on Children: A Review of Progress Since the 1996 United Nations Report on the Impact of Armed Conflict on Children*, Palgrave MacMillan, Basingstoke, 2001, 80.

202 Office of the Special Representative of the Secretary-General for Children and Armed conflict, Working Paper No 3, above note 152.

203 See in general Redress, 'Victims, Perpetrators or Heroes: Child Soldiers before the International Criminal Court', September 2006, at 27, available at: http://www.redress.org/downloads/publications/childsoldiers.pdf. See Drumbl, above note 20, in particular chapter 2, where the author provides an overview of child soldiers in each of the world's regions.

204 Child Soldiers International, 'Louder than Words: An Agenda for Action to End State Use of Child Soldiers', 2012, at 44, available at: http://child-soldiers.org/global_report_reader.php?id=562.

205 Drumbl, above note 20, at 132.

206 Ibidem, at 62.

and their pregnancy is the outcome of sexual violence/slavery. Predictably, when the armed conflict ends the children born into armed forces or groups, also known as 'war babies' tend to face stigmatisation and exclusion on a larger scale than do their peers.[207]

Concerning the first two paths to militarisation, children are either recruited 'by force' or 'voluntarily', and in both cases they generally undergo strenuous initiation and training. In many instances initiation requires recruits to perpetrate atrocities towards loved ones, such as parents or siblings, or younger members of the group as a means of breaking family bonds and hindering possible return.[208] It is almost inevitable that the armed group becomes the child's new community, regardless of how he or she has been admitted into its ranks. Children who join a party involved in an armed conflict do not necessarily participate in hostilities. Therefore the term 'child soldier' appears to be too narrow to describe a phenomenon which goes beyond placing children in the frontline to fight. For this reason the Paris Principles, a non-binding document that lays out detailed guidelines for protecting children from recruitment and for providing assistance to those already involved with armed groups or forces, adopted a far-reaching and more nuanced terminology, i.e. 'children associated with armed forces or armed groups'.[209] According to the Principles, a 'child associated with an armed force or armed group' refers to any person below 18 years of age who is or who has been recruited or used by an armed force or armed group in any capacity, including but not limited to children, boys and girls, used as fighters, cooks, porters, messengers, spies or for sexual purposes. It does not only refer to a child who 'is taking or has taken a direct part in hostilities'. This book privileges the use of the term 'children associated with an armed force or armed group', but for reasons of convenience it adopts also the term 'child soldiers', as encompassing minors taking a direct part in the hostilities as well as those who are used for auxiliary activities.[210]

---

207 See T.A. Salzman, 'Rape Camps as a Means of Ethnic Cleansing: Religious, Cultural and Ethical Responses to Rape Victims in the Former Yugoslavia', (1998) 20 *Human Rights Quarterly* 348, at 348–378; R. Charli Carpenter (ed.), *Born of War: Protecting Children of Sexual Violence Survivors in Conflict Zones*, Kumarian Press, Bloomfield, 2007; see also in general D. Buss, J. Lebert, B. Rutherford, D. Sharkey and O. Aginam (eds.), *Sexual Violence in Conflict and Post-Conflict Societies: International Agendas and African Contexts*, Routledge, London, 2014.

208 Redress, above note 203, at 7.

209 UNICEF, 'The Paris Principles', above note 200.

210 The term 'child soldiers', in fact, places particular emphasis on the combat functions carried out by children, to the detriment of the girls associated with armed forces or groups who usually perform different tasks.

2.6.1. CONSCRIPTING, ENLISTING AND USING CHILDREN TO PARTICIPATE IN HOSTILITIES UNDER INTERNATIONAL HUMAN RIGHTS LAW AND INTERNATIONAL HUMANITARIAN LAW

The obligations set forth under the current international legal framework address the prohibition on recruiting children and using them to participate in hostilities. The existing norms belong to three fields of international law, namely IHL, IHRL and ICL. Under IHL, Article 77(2) of the Additional Protocol to the Geneva Conventions relating to the Protection of Victims of International Armed Conflicts ('Protocol I') states that 'The Parties to the conflict shall take all feasible measures in order that children who have not attained the age of fifteen years do not take a direct part in hostilities and, in particular, they shall refrain from recruiting them into their armed force ....'[211] This obligation is reasserted in Article 4(3) of Additional Protocol II relating to the Protection of Victims of Non-International Armed Conflicts ('Protocol II').[212] While the text of Article 4(3) is generally described as a simplified version of the comparable list enshrined in Articles 77 and 78 of Protocol I,[213] with regard to the prohibition on recruiting and use of child soldiers Protocol I seems to provide children with a higher degree of protection. Article 4(3)(c) in fact states that children who have not attained the age of 15 years shall neither be recruited into the armed forces or groups nor allowed to take part in hostilities. Unlike Article 77(2), the provision regulating child soldiering in armed conflicts not of an international character does not request States to take 'all feasible measures',[214] but it rather expresses a clear duty incumbent upon the States parties to Protocol II. Furthermore, the fact that this provision does not draw any distinction between 'direct' and 'indirect' participation in hostilities has been read by some authors as an attempt at broadening the scope of the protection awarded.[215] Even though the provision enshrined in Additional Protocol II is firmer than the one spelled out in Article 77 of Additional Protocol II,[216] when it comes to the scope of the prohibition it should be noted that both Protocols refer to direct participation in hostilities,

211 Art. 77(2) of Protocol I.

212 On the legal distinction between international and non-international armed conflicts see Fleck above note 62, at 603.

213 Kalshoven and Zegveld, above note 33, at 145.

214 The term 'feasible' indicates that the implementation of the provision is a matter of judgement. S.C. Grover, *Child Soldier Victims of Genocidal Forcible Transfer*, Springer, Heidelberg, 2012, 6.

215 McBride above note 195, at 22.

216 L. Doswald-Beck, *Human Rights in Times of Armed Conflict and Terrorism*, Oxford University Press, Oxford, 2011, 526.

even when the term direct (or active) is omitted.[217] Finally, the prohibition has attained the status of customary international law, binding upon all parties to an armed conflict, i.e. both States and NSGAs, and providing that 'children under 15 years of age must not be recruited into armed forces or armed groups' and also that 'children must not be allowed to take part in hostilities'.[218]

IHRL also prohibits children's recruitment and direct involvement in armed conflicts. Binding treaties as well as several non-binding documents deal with this issue and enshrine a number of specific provisions. Pursuant to the CRC States parties shall take all feasible measures to ensure that persons who have not attained the age of 15 years do not take a direct part in hostilities and they shall refrain from recruiting any person below the age of 15 years into their armed forces.[219] This Article seemingly does not provide adequate protection to children associated with armed forces or groups. *In primis* Article 38 is the only one in the entire CRC that places on States a limited responsibility to achieve the goal set in the provision, as expressed by the wording 'feasible measures'. Furthermore, in spite of the fact that the Article deals with one of the most dangerous situations that children can be exposed to, it creates a 'loophole of non-protection'[220] targeting children under the age of 15 years even though the CRC defines a child as every human being under the age of 18 years. Finally, Article 38 repeats the distinction between 'direct' versus 'indirect' participation, to the detriment of all children who play subsidiary roles.

In order to remedy some of the CRC's perceived inadequacies an Optional Protocol on the Involvement of Children in Armed Conflict was adopted in 2000.[221] The goal of rectifying the mistakes of the CRC, however, has not been fully met. Article 1 of the Optional Protocol affirms that States parties shall take all feasible measures to ensure that members of their armed forces who have not attained the age of 18 years do not take a direct part in hostilities. If, on the one hand, this provision has the merit of raising the age limit from 15 to 18 years, overcoming the loophole of protection noted with regard to Article 38

---

217 As explained by Wagner, 'That the term "direct", or indeed "active", is omitted in a certain part of an article should not be taken to mean that the prohibition is one other than direct. This is all the more so given the lack of the word "direct" in the Commentary of Article 77(2) of API when discussing that the Parties to the conflict are to take "all feasible measures" that those who have not attained the age of 15 do not take a direct part in hostilities'. See N. Wagner, 'A Critical Assessment of Using Children to Participate Actively in Hostilities in Lubanga: Child Soldiers and Direct Participation', (2013) 24 *Criminal Law Forum* 145, at 166. See also Y. Sandoz, C. Swinarski and B. Zimmermann (eds.), *Commentary to the Additional Protocols to the Geneva Conventions*, Martinus Nijhoff Publishers, The Hague, 1987, 901, §3185.

218 J.M. Henckaerts and L. Doswald-Beck, (eds.), *Customary International Humanitarian Law*, Cambridge University Press, Cambridge, 2006, Rule 136 and Rule 137.

219 Art. 38 of the CRC.

220 McBride, above note 195, at 26.

221 Optional Protocol to the Convention on the Rights of the Child on the Involvement of Children in Armed Conflict, above note 134.

of the CRC, on the other hand the obligation imposed on States is again one of conduct rather than of result. Moreover the provision protects children against taking 'direct' part in hostilities, offering weaker protection than Article 4(3)(c) of Protocol II. Concerning the recruitment of children, Article 2 of the Optional Protocol imposes on States parties the obligation to refrain from compulsory recruiting of persons who have not attained the age of 18 years. Article 3, instead, provides for gradually raising the age for the voluntary recruitment of children, recognising that under the CRC, human beings under the age of 18 years are entitled to special protection. Finally, Article 4 places an absolute prohibition on the recruitment, compulsory and voluntary, of children under 18 years of age by NSAGs, and imposes on governments the obligation to, again, use all feasible measures to prevent such recruitment. NSAGs are thus not only subject to norms agreed on without consent, but they must also comply with a higher standard than the States' armed force. This asymmetry, which permits sovereign States to recruit child soldiers but bars NSAGs from doing the same, has been strongly criticised.[222] Concerning the scope of IHRL rules concerning the prohibition to recruit and use child soldiers, Article 2 of the CRC calls on States to respect and ensure rights to each child in their 'jurisdiction', requiring a jurisdictional reach that surmounts State borders and therefore applies extraterritorially.[223] The Committee on the Rights of the Child has also determined that the Convention applies beyond the territory of a State party, a position that was also supported by the International Court of Justice ('ICJ').[224] The Committee in General Comment No. 6 on the Treatment of Unaccompanied and Separated Children Outside their Country of Origin has stressed that as under-age recruitment and participation in hostilities entails a high risk of irreparable harm involving fundamental human rights, including the right to life, State obligations deriving from Article 38 of the Convention, in conjunction with Articles 3 and 4 of the Optional Protocol to the Convention on the Rights of the Child on the involvement of children in armed conflict, implies extraterritorial effects.[225] The General Comment went even further, asserting that States shall refrain from returning a child in any manner whatsoever to the borders of a State where there is a real risk of under-age

222 D.M. Rosen, *Armies of the Young: Child Soldiers in War and Terrorism*, Rutgers University Press, New Brunswick, 2005, 146.

223 See the Maastricht Principles on Extraterritorial Obligations of States in the area of Economic, Social and Cultural Rights, 2011, available at www.icj.org/dwn/database/Maastricht%20ETO%20Principles%20-%20FINAL.pdf.

224 Committee on the Rights of the Child, Concluding Observations: Israel, §§2, 5, 52–57. See also §58, where the Committee considered that the CRC also applied to Israeli army activities in Lebanon. See also Advisory Opinion of 8 July 1996, (On the Legality of the Threat or Use of Nuclear Weapons), (1996) ICJ Reports, p. 226, §113.

225 UN Committee on the Rights of the Child, General comment No. 6 (2005): Treatment of Unaccompanied and Separated Children Outside their Country of Origin, 1 September 2005, UN doc. CRC/GC/2005/6, at 10.

recruitment, including recruitment not only as a combatant but also to provide sexual services for the military or where there is a real risk of direct or indirect participation in hostilities, either as a combatant or through carrying out other military duties. As a result, in light of the extraterritorial application of the CRC and its Optional Protocols, the obligations enshrined in Article 38 and in Article 4(2) do not cease to exist only because the children are no longer in the territory of the States. On the contrary, States parties must still take all feasible measures to prevent children's recruitment and use by NSAGs, including the adoption of legal measures necessary to prohibit and criminalise such practices.[226]

What ultimately emerges from the analysis of the provisions enshrined in the key binding treaties is that military considerations and sovereignty concerns keep prevailing over children's well-being. Instead, non-binding documents, due to their inherently aspirational nature, pursue a different approach by enhancing the level of protection and putting children's interest in a prominent position. Examples of this attitude can be found in the Machel Report, which advocates 18 as the minimum age for children's involvement in armed forces or groups, as well as in the Cape Town Principles and in the Paris Principles.[227] While these instruments invoke a 'straight 18' approach to recruitment, as a matter of binding law this position is not settled in either IHL or IHRL. As noted by Ni Aolàin, legally speaking the issue of effectively protecting child soldiers is far from being addressed and 'the difficulties are rife as treaty provisions continue to make a distinction between persons under 15 years of age, for whom the prohibitions are generally robust and absolute and those between 15–18 years old, who can be voluntarily conscripted into military forces'.[228]

2.6.2. CHILD SOLDIERS UNDER THE INTERNATIONAL CRIMINAL LAW FRAMEWORK

International criminal law involves the substantive and procedural frameworks that prosecute core crimes of concern to the global community through a number of mechanisms, ranging from national courts (civil and military), international courts and tribunals, and mixed or hybrid judicial bodies. Regardless of whether they are perpetrated during an international or a non-international armed conflict, the conscription, enlistment or use of children under the age

226 Article 4(2) of the Optional Protocol on the Involvement of Children in Armed Conflict (emphasis added).

227 Drumbl, above note 20, at 140. Cape Town Principles and Best Practices on the Recruitment of Children into the Armed Forces and on Demobilization and Social Reintegration of Child Soldiers in Africa, UNICEF, 1997.

228 See F. Ni Aolàin, N. Cahn and D. Haynes, 'Masculinities and Child Soldiers in Post-Conflict Societies', in F.R. Cooper and A.C. McGinley (eds.), *Masculinities and the Law: A Mutual Approach*, New York University Press, New York, 2012, 240.

of 15 to participate in hostilities is a war crime, which entails the individual criminal responsibility of those who commit it.[229] This specific war crime was not incorporated in the Statutes of the ICTR and the ICTY, but it is listed in the Statutes of the Special Court for Sierra Leone ('SCSL')[230] and the ICC.[231] Article 8(2)(b)(xxvi) and Article 8(2)(e)(vii) of the Rome Statute proscribe, respectively within international armed conflicts and non-international armed conflicts, conscripting or enlisting children under the age of 15 into the armed forces or groups and using them to participate *actively* in hostilities.[232]

There is a difference between conscription and enlistment. The first refers to the compulsory entry into the armed forces, the latter instead refers to the generally voluntary act of joining armed forces by enrolment, typically on the 'list' of a military body or by engagement indicating membership and incorporation in the forces.[233] The specific mode of admitting a child into an armed force or group is, however, legally irrelevant and the distinction between the means of committing the material element of the war crimes under Article 8(2)(b)(xxvi) and Article 8(2)(e)(vii) may become pertinent only during sentencing.[234] In fact in the *Lubanga* case Trial Chamber I sentenced Mr Lubanga Dyilo to a total term of 14 years, but the majority concurrently sentenced him to 13 years' imprisonment for the crime of conscription, 12 years for the crime of enlistment, and 14 years

229 Drumbl, above note 20, at 143.

230 Art. 4(c) of the Statute of the Special Court for Sierra Leone, 16 January 2002, 2178 UNTS, 'Conscripting or enlisting children under the age of 15 years into armed forces or groups or using them to participate actively in hostilities'.

231 See Van Bueren, above note 112, at 44. Van Bueren stressed that the Rome Statute has substantially advanced international law relating to the protection of children in armed conflict and the prosecution of violence against them.

232 Rome Statute of the ICC, 1998, UN doc. A/CONF.183/9 (emphasis added).

233 R.S. Clark and O. Triffterer, 'Article 26: Exclusion of Jurisdiction over Persons under Eighteen', in O. Triffterer (ed.), *Commentary on the Rome Statute of the International Criminal Court: Observers' Notes, Article by Article*, Nomos, Baden-Baden, 1999, 261.

234 M. Happold, 'The Age of Criminal Responsibility in International Criminal Law', in K. Arts and V. Popovski (eds.), *International Criminal Accountability and the Rights of Children*, TMC Asser Press, The Hague, 2006, 69. In an *amicus curiae* brief submitted in the *Lubanga* case by the Special Representative of the Secretary-General on Children and Armed Conflict it was stressed that 'the line between voluntary and forced recruitment is therefore not only legally irrelevant but practically superficial', cited in Drumbl, above note 20, at 155. In the *Lubanga* case Trial Chamber I ultimately determined that although conscription and enlistment are separate offences, the consent of the child could never be a defence. As a matter of establishing criminal responsibility, therefore, it does not matter whether the child was forcibly abducted or was enlisted after coming forward to volunteer. Trial Chamber I did state, however, that the manner of recruitment may be taken into consideration in sentencing *or reparations*; hence, an abductor might be punished more harshly than a commander who enrols child volunteers. See M.A. Drumbl, 'The Effects of the Lubanga Case on Understanding and Preventing Child Soldiering', in T. Gill, R. Geiß, R. Heinsch, T. McCormack and C. Paulussen (eds.), *Yearbook of International Humanitarian Law*, T.M.C. Asser Press, The Hague, 2013, 90, at 101.

for the crime of using children to participate actively in hostilities.[235] These distinctions, however mild, are pertinent insofar as they recognise that the three offences may differ in terms of inherent gravity.[236]

Moving on to the analysis of the provisions enshrined in the Rome Statute, the first issue that emerges is related to the age limit, set at 15 years. Article 26 of the Rome Statute specifies that the Court excludes children, as defined under Article 1 of the CRC, from its jurisdiction and this gap between the jurisdiction *ratione personae* and the criminalisation of the conducts at stake can produce a disturbing, indirect effect by encouraging adult soldiers to prefer children above the age of 15 years and making them a target for brutal abductions, enlistment and the commission of dreadful acts. The second key problem that arises is the use of the adverb 'actively' in lieu of 'directly', which appears in Article 77(2) of Protocol I to the Geneva Conventions and Article 38 of the CRC. This issue was only partially addressed during the negotiations of the Rome Statute. According to the Report of the Preparatory Committee on the Establishment of an International Criminal Court the words 'using' and 'participate' have been adopted to

> cover both *direct participation in combat* and also *active participation in military activities* linked to combat such as scouting, spying, sabotage and the use of children as decoys, couriers or at military checkpoints. It would not cover activities *clearly unrelated to the hostilities* such as food deliveries to an airbase or the use of domestic staff in an officer's married accommodation. However, use of children in a direct support function such as acting as bearers to take supplies to the front line, or activities at the front line itself, would be included within the terminology.[237]

In order to establish the alleged difference between active and direct participation it would be useful to rely on a clear definition of what 'direct' participation means under the IHL framework. Remarkably, IHL fails to properly determine the scope of direct participation in hostilities, nor does a clear interpretation of the concept emerge from State practice or international jurisprudence.[238]

---

235 Judgment of 14 March 2012 (Judgment Pursuant to Article 74 of the Statute), (2012) ICC, Case No. ICC-01/04-01/06, §98.

236 See also Judgment of 1 December 2014 (Judgment on the appeal of Mr Thomas Lubanga Dyilo against his conviction), (2014) ICC, Case No. ICC-01/04-01/06-3121, §§37–38.

237 Draft Statute of the International Criminal Court, Report of the Preparatory Committee on the Establishment of an International Criminal Court, Addendum, Part One, 14 April 1998, UN doc. A/CONF.183/2/Add.1, p. 21 (cited in Vol. II, Ch. 39, §513) (emphasis added).

238 See N. Melzer, 'Interpretive Guidance on the Notion of Direct Participation in Hostilities under International Humanitarian Law', February 2009, at 42, available at: https://www.icrc.org/eng/assets/files/other/icrc-002-0990.pdf. 'Participation' in hostilities refers to the (individual) involvement of a person in these hostilities. Depending on the quality and degree of such involvement, individual participation in hostilities may be described as 'direct' or 'indirect'.

To shed light on this crucial matter the International Committee for the Red Cross ('ICRC') Interpretive Guidance on the Notion of Direct Participation in Hostilities under International Humanitarian Law has clarified that the concept of 'direct participation' refers to specific hostile acts carried out by individuals as part of the conduct of hostilities between parties to an armed conflict.[239] Acts amounting to direct participation in hostilities must meet three cumulative requirements: (1) a threshold regarding the harm likely to result from the act, (2) a relationship of direct causation between the act and the expected harm, and (3) a belligerent nexus between the act and the hostilities conducted between the parties to an armed conflict. The Interpretative Guidance also stressed that the terms 'direct' and 'active' indicate the same quality and degree of individual participation in hostilities under IHL. Moreover, the ICRC Interpretive Guidance sets out a broader definition of direct participation, capable of incorporating many of the examples given by the ICC of 'active participation' such as scouting, sabotage, and guarding military objectives. Since neither the Rome Statute nor the Elements of Crimes outline further the criminal conducts under scrutiny, the scope of the activities covered by Article 8(2)(b)(xxvi) and Article 8(2)(e)(vii) of the Statute must be determined in accordance with Articles 21 and 22(3), which compel the Chambers to interpret and apply the law consistently with internationally recognised human rights.[240] Trial Chamber I, which delivered the first judgment issued by the ICC, was expected to differentiate between 'use to participate actively in hostilities' and 'direct participation in hostilities' in the *Lubanga* case. According to the Court:

> Those who participate actively in hostilities include a wide range of individuals, from those on the front line (*who participate directly*) through to the boys or girls who are involved in a myriad of roles that *support* the combatants. All of these activities, which cover either direct or indirect participation, have an underlying common feature: *the child concerned is, at the very least, a potential target*. The decisive factor, therefore, in deciding if an 'indirect' role is to be treated as active participation in hostilities is whether the support provided by the child to the combatants exposed him or her to real danger as a potential target.[241]

---

239 Ibidem, at 45–46.

240 See Judgment of 14 March 2012, (Judgment pursuant to Article 74 of the Statute), (2012) ICC, Case No. ICC-01/04-01/06, §600. Art. 21 (*Applicable Law*) of the Rome Statute makes the interpretation, as well as the application of the law applicable under the Statute, subject to internationally recognised human rights. It requires the exercise of the jurisdiction of the Court in accordance with internationally recognised human rights norms. Art. 22(3) (*nullum crimen sine lege*) of the Rome Statute requires that the definition of a crime must be strictly construed and that it cannot be extended by analogy.

241 Ibidem, §628, (emphasis added). The idea of linking the active participation of the child to his or her risk of becoming a potential target stems from the SCSL's interpretation of the term 'active participation'. The SCSL has held that active participation is 'not restricted to children directly involved in combat' but 'encompasses the use of children in functions other than

The Majority of the Chamber has thus found that 'active participation' under Article 8(2)(e)(vii) ICC Statute is a concept distinct from, and broader than, 'direct participation in hostilities'. However, the judges in this instance declined to enter a legal definition of the concept of 'participating actively', leaving it to a case-by-case determination, which is limited by the charges and evidence brought by the prosecution against the accused. The approach followed by Trial Chamber I in the *Lubanga* case has triggered the reaction of several commentators. Some authors affirm that the two terms should still be considered synonymous and the recourse to supplementary meanings of interpretation was 'unnecessary and misleading';[242] others warn the Court about the danger of maintaining such separation without duly clarifying it.[243] According to the principle of distinction, in fact, children associated with armed groups are protected under IHL unless they take direct part in hostilities. Broadening the scope of Article 8(2)(e)(vii) on the one hand criminalises the conduct of using children who do not participate in front line combat; on the other hand, however, it narrows the protection available under Common Article 3 of the Geneva Conventions, making such children a legitimate target of attacks and potentially giving rise to a serious and unnecessary conflict between the provisions of the Rome Statute and IHL.

The problems raised by the Trial Chamber's interpretation of 'active participation' were, at least in part, addressed in the judgment issued by the Appeals Chamber on 1 December 2014. The Appeals Chamber ultimately stressed that Trial Chamber I erred in law in finding that '[t]he decisive factor … in deciding if an "indirect" role is to be treated as active participation in hostilities is whether the support provided by the child to the combatants exposed him or her to real danger as a potential target'. According to the Appeals Chamber, in assessing whether an activity or role falls within the scope of Article 8(2)(e)(vii) of the Statute, it is necessary instead to analyse the link between the activity for which the child is used and the combat in which the armed force or group of the perpetrator is engaged. Unfortunately, the Appeals Chamber did not consider it appropriate to give further guidance on the parameters of the notion of 'active participation in hostilities' in the abstract 'in view of the complex and unforeseeable scenarios presented by the rapidly changing face of warfare in the modern world'.[244] To justify the refusal to finally shed light on this issue the Appeals Chamber underlined that the determination as to whether a particular activity falls within this definition must be made, again, on a case-by-case basis.

as front line troops … including support roles within military operations'. But to constitute active participation, the support roles would need to put the child soldiers' lives 'directly at risk in combat'. See Judgment of 20 June 2007, (2007) SCSL, Case No. SCSL-04-16-T.

242 Wagner, above note 217, at 150.

243 R. Graf, 'The International Criminal Court and Child Soldiers: An Appraisal of the Lubanga Judgment', (2012) 10 *Journal of International Criminal Justice* 945, at 963.

244 Judgment of 1 December 2014, ICC, above note 236, §329 et seq.

Concerning the possibility of a conflict between the Rome Statute and the law of armed conflict, the Appeals Chamber has clarified that

> ...Despite the use of similar terminology, the purpose of Article 8 (2) (e) (vii) of the Statute is different from that of Common Article 3 of the Geneva Conventions. The latter provision establishes, inter alia, under which conditions an individual loses protection as a civilian because he or she takes direct part in hostilities. On the other hand, Article 8(2)(e)(vii) of the Statute seeks to protect individuals under the age of fifteen years from being used to 'participate actively in armed hostilities' and the concomitant risks to their lives and well-being. Therefore, the Appeals Chamber finds that the interpretation given to Common Article 3 of the Geneva Conventions in the context of the principle of distinction cannot be simply transposed to that of Article 8(2)(e)(vii) of the Statute. Rather, the term 'participate actively in hostilities' must be given *an interpretation* that bears in mind that provision's purpose.[245]

The difference therefore lies in the interpretation of the two terms, which must reflect the purposes of the provisions (and of the treaties) in which they are enshrined, rather than in their meaning, which is identical. In other words not interpreting the term 'active participation' against the principle of distinction would allow the Court to overcome potential frictions with IHL and draw a line between the sets of values that the two regimes seek to protect. Notably though, if ultimately what matters is the link between the activity for which the child is actually used and the combat in which the armed force or group of the perpetrator is engaged, the 'reality check' will probably have the effect of ironing out the alleged difference between active and direct participation. In other words, in a court of law the requirements identified by the Appeals Chamber are likely to match the cumulative conditions singled out by the ICRC, making the distinction elaborated both unnecessary and redundant.

In conclusion, the prohibition on conscripting, enlisting or using children under the age of 15 years to take part in hostilities is also embedded in the ICC Statute and it is framed as a war crime, regardless of whether it is committed in the context of an international or internal armed conflict. The important step of criminalising a course of conduct that was neglected by the Statutes of the previous international tribunals, risks, nonetheless, being overshadowed by the decision to abide by the age limit of 15 years. Moreover, the adoption of the term 'active participation' in lieu of 'direct participation' and the lack of a decisive argument to fully explain and justify the ICC's departure from the traditional understanding of this concept have contributed to increasing the level of uncertainty in this delicate field.

245 Ibidem, §324.

2.6.3. WHY VICTIMS INSTEAD OF PERPETRATORS?

In his thought-provoking book Drumbl singled out the four stereotypical images of child soldiers: the first typifies the child soldier as a faultless passive victim, the second is that of child soldiers as irreparable damaged goods, the third posits the child soldiers as heroes who fought for a just cause, and the fourth characterises child soldiers as demons and bandits.[246] None of these images can be regarded as accurate or able to provide a truthful snapshot of such a multifaceted and nuanced phenomenon. The reality offers a much more complicated scenario, hardly explicable through the adoption of strict categories.

Often the crimes committed by child soldiers are imposed by their adult commanders and result from threats and violence. Traditionally, in fact, the reason behind the choice to recruit minors lies with the assumption that they can be easily intimidated and indoctrinated.[247] Due to their age and immaturity very young children do not fully understand the consequences and the implications of their actions. Also, in order to distort their state of mind prior to committing terrible crimes, child soldiers are sometimes forced to consume alcohol and drugs.[248] In those cases the lack of *mens rea* and the objective impossibility to escape or disobey the orders *per se* justifies child soldiers' categorisation as victims rather than as perpetrators.[249] In other instances, instead, the wrongful acts committed by child soldiers who are not coerced, nor necessarily motivated by survivalism, originate from ordinary criminal backgrounds, proclivities and propensities.[250] As underlined by Happold, the debate concerns the extent to which 'these children should be held responsible for their actions or simply seen as innocent tools of their superiors'.[251] The fact that this issue is not properly regulated at the international level, even with regard to the crimes which fall within the category of international crimes, has vastly contributed to increasing the degree of uncertainty which characterises the status of child soldiers.

The general provision to take into account is Article 40(3) of the CRC, which affirms that States parties to the Convention shall seek to establish the minimum age below which children are presumed to be not capable of violating penal

---

246 Drumbl, above note 20, at 6.

247 For example Beber and Blattman argue that children are recruited because they are easier and cheaper to retain, or more responsive to coercive methods. B. Beber and C. Blattman, 'The Logic of Child Soldiering and Coercion', 2011, at 4, available at: http://chrisblattman.com/documents/research/2011.LogicOfChildSoldiering.pdf.

248 Amnesty International, 'Liberia: Demand Justice for Child Soldiers', 2004, available at: https://www.amnesty.org/en/documents/AFR34/013/2004/en/.

249 According to Justice Devlin *mens rea* consists of two elements 'It consists first of all of the intent to do an act and secondly of the knowledge and the circumstances that makes that act a criminal offence', cited in van Sliedregt, above note 83, at 43.

250 See I. Abdullah, 'Bush Path to Destruction: the Origin and Character of the Revolutionary United Front/Sierra Leone', (1998) 36 *Journal of Modern African Studies* 203, at 213–222, cited by Drumbl, above note 20, at 93.

251 See Happold, above note 234, at 70.

law.[252] Unfortunately, the provision does not go any further: without imposing the establishment of a common standard it leaves to each State the duty to set a minimum age.[253] As a result the global overview of the minimum age of criminal responsibility ('MACR') provides a very heterogeneous picture,[254] which reflects the lack of a uniform approach to childhood. The Commentary to Rule 4 of the Beijing Rules states that:

> The minimum age of criminal responsibility differs widely owing to history and culture. The modern approach would be to consider whether a child can live up to the moral and psychological components of criminal responsibility; that is, whether a child, by virtue of her or his individual discernment and understanding, can be held responsible for essentially anti-social behaviour. If the age of criminal responsibility is fixed too low or if there is no lower age limit at all, the notion of responsibility would become meaningless. In general, there is a close relationship between the notion of responsibility for delinquent or criminal behaviour and other social rights and responsibilities (such as marital status, civil majority, etc.).[255]

Cipriani has identified only 19 out of over 200 States[256] with an MACR of zero; in other words, effectively, no age of criminal responsibility so that all children, however young, can, potentially, be held criminally liable.[257] The remaining States have adopted national legislation more in line with the standard proposed by the Beijing Rules and other non-binding instruments, setting an MACR

---

252 According to Art. 40(3) of the CRC, 'States Parties shall seek to promote the establishment of laws, procedures, authorities and institutions specifically applicable to children alleged as, accused of, or recognised as having infringed the penal law, and, in particular: (a) The establishment of a minimum age below which children shall be presumed not to have the capacity to infringe the penal law ...'.

253 For example in England and Wales the minimum age for criminal responsibility is as low as ten years old. See, for instance, *T. and V. v United Kingdom*, Judgment of 16 December 1999, [1999] ECtHR, Application No. 24724/94.

254 See in general D. Cipriani, *Children's Rights and the Minimum Age of Criminal Responsibility: A Global Perspective*, Ashgate, Farnham, 2009.

255 See the Commentary to the United Nations Standard Minimum Rules for the Administration of Juvenile Justice, adopted by General Assembly Resolution 40/33 of 29 November 1985, ('the Beijing Rules').

256 The States are Bahrain, Cambodia, Cuba, Democratic Republic of Congo, France, Luxembourg, Malaysia, Marshall Islands, Mauritius, Micronesia, Mozambique, Nauru, Nepal, Pakistan, Poland, Solomon Islands, Somalia, Sudan and some US states. See C. McDiarmid, 'An Age of Complexity: Children and Criminal Responsibility in Law', (2013) 13 *Youth Justice* 145, at 150–160.

257 With regard to France, for example, 'persons under the age of 18 "able to understand what they are doing" are criminally responsible for the felonies, misdemeanours or petty offences of which they have been found guilty, and may be subject to measures of protection, assistance, supervision and education according to the conditions laid down by specific legislation. There is no absolute minimum age set at which children become able to be held criminally responsible, but a child will usually be considered to have "discernment" between the ages of 8 and 10'. See CRIN, 'Policy Work on the Minimum Age of Criminal Responsibility', available at: https://www.crin.org/en/home/ages.

under which children do not face the imposition of penal measures.[258] The majority of States have opted for fixing the limit at 14 or 16 years of age, but generally speaking the spectrum goes from seven, e.g. in Qatar and Pakistan, to 18, e.g. Brazil and Chile. This data, however, mainly refers to so-called ordinary common crimes, whereas in relation to war crimes often a different approach prevails.[259]

According to Happold it has occasionally been argued that the minimum age set by Article 77(2) of AP I to the Geneva Convention for the lawful recruitment of children should be read also as the MACR for IHL violations. Such a statement is, in the first place, not supported by the text itself and, secondly, the negotiators explicitly decided not to include this kind of provision within the Protocol.[260] Even though many domestic jurisdictions permit the prosecution of children on charges of extraordinary international crimes,[261] such prosecutions in reality tend to be very infrequent. In the Democratic Republic of the Congo ('DRC'), for example, children under the age of 18 years cannot be prosecuted by military courts;[262] in Colombia, despite the fact that former child soldiers are not automatically excluded from criminal prosecution,[263] not a single case has been brought against this category of children.[264] This trend can be noted in several post-conflict countries, including Liberia[265] and Sudan,[266] and it derives

---

258 In General Comment No. 10, the Committee on the Rights of the Child concludes that 'a minimum age of criminal responsibility below the age of 12 years is considered by the Committee not to be internationally acceptable'. UN Committee on the Rights of the Child, CRC General Comment No. 10 (2007), Children's Rights in Juvenile Justice, 25 April 2007, UN doc. CRC/C/GC/10, §32.

259 Drumbl, above note 20, at 175.

260 See Happold, above note 234, at 71–72.

261 Drumbl, above note 20, at 175.

262 Ibidem.

263 In March 2005 the Colombian Constitutional Court handed down Judgment 203, which revoked another provision of Law 782 allowing the prosecution of minors involved in armed groups (Art. 19). However, according to Art. 175 of the Childhood and Adolescence Code, which entered into force in 2006, prosecution for membership of, or for acts committed during membership of, an armed group could be waived for all but the most serious acts – those 'which may constitute grave breaches of international humanitarian law, crimes against humanity or genocide under the Rome Statute'. See Child Soldiers, Global Report 2008.

264 C. Aptel and V. Ladisch, 'Through a New Lens: A Child-Sensitive Approach to Transitional Justice', ICTJ, August 2011, at 24, available at: http://ictj.org/sites/default/files/ICTJ-Children-Through-New-Lens-Aptel-Ladisch-2011-English.pdf.

265 According to the Liberian Truth and Reconciliation Commission, 'Children were among the main victims of the Liberian conflict. They were forced to participate in fighting and to commit grave human rights violations under the direction of their commanders. Refusing to take part in hostilities was not an option for children. Therefore, children under the age of 18 do not have any criminal responsibility for their actions and they cannot be held accountable for crimes committed under international human rights or international humanitarian law.' See Final Report of the Truth and Reconciliation Commission of Liberia, Volume Three: Appendices, Title II: Children, the Conflict and the TRC Children Agenda, June 2009, at 105.

266 Drumbl, above note 20, at 176.

from the influx exercised by ICL bodies. In fact, even though they actually had jurisdiction over children,[267] none of the *ad hoc* or hybrid tribunals established so far has ever prosecuted anyone under the age of 18 years. This is mainly due to the limited resources available and to the endemic constraint deriving from these bodies' focus on the perpetrators who 'bear the greatest responsibility' for the crimes under scrutiny. The ICC has departed from the other ICL mechanisms and included in its Statute an explicit age-exclusion clause, which automatically renders meaningless any explanation based on prosecutorial strategies and economic considerations. The ICC, thus, has 'set out a model standard for the preferred approach regarding children involved in conflict-related international crimes',[268] influencing also domestic courts and discouraging the criminal prosecution of child soldiers for the violations committed while associated with armed forces or groups. In the absence of a straightforward international norm regulating children's criminal responsibility for war crimes and crimes against humanity perpetrated during an armed conflict, ICL has eventually determined its own 'golden rule'. This rule refers to child soldiers who have not attained the age of 18 years old at the time of the commission of the crimes under the ICC's jurisdiction and it does not apply to former child soldiers who are now adults. This crucial point was made clear when the ICC indicted and apprehended Mr Dominic Ongwen, a commander of the Lord's Resistance Army ('LRA') who in 1988 was abducted on the way to school at the age of 14 years and eventually become a brutal leader, currently facing three counts of crimes against humanity and four counts of war crimes arising out of an attack on an internally displaced persons' ('IDPs') camp in 2004.[269] Certainly, even though Ongwen is going to be prosecuted for crimes committed as an adult, this trial will contribute to the discussion on children associated with armed forces or groups and it will help shed light on the complicated reality of child soldiering.

With regard to the domestic level, relying first on the jurisprudence of the international and hybrid tribunals, which *de facto* excluded child soldiers' accountability, and then on the ICC Statute, many States started to implement

---

[267] The SCSL had jurisdiction over children aged 15 to 18 as stated in Article 7 of the SCLS's Statute, however the Chief Prosecutor, David Crane, clarified from the outset that he would have not indicted children as 'the children of Sierra Leone have suffered enough both as victims and as perpetrators'. See A. McDonald, 'Correspondents' Report', *Yearbook of International Humanitarian Law*, TMC Asser Press, The Hague, 2002, 591.

[268] See Grover, above note 214, at 80.

[269] Decision of 6 March 2015 (Decision Postponing the Date of the Confirmation of Charges Hearing), (2015) ICC, Case No. ICC-02/04-01/15.

domestic laws in line with this trend.[270] The rationale behind the choice not to prosecute child soldiers for the crimes committed while in the ranks of armed forces or groups has been discussed in detail by several distinguished scholars. Grover, for example, built the argument against the criminal prosecution of child soldiers 'on the proximate cause of children's commission of war-related atrocities as part of an armed force or group'.[271] In other words the proximate cause consists in the failure by States to meet their IHL obligation to protect children from direct involvement in the hostilities as members of armed groups or forces that commit violations of the law of armed conflict. As a result children cannot be prosecuted because their crimes are the consequence of a wrongful act. The other dominant argument, mainly advanced by children's rights campaigners,[272] resists the criminal prosecution of child soldiers on the grounds that it is not in children's best interests. Rather than criminal prosecution it is child recruitment *per se* that – as highlighted by Ms Radhika Coomaraswamy, the former UN Special Representative for Children and Armed Conflict and expert witness in the *Lubanga* case – is against the best interests of the child. During her testimony, Ms Coomaraswamy described her experience with former child soldiers. In particular she stressed that all the victims of child recruitment, even those who had the resilience to come up and share their stories, tended to emphasise how their education and livelihood have been deeply damaged, and how they need some kind of psychosocial support. The expert witness went on to say that she had never met one child soldier, including the ones who have survived and tried to move on, who would depict his or her experience as positive.[273] There are, clearly, no doubts with regard to the danger inherent to child recruitment. To use Judge Odio Benito's words:

> Children are protected from child recruitment not only because they can be at risk for [*sic*] being a potential target to the 'enemy' but also because they will be at risk from their 'own' armed group which has recruited them and will subject these children to brutal trainings, torture and ill-treatment, *sexual violence* and other activities and living conditions that are incompatible and in violation to [*sic*] these children's fundamental rights. The risk for children who are enlisted, conscripted or used by an armed group inevitably also comes from within the same armed group.[274]

---

270 This is true also for countries such as Rwanda, which in the past prosecuted all the persons responsible for the genocide that occurred in 1994, including child perpetrators. According to Drumbl the Rwandan President has released all those incarcerated for genocide-related crimes committed when they were minors, DRUMBL, above note 20, at 176.

271 See GROVER, above note 214, at 85.

272 HAPPOLD, above note 234, at 84.

273 See Radhika Coomaraswamy, former United Nations Special Representative of the Secretary-General for Children and Armed Conflict, as expert evidence in: *Prosecutor v. Lubanga*, Situation in the Democratic Republic of the Congo, Case No. ICC-01/04-01/06, Transcript ICC-01/04-01/06-T-223-ENG.

274 See Judgment of 14 March 2012 (Separate and Dissenting Opinion Judge Elizabeth Odio Benito), (2012) ICC, Case No. ICC-01/04-01/06-2842 14-03-2012, §19.

The blatant violation of the child's best-interests principle and the crimes perpetrated against children while in the ranks of armed groups or forces do not, however, provide a legal answer to the question why these children should not be held accountable for the wrongful acts that they have committed. Similarly, the proximate cause argument does not fully justify the choice to exempt child soldiers from criminal liability as it simply shields their actions behind the State's failure to protect them. This book's rationale for qualifying child soldiers as victims rather than perpetrators departs from the legal and moral basis upon which other authors have built their arguments. In fact, since the main goal of this study is to discuss the right to reparation for child victims of armed conflict, in light of this the minors *unlawfully* recruited into armed forces or groups, or used to participate in hostilities, are identified as individuals or groups who have suffered harm as a result of the violation of a primary norm, well rooted in IHRL, IHL and ICL. The recognition of child soldiers' victimhood entails that they should become the beneficiaries of reparative measures able to address, to the maximum extent possible, both the causes of the recruitment and the consequences of the harm suffered while associated with armed forces or groups. Qualifying child soldiers as victims entitled to reparations does not, however, automatically exclude their liability for the crimes committed. The victim/perpetrator dichotomy, which tends to be neat in several other instances concerning child victims, is rather blurred with regard to child soldiers. Adopting a blanket approach, which erases children's responsibility for the crimes committed while under the influence of an armed group, is understandable on the one hand, but on the other hand it exacerbates a gap in the way juvenile justice is implemented in post-conflict countries.[275] The idea that 'when the child inflicts horrors, responsibility passes entirely to the adult abductor, enlister, recruiter or commander'[276] is applicable, and should be applied, whenever children are *truly* faultless victims, whereas in all the other instances more thorough and balanced considerations should be undertaken in order to attach the right importance to the relevant factors,[277] including, for example, the individual's path to militarisation,[278] that shape

---

275 For example the Committee on the Rights of the Child has stressed with regard to Colombia that children living in the streets or associated with BACRIM (i.e. *bandas criminales emergentes*) are generally stereotyped as criminals and subjected to disproportionate use of the punishment of deprivation of liberty. Committee on the Rights of the Child Concluding Observations on the Combined Fourth and Fifth Periodic Reports of Colombia, adopted by the Committee at its sixty-eighth session (12–30 January 2015), UN doc. CRC/C/COL/CO/4-5.

276 Drumbl above note 20, at 18.

277 It is, in fact, very unlikely that States will implement a zero-accountability policy against the large number of adolescents flocking to Syria and Iraq to fight in the ranks of the Islamic State. See F. Capone 'Child Soldiers: The Expanding Practice of Minors Recruited to Become Foreign Fighters', in de Guttry, Capone and Paulussen, above note 39, 187.

278 As noted by Drumbl, since child soldiers are not interchangeable equals, 'it would be preferable to appreciate heterogeneity within the protected group rather than assume bland homogeneity and prosaic uniformity'. Drumbl, above note 20, at 94.

and personalise each child soldier's experience. After all, depicting all former child soldiers as 'emotionally crippled and damaged for life' is not in their best interests and risks emphasising defects,[279] while overlooking the reality that many child soldiers exhibit considerable resilience and could be able to deal with the consequences of their actions. As suggested by Drumbl, ICL, be it through international or national trials, cannot be the way forward to deal with child soldiers' accountability. However, once it is agreed that criminal law must recede (and as shown in this paragraph, it is actually receding), post-conflict justice, which includes diverse accountability modalities and a greater sensitivity to the context, must necessarily step up.[280]

2.7. CONCLUSIONS

This chapter has contributed to laying down the theoretical foundations of the current study. In particular it has explored the victimhood of children affected by violations of IHRL and IHL perpetrated during an international or non-international armed conflict. The analysis has covered a number of important aspects. *In primis* it has covered the taxonomy of the violations and crimes committed against children, which is essential to understanding the kinds of intervention that the actors involved in the reparations discourse must undertake in order to implement meaningful measures. Secondly the chapter has provided an overview of the concept of 'victim' within the existing international legal framework, focusing in particular on the three regimes that are relevant to the study. Several paragraphs have introduced the provisions of the CRC that underpin children's right to reparation. The importance of such rights can be summarised as follows: 'without rights children can make requests, they can beg or implore, they can be troublesome; they can rely on what has been called *noblesse oblige*, or on others being charitable, generous, kind, co-operative or even intelligently foresighted. But they cannot demand, for there is no entitlement'.[281] This chapter has also shed light on the concept of vulnerability, explaining the factors that exacerbate children's exposure to violence in armed conflict and in particular the risk of polyvictimisation. Alongside vulnerability, the assessment of which is crucial to determine what kinds of measures should be implemented in order to provide effective redress to child victims, it is also

---

279 See M. Wessells, *Child Soldiers: From Violence to Protection*, Harvard University Press, Cambridge, MA, 2006, 4.

280 See Drumbl, above note 20, at 215.

281 M. Freeman, 'Why It Remains Important to Take Children's Rights Seriously?', (2007) 15 *International Journal of Children's Rights* 5, at 5–23.

necessary to take into account children's resilience, which represents the other end of a spectrum worth investigating in its entirety and complexity. Children's vulnerability, although to some extent entwined with women's, should be read in light of the characteristics that make child victims different from any other groups in need of additional protection. Finally, this chapter has presented the relevant provisions that prohibit the recruitment and use of child soldiers, providing an overview of the current limitations and clarifying the rationale for their recognition as victims against the backdrop of the right to reparation.

CHAPTER 3

THE RIGHT TO REPARATION IN INTERNATIONAL LAW: DEVELOPMENTS, SHORTCOMINGS AND THEIR RELEVANCE TO CHILD VICTIMS OF ARMED CONFLICT

3.1. INTRODUCTION

The key principles that traditionally govern the right to reparation are spelled out in the judgment of the case concerning the *Factory at Chorzów*, issued by the Permanent Court of International Justice ('PCIJ') in 1928. According to the Court:

> It is a principle of international law that the breach of an engagement involves a [State's] obligation to make reparation in an adequate form [and] reparation must, as far as possible, *wipe out all the consequences* of the illegal act and re-establish the situation which would, in all probability, have existed if that act had not been committed.[282]

On that occasion the PCIJ clearly described the common approach to reparations in an inter-State dispute. Such approach has been reiterated several times and has been enshrined in the International Law Commission ('ILC') Articles on Responsibility of States for Internationally Wrongful Acts ('Articles on State Responsibility').[283] These Articles explain that a State responsible for the commission of a wrongful act is under an obligation to cease the conduct and to offer appropriate assurances, normally given verbally, and guarantees of non-repetition, such as preventive measures to be taken to avoid repetition of the breach. The responsible State is also under an obligation to make reparation for the injury caused by the internationally wrongful act. The forms of reparations, identified in the Articles on State Responsibility and endorsed by the jurisprudence of the ICJ and its predecessor are restitution, compensation and satisfaction, either singly or in combination and, where appropriate,

---

282 Judgment of 13 September 1928 (Merits), (1928) PCIJ, Ser. A, No. 17, §78 (emphasis added).

283 Articles on Responsibility of States for Internationally Wrongful Acts, above note 17.

accompanied by interest.[284] The evolution of the right to reparation, marked, *inter alia*, by the adoption of the Basic Principles and Guidelines, has led to the identification of other forms of reparation, including rehabilitation and guarantees of non-repetition.[285] Unlike the Articles on State Responsibility, the UNBPG focuses on the right to reparation for victims (not States), meaning individuals or collectives who have suffered harm including physical or mental injury, emotional suffering, economic loss or substantial impairment of their fundamental rights, through acts or omissions that constitute violations of international law. Until quite recently, the existence of an individual's right to reparation was questioned, mainly due to the limited practice supporting the concrete exercise of this right.[286] However, the debate over the possibility for individuals or groups to claim for reparations has eventually been overcome in light of the increasing importance that reparations' awards to victims have gained in judicial and non-judicial settings,[287] e.g. the judgments of the regional human rights courts and the national reparations programmes set up in various post-conflict States. The practice concerning the implementation of child victims' right to reparation will be discussed in detail in the next part of the book; the current chapter instead focuses on the international legal framework, highlighting in particular the limitations therein as well as the most recent developments. This analysis will help assess whether the legal basis governing child victims' right to reparation allows for an adequate, prompt and effective design and enforcement of redress measures as a result of IHRL and IHL violations perpetrated in correlation with an armed conflict. Reparation is a dynamic concept, which has been subject to constant evolution in order to keep up with the newest international law developments. As noted by Judge Cançado Trindade, 'in modern times it has been clearly reckoned that there are no "'immutable'" rules of international law, as erroneously assumed in times long past'.[288] This statement could refer also to the traditional inter-State dimension of the right to reparation,[289] which, as discussed above, was first challenged

---

[284] See also J. Crawford, *The International Law Commission's Articles on State Responsibility: Introduction, Text and Commentaries*, Cambridge University Press, Cambridge, 2002, 201.

[285] See UNBPG, above note 2, §9.

[286] See Tomuschat, above note 1, at 157–159.

[287] A significant example is found in the advisory opinion on the Legal Consequences of the Construction of a Wall in the Occupied Palestinian Territory, in which the ICJ clarified that Israel has the obligation under international law to make reparation for the damage caused to 'all natural or legal persons having suffered any form of material damage as a result of the wall's construction'. Advisory Opinion of 9 July 2004 (Legal Consequences of the Construction of a Wall on the Occupied Palestinian Territory), above note 153, p. 136.

[288] Judgment of 3 February 2012, (2012) ICJ, Judgment, ICJ Reports 2012, p. 99.

[289] See generally R.M. Buxbaum, 'A Legal History of International Reparations', (2005) 23 *Berkeley Journal of International Law* 313, at 313–346; M. Iovane, *La Riparazione nella Teoria e nella Prassi dell'Illecito Internazionale*, Giuffrè Editore, Milano, 1990; and G. Bertolini, *Riparazione per Violazione dei Diritti Umani e Ordinamento Internazionale*, Jovene, Naples, 2009.

and ultimately overcome by the recognition of an individual's right to claim for redress as a result of the harm caused to the victim by the violation of his or her rights. The overview of the existing legal framework regulating the right to reparation within the three regimes relevant to this study will highlight the main issues at stake. The attention placed on the urge to redress violations of international law, in particular those defined as gross violations of human rights law[290] and serious violations of IHL, has not lost momentum and new issues keep emerging, for example with regard to the actors responsible as well as the different reparative measures available and the scope of reparations.

3.2. REPARATIONS UNDER INTERNATIONAL HUMAN RIGHTS LAW, INTERNATIONAL HUMANITARIAN LAW AND INTERNATIONAL CRIMINAL LAW

3.2.1. INTERNATIONAL HUMAN RIGHTS LAW

Since the aftermath of WWII the right to reparation has been firmly entrenched in several international human rights treaties. To use Zegveld's words 'a victim's right to reparation depends in the first place on his rights, as recognised under international law, having been breached. A victim's right to reparation therefore presupposes rights of victims in international law'.[291]

Human rights violations create a right to obtain a remedy and, at the same time, a duty on individual perpetrators and/or States to satisfy this right. As will be explained in the course of this section, human rights law is the field of international law which has mainly contributed to the recognition of individuals as holders of the right to reparation, as it emerges from the analysis of the human right treaties and the jurisprudence of the human rights bodies.[292]

Article 8 of the UDHR provides that 'everyone has the right to an effective remedy by the competent national tribunals for acts violating the fundamental

290 'No agreed definition exists of the term "gross" violations of human rights. It appears that the word gross qualifies the term "violations" and indicates the serious character of the violations but that the word "gross" is also related to the type of human right that is being violated'. See Study Concerning the Right to Restitution, Compensation and Rehabilitation for Victims of Gross Violations of Human Rights and Fundamental Freedoms, final report submitted by Professor Theo van Boven, Special Rapporteur, UN doc. E/CN.4/Sub.2/1993/8, Commission on Human Rights, Sub-Commission on Prevention of Discrimination and Protection of Minorities Forty-fifth session.

291 L. Zegveld, 'Victims' Reparations Claims and International Courts', (2010) 8 *Journal of International Criminal Justice* 79, at 80–85.

292 See A.A. Cançado Trindade, *Évolution du Droit International au Droit des Gens. L'Accès des Individus à la Justice Internationale: Le regard d'un Juge*, Pédone, Paris, 2008.

rights granted him by the constitution or the laws'.[293] The principle prescribed in Article 8 became part of the Declaration only at a very late stage of the drafting process. The proposal was made by delegates coming from Latin American countries and reflected a principle already recognised by many States. A strong argument in favour of it was the lack of other Articles in the UDHR which could be invoked by an individual against the State if his/her human rights had been violated. It is self-evident that the compilation of Article 8 was strongly influenced by this need and also by the principles of *recurso de amparo* and *habeas corpus*. These two principles, in fact, represent an example of local remedies, the first being typical of Latin American countries, and the second recognised as the Anglo-Saxon fundamental instrument for safeguarding individual freedom against unlawful detention. As pointed out by Shelton, 'it is thus appropriate and probably inevitable that international tribunals draw upon national law, as well as international law, to develop remedies'.[294] With the proclamation of the UDHR, eventually the protection of individuals moved from the local to the international stage, allowing, in theory, all human beings to have access to some kind of remedies. It is noteworthy that Article 8 of the UDHR adopts the term 'remedy' and does not make any explicit reference to 'reparation'. Although the two concepts are often confused, 'remedy' and 'reparation' are not synonyms: in an unsophisticated way it would be possible to affirm that they are involved in a 'genus–species' relationship. The definition of remedies provided by the Basic Principles and Guidelines includes the right to equal and effective access to justice, the access to relevant information concerning violations and redress mechanisms, *and* the right to adequate, effective and prompt reparation.[295] Under international law, the concept of remedies appears to be more complex as it not only refers to the kind of remedies claimable by individuals, which are those enshrined within the UNBPG, but it also governs inter-State disputes and the consequences of a State's misconduct towards another State.[296] In national legal systems remedies are secured by the existence of third-party enforcers; in contrast, international law, relying mostly on self-enforcement, has not yet designed a uniform and coherent framework. The key principle governing controversies arising among states is enshrined in Article 2(3) of the UN Charter,

---

293 UN General Assembly, Universal Declaration of Human Rights, 10 December 1948, 217 A (III).

294 See in general Shelton in De Feyter et al. above note 22.

295 For the purpose of the current work 'redress' shall mean 'the act of receiving satisfaction for an injury sustained'. *Bouvier's Law Dictionary*, revised 6th edn., 1856.

296 See F. Capone, 'Remedies', in R. Wolfrum (ed.), *Max Planck Encyclopedia of Public International Law*, Oxford University Press, Oxford, 2012. 'Remedies is the field of law dealing with the means by which a right is enforced or the violation of a right is prevented or redressed. Remedies are of four kinds: by act of the party injured, by operation of law, by agreements between parties and by judicial remedies'.

which requires Member States to settle their international disputes by peaceful means in such a manner that international peace and security, and justice, are not endangered.[297] As for the possible remedies, the existing framework is crystallised in the ILC's Articles on State Responsibility, whose provisions apply to breaches of both customary law and treaty law, unless the treaty provides otherwise.

The ICCPR regulates the right to a remedy in a more comprehensive way. It is included in three different Articles, addressing in Article 2(3) the right to access an authority competent to afford remedies and in Articles 9(5) and 14(6) narrowing the focus to the situation of unlawful arrest, detainment or conviction, stating that everyone unlawfully arrested, detained or convicted shall have an enforceable right to compensation or to be compensated according to law. On 26 May 2004 the Human Rights Committee adopted General Comment No. 31 (which replaced General Comment No. 3, reflecting and developing the same principles) on Article 2 of the ICCPR. According to the Human Rights Committee:

> Article 2 is couched in terms of the obligations of the State parties towards individuals as the rights holders under the Covenant, every State party has a legal interest in the performance by every other State Party of its obligations. This follows from the fact that the 'Rules concerning the basic rights of the human person' are *erga omnes* obligations and that, as indicated in the fourth preambular paragraph of the Covenant, there is a United Nations Charter obligation to promote universal respect for, and observance of, human rights and fundamental freedoms.[298]

Article 2(3) requires that, besides guaranteeing that individuals enjoy an effective protection of the Covenant rights, States parties have to provide accessible and effective remedies to vindicate those rights. Moreover, the General Comment stressed that 'such remedies must be appropriately adapted in order to take into account the special vulnerability of certain categories of person, *including in particular children*'.[299] Paragraph 16 of the General Comment focuses on the right to reparation for the victims who experienced violations of the rights protected by the Covenant:

> Without reparation to individuals whose Covenant rights have been violated, the obligation to provide an effective remedy, which is central to the efficacy of Article 2(3) is not discharged. In addition to the explicit reparation required by Articles 9(5) and 14(6) the Committee considers that the Covenant generally entails appropriate

297 See United Nations, Charter of the United Nations, 24 October 1945, 1 UNTS XVI.

298 See UN Human Rights Committee, General Comment 31, Nature of the General Legal Obligation Imposed on States Parties to the Convention, 13, 26 May 2004, UN doc. CCPR/C/21/Rev.1/Add., §2.

299 Ibidem (emphasis added).

> compensation. The Committee notes that, where appropriate, reparation can involve restitution, rehabilitation and measures of satisfaction, such as public apologies, public memorials, guarantees of non-repetition and changes in relevant laws and practices, as well as bringing to justice the perpetrators of human rights violations.[300]

The 'practice' of the Human Rights Committee and the other UN treaty bodies with regard to reparations in cases brought under the Optional Protocols will be analysed in due course. Nonetheless it is important to stress that the UN Human Rights Committee ('HRC') has placed specific attention on child victims' vulnerability as well as on the different forms of reparations that can be implemented by the States parties responsible for violations of the ICCPR's rights.

Provisions on the right to a remedy are present also in Article 2(c) of the CEDAW[301] and in Article 14 of the CAT. The latter in particular establishes that

> each State party shall ensure in its legal system that the victim of an act of torture obtains redress and has an enforceable right to fair and adequate compensation including the means for as full rehabilitation as possible. In the event of the death of the victim as a result of an act of torture, his dependants shall be entitled to compensation.

In General Comment No. 3 the Committee against Torture has highlighted the

> importance that appropriate procedures are made available to address the needs of children, taking into account the best interests of the child and the child's right to express his or her views freely in all matters affecting him or her, including judicial and administrative proceedings, and that the views of the child are given due weight in accordance with the age and maturity of the child. States parties should ensure the availability of *child sensitive measures for reparation, which foster the health and dignity of the child.*[302]

The Committee against Torture has thus recognised the particular status of child victims and the need to promote the enjoyment of the rights enshrined in the CRC while providing access to remedies and reparations, which, in order to be effective and adequate, must take into account children's vulnerability and resilience.

Finally, at the regional level, human rights treaties promote the right to a remedy and reparation in various provisions: Article 13 of the ECHR,

---

300 Ibidem, §16.

301 Art. 2(c) of the CEDAW 'to establish legal protection of the rights of women on an equal basis with men and to ensure through competent national tribunals and other public institutions the effective protection of women against any act of discrimination'.

302 See Committee against Torture, General Comment No. 3 Implementation of Article 14 by States parties, 19 November 2012, UN doc. CAT/C/GC/3, at 8, §36 (emphasis added).

Article XVII of the American Declaration on the Rights and Duties of Man, Articles 10 and 25 of the ACHR, and Articles 7 and 21 of the ACHPR. In many treaties it is also possible to encounter references to the right to legal protection for violations of privacy, family, home and correspondence or for attacks on honour and reputation, which also trigger the right to obtain satisfactory remedies. Some examples can be found in Article 11(3) of the ACHR, Article 8 of the ECHR and Article 5 of the ACHPR.

In particular with the regard to the African human rights system it is striking to note that the ACRWC does not contain any provision concerning the right to a remedy and reparation. The wording of Article 22(3) of the ACRWC recalls Article 38(4) of the CRC and stresses States parties' obligation to take all feasible measures to ensure the protection and care of children who are affected by armed conflicts. However, unlike its universal counterpart, the ACRWC does not encompass the duty to provide children with redress measures.[303] The African Youth Charter,[304] which focuses specifically on young persons between the ages of 15 and 35 years and hence on children between 15 and 18 years, contains instead a specific provision that requires States parties to consider youth both as active stakeholders in post-war reconstruction[305] and as a group of victims entitled to physical and psychological recovery and social reintegration through access to education and skills development, such as vocational training, which are indispensable to resuming social and economic life.[306] Unlike the CRC, therefore, the African Youth Charter provides further indications as to the means that States should adopt in order to promote young people's rehabilitation. Furthermore, its scope is limited to a precise category of children, i.e. adolescents, leaving open the question of whether other kinds of measures should be implemented for younger children and, if so, which ones.

3.2.2. INTERNATIONAL HUMANITARIAN LAW

According to Gattini 'it is a widespread belief that the consequences of war, particularly of major wars, inevitably escape the strict judicial appraisal. For various and often contradictory extrajudicial reasons, factors above and beyond

303 See Art. 39 of the CRC.

304 The African Youth Charter was adopted at the Seventh ordinary Session of the Assembly of Heads of State and Government of the African Union in Gambia, in July 2006. So far the African Youth Charter has been ratified by 36 States.

305 Art. 17(f) of the African Youth Charter: 'Mobilise youth for the reconstruction of areas devastated by war, bringing help to refugees and war victims and promoting peace, reconciliation and rehabilitation activities'.

306 See Art. 17(g) of the African Youth Charter.

the law seem to determine how the consequences of war are dealt with'.[307] As reported by Titus Livy, the practice of war reparations dates back to the First Punic war and, ever since, it has been steered by political decisions rather than by legal considerations.[308] Traditionally, war settlements have been sorted out as they were different from any other international dispute settlement and this also led to far-reaching implications with regard to reparations, intended as the payments and transfer of goods imposed on the defeated party by the triumphant side.

Examples of this approach can be found in the reparations awarded in the aftermath of the two World Wars. The reparations regime established after WWI has been described as a 'constant source of tension during the inter-war period' and also one of the main causes of WWII.[309] According to Trachtenberg, 'the Allies tried to make Germany compensate them for some of the damages they had suffered; this attempt to extract reparation dominated European politics during the critical period immediately following the conclusion of peace'.[310] In this context little attention was paid to the population's needs since reparations, understood only as monetary compensation, were seen as a means to punish the German government, to cement the victors' justice and to solve France's economic problems through what was labelled as the inter-Allied economic cooperation.[311] After WWI the reparations clauses settled under the Versailles peace treaty also established a Reparation Commission representing the victorious powers, which was in charge of determining the amount of damages to be paid by Germany.[312]

The 'economic vivisection' that characterised the reparation regime set up post-WWI, was not reiterated when WWII came to an end, in the first place because, unlike WWI, WWII seriously damaged the infrastructure and the economy of the defeated nations since the Allied powers reacted to the Axis aggressions triggering what was known as a 'total war',[313] and secondly because the political division of the world, agreed at the Potsdam Conference in 1945, led to a military occupation of the territories of the defeated nations. As a result the occupying powers did not want to impoverish the resources under their control through the establishment of an unsustainable reparation regime. Rather

---

307 A. Gattini, 'The UN Compensation Commission: Old Rules, New Procedures on War Reparations', (2002) 13 *European Journal of International Law* 161. By the same author see also 'To What Extent are State Immunity and Non- Justiciability Major Hurdles to Individuals' Claims for War Damages?', (2003) 1 *Journal of International Criminal Justice* 348, at 349–367.

308 T. Livy, *The Early History of Rome: Books I–V of the Ab Urbe Condita*, Penguin, London, 2002.

309 See P. D'Argent, 'Reparations after WWII', in R. Wolfrum (ed.), *Max Planck Encyclopedia of International Law*, Oxford University Press, Oxford, 2012.

310 See M. Trachtenberg, *Reparation in World Politics*, Columbia University Press, New York, 1980, Preface.

311 Ibidem, at vii.

312 See Treaty of Peace of Versailles, 28 June 1919, Arts. 231–247. Germany-Allies, 225 Consol. T.S. 188.

313 See D'Argent, above note 309, at §2.

than focusing on monetary compensation, as occurred after WWI, the Western countries decided to target the German industries to better comply with the 'first charge'[314] principle. In particular they dismantled the existing industries in order to move them to France and the UK and they harvested the scientific knowledge by 'acquiring' most of the German patents and prominent scientists.[315]

As for the other States that joined forces with Germany, the reparations imposed on Japan and on the European allies of the Nazi regime were also made through the dismantling of the factories and the deliveries of goods or raw materials. The reparations regime set in the aftermath of WWI was aimed at humiliating and punishing Germany by decreasing its national wealth, while the reparation strategies stemming from WWII focused on making Germany finally harmless, damaging its scientific and technological resources. What is truly relevant, and to some extent revolutionary, with regard to the post-WWII reparations regime is the West German payments to the State of Israel and the Jewish victims of the Holocaust.[316] A 1993 United Nations report examined the German compensation scheme and concluded that 'the most comprehensive and systematic precedent of reparation by a government to groups of victims for redress of wrongs suffered is provided by the Federal Republic of Germany to the victims of Nazi persecution'.[317] Departing from the traditional scheme of war reparations, these awards compensated two categories of people: individual victims of the Holocaust, including citizens of the State paying reparations; and citizens of a new country, Israel.[318] In more detail, the agreement reached envisaged two broad categories of measures. The first category compensated Israel for the pain suffered by survivors of the Shoah who migrated to the new State. The funds in this case where allocated by the German government to Jewish organisations to support an outreach programme for the victims of Nazi persecution. The second category of measures enshrined in the agreement

314 According to such principle 'in working out the economic balance of Germany reparations payments were to be made only if means were provided to pay for any needed essential imports into Germany. In short, Great Britain and the United States wanted Germany to pay its bills before reparations were taken from it. Exports were first to pay for imports; only thereafter could they be considered reparations.' See B. Kuklick, 'The Division of Germany and American Policy on Reparations', (1970) 23 *The Western Political Quarterly* 276, at 283–293.

315 See D'Argent, above note 309, at §37. 'The dismantling of industrial plants was a way to exact reparations in the short term and at the same time to pursue long term security goals by disarming the former enemies'.

316 See K.R. Grossmann, *Germany and Israel: Six Years Luxemburg Agreement*, Herzl Press, New York, 1958. See also R. Ludi, *Reparations for Nazi Victims in Postwar Europe*, Cambridge University Press, Cambridge, 2012.

317 Study Concerning the Right to Restitution, Compensation and Rehabilitation for Victims of Gross Violations of Human Rights and Fundamental Freedoms, above note 290, §107.

318 See A. Colonomos and A. Armstrong, 'German Reparations to the Jews after World War II', in P. de Greiff, above note 22, 390, at 391.

obligated Germany to enact a series of laws that allowed individuals to request reparations because of physical and moral suffering during the time of the Nazi persecution. In 1957 the Bundestag, the West German Parliament, also enacted a restitution law that allowed individuals to reclaim confiscated property.[319]

The first category was implemented through the Claims Conference, which distributed the reparations money through the American Joint Distribution Committee ('JDC'), the Jewish Relief Survivor Organisation ('JRSO') and the Jewish Agency ('JA'). The relief programmes organised by the JDC fell into different categories, for example cash relief, medical aid, childcare and care for the elderly. The JA instead financed its own resettlement and rehabilitation programmes as well as other Israeli organisations. The reparation money, thus, did not directly support the resettlement of the half-million Holocaust survivors as the funds received were rather used to foster economic development. The allocation of the funds was subjected to criticism and it resulted in claims brought by victims or groups of victims, including orphan children, before the Israeli courts.[320]

Concerning the second category, Germany enacted the first Federal Supplementary Law for the compensation of Victims of National Socialist Persecution ('Federal Compensation Law') and then amended it in 1956 and 1965 to try to remedy some of its shortcomings, for example the exclusion of certain victims and the very complex procedure to request compensation. Children were not considered as a specific category of victims and they were mentioned in the Federal Compensation Law among 'the dependent relatives who could apply for an annuity for wrongful death'.[321] Furthermore, despite the attempts to simplify it, the procedure envisaged to claim for reparations remained very complex and challenging for the victims. Colonomos and Armstrong described the process as follows:

> Victims had to file individual claims that would be sent to provincial (Land) reparations agencies. They had to follow very precise bureaucratic procedures and notably be interviewed by doctors if they wanted to be compensated for physical or psychological damages. If the claimant disagreed with the agency's decision, he or she could contest the settlement first in provincial courts (Landgerichte), then courts of appeal (Oberlandsgerichte), and finally the Federal Supreme Court (Bundesgerichthof).[322]

The lengthy and slow procedure leading to compensation has been depicted as strenuous for the victims,[323] in particular for those who suffered from physical

---

319 Ibidem.

320 See below Section 3.3.1.

321 See N. Balabkins, *West German Reparations to Israel*, Rutgers University Press, New Brunswick, NJ, 1971, 138.

322 See Colonomos and Armstrong, above note 318, at 402.

323 Ibidem.

and psychological damage. In fact, whereas in the case of property restitution the applicant had to provide objective evidence of the looting, for the compensation of damage to body and health the victims were obliged to undergo examination by various doctors in order to access reparations benefits.

After the victim had filed a claim for body and health damages, the file was sent to the reparations office in Germany, where it was processed and was either accepted or denied. If it was denied, the victim could bring his or her case to court. The victim had to hire a lawyer and the court nominated experts. The victim would be interviewed by regular physicians, specialists, and in the case of psychological problems, by psychiatrists. Such an experience by definition brings back memories of the war. This process also obliged victims to face the judgment of evaluators, bureaucrats, doctors, and sometimes court judges.[324]

This explains why in the end the German government approved 'only' 2 million applications for individual reparations out of over 4.3 million received.[325]

The German reparations towards Jewish persons and the State of Israel, despite the weaknesses highlighted above, still represent a landmark milestone in the history of individual reparations for violations of the law of armed conflict. This is a trivial consequence stemming from the traditional understanding and implementation of war reparations. Unlike IHRL, the framework governing reparations for violations of IHL is much more limited and the provisions therein are far less specific and certainly not focused on victims' rights. According to Article 3 of the 1907 Hague Convention (IV) respecting the Laws and Customs of War on Land 'a belligerent Party which violates the provisions of the Regulations respecting the Laws and Customs of War on Land shall, if the case demands, be liable to pay compensation ...'.[326] A similar requirement to pay compensation for violations of IHL is expressly established in Article 91 of Additional Protocol I to the Geneva Conventions.[327] According to Kalshoven, the word 'compensation' instead of, for example, 'reparation' should be understood as referring especially to individuals as beneficiaries of the rule.[328] Even though both the Hague

---

324 C. Pross, *Paying for the Past: The Struggle over Reparations for the Surviving Victims of the Nazi Terror*, Johns Hopkins University Press, Baltimore, MD, 1998, Appendix A, cited by Colonomos and Armstrong, above note 318, at 402.

325 Ibidem, at 408.

326 1907 Hague Convention (IV) Respecting the Laws and Customs of War on Land and its Annex: Regulation concerning the Laws and Customs of War on Land, 187 CTS 227.

327 Art. 91 of Protocol I: 'A Party to the conflict which violates the provisions of the Conventions or of this Protocol shall, if the case demands, be liable to pay compensation. It shall be responsible for all acts committed by persons forming part of its armed forces.'

328 See expert opinion by F. Kalshoven, 'Article 3 of the Convention (IV), Respecting the Laws and Customs of War on Land', in H. Fuijta, I. Suzuki and K. Nagano (eds.), *War and Rights of Individuals*, Nippon Hyoronsha Co, Ltd. Publishers, Tokyo, 1999, 37. Cited by Zegveld, above note 13.

Convention and Additional Protocol I speak exclusively of 'compensation', reparations for violations of IHL can take various forms, namely all the five forms enshrined in the Basic Principles and Guidelines. In the armed conflict context and according to the Protocol to the 1954 Convention for the Protection of Cultural Property in the Event of Armed Conflict, one of the most common is 'restitution', which is meant as the return of unlawfully taken property.[329] As underlined by Gillard:

> While there is general consensus that there is no reason for limiting the right to compensation referred to in the Hague Convention and Additional Protocol I to States and that individual victims should also benefit, problems have arisen when such persons have attempted to enforce this right to reparation directly before national courts.[330]

As noted by Zegveld, while Article 3 of the 1907 Convention, Article 91 of Protocol I and customary law arguably confer secondary rights, including a right to compensation, upon individuals in the event of a violation of a primary norm, the question remains as to whether an individual can, in practice, assert his/her right against the State or the wrongdoer. In other words, once it is ascertained that individual victims do have legal standing to claim for reparations under IHL, historically geared towards regulating warfare between States, are there adequate implementation mechanisms in place?

Article 3 of the 1907 Convention and Article 91 Protocol I are silent in this regard, leaving it to customary international or domestic law to empower international organs or domestic courts to give effect to that right.[331] Some authors, *inter alia* Kalshoven, Zegveld and Greenwood,[332] suggest that the lack of implementation mechanisms for humanitarian law may be remedied by human rights instruments because, in contrast to IHL, human rights treaties are commonly equipped with committees, commissions or courts that are competent to receive complaints from individuals. Other authors[333] have highlighted that claims commissions, i.e. special arbitral tribunals which are usually set up by

329 Protocol to the 1954 Convention for the Protection of Cultural Property in the Event of Armed Conflict in Art. 1(3) states that 'Each high contracting Party undertakes to return at the close of hostilities to the competent authorities of the territory previously occupied, cultural property which is in its territory if such property has been exported in contrast with the principles laid down in the first Paragraph. Such property shall never be retained as war reparation.'

330 See Gillard, above note 15.

331 See generally R. Dolzer, 'The Settlement of War-Related Claims: Does International Law Recognise a Victim's Private Right of Action? Lessons after 1945', (2002) 20 *Berkeley Journal of International Law* 212, at 220–232.

332 See also C. Greenwood, 'International Humanitarian Law' in F. Kalshoven (ed.), *The Centennial of the First International Peace Conference: Reports and Conclusions*, Kluwer Law International, The Hague, 2000, at 240–241 and 251–252.

333 See Gillard, above note 15, at 529.

bilateral or multilateral treaty after revolutions and conflicts, have traditionally been a more successful way for individuals to assert their claims for compensation than national courts and other international fora. There are many examples of such commissions over the course of the last century, e.g. the Mixed Claims Commissions set up after World War I, the Iran-US Claims Tribunal, which was set up by the Algiers Accords between the US and Iran in 1981, the United Nations Compensation Commission ('UNCC') and the Eritrea-Ethiopia Claims Commission ('EECC'). Claims Commissions have operated with considerable success, but of course their *ad hoc* nature makes their establishment subject to political and economic considerations and to the willingness of the States involved.

The lack of implementation and monitoring mechanisms to restore victims' rights in the aftermath of IHL violations affect all the persons potentially entitled to reparations and in particular children and other vulnerable groups that find themselves even more impaired by this deficiency. States' responsibility for IHL violations represents only one side of the coin, in fact under certain circumstances IHL also gives rise to individual perpetrator(s)' accountability, which is addressed within the ICL framework.

3.2.3. INTERNATIONAL CRIMINAL LAW

As noted by Crane, 'the previous century was remarkable in its propensity to commit atrocity'.[334] As a result, the last decade of the twentieth century witnessed major efforts at different levels in the pursuit of 'justice' for international crimes. Developments are evident on a range of fronts, including the institution of the so-called *ad hoc* tribunals for the former Yugoslavia and Rwanda, the creation of hybrid tribunals such as the SCSL, the Special Tribunal for Lebanon ('STL'), the Extraordinary Chambers in the Courts in Cambodia ('ECCC') and, finally, the establishment of the ICC. To use Drumbl's words, one could easily conclude that nowadays 'international criminal law is everywhere'.[335] What is meant by ICL is 'a body of international Rules designed both to proscribe international crimes and to impose upon States the obligation to prosecute and punish at least some of those crimes. It also regulates international proceedings for prosecuting and trying persons accused of such crimes.'[336] This branch of international law includes both substantive and procedural rules. The first set

---

334 D. M. Crane, 'Back to the Future. Reflections on the Beginning: International Criminal Law in the Twenty-first Century', (2008) 32 *Fordham International Law Journal* 1761, at 1761.

335 M. Drumbl, 'International Criminal Law: Taking Stock of a Busy Decade', (2009) 4 *Melbourne Journal of International Law* 38, at 38–49. On international criminal law in general, see A. Cassese, *International Criminal Law* 3rd edn., Oxford University Press, Oxford, 2013.

336 Cassese, above note 335, at 15.

of rules establishes which acts fall within the definition of international crimes; it specifies the criteria according to which such acts are prohibited, but also the circumstances that exclude perpetrators' criminal liability. The set of rules that constitutes procedural criminal law 'governs the action by prosecuting authorities and the various stages of international trials'.[337] The entire body of ICL 'simultaneously derives its origins from, and continuously draws upon, international humanitarian law, international human rights law and national criminal law'.[338] In particular, with regard to the latter, it is worth stressing that ICL originally evolved from the so-called municipal case law (intra-State law) and it can, therefore, be considered as the 'transposition on to the international level of Rules and legal constructs proper to national criminal law or to national trial proceedings'.[339]

National criminal law, though, is difficult to classify as uniform. In fact, as noted by Cassese, 'amongst the different systems, the two principal ones emerged so far: namely the common law legal system and the civil law one'.[340] Since ICL is not yet sufficiently developed to autonomously supply a solution for every substantive or procedural issue, it has to rely on national criminal law, especially when it comes to reparations. In many civil law countries victims have a role in the criminal proceedings. As Sarkin pointed out, 'in Latin American a victim or his/her representative can participate as private prosecutor or *querellante adhesivo*, with the ability to initiate a prosecution or to attach as co-prosecutor to a case initiated by the Public Ministry'.[341] In other civil law countries, such as, for example, Italy, France and Germany, the criminal and the civil aspects of a case are brought together thanks to the so-called *partie civile* institute. As a consequence, the victim has the right to be represented in the trial, to be fully informed and to contribute to the resolution of the case, bringing witnesses and/or experts. If the criminal case is unsuccessful the civil claim normally follows its fate. In most jurisdictions if the accused is acquitted the victim's case also fails, while in others, e.g. France, Norway and Sweden, 'the failure of the criminal aspect of the case does not mean automatic failure for the victim' and the civil case can be transferred to a civil court.[342] Despite its undeniable positive aspects, the civil law system is far from being perfect. In particular victims are often not aware of their rights and they choose not to join the criminal proceedings, moreover there is also a need to comply with specific rules and a range of

337 Ibidem.
338 Ibidem, at 189.
339 Ibidem, at 3.
340 Ibidem, at 15.
341 Sarkin, above note 27, at 157.
342 Ibidem, at 173. See also C.P. Trumbull IV, 'The Victims' Participation in International Criminal Proceedings', (2008) 29 *Michigan Journal of International Law* 777, at 778–826.

limitations that affect the reparations awarded, which most likely take the form of compensation.[343]

In countries regulated by common law the relationship between the State and the offender is the only one under the spotlight. The purpose of criminal law is to punish the perpetrator and the victims thus only play a limited role. They may not even be called to testify and certainly they are not considered as an important party in the process. The award of reparations, therefore, depends on the single State's legislation, since it cannot be regarded as a cornerstone of common law. More than one-third of the US courts, for example, are required by statute to order restitution, unless there are compelling or extraordinary circumstances, and the United Kingdom has also slowly changed its traditional attitude to compensation.[344]

At the international level, the influence of the common law systems has been always quite strong. During the first international trials held before the Nuremberg Tribunal there was no room left for victims and punishment was the one and only goal pursued.[345] This approach was embraced by the later *ad hoc* international tribunals and has only recently been questioned and finally overcome. The lack of victims' participation and recognition in post-WWII international proceedings has contributed to spreading the perception of justice as a 'far-away concept not available … on a personal or local level'[346] and to enhance what has been defined as the 'conspiracy of silence'.[347] These shortcomings have been, to some extent, remedied through the establishment of the ICC in 2002. As for the other international courts and tribunals, it is worthy of note that still very little attention has been placed on victims' rights and needs. These international mechanisms, either *ad hoc* or hybrid, have not provided for

---

343 See E. Hoegen, M. Brienen, *Victims of Crime in 22 European Criminal Justice Systems: The Implementation of Recommendation (85) 11 of the Council of Europe on the Position of the Victim in the Framework of Criminal Law and Procedure*, Wolf Legal Publishers, Eindhoven, 2003.

344 Sarkin, above note 27, at 168.

345 C. Tomuschat, 'The Legacy of Nuremberg', (2006) 4 *Journal of International Criminal Justice* 830, at 830–844. See also in general Y. Shany, *The Competing Jurisdiction of International Courts and Tribunals*, Oxford University Press, Oxford, 2003. See also M.J. Kelley and T.L.H. McCormack, 'The Nuremberg Trial and the Subsequent Development of International Law', in D. Blumenthal and T.L.H. McCormack, *The Legacy of Nuremberg: Civilising Influence or Institutionalised Vengeance?*, Martinus Nijoff Publishers, Leiden, 2008, 102. See in general T. Meron, 'The Ad Hoc International Tribunals and the Proposed International Criminal Court', (1995) 9 *ASIL Bulletin* 5, at 5–34.

346 Y. Danieli, 'Reappraising the Nuremberg Trials and their Legacy: The Role of Victims in International Law', (2006) 27 *Cardozo Law Review* 1634, at 1634–1636.

347 Y. Danieli, *The International Handbook of Multigenerational Trauma*, Springer, New York, 1998.

a reparations scheme.[348] Article 25 of the STL's Statute, for example, mirrors the equivalent provision of the RPE of the ICTY and stipulates that

> [t]he Special Tribunal may identify victims who have suffered harm as a result of the commission of crimes by an accused convicted by the Tribunal. Subsequently, when the Tribunal has found the accused guilty, a victim may bring an action in a Lebanese or other national court or other competent body to obtain compensation, based on the judgment of the Lebanon Tribunal which shall be final and binding as to the criminal responsibility of the convicted person.[349]

In other words, the issue of reparations is devolved entirely to the national courts, which can use as a legal basis the judgments issued by the STL. A more lenient approach to victims has been envisaged by the ECCC, which was the first international court to give victims a formal voice in a major atrocities trial.[350] According to the Internal Rules of the ECCC there is a distinction between 'victims' and 'civil parties'. The former term refers to 'any person or legal entity who has suffered from physical, psychological, or material harm as a direct consequence of the crimes committed in Cambodia by the Democratic Kampuchea regime between 17 April 1975 and 6 January 1979 that are under the jurisdiction of the ECCC'.[351] Victims can decide to file a complaint before the ECCC, i.e. they can fill in the Victim Information Form and submit it to the Victims Support Section in order to provide information about the crimes committed by the Khmer Rouge. The information enshrined in the complaint may then be used to help in the investigations. The victims who have submitted a complaint do not participate as parties in the hearings, and they are not entitled to ask the court for reparations. They may, however, be requested to give evidence or testify as witnesses. If they wish to, victims may also apply to become civil

---

348 See D. Jacobs, 'The Unique Rules and Procedures of the STL', in A. Alamuddin, N.N. Jurdi and D. Tolbert (eds.) *The Special Tribunal for Lebanon: Law and Practice*, Oxford University Press, Oxford, 2014, 121.

349 In May 2007 the UNSC adopted resolution 1757, which authorised the creation of the Special Tribunal for Lebanon UNSC Res. 1757, 30 May 2007, UN doc. S/RES/1757.

350 The ECCC was set up in 2006 to bring to trial senior leaders and those most responsible for crimes committed during the time of Democratic Kampuchea. During that period, at least 1.7 million people are believed to have died from starvation, torture, execution and forced labour. The ECCC was established by domestic law following a 2003 agreement between the Cambodian government and the UN. The Court's personal jurisdiction is limited to two categories of perpetrators, i.e. senior leaders of Democratic Kampuchea and those who are most responsible for crimes committed during Democratic Kampuchea. Internal Rule 23(1) of the ECCC provides that 'The purpose of Civil Party action before the ECCC is to: a) Participate in criminal proceedings against those responsible for crimes within the jurisdiction of the ECCC by supporting the prosecution; and b) Seek collective and moral reparations, ... '.

351 See the Glossary attached to the ECCC Internal Rules (Rev.9), 16 January 2015.

parties. This status provides victims with the opportunity to participate in the proceedings and to claim for 'collective and moral reparations'.[352] A position paper issued by Open Society Initiatives has clarified that the ECCC reparations are limited to 'collective and moral reparations',[353] to 'acknowledge the harm suffered by civil parties as a result of the commission of the crimes … and provide benefits to the civil parties which address this harm'. The Court's rules say that these benefits shall not take the form of monetary payments to civil parties themselves, and that sufficient funding shall be secured from outside sources if the accused cannot pay for reparations. Civil parties are represented collectively at trial and for the purpose of requesting reparations, by a team of lawyers designated as the Co-Lead Lawyers.[354] In Case 002/01, which ended in August 2014 with the conviction of Mr Nuon Chea and Mr Khieu Samphan,[355] a total of 3,869 civil parties were admitted and comprised the consolidated group of Civil Parties at trial.[356] The Civil Party Lead Co-Lawyers requested the Trial Chamber to recognise that specific reparations measures, designed or identified in coordination with the Victims Support Section, were appropriate for implementation using external resources since the convicted persons were deemed indigent.[357] As clarified by the ECCC in the judgment of Case 002/01:

> The Chamber has no jurisdiction to order the implementation or the payment of reparation measures against Cambodian or other national authorities or international bodies. Nor can it properly impose obligations on persons or entities that were not parties to the proceedings before it. However, the adoption of Internal Rule 23quinquies (3)(b) has enabled the Chamber to recognise that specific projects give appropriate effect to an award sought on the behalf of the consolidated group of Civil Parties to contribute to their rehabilitation, reintegration and restoration of dignity where national or international authorities, non-governmental organisations or other potential donors,

352 See Rule 23 of the ECCC.

353 The Supreme Court Chamber has interpreted the term 'moral' to mean repairing moral damages rather than material ones, and 'collective' as confirming the unavailability of individual financial awards. *KAING Guek Eav Appeal Judgment*, §658.

354 Open Society Initiative, Reparations for Khmer Rouge Crimes, September 2013, available at: http://www.opensocietyfoundations.org/sites/default/files/PositionPaper-ECCC-reparations-09–10-2013.pdf.

355 See Judgment, 7 August 2014, (2014) ECCC, Case 002/01, E313.

356 At the pre-trial stage, Civil Parties participate individually. Civil Parties at the trial stage and beyond shall comprise a single, consolidated group, whose interests are represented by the Civil Party Lead Co-Lawyers. See Internal Rules 12*ter*, 23(3), 23*bis*, 23*ter* and 23*quinquies*.

357 Art. 39 of the Law on ECCC states that '… In addition to imprisonment, the Extraordinary Chamber of the trial court may order the confiscation of personal property, money, and real property acquired unlawfully or by criminal conduct. The confiscated property shall be returned to the State', thus highlighting that in any case the assets of the convicted persons will not necessarily be devoted to compensating the victims, but it will be up to the State to decide how to use them.

provide financial support and other forms of assistance to show solidarity with the victims of Khmer Rouge era crimes.[358]

Over the course of the trial in Case 002/01, the Victims Support Section and Lead Co-Lawyers sought funding for reparations from donor contributions and developed a number of projects in collaboration with governmental and non-governmental organisations external to the ECCC.[359]

The ECCC evaluated 13 projects proposed by the Lead Co-Lawyers and in the end it authorised the implementation of 11 projects, which met the requirements of Internal Rule 23*quinquies*(3)(b).[360] Only two projects were not endorsed,[361] i.e. numbers 2 and 4, the former because the information provided was not sufficiently detailed and the latter because the necessary funding had not yet been secured.[362] The crimes related to the forced movements of the population from Phnom Penh that were committed from April to September 1975 and, according to the testimonies collected during the hearings of Case 002/01, young children were among the most affected by the exodus.[363] Of course, as explained above, only victims who took part in the proceedings can claim for reparations, but the projects approved will clearly reach a much broader audience. In particular project 9 will allow for the inclusion of an additional chapter on forced transfer and the Tuol Po Chrey execution site in the Teacher's Guidebook: *The Teaching of A History of Democratic Kampuchea (1975–1979)*, which is used in all genocide education programmes. The chapter will provide the schools with an accurate basis for the discussion of events during the Democratic Kampuchea era and it will especially target those children who have been indirectly victimised by the experiences suffered by their parents, relatives and Cambodian society at large.

---

358 See Judgment of 7 August 2014, ECCC, above note 355, §1116.

359 Annex Case 002/01, 'Overview of Civil Party Reparation Requests in Case 002/01', available at: http://www.eccc.gov.kh/sites/default/files/articles/Annex%20Case%20002-01%20ReparationProjects.pdf.

360 See ECCC, Case 002/01, Judgment, 7 August 2014, E313, §§1551–1664.

361 Project 2 aimed at developing a small number (~6) of public memorial sites with related truth-telling and educational activities through a consultative process with civil parties, local communities and other stakeholders at sites distributed throughout Cambodia. Project 4 was about the construction of a monument for victims of the Khmer Rouge living in France in order to provide a space where survivors and relatives of the victims could hold ceremonies and honour the memory of those lost.

362 See Judgment of 7 August 2014, ECCC, above note 355, §§1662–1664.

363 Ibidem, footnote 1469: T. 19 October 2012 (YIM Sovann), p. 87 (a child at the time, they had to travel on foot the whole day and were exhausted); T. 5 December 2012 (KIM Vanndy), pp. 100–103 (a child at the time, his family had been travelling for three or four days and their feet were so tired they could barely walk; when they could no longer walk, they rested in that location for a day or two to gain some strength and then continued); T. 27 May 2013 (AUN Phally), p. 44 (could see that people had a lot of difficulties during the evacuation, young and old people alike struggled to walk because of tiredness and lack of food).

3.3. WHOSE RESPONSIBILITY?

3.3.1. STATES

The right to reparation in its traditional connotation, i.e. as part of the inter-State dispute settlement process, has never been questioned. The dissenting opinion of the Polish national judge Ludwik Ehrlich in the *Factory at Chorzów* case corroborates this statement, highlighting how

> [i]t followed from Judgment No.7, without the necessity of an explicit statement, that the Polish Government *was bound to make reparation* for any damage which may actually and unlawfully have been inflicted ... This is a consequence of the principle that the violation of an international obligation entails the duty of reparation, a principle *generally accepted in the classification of international disputes of a legal character*, which was embodied in Article 13 of the Covenant of the League of Nations, and in Article 36 of the Statute of the Court.[364]

Although the dissenting opinion contested the jurisdiction of the PCIJ on this specific case and therefore its power to grant reparation to the German State, at the same time it stressed the existence under international law of the duty to fully repair, in principle through economic compensation, the breach of an international obligation. Since, by tradition, under international law States have been identified as the main actors, they were thought to be the only ones entitled to this duty and the corresponding right.[365] This concept is further stressed in another famous passage of the *Factory at Chorzów* ruling, which affirms that

> [i]t is a principle of international law that the breach of an engagement involves an obligation to make reparation in an adequate form. Reparation, therefore, is the indispensable complement of a failure to apply a convention and *there is no necessity for this to be stated in the convention itself.*[366]

The idea of reparation as the 'complement of a failure' rather than as 'a right', expresses *in toto* the way the principle was used as a meaning to 'solve inter-States disputes' and to prevent the emergence of new ones.[367]

---

364 Judgment of 13 September 1928 (Merits), PCIJ, above note 282, §228.

365 As Oppenheim stated in the first edition of his famous treatise, 'Since the Law of Nations is a law between States only, and since States are the sole exclusive subjects of International Law, individuals are mere objects of International Law, and the latter is unable to confer directly rights and duties upon individuals'. See L. Oppenheim, *International Law: A Treatise*, Longmans, Green and Co., London, 1905.

366 Judgment of 13 September 1928 (Merits), PCIJ, above note 282, p. 21.

367 In particular before the enhancement of individuals' rights within the international arena, the idea of reparation was simply assimilated to the concept of 'remedies'.

Since the PCIJ, the ICJ has implemented its decisions on reparations in several cases, e.g. in the *LaGrand* case and in the *Advisory Opinion on the Legal Consequences of the Construction of a Wall in the Occupied Palestinian Territory.*[368] Given its role as the most prominent and authoritative judicial body worldwide, through the rulings issued by the ICJ it is possible to explain the evolution of the right to reparation under public international law and some of its recent developments. In particular, in the advisory opinion on the Israeli separation wall the Court affirmed that Israel had a duty to make reparation for the damage caused. In fact, according to the ICJ, Israel was under an obligation to return the land, orchards, olive groves and other immovable property seized from any natural or legal person for purposes of construction of the wall in the Occupied Palestinian Territory. In the event that such restitution should prove to be materially impossible, Israel was compelled to compensate the natural and legal persons in question for the damage suffered.[369]

Notwithstanding its 'openness' to the recognition of individuals as victims of the State's misconduct and as subjects entitled to obtain reparations, the ICJ has showed that, ultimately, when a choice is to be made between States' rights and immunities versus victims' rights, the former still prevail. In February 2012 the ICJ gave a landmark judgment in respect of a dispute originating in 'violations of obligations under international law committed by Italy through its judicial practice in that it has failed to observe the jurisdictional immunity, which Germany enjoys under international law'.[370] Germany's application was filed on the grounds that Italy, by allowing its nationals' civil claims[371] based on the violations of IHL committed by the German Reich during WWII from September 1943 to May 1945 to be brought against the Federal Republic of Germany, had breached its above-mentioned obligations.[372] The Court thus was called to determine whether or not, in proceedings regarding claims for compensation

368 'The Court here abandoned the view that reparation was to be made to States with individuals as ultimate beneficiaries. Rather, it found it incumbent upon the responsible party to grant reparation directly to the individuals themselves. For this reason, the judgment has been interpreted as endorsing an individual right to reparation, even if it is drafted in the language of obligations'. According to the Committee on the Right to Reparation for Victims of Armed Conflict, International Law Association (ILA), The Hague, August 2010. See Commentary on Article 6, §2(h) of the Draft declaration, available at: http://www.ila-hq.org/en/committees/index.cfm/cid/1018.

369 Advisory Opinion of 9 July 2004, ICJ, above note 153.

370 Judgment of 3 February 2012, (2012) ICJ Reports 2012, p. 99.

371 Ibidem, at §27: 'On 11 March 2004, the Italian Court of Cassation held that Italian courts had jurisdiction over the claims for compensation brought against Germany by Mr. Luigi Ferrini on the ground that immunity does not apply in circumstances when the act complained of constitutes an international crime (Ferrini v. Federal Republic of Germany, Decision No. 5044/2004), *Rivista di diritto internazionale*, Vol. 87, 2004, at 539; *International Law Reports* (ILR), Vol. 128, at 658.'

372 Ibidem, at §15.

arising out of the acts perpetrated by the German forces, the Italian courts were obliged to accord immunity to Germany.[373] In its ruling the ICJ found that the acts committed by the German army fell within the so-called *acta jure imperii* and as such were entitled to jurisdictional immunity, notwithstanding both their unlawfulness and gravity.[374]

In addition to that, the Court also ruled that immunity from jurisdiction is an immunity 'not merely from being subjected to an adverse judgment *but from being subjected to the trial process*', which means that the issue of immunity should be determined prior to the enquiry on the merits. The Court stated that under current international customary law it is not possible to affirm that a State is deprived of its immunity 'by reason of the fact that it is accused of serious violations of international human rights law or of international law of armed conflict'.[375] Finally, the Court did not detect any conflict between a rule, or rules,

---

373 'The Court must determine whether, as Italy maintains, the failure of a State to perform completely a duty of reparation which it allegedly bears is capable of having an effect, in law, on the existence and scope of that State's jurisdictional immunity before foreign courts. This question is one of law on which the Court must rule in order to determine the customary international law applicable in respect of State immunity for the purposes of the present case' §50.

374 *Acta jure imperii* are traditionally distinguished from *acta jure gestionis*. The former are recognised as the outcomes of the exercise by a State of its sovereign power, while the latter concern the non-sovereign activities of a State, in particular private and commercial activities. On the distinction between *acta jure imperii* and *acta jure gestionis* see generally M. Frulli, *Immunità e Crimini Internazionali. L'Esercizio della Giurisidizione Penale e Civile nei confronti degli Organi Statali Sospettati di Gravi Crimini Internazionali*, G. Giappichelli editore, Turin, 2007. See also M. Krajewski and C. Singer, 'Should Judges be Front–Runners? The ICJ, State Immunity and the Protection of Fundamental Human Rights', in A. von Bogdandy and R. Wolfrum (eds.) *Max Planck UNYB*, Martinus Nijhoff Publishers, Leiden, 2012, volume 16, 1, at 17–18.

375 The Court further dwells on this point, referring to the judicial practice of national courts worldwide and also of the European Court of Human Rights: 'There is a substantial body of State practice from other countries which demonstrates that customary international law does not treat a State's entitlement to immunity as dependent upon the gravity of the act of which it is accused or the peremptory nature of the Rule which it is alleged to have violated. That practice is particularly evident in the judgments of national courts. Arguments to the effect that international law no longer required State immunity in cases of allegations of serious violations of international human rights law, war crimes or crimes against humanity have been rejected by the courts in Canada (Bouzari v. Islamic Republic of Iran, Court of Appeal of Ontario, (2004) Dominion Law Reports (DLR) 4th Series, Vol. 243, p. 406; ILR, Vol. 128, p. 586; allegations of torture), France (Judgment of the Court of Appeal of Paris, 9 September 2002, and Cour de cassation, No. 02-45961, 16 December 2003, Bull. civ., 2003, I, No. 258, p. 206 (the Bucheron case); Cour de cassation, No. 03-41851, 2 June 2004, Bull. civ., 2004, I, No. 158, p. 132 (the X case) and Cour de cassation, No. 04-47504, 3 January 2006 (the Grosz case); allegations of crimes against humanity), Slovenia (case No. Up-13/99, Constitutional Court of Slovenia; allegations of war crimes and crimes against humanity); European Court of Human Rights: Kalogeropoulou and others v. Greece and Germany (Application No. 59021/00, Decision of 12 December 2002, ECHR Reports 2002-X, p. 417; ILR, Vol. 129, p. 537.) and Al-Adsani v. United Kingdom [GC], Application No. 35763/97, Judgment of 21 November 2001, ECHR Reports 2001-XI, p. 101, Para. 61; ILR, Vol. 123, p. 24'.

of *jus cogens*, and the rule of customary law which requires a State to accord immunity to another. In particular, according to the Court the rules that govern a State's jurisdictional immunity are 'procedural in character' and their sphere of activity is confined to determining whether or not the courts of one State may exercise jurisdiction in respect of another State. Given their procedural status, such rules do not have a bearing upon the question of whether the conduct which triggered the proceedings was lawful or unlawful and therefore they address different matters from those addressed by the *jus cogens* rules. With regard to reparations, the Court specified that the duty to make reparation to restore the victims of a State's misconduct is not dependent on those rules that concern the means by which it is to be effected,[376] meaning that, again, there is no conflict between the rules on jurisdictional immunities and the rules that impose the obligation to repair the wrongdoings.

The Court also stressed that international law does not contain a rule requiring the payment of full compensation to each and every individual victim and accepted by the entire community of States as a rule completely exempt from derogation.[377] In particular, if a State, which received funds as the outcomes of a comprehensive settlement in the aftermath of an international armed conflict, decides to use such funds to rebuild its national economy and infrastructure instead of distributing them among the victims, it is, then, not entitled to allow further claims by individual victims against the State which already 'transferred the money'.[378]

In other words, the Court saw the lack of compensation to the victims as a misdeed attributable to Italy rather than as a breach of the obligation to make adequate and prompt reparation perpetrated by Germany. This judgment, the most recent in which the ICJ has addressed, even though only incidentally,[379]

---

376 Judgment of 3 February 2012, (2012) ICJ, §94.

377 On this point see Tomuschat above note 1. Professor Tomuschat was one of the three legal representatives of the Federal Republic of Germany in this case before the ICJ. See also the Dissenting Opinion of Judge Cancado Trindade, according to whom '[T]he finding of the particularly grave violations of human rights and of international humanitarian law provides, in my understanding, a valuable test for the removal of any bar to jurisdiction, in pursuance of the necessary realization of justice. In sum and conclusion on this point: (a) there is no State immunity in such cases of extreme gravity, cases of *delicta imperii*; and (b) grave breaches of human rights and of international humanitarian law *ineluctably entail the duty to provide reparation to the victims*', §213, (emphasis added).

378 The Court referred to the two agreements signed in 1961 between the Federal Republic of Germany and Italy, the first concerned with the 'Settlement of certain property related, economic and financial questions' and the second concerned with 'Compensation for Italian Nationals subjected to National-Socialist measures of persecution'.

379 The Counter-Memorial of Italy included a counterclaim 'with respect to the question of the reparation owed to Italian victims of grave violations of international humanitarian law committed by forces of the German Reich'. By an Order of 6 July 2010, the Court decided that the counterclaim presented by Italy was inadmissible as such under Art. 80, §1, of the Rules of the Court.

the issue of reparation, represents a relevant example of the procedural hurdles that a claim for reparation has to overcome before the international judicial bodies, in particular with regard to the jurisdictional immunities which still hinder the individuals' exercise of the right to reparation in the aftermath of a State's misconduct. Notably, in the aftermath of a reparations settlement between States, when the claim concerns the victims vis-à-vis their own State and therefore no immunity and States' privileges are at stake, the survivors have a better chance of challenging the distribution of the award received. For example, in August 2012, therefore less than six months after the judgment issued by the ICJ, the Tel Aviv District Court ruled that the State must pay out compensation, totalling NIS 17 million, to a group of 217 Holocaust survivors who sued Israel for unpaid reparations. The claimants, who are mostly in their 80s, belong to a group of survivors known as the 'Tehran Children', i.e. Jewish orphans who, after the Nazis massacred their parents, fled Poland and lived in a refugee camp in Tehran until the JA rescued them and brought them to Israel in 1943. The civil suit brought by 217 Tehran Children focused on whether the claimants, formally recognised as Holocaust survivors only in 1997, were personally entitled to receive compensation payments from the monies that Israel received under the Reparations Agreement signed in Luxembourg on 10 September 1952. According to the Reparations Agreement, West Germany committed itself to paying Israel about DM 3 billion in annual instalments over 12 years in the form of goods and services – plus another DM 450 million over 12 years 'to be used for the relief, rehabilitation and resettlement of Jewish victims of Nazi persecution'.[380] As stressed by one of the victims the lack of assistance from the State, which in turn received plenty of funds from Germany, had impaired their ability to become part of Israeli society and receive an education.[381] The survivors were forced to '[leave] the educational system without an education or profession. They tried to rehabilitate without the help of the State and the reparations.'[382] It is the case, thus, that the Tel Aviv District Court has addressed an issue raised, but not solved, by the ICJ, arguing that it is possible for the victims of an armed conflict to question the way inter-State reparations awarded to the their State of origin have been allocated. According to the ICJ:

> Where the State receiving funds as part of what was intended as a comprehensive settlement in the aftermath of an armed conflict has elected to use those funds to rebuild its national economy and infrastructure, rather than distributing them to individual victims amongst its nationals, it is difficult to see why the fact that those individuals had

---

380 See Colonomos and Armstrong, above note 318.

381 Professor Zeev Schuss, a science professor who currently teaches at Tel Aviv University, has acted as a *de facto* spokesperson for the Tehran Children. See G. Morag, '"Tehran children" Holocaust survivors finally win compensation', 5 August 2014, *Jewish World*, available at: http://www.ynetnews.com/articles/0,7340,L-4517670,00.html.

382 Ibidem.

> not received a share in the money should be a reason for entitling them to claim against the State that had transferred money to their State of nationality.[383]

In other words, while on the one hand the responsibility cannot be attributed to the State that has transferred the money, on the other hand the State of nationality, which has received the funds and decided to exclude certain victims, including children, from the distribution of the monies, could (and should) be held accountable. This landmark judgment thus provided an interesting twist on victims' legal standing in relation to war claims originally conceived as inter-State and indicated a new path to those who have been neglected by the domestic implementation of reparations awards, especially child victims and other vulnerable groups to whom justice is very often denied. Furthermore, also worth noting is the fact that the Tel Aviv Court ruled that all the Tehran Children, not just the 217 who sued the Finance Minister and the JA, were each entitled to a compensation payment of NIS 50,000.[384] The Court therefore deemed it important to confer the status of reparations beneficiaries also to those victims who did not participate in the proceedings.

3.3.2. NON-STATE ACTORS' ABIDANCE BY INTERNATIONAL HUMAN RIGHTS LAW AND INTERNATIONAL HUMANITARIAN LAW

If on the one hand it is trivial to affirm that States are bound by international law and thus accountable for violations committed, on the other hand applying this basic, and *prima facie* obvious, concept also to non-State actors poses several issues.

Broadly speaking the term 'non-State actor' may refer to 'an individual or organisation that has significant political influence but is not allied to any particular country or State'.[385] In the context of an armed conflict this all-encompassing definition can be narrowed so as to include:

(1) regularly constituted groups of combatants with a military command structure and a political structure;
(2) non-regularly constituted groups of combatants with or without a command structure and with or without a political hierarchical structure;

---

383 Judgment of 3 February 2012, (2012) ICJ, §102.
384 See J. Paraszczuk, The Jerusalem Post, reported in 'Martyrdom and Resistance', Vol. 39 January/February 2013, at 7, available at: http://www.yadvashemusa.org/documents/MR/2013_Jan_Feb.pdf.
385 'Non-State Actor', OED online, Oxford University Press, 22 June 2015, available at: http://www.oxforddictionaries.com/definition/english/non-state-actor?q=nonstate+actor.

(3) spontaneously gathered groups who engage in combat or who engage in sporadic acts of collective violence with or without a command structure and with or without political leadership;
(4) mercenaries acting as an autonomous group or as part of other groups of combatants; and
(5) expatriate volunteers who engage for a period of time in combat or in support of combat operations, either as separate units or as part of duly constituted or *ad hoc* units.[386]

The list is certainly not exhaustive, but provides an account of the variety of stakeholders which can generally be described as Armed Non-State Actors ('ANSAs'), potentially involved in an armed conflict.[387] NSAGs are a specific sub-category within ANSAs, encompassing 'those who articulate a political agenda rather than private (including economic) goals, though without a requirement of elaborated political manifestos'.[388] NSAGs are the most relevant non-State actors for the purposes of the present book.

The question remains as to whether such actors are, at least to some extent, required to comply with IHRL and IHL and what consequences, if any, are envisaged in case of violations. The first part of the question has been thoroughly and exhaustively discussed among scholars and practitioners and it can arguably be answered with a, for some still cautious, yes.[389] In more detail, under IHRL States are traditionally thought of as the only subjects committed to the protection of the rights enshrined in the treaties that they have ratified or accessed. However, as affirmed by several authors,[390] NSAs are also bound to respect IHRL when they exercise 'effective power over a significant segment of

386 See M.C. Bassiouni, 'The New Wars and the Crisis of Compliance with the Law of Armed Conflict by Non-State Actors', (2008) 98 *Journal of Criminal Law and Criminology* 712, at 715.

387 'Armed Non-State Actor [refers to] any armed group, distinct from and not operating under the control of, the State or States in which it carries out military operations, and which has political, religious, and/or military objectives'. See A. Bellal, G. Giacca, and S. Casey-Maslen, 'International Law and Armed Actors in Afghanistan', (2011) 93 *International Review of the Red Cross* 47, at 48, footnote 4.

388 DCAF & Geneva Call, Armed Non-State Actors: Current Trends & Future Challenges, Horizon 2015 Working Paper No. 5, 2011, available at: http://www.dcaf.ch/Publications/Armed-Non-State-Actors-Current-Trends-Future-Challenges.

389 See for instance R. McCorquodale, 'An Inclusive International Legal System', (2004) 17 *Leiden Journal of International Law* 477, at 478–504. S. Sivakumaran, 'Binding Armed Opposition Groups', (2006) 55 *International and Comparative Law Quarterly* 369, at 370–371. M. Sassòli, 'The Implementation of International Humanitarian Law: Current and Inherent Challenges', (2007) 10 *Yearbook of International Humanitarian Law* 45, at 63.

390 N.S. Rodley, 'Can Armed Opposition Groups Violate Human Rights?', in K.E. Mahoney and P. Mahoney (eds.), *Human Rights in the Twenty-first Century*, Martinus Nijhoff Publishers, Dordrecht, 1993, 297, at 300–318. See also L. Zegveld, *The Accountability of Armed Opposition Groups in International Law*, Cambridge University Press, Cambridge, 2002, 38.

population'[391] and act in a way comparable to a government.[392] This approach has eventually been replaced by a more empirical and progressive one according to which, even though all NSAGs in principle are bound by IHRL obligations, the degree of compliance is not standardised as it depends on how much power each NSAG exercises on a given territory and how organised and well structured it is.[393]

With regard to IHL, it is authoritatively accepted that the law of armed conflict can bind NSAGs.[394] Several theories have been developed and used over the years to understand the legal basis underpinning this attribution.[395] Two of them have ultimately prevailed. The first theory is the 'third-party consent theory', which holds that in order for an international treaty to bind third parties the drafters must have intended to bind the third parties and those third parties must consent to be so bound.[396] The second theory, known as the doctrine of legislative/prescriptive jurisdiction, affirms that a State may pass binding legislation applicable to persons or entities on its territory. According to this theory, any international obligation entered into by a State binds the State itself as well as the actors that operate on its territory, including NSAGs.[397] Both theories of course have strengths and shortcomings. The former, putting the accent on NSAGs' consent to be bound, seems less rooted in the existing IHL framework and more aspirational than the latter, which in turn downsizes the role played by non-State

---

391 Rodley, above note 390, at 298.

392 See UN Assistance Mission in Afghanistan ('UNAMA'), Afghanistan: Annual Report 2011, Protection of Civilians in Armed Conflict, Kabul, February 2012, at iv, 'While non-State actors in Afghanistan, including non-State armed groups, cannot formally become parties to international human rights treaties, international human rights law increasingly recognises that where non-State actors, such as the Taliban, exercise *de facto* control over territory, they are bound by international human rights obligations'.

393 A. Clapham, *Human Rights Obligations of Non-State Actors*, Oxford University Press, Oxford, 2006, 284.

394 Judgment of 27 June 1986 (Merits), (1986) ICJ Reports p. 14, §218. See also J.K. Kleffner, 'The Applicability of International Humanitarian Law to Organised Armed Groups', (2011) 93 *International Review of the Red Cross* 443, at 453–461.

395 See D. Murray, 'How International Humanitarian Law Treaties Bind Non-State Armed Groups', (2014) 20 *Journal of Conflict and Security Law* 101, at 102. The author identifies five theories, namely customary law, general principles, State succession, third-party consent and legislative (or prescriptive) jurisdiction.

396 Ibidem, at 112.

397 This theory is far more traditional and supported by several authors, *in primis* Professor Brownlie. See I. Brownlie, *Principles of Public International Law* 7th edn., Oxford University Press, Oxford, 2008, 299. See also C. Ryngaert, 'Non-State Actors and International Humanitarian Law', University of Leuven, Working Paper No. 1, 2008. According to the author, 'In what is seen as the majority view, non-State actors are bound by IHL by reason of their being active on the territory of a Contracting Party (a State Party to the Geneva Conventions and/or its Additional Protocols). This theory is also referred to as the "principle of legislative jurisdiction", pursuant to which the agreements which a State enters into are automatically binding on all (non-State) actors within its jurisdiction.'

actors, including NSAGs, but has the advantage of potentially paving the way for the future application of international treaty law to non-State actors in general. The wording of Article 3 Common to the Geneva Conventions directly imposes upon each party, thus also NSAGs, the obligation to respect the minimum standards of humanitarian principles applicable in NIACs. Whereas the text of Article 3 explicitly envisages its relevance to NSAGs, Additional Protocol II is deliberately silent on the issue. Nonetheless, the Commentary on the Additional Protocols stresses that 'the commitment made by a State not only applies to the government but also to any established authorities and private individuals within the national territory of that State and certain obligations are therefore imposed upon them'.[398] It seems, then, that elements of both theories emerge in relation to the reading and the interpretation of the relevant IHL provisions. The case law of the relevant courts and tribunals also supports NSAGs' abidance by IHL and IHRL. In the *Hinga Norman* case the SCSL stated that '[i]t is well settled that all parties to an armed conflict, whether States or non-State actors, are bound by international humanitarian law, even though only States may become parties to international treaties'.[399]

3.3.2.1. *Non-State Armed Groups' Secondary Obligations*

Once it is established that NSAGs are bound by primary norms under IHRL and IHL, the main issue to address for the purpose of the present work is to determine whether the breach of such norms gives rise to secondary obligations, including the duty to provide reparations to the victims. The traditional approach in this regard can be summarised as follows: 'the [NSAG] either wins and then its international responsibility is absorbed into that of a State, or is defeated and then its international responsibility can hardly yield any results since the movement ceases its existence'.[400] As reported by Ryngaert and d'Aspremont, 'the long duration of many non-international armed conflicts and the ability of many Armed Organised Groups ('AOGs') to survive the end of armed conflicts have however proved this assumption largely incorrect'.[401] As a result there is increasing support for the idea that NSAGs need to be held responsible under international law for violations of what should be recognised as their collective (group) primary obligations. Ryngaert and d'Aspremont noted that this opinion benefits from indirect support by the ILC, which speaks of 'a ... possibility ... that

---

398 See Sandoz, Swinarski and Zimmermann, above note 217, at 1345.

399 Decision of 31 May 2004 (Decision on Preliminary Motion Based on Lack of Jurisdiction), (2004) SCSL Case No. SCSL-2004-14-AR72(E), §22.

400 E. David, *Principes de Droit des Conflits Armés*, 3rd edn., Bruylant, Brussels, 2002, 643.

401 C. Ryngaert and J. d'Aspremont, 3rd Report of the ILA Non-State Actors Committee, 2014, available at: http://www.ila-hq.org/en/committees/index.cfm/cid/1023.

the insurrectional movement may itself be held responsible for its own conduct under international law, for example for a breach of international humanitarian law committed by its forces'.[402] Further confirmation may be found in UNSC resolutions calling for the responsibility of specific NSAGs engaged in NIACs.[403] Moreover, as stressed by Amoroso, 'an impetus in this direction could come precisely from UN practice relating to the civil wars in Syria and Iraq'.[404] The joint reports of the UN monitoring bodies, United Nations Assistance Mission for Iraq ('UNAMI') and the Office of the United Nations High Commissioner for Human Rights ('OHCHR'), currently documenting the situation of human rights in these countries, concluded with a call to all parties (including, therefore, NSAGs) to 'cease immediately' violence and abuses against civilians 'in violation of applicable international … human rights law'.[405] The cessation of wrongful conduct is one of the remedies envisaged by the Draft Articles on State Responsibility and in this case it has been imposed directly on the NSAGs involved in the conflict.[406] The Commission of Inquiry on Syria alluded to an obligation of reparation incumbent on armed groups when it recommended, in its fourth report, that anti-government forces 'provide effective redress for victims based on international standards'.[407] In a previous report, the Commission, after establishing that the Free Syrian Army ('FSA') had committed acts of torture, unlawful killings and enforced disappearances, invited the insurgent group to provide a series of guarantees of non-repetition, consisting in the adoption and the public announcement of 'rules of conduct that are in accordance with international human rights law … ', and in the public pledge not to commit these acts again.[408]

Three years after the second report the situation in Syria has further deteriorated, also due to the increasing role played by new actors like the Islamic State of Iraq and Syria ('ISIS') and Jabhat Al-Nusra. With regard to the

402 See Articles on Responsibility of States for Internationally Wrongful Acts, above note 17, at 118, §16.

403 UN doc. S/RES/43 (1948), 1 April 1948, §2; UN doc. S/RES/954 (1994), 4 November 1994, §7; UN doc. S/RES/1316 (2000), 13 August 2000, §. 9 of the preamble, cited by Ryngaert and d'Aspremont, above note 401.

404 Amoroso, above note 39, at 217.

405 UNAMI-OHCHR Report on the Protection of Civilians in the Armed Conflict in Iraq: 6 July to 10 September 2014 at 21, available at: http://www.ohchr.org/Documents/Countries/IQ/UNAMI_HRO_DP_1Oct2014.pdf; UNAMI-OHCHR, Report on the Protection of Civilians in the Armed Conflict in Iraq: 11 September to 10 December 2014, at 27, available at: http://www.ohchr.org/Documents/Countries/IQ/UNAMI_OHCHR_Sep_Dec_2014.pdf.

406 Art. 30(a) of the ILC Articles on State Responsibility.

407 Human Rights Council, Report of the Independent International Commission of Inquiry on the Syrian Arab Republic, 5 February 2013, UN doc. A/HRC/22/59, §177(d).

408 Human Rights Council, Second Report of the Independent International Commission of Inquiry on the Syrian Arab Republic, UN doc. A/HRC/19/69, §133(a)(b).

former, the ninth report of the Commission of Inquiry, issued on February 2015, highlighted that

> ISIS has instrumentalised and abused children on a scale not seen before in the Syrian conflict. It has established 'cubs camps' across areas under its control, where children are taught how to use weapons and trained to be deployed as suicide bombers. In September and October 2014, minors were part of ISIS forces during its assault on Ayn al-Arab (Kobane). Children have been deliberately targeted for indoctrination and instrumentalised by ISIS. ISIS has also used schools for military purposes, endangering children and preventing their access to education.[409]

Similarly, Jabhat Al-Nusra has been accused of infringing the rights of children and breaching all obligations to afford them necessary protections from harm and abuse.[410] The report affirms that of the 6.5 million internally displaced persons in Syria, half are children. Many IDPs keep fleeing into areas under NSAGs' control and become vulnerable to their conduct. Children, in particular if separated from their families and communities, are at risk of being targeted, recruited and used in hostilities. The Commission of Inquiry in its recommendations to the parties involved in the armed conflict has stressed the necessity to

> strengthen measures to help specific groups, such as women, children, persons with disabilities and minorities, including more programmes to provide socio-psychological support for rehabilitation/social reintegration, with due regard for the effective participation of beneficiaries.[411]

This recommendation, recalling the wording of Article 39 of the CRC, imposed on all parties a duty to provide redress to the most vulnerable groups affected by the violations committed. However, rather than hinting at a proper obligation to award reparations to the victims, the text seems to promote the adoption of some sort of assistance measures. Despite the mild language adopted, the work of the Commission of Inquiry paves the way for the recognition of secondary norms incumbent on actors other than States for breaches of IHRL and IHL.

The 'push' by the Commission of Inquiry is particularly relevant as there is no norm within the existing framework that corroborates the existence of an obligation to repair the harm suffered by the victims of NSAGs' misconduct. Some authors refer to Article 10 of the ILC Articles on State Responsibility as

---

409 Human Rights Council, Ninth Report of the Independent International Commission of Inquiry on the Syrian Arab Republic, UN doc. A/HRC/28/69, §70.

410 Ibidem, §204.

411 Ibidem, §143.

the primary rule in international law for holding armed groups responsible.[412] However, the provision contained in Article 10 is strictly limited to those groups that successfully overthrow the government or form a new State, thereby excluding the responsibility of groups who fail to do so. The boldest and clearest attempt to hold NSAGs accountable for reparations can be found in the UNBPG. Principle 15 affirms that 'in cases where a person, a legal person, *or other entity* is found liable for reparation to a victim, such party should provide reparation to the victim or compensate the State if the State has already provided reparation to the victim'.[413] Principle 16 further underlines States' subsidiary role in cases where the parties liable for the harm suffered are *unable or unwilling* to meet their obligations, whereas Principle 17 clarifies that States must enforce domestic judgments for reparation against individuals or *entities liable* for the harm suffered and endeavour to enforce valid foreign legal judgments for reparation.[414] *In abstracto*, then, NSAGs bear the responsibility for the violations committed and are accountable for reparations; *in concreto*, however, the practice supporting this statement is, at the very least, scant. The ILA Committee on non-State actors reported some examples of NSAGs voluntarily committing themselves to provide reparations to victims.[415] In Uganda, for instance, the Lord's Resistance Army pledged itself to provide reparations as part of the Juba Peace Process, and the State agreed to facilitate and provide a subsidiary role in cases where members of the LRA were indigent.[416] The leader of the LRA, Joseph Kony, failed to sign the final agreement and the peace talks were ultimately aborted. Even though several agenda items were agreed upon, including agenda item three on accountability and reconciliation, reparations have never been implemented. Nonetheless, it is noteworthy that the agreement acknowledged the particular vulnerability of some segments of the population, including children, and it highlighted the need to prioritise reparations for the members of these groups.[417]

In Colombia, a series of transitional justice laws has been promulgated in which NSAGs have voluntarily provided reparations to victims in order to avail themselves of reduced sentences. This scheme was first enacted through the

---

412 See L. Moffett, 'Beyond Attribution: Responsibility of Armed Non-State Actors for Reparations in Northern Ireland, Colombia and Uganda', (2013) 20 Queen's University Belfast School of Law: Research Paper, at 1–19.

413 See UNBPG, above note 2, §15 (emphasis added).

414 Ibidem.

415 See Ryngaert and d'Aspremont, above note 401.

416 See Clauses 6.4, 8.1, and 9, 'Juba Peace Agreement on Accountability and Reconciliation', 29 June 2007; and Clauses 16–18, 'Annexure to the Agreement on Accountability and Reconciliation', 19 February 2008.

417 'Juba Peace Agreement on Accountability and Reconciliation', 29 June 2007, Clause 9.1.

adoption of the Justice and Peace Law ('JPL') in 2005.[418] With the entry into force of the JPL the legislator tried to purse a manifold goal, namely to achieve demobilisation, disarmament and reintegration of illegal armed groups, to recognise and enforce the rights of the victims to truth, justice and reparation and to conduct criminal proceedings against the leaders of those groups that are responsible for the commission of serious crimes.[419] Despite its ambitious scope and the far-reaching breadth, the JPL has been strongly criticised for prioritising 'neutralisation' of the State's opponents over the rights and the needs of victims, including children.[420] Some of these limitations have been remedied through the adoption of the Victims and Land Restitution Law in 2011 (Victims' Law), which complements the JPL. Within the Victims' Law acquiring victim status is explicitly divorced from the process of condemning the person responsible for victimisation.[421] The JPL, instead, has been developed retaining its core element, namely that of alternative sentences for perpetrators,[422] and it deals only incidentally with reparations for the victims.

As stated in the JPL, in order to be eligible for benefits, individual demobilised paramilitary candidates must: provide information about the paramilitary organisation, sign a statement of commitment to the government; and turn over all illegally obtained assets which are then collected in the *Fondo de Reparación* (i.e. the Reparation Fund).[423] If the candidate fulfils these requirements, judicial proceedings are initiated which involve the following: investigations by a prosecutor; a confessions process, including the delivery of *versiones libres* (i.e. voluntary depositions) in which the person provides a list and details of confessed crimes; arraignment following the completion of the prosecutor's investigation; acceptance of charges by the candidate; a public hearing before a Justice and Peace Tribunal to determine whether the acceptance of charges by the individual was free and voluntary; delivery of the verdict; and sentencing.[424]

Article 42 of the JPL stipulates that members of armed groups who 'benefit from the provisions of this law, i.e. demobilisation and reduced sentence, are

---

418 JPL, Arts 24, 29; P. Alston, *Report of the Special Rapporteur on Extrajudicial, Summary or Arbitrary Executions*, Addendum, Mission to Colombia, 31 March 2010, UN doc. A/HRC/14/24/Add.2, Appendix C, Justice and Peace Law §3. See also J. García-Godos and K.A.O. Lid, 'Transitional Justice and Victims' Rights before the End of a Conflict: The Unusual Case of Colombia', (2010) 42 *Journal of Latin American Studies* 487, at 490–516.

419 Review Conference of the Rome Statute, 'Transitional Justice in Colombia, Justice and Peace Law: An Experience of Truth, Justice and Reparation', 1 June 2010, UN doc. RC/ST/PJ/M.1.

420 See Alston, above note 418, §56.

421 N. Summers, 'Colombia's Victims' Law: Transitional Justice in a Time of Violent Conflict?', (2012) 25 *Harvard Human Rights Journal* 219, at 226.

422 Evans, above note 47, at 212.

423 See JPL, Art. 11.

424 JPL, Arts. 16–25; see also Alston, above note 418, §50, Appendix C, Justice and Peace Law, §§4–6.

under a duty to make reparation to the victims of said criminal conduct for which they were convicted by judicial verdict'. Furthermore, Article 44 outlines appropriate reparations individuals can be held responsible for, which include

> surrendering to the State illegally obtained assets for making reparation to the victims; a public statement that re-establishes the dignity of the victim and of the persons closest to him or her; public recognition of having caused harm to the victims, the public statement of repentance, the request for forgiveness directed to the victims, and the promise not to repeat such criminal conduct; and effective collaboration in locating persons kidnapped or disappeared and in locating the victims' remains.[425]

One of the main shortcomings of the framework envisaged by the JPL to hold members of the paramilitary groups accountable for reparations is the caveat that reparations ought to be paid to the victims only pursuant to individual conviction. Moreover, the provisions enshrined in the JPL make the award of reparations conditional upon a number of factors: 'the outcome of the investigation; the ability of the victim to present proof to support his or her claim; if property was relinquished by the perpetrator to the Reparations Fund; and whether the Reparations Fund held sufficient resources to distribute'.[426] According to the Colombian Constitutional Court these requirements curtail significantly victims' access to remedies. To partially redress this shortcoming the Constitutional Court has determined in a landmark judgment that the collective civil responsibility of the whole armed group should arise whenever one of its members is convicted.[427] Furthermore, the Constitutional Court has also affirmed that all the individuals affiliated with a paramilitary group have a duty to provide reparations from both their illegal and legal resources.[428]

Despite these significant steps forward, Human Rights Watch reported that as of September 2014, only 37 of the more than 30,000 paramilitaries who officially participated in the demobilisation process had been convicted of crimes under the JPL.[429] The convictions covered only a small portion of the nearly 70,000 crimes confessed by defendants seeking the JPL benefits.[430] With regard in particular to child victims, to date there have been 69 convictions for child recruitment, of which only five were under the JPL, and 64 by the

---

425 Art. 44 of the JPL.

426 See Evans, above note 47, at 214.

427 Judgment of 18 May 2006, Gusavo Gallón y otros, Corte Constitucional C-370/2006, §.6.2.4.4.7–6.2.4.4.13. See also Judgment of 29 June 2010, Tribunal Superior del Distrito Judicial de Bogotá, Sala de Justicia y Paz, Edwar Cobos Téllez y Uber Enrique Banquéz M., §§252–253.

428 Ibidem.

429 Human Rights Watch, 'World Report – 2015: Colombia', 2015, available at: www.hrw.org/world-report-2015/Colombia.

430 Ibidem.

Human Rights Unit of the Office of the Attorney General.[431] The most famous conviction under the JPL was issued in December 2011, against a top United Self-Defense Forces of Colombia ('Autodefensas Unidas de Colombia', 'AUC') commander, Mr Fredy Rendón Herrera, alias *El Alemán* (i.e. the German).[432] He had a direct role in overseeing the illegal recruitment between 1997 and 2002 of 309 children in Chocó and Antioquia, by visiting schools to promote enlistment and authorising the admission of minors into the group. The Court ordered the payment of individual monetary compensation including 'for approximately 15 months of work at minimum wage for children who were recruited between 15 and 17 years old, with higher payments to those who were recruited at an earlier age' as well as medical and psychological care.[433] The responsibility to award reparations under the JPL framework still stems from the individual criminal conviction, but, since the intervention of the Colombian Constitutional Court the whole NSAG to which the convicted person belongs has a collective civil responsibility to provide reparations. In the *El Alemán* case, therefore, the obligation to provide reparation pertains to the culprit as well as the other AUC members,[434] whereas the State has been called upon by the Court to support the victims' other needs of rehabilitation and prevention. Moreover, concerning the monetary compensation, the Court has ordered the Reparations Fund to proceed with the actual payments only when the victims have proved that they have successfully completed the reintegration plan envisaged. The Court, thus, deems it important for the victims to understand that the only way to earn money is through honest work and individual efforts.[435]

Despite the significant achievements made, especially within the Colombian framework, to strengthen NSAGs' accountability and attribution of secondary obligations, the situation is still uncertain and many important issues need to be clarified. *In primis* it is not clear whether the direct responsibility of NSAGs should be framed in analogy with State responsibility or individual criminal responsibility.[436] According to Moffett none of these options would be able to

---

431 Report of the Secretary-General on Children and Armed Conflict, 15 May 2014, A/68/878–S/2014/339.

432 Judgment of 16 December 2011 (Sentencia), Fiscalía 44 Unidad Nacional de Justicia y Paz, Bogota D.C., Proceso 2007 82701, §2.3, part 6.

433 See L. Moffett, 'Beyond Attribution: Responsibility of Armed Non-State Actors for Reparations in Northern Ireland, Colombia and Uganda', in N. Gal-Or, C. Ryngaert and M. Noortmann, *Responsibilities of the Non-State Actor in Armed Conflict and the Market Place: Theoretical Considerations and Empirical Findings*, Brill, Leiden, 2015, 323, at 341.

434 The original text of the judgment reads: 'Condenar al postulado FREDY RENDON HERRERA de manera solidaria con los demás integrantes del bloque Elmer Cárdenas de las Autodefensas Unidas de Colombia, al pago de los daños y perjuicios materiales y morales, en los montos y condiciones establecidos en la parte motiva de la providencia'. Judgment of 16 December 2011 (Sentencia), above note 432, p. 413.

435 Ibidem.

436 See Ryngaert and d'Aspremont, above note 401.

tackle the peculiarities of a different form of responsibility that he defines as 'organisational'.[437] As a result the problem cannot be solved *de lege lata*, but it requires some substantial efforts *de lege ferenda*. In fact, while under the existing framework a variety of international, regional and national mechanisms are available to victims of States' abuses who seek to bring a reparation claim against a State, there are no equivalent mechanisms in relation to NSAGs.[438]

Another crucial aspect that needs to be addressed is NSAGs' lack of capacity and resources to provide reparations.[439] In the aftermath of a conflict, such groups may be indigent, preventing them from providing any monetary awards to victims; or they may have hidden such assets in off-shore accounts or laundered their resources through legitimate businesses, making them difficult to trace. Furthermore, the organisational structure of the group itself may have dissolved or fragmented, preventing the organisation from carrying out structured engagement with reparation mechanisms.[440] These hurdles clearly hamper NSAGs' capacity to provide reparations, but in many instances the same reasoning could be applied to war-torn States struggling to fulfil their duties to the victims. In the end financial, political and economic constraints do not justify States' inertia towards reparations and, similarly, once it has been established that victims have a right to obtain redress from the person or entity responsible for the harm suffered, such aspects should not curtail a legitimate and timely discussion on the means to hold non-State actors, including NSAGs, directly accountable.

De Greiff noted that 'broadly speaking, there are two main models for (States') financing of reparations: creating special trust funds or introducing a dedicated line in the yearly national budget',[441] the latter guarantees more stability in financing and shows a clear political commitment,[442] but the former also represents a viable alternative, in line with the States' subsidiary role envisaged by the UNBPG.[443] In other words, NSGAs should in principle be

---

437 See Moffett, above note 433, at 325.

438 See R. Dudai, 'Closing the Gap: Symbolic Reparations and Armed Groups', (2011) 93 *International Review of the Red Cross* 783, at 786.

439 See C. Rose, 'An Emerging Norm: The Duty of States to Provide Reparations for Human Rights Violations by Non-State Actors', (2010) 32 *Hastings International Comparative Law Review* 307, at 309.

440 Moffett, above note 433.

441 See. A. Segovia, 'Financing Reparations Programmes', in de Greiff, above note 22, at 660. See also de Greiff, above note 23, at 32.

442 Ibidem, de Greiff.

443 See Report of the International Commission of Inquiry on Darfur to the United Nations Secretary-General, above note 7, §166. The UN Commission of Inquiry on Darfur suggested that NSAGs should provide reparations. The Commission documented abuses committed by the government of Sudan as well as several rebel armed groups, and thus proposed the establishment of a compensation mechanism ('Compensation Commission') to redress the victims. The Commission noted, alongside the obligation of the Sudanese government to pay compensation for crimes perpetrated in Darfur by its agents, that '[a] similar obligation is incumbent upon rebels for all crimes they may have committed'.

held responsible for providing and implementing all forms of reparations, not necessarily symbolic as suggested by Dudai,[444] but, whenever such groups are not able to comply with this obligation States should intervene to ensure that victims receive redress.

3.3.2.2. Non-State Armed Groups and Children in Armed Conflict

There is a sense of urgency concerning the need to define the contours of non-State actors' responsibility and establish mechanisms to implement their obligation to award reparations. Children, being among the most victimised segments of the population during or in the wake of an armed conflict, are also extremely affected by the misconduct of NSAGs. The Annual Report on children and armed conflict submitted by the Secretary-General to both the General Assembly and the Security Council,[445] begins by highlighting the recent trends and development:

> There were unprecedented challenges in 2014 with regard to the protection of tens of millions of children growing up in situations affected by conflict. In particular, children in several countries affected by major crises, namely, the Central African Republic, Iraq, Israel/State of Palestine, Nigeria, South Sudan and the Syrian Arab Republic, were exposed to the most egregious violations.[446]

As most of the countries mentioned in the Report are currently affected by NIACs it follows that these egregious violations have not been solely committed by States and their agents. On the contrary, many of them are directly attributable to NSAGs. In order to foster NSAGs' compliance with child protection standards the UN has established the MRM,[447] which has the purpose to provide for the systematic gathering of accurate, timely and objective information on grave violations committed against children in armed conflict. Once the MRM is activated in a given country, a task force is created. The task force is chaired by the highest UN authority on the ground and composed of relevant UN agencies and is responsible for collecting information on all six grave violations against children. Annual country reports are prepared by the task force, reviewed and vetted by the Office of the Special Representative of the Secretary-General on Children and Armed Conflict ('OSRSG-CAAC') as convener of the UN system on children and armed conflict, and submitted by the Secretary-General to

444 See Dudai, above note 438, at 807.
445 See the Annual Report of the Secretary-General on Children and Armed Conflict, above note 11.
446 Ibidem, at 2.
447 See above Chapter 2, Section 2.1.

the Security Council Working Group. The information is then included in the Annual Report of the Secretary-General on Children and Armed Conflict.

Another crucial piece of the UN children and armed conflict architecture involves the preparation and implementation of action plans, which are concrete, time-bound commitments by a listed party to a conflict to halt recruitment and use of child soldiers, sexual violence, killing and maiming, or attacks on schools and hospitals. The completion of an action plan and the subsequent cessation of violations is the only officially defined way to be delisted from the annexes to the Secretary-General's report on children and armed conflict, although factual developments may lead to the same end result (e.g. if a party ceases to exist).[448] At the time of writing 23 listed parties have signed action plans, including 11 government forces and 12 NSAGs.[449] Of those, to date nine parties have fully complied with their action plan and have subsequently been de-listed.

The efforts to quantify and monitor violations committed against children, not only by States, but also, and foremost, by NSAGs, stem from the overwhelming need to limit and prevent the disproportionate victimisation of children in armed conflict. Despite the importance of this mechanism, there are a number of weaknesses that hamper its potentially positive impact. In the first place the action plans can be signed exclusively between the UN and the parties listed in the Annual Report's annexes, meaning that five of the six grave violations identified can be the object of the agreement. Denial of humanitarian access to children is currently excluded, thus creating a loophole in protection. Concerning children's abduction the Secretary-General in his Annual Report has stressed that

> [m]ass abductions of civilians, including children, have become an increasingly prevalent feature of conflict in many situations described in the present report. The abduction of children had primarily been a precursor to other violations, such as killing and maiming, recruitment and use, or sexual violence … In Iraq and the Syrian Arab Republic, over one thousand girls and boys were abducted by the Islamic State of Iraq and the Levant (ISIL). In one incident in the Syrian Arab Republic, ISIL abducted approximately 150 young boys on their way home from having taken school exams in Aleppo. They were released from captivity after a few months, during which they were physically abused, indoctrinated and made to observe violent practices … In Nigeria, Boko Haram abducted hundreds of women and girls in major attacks in Chibok and across the country's north-eastern region.[450]

---

448 See International Peace Institute, 'Engaging Non-State Armed Groups on the Protection of Children: Towards Strategic Complementarity', April 2012, available at: http://www.genevacall.org/resources/research/f-research/2001-2010/IPI_E_Pub_ENGAGING_NONSTATE.pdf.

449 Further information is available at: https://childrenandarmedconflict.un.org/our-work/action-plans/.

450 See the Annual Report of the Secretary-General on Children and Armed Conflict, above note 11, §7.

Consequently, in his final recommendations the Secretary-General has called upon the Security Council to expand the tools available to child protection actors to gather information and report on the abduction of children, including through adding abduction as a trigger violation for listing in the annexes.[451] With regard to denial of humanitarian access, despite the numerous episodes occurring in many of the countries included in the Annual Report, this violation has not been the subject of a specific recommendation yet.

Another important aspect is the lack of effective enforcement mechanisms. The parties that are listed in the annexes for five years or more are labelled as 'persistent violators' and no further measures are currently envisaged to strengthen compliance with children's rights. In order to effectively address this issue the OSRSG-CAAC has been advocating for the adoption of sanctions by the Security Council to end impunity and to halt children's victimisation.[452] In several resolutions the Security Council has expressed its intention to consider imposing targeted and gradual measures against parties to conflicts violating the rights of children.[453] However, the sanctions system established within the UN is extremely complex. In particular sanctions can be adopted against individuals and entities if two cumulative criteria are met, namely the existence of a Sanctions Committee already in place and the explicit mention of violations against children in its mandate.

Out of the 13 existing UN sanctions regimes, only the Sanctions Committees[454] dealing with the situations in Côte d'Ivoire, Somalia and the Democratic Republic of the Congo fulfil these criteria. Currently two perpetrators in Côte d'Ivoire and 14 in the DRC have been sanctioned for grave violations committed against children. With regard to the DRC, the Security Council in 2006 expanded the mandate of the Sanctions Committee to include also 'political and military leaders recruiting or using children in armed conflict in violation of applicable international law and individuals committing serious violations of international law involving the targeting of children in situations of armed conflict, including killing and maiming, sexual violence, abduction and forced displacement'.[455] The perpetrators designated by the Committee have been subject to travel bans

451 Ibidem, §273. On 18 June 2015, the UNSC, Adopting Resolution 2225 (2015), added parties abducting children during armed conflict to the list monitoring grave human rights violators.

452 The basis for UN sanctions under international law derives from Chapter VII of the UN Charter, and more specifically, Article 41, which covers enforcement measures not involving the use of armed force. See generally J.M. Farrall, *United Nations Sanctions and the Rule of Law*, Cambridge University Press, Cambridge, 2007.

453 UNSC, S/RES/1539 (2004); UNSC, S/RES/1612 (2005); UNSC, S/RES/1882 (2009); and UNSC, S/RES/1998 (2011).

454 Sanctions committees are subsidiary organs of the Security Council for the purpose of administering sanctions regimes. They are created under Art. 29 of the UN Charter or Rule 28 of the Provisional Rules of the Security Council.

455 UNSC, S/RES/1698 (2006), §13.

and asset freezing, in accordance with Resolution 1596 (2005).[456] So far UN sanctions have been applied exclusively to individuals who committed violations against children, but nothing in the UN sanctions framework would prevent the extension of these measures to the entities of which those individuals are members. Furthermore, there are only five main types of targeted UN sanctions: diplomatic, travel ban, asset freezing, arms embargo and commodity interdiction. Since the designation criteria keep evolving, to include also violations of IHRL and IHL, obstructing access to humanitarian assistance, targeting of civilians for human rights violations, recruiting of child soldiers, and committing rape and gender-based violence,[457] the question remains as to whether it would be logical at this point to also design different forms of targeted sanctions in order to better tackle the specificity of each situation. Finally, the current UN children in armed conflict architecture is confined to investigating and reporting the violations of primary norms enshrining children's rights, but it does not address the issue of secondary obligations arising from such breaches. In other words, the scope of the MRM and the action plans could, and should, be further expanded in order to encompass also reparative measures.

3.3.3. INDIVIDUALS

It is only under ICL that it is possible to find mechanisms, such as international tribunals, able to enforce international law against the members of an armed group.[458] Notwithstanding the fact that at least half of the belligerents in the most victimising armed conflicts around the world are NSAGs, as discussed above the violations committed cannot be addressed through organisational responsibility. The two options remain States' and individuals' accountability and the issue of reparation is dealt with accordingly.[459] Individuals can be held responsible through ICL mechanisms, e.g. domestic courts, *ad hoc* and hybrid tribunals, and the ICC. All these settings are primarily functional to the scope of punishing the culprits as well as deterring further violations, with the notable exception of the ICC, which foresees the possibility of also adding victims to the justice equation. From the point of view of victims, attaching responsibility for reparations to perpetrators, whether individuals, entities or States, fulfils an important psychological function in appropriately directing blame at those

---

456 UNSC, S/RES/1596 (2005), §§13–16.

457 Special Research Report, 'UN Sanctions', November 2013, available at: http://www.securitycouncilreport.org/atf/cf/%7B65BFCF9B-6D27-4E9C-8CD3-CF6E4FF96FF9%7D/special_research_report_sanctions_2013.pdf.

458 See M. Sassòli, 'Taking Armed Groups Seriously: Ways to Improve their Compliance with International Humanitarian Law', (2010) 1 *International Humanitarian Legal Studies*, 5, at 12.

459 Ibidem.

who committed the atrocity against them and to relieve their guilt. As noted by Hamber, 'reparations thus represent or indirectly express something abstract or invisible to victims about those giving or granting the reparations, for example, an admission of guilt, benevolence, care for citizens by society, and/or a willingness to pay back what has been lost'.[460]

In the context of a criminal proceeding, reparation orders are intrinsically linked to the individual whose criminal liability is established in a conviction and whose culpability for those criminal acts is determined in a sentence.[461] Of course in other settings the standard required to ascertain individuals' responsibility is much lower, as explained by the Liberian Truth and Reconciliation Commission ('TRC'), which

> decided that the corresponding standard of proof should be a preponderance of the evidence (that the accused 'more likely than not' is responsible for committing the violation or crime). Since the TRC is not a criminal court or tribunal, no higher standard of proof is necessary. If a prosecution mechanism is established after the TRC process is complete, it will be for Government to determine the requisite prosecutorial standard of proof, which, in accordance with Liberian law, would be 'beyond a reasonable doubt'.[462]

Within the ICC framework, reparations proceedings are fundamentally different from proceedings at trial and therefore 'a less exacting standard should apply',[463] meaning that the applicant must provide sufficient proof of the causal link between the crime and the harm suffered, based on the specific circumstances of the case. In the *Lubanga* case, for example, the ICC ultimately applied the standard of proof of a balance of probabilities, both to reparations made through the TFV and to the convicted person.[464] Ultimately, the imposition of liability for reparations on the convicted person is consistent with the UNBPG, pursuant to which '[i]n cases where a person, a legal person, or other entity is found liable for reparation to a victim, such party should provide reparation to the victim ... '.[465]

460 See B. Hamber, 'Narrowing the Micro and Macro: A Psychological Perspective on Reparations in Societies in Transition', in de Greiff above note 22, 560, at 566.

461 See Judgment of 3 March 2015 (*Lubanga* case) above note 50, §65.

462 Final Report of the Truth and Reconciliation Commission of Liberia, Volume I: Findings and Determinations, June 2009, at 33.

463 Decision of 7 August 2012 (Decision Establishing the Principles and Procedures to be Applied to Reparations), above note 24, §251.

464 See Judgment of 3 March 2015 (*Lubanga* case) above note 50, §83. In the impugned decision the Trial Chamber established a different standard of proof in cases where reparations were made 'through the Trust Fund' (i.e. 'wholly flexible approach') versus where reparations were ordered against Mr Lubanga (i.e. 'balance of probabilities').

465 UNBPG, above note 2, §15.

3.4. CONCLUSIONS

It does not come as a surprise that the existing international law framework governing the right to reparation is not satisfactory, at least from the victims' point of view. Even though reparations are recognised as a legally inseparable corollary to international law violations,[466] the regimes relevant to this study show that there is a significant gap in terms of legal sources and mechanisms to enforce the responsibility of the actors involved. With regard to the first point, IHRL appears to be the field of international law better equipped to deal with victims' rights, although it does so through a number of provisions scattered over different conventions and non-binding documents. The IHRL framework does not encompass specific norms that focus on child victims, whose right to obtain adequate redress is spelled out only in Article 39 of the CRC, and even then not explicitly. Under IHL, the traditional inter-State dimension of war reparations keeps prevailing over individuals' rights and needs, to the detriment of the most vulnerable members of the population, including children. In the entire corpus of IHL only two provisions deal with reparations and none of them refer to individual victims. A conservative interpretation of both Article 3 of the 1907 Hague Convention and Article 91 of Additional Protocol I to the Geneva Conventions would still suggest that reparation should be thought of as an inter-State mechanism, however this approach has eventually been overcome in favour of a new reading, more lenient towards individual victims. Several scholars, in particular Kalshoven,[467] have contributed to significantly broadening the scope of those provisions in order to create a direct right to compensation for individuals. Despite the recognition of such right, the problem remains as to what kind of mechanisms victims can resort to in order to effectively claim for reparations. Under IHL it is still very difficult to identify judicial fora able to promote the enjoyment of the right to reparation.

This gap has been partially remedied due to the rise of ICL and the creation of the ICC. Holding individual perpetrators responsible for the international crimes committed has been for a long time detached from any kind of efforts to recognise victims' right to participate in the proceedings and demand reparations. The establishment of the ICC has finally wiped out this last legal taboo.

---

466 Evans, above note 47, at 42.

467 See expert opinion by Kalshoven, above note 328, at 37. See F. Kalshoven, 'State Responsibility for Warlike Acts of the Armed Forces: From Article 3 of the Hague Convention IV of 1907 to Article 91 of Additional Protocol I and Beyond', (1991) 40 *International and Comparative Law Quarterly* 827, at 828–832. See also Evans, above note 47, at 32. See R. Pisillo Mazzeschi, 'Reparations Claims by Individuals for State Breaches of International Humanitarian Law and Human Rights: An Overview', (2003) 1 *Journal of International Criminal Justice* 339, at 340–347.

In terms of the regime of responsibility governing the right to reparation, States and individual perpetrators still represent the two main categories of actors involved in the remedial discourse. It goes without saying that this framework fails to address the reality, which is populated by a wider number of relevant actors. In the field of reparations awarded in the aftermath of an armed conflict it is simply impossible to keep overlooking the role played by NSAGs. Promoting individual members' responsibility and enhancing States' subsidiary intervention are important steps forward, but they are not able to fill the absence of a third responsibility regime or at least the full assimilation of organisational responsibility with either State or individual responsibility. In other fields of law there is currently an impetus towards the recognition of the direct responsibility of non-State actors, thus paving the way for a more comprehensive and realistic approach to reparations.[468] In the case of NSAGs the discussion on secondary obligations seems to be at an embryonic stage. Efforts have been made by NGOs, in particular Geneva Call,[469] and the UN children and armed conflict framework in order to engage NSAGs and develop time-bound commitments to foster their abidance by IHRL and IHL norms. Such efforts, however, do not yet encompass the possibility to make NSAGs accountable for the violations committed and, thus, directly responsible for reparations.

---

468 Consider, for example, the 'Ruggie Principles on Business and Human Rights'. In the principles the remedy pillar advances the concept that companies as well as public authorities should provide effective courses of action and remedies to victims, that is to say both legal and non-legal recourse, including in-company grievance mechanisms. This is not an accepted principle at the international level, but, as noted by the ILA Committee on non-State actors 'the legal development at the domestic level has seen greater integration of the juridical person in alignment with that of the natural person for the purpose of criminal liability. In many domestic legal systems, corporations can indeed be sanctioned … this may create a bottom-up groundswell, from the domestic to the international legal level that may result in the ultimate recognition of corporate international criminal responsibility': Ryngaert and d'Aspremont, above note 401, at 14. See HRC, Report of the Special Representative of the Secretary-General on the Issue of Human Rights and Transnational Corporations and other Business Enterprises, *Guiding Principles on Business and Human Rights: Implementing the United Nations 'Protect, Respect, Remedy' Framework*, Introduction to the principles, 21 March 2011, UN doc. A/HRC/17/31, §6. C. Rees, 'Grievance Mechanisms for Business and Human Rights, Corporate Social Responsibility Initiative', Working Paper No. 40, January 2008, Cambridge, MA, John F. Kennedy School of Government, Harvard University, available at: http://www.hks.harvard.edu/m-rcbg/CSRI/publications/workingpaper_40_Strengths_Weaknesses_Gaps.pdf.

469 On Geneva Call and its Deeds of Commitment see A. Clapham, 'Non-State Actors', in D. Moeckli, S. Shah and S. Sivakumaran (eds.), *International Human Rights Law*, Oxford University Press, Oxford, 2014, 531, at 535–540.

CHAPTER 4

FORMS AND SCOPE OF REPARATIONS FOR CHILD VICTIMS OF ARMED CONFLICT

4.1. INTRODUCTION: OVERVIEW OF THE DIFFERENT FORMS OF REPARATION FOR CHILD VICTIMS

Reparations can take different forms as explained in the UNBPG. Whereas within the traditional international law framework the options envisaged are solely restitution, compensation and satisfaction, reparations for individuals or groups who have suffered from IHRL and IHL violations include also rehabilitation and guarantees of non-repetition. In addition to the specific kinds of reparation that can be awarded it is also important to discuss the scope and breadth of the measures available and their potential impact on child victims' current and future situation. As stressed by the Liberian TRC, 'children expect to receive reparations as an acknowledgement of their suffering, a means to make up for lost out opportunities and as concrete assistance for their rebuilding of their shattered lives'.[470] In the case of former child soldiers, the expectations placed on reparations are even more demanding:

> Reparation orders and programmes in favour of child soldiers, should guarantee the development of the victims' personalities, talents and abilities to the fullest possible extent and, more broadly, they should ensure the development of respect for human rights and fundamental freedoms. For each child, the measures should aim at developing respect for their parents, cultural identity and language. Former child soldiers should be helped to live responsibly in a free society, recognising the need for a spirit of understanding, peace and tolerance, showing respect for equality between the sexes and valuing friendship between all peoples and groups.[471]

---

470 Final Report of the Truth and Reconciliation Commission of Liberia, Volume Three: Appendices, Title II: Children, the Conflict and the TRC Children Agenda, June 2009, at 98.

471 Judgment of 3 March 2015, ICC, above note 50, Order for Reparations, Annex A, §26.

On the one hand it is desirable for reparations to broaden their scope in order to better address victims' needs; however, on the other hand it is crucial to bear in mind that several factors come in to play when redress measures are designed and implemented. Furthermore, it is important to distinguish between reparations and other forms of aid and assistance to which child victims may also be entitled. Whereas reparations have a specific legal meaning and infer the commission of a violation, the existence of a causal link, and the recognition/personification of the victim, assistance measures can be simply put in place to fill a gap in the States' capability of guaranteeing access to basic rights.

4.1.1 RESTITUTION

Restitution is the first form listed in the UNBPG and

> [it] should, whenever possible, restore the victim to the original situation before the gross violations of international human rights law or serious violations of international humanitarian law occurred. Restitution includes, as appropriate: restoration of liberty, enjoyment of human rights, identity, family life and citizenship, return to one's place of residence, restoration of employment and return of property.[472]

In the traditional inter-State context, restitution may take the form of material restoration or return of territory, persons or property or the reversal of some juridical act (or a combination of the two). Restitution (also called *restitutio in integrum* or 'full restitution') seeks to re-establish the situation that existed before the wrongful act was committed by restoring the original condition. Article 35 of the Articles on State Responsibility adopts a narrow definition of restitution as it refers to the re-establishment of the *status quo ante*, namely the situation that existed prior to the occurrence of the wrongful act, to the extent to which restitution is not materially impossible and the principle of proportionality is respected.[473]

In general, under IHRL, restitution encompasses the re-establishment of the situation that existed prior to the occurrence of the human rights violation, but in case of gross violations, as discussed above, it is often impossible to bridge the gap between the current situation of the victim and the one that pre-existed the wrongful act. Furthermore, in many instances bridging this gap is not even desirable. In the case of Sierra Leone, for example, most of the children who joined the army or the RUF were 'raray boys', i.e. street boys, for whom

472 UNBPG, above note 2, §19.

473 See Capone et al., above note 161, at 30.

recruitment meant a meal ticket and an alternative to education. According to Zack-Williams:

> Children in stable family relationship are not impelled to become child combatants, simply because the route to child soldiering, i.e. the status of street children, is one that is not an option for the children of the rich and privileged … The failed economic policies that have typified post-colonial Sierra Leone have hardened the children and young people as many of them have gone without the basic necessities of life, and they feel a sense of betrayal.[474]

Similarly, in Colombia different studies have shown that there exists a close link between displacement and sexual violence,[475] as well as between displacement and recruitment and abduction of child soldiers,[476] thus stressing how being in a vulnerable situation increases the possibility of being further victimised and thus exposed to polyvictimisation. Restoring the situation that was in place prior to the violation is far from being in the best interests of the child and therefore, in many instances, restitution is not a viable or adequate option for child victims.

4.1.2. COMPENSATION

The second form of reparation envisaged by the UNBPG is compensation. In its Commentary on the Articles on State Responsibility, the ILC stated that 'of the various forms of reparation, compensation is perhaps the most commonly sought in international practice'.[477] Under international law in general, compensation covers any financially assessable damage, insofar as it is established.[478] Compensation has been sought and, awarded, before several international courts and tribunals.[479] For example, loss of life or loss of profits

---

474 See T. Zack-Williams, 'When Children Become Killers: Child Soldiers in the Civil War in Sierra Leone', in Fernando and Ferrari, above note 180, 83, at 92.

475 D. Meertens, 'Forced Displacement and Gender Justice in Colombia: Between Disproportional Effects of Violence and Historical Injustice', Case Studies on Transitional Justice and Displacement, Brookings-LSE, Project on Internal Displacement, July 2012, at 10, available at: https://www.ictj.org/sites/default/files/ICTJ-Brookings-Displacement-Gender-Colombia-CaseStudy-2012-English.pdf.

476 L. Alfredson, 'Child Soldiers, Displacement and Human Security', Disarmament Forum: Children and Security, UNIDIR No. 3, 2002, at 17–27.

477 As quoted in B. Saul, 'Compensation for Unlawful Death in International Law: A Focus on the Inter-American Court of Human Rights', (2004) 19 *The American University International Law Review* 523, at 545.

478 See Art. 36 ILC Articles on State Responsibility.

479 Including the International Tribunal for the Law of the Sea, the ICSID Tribunals, the Iran-United States Claims Tribunal and the ICJ where, in the *Gabcíkovo-Nagymaros Project* case, for example, the ICJ affirmed it to be 'a well-established rule of international law that an

due to unlawful detention can be financially assessed through established formulas.[480] The approach to compensation developed at the inter-State level has, by and large, been adopted within the IHRL framework, with the significant difference that under IHRL the award of moral damage (or 'non-pecuniary loss') is also provided, whereas it is excluded under the ILC Articles on State Responsibility.[481] A declaratory judgment combined with compensation for the pecuniary and non-pecuniary damages suffered by the victims are the forms of reparation usually awarded by the ECtHR, also in cases where children's rights are at stake and the violations committed are particularly grave.[482] The IACtHR, consistently with its inclusive and far-reaching approach to reparations, has compensated the victims' relatives also in cases of consequential, and not direct, harm.[483] In the *Bulacio* case, concerning the unlawful detention of a 17-year-old who died after being beaten by the police, the IACtHR awarded reparations to the victim's grandmother and sister to treat their illnesses of cancer and bulimia, which resulted from the depression arising from their loss.[484]

---

injured State is entitled to obtain compensation from the State which has committed an internationally wrongful act for the damage caused by it'. See Judgment, 25 September 1997 (Merits), (1997) ICJ Reports 1997, p. 7, §114.

480 See, for example, a discussion of the *Lusitania* cases in Shelton, above note 21, at 852, explaining that the formula coined by Umpire Parker to calculate the compensation due as result of wrongful death and unlawful detention has been used in both human rights and diplomatic protection claims.

481 According to the UNBPG, above note 2, §20, 'compensation should be provided for any economically assessable damage, as appropriate and proportional to the gravity of the violation and the circumstances of each case, resulting from gross violations of international human rights law and serious violations of international humanitarian law, such as: (a) Physical or mental harm; (b) Lost opportunities, including employment, education and social benefits; (c) Material damages and loss of earnings, including loss of earning potential; (d) Moral damage; (e) Costs required for legal or expert assistance, medicine and medical services, and psychological and social services'. Art. 36(2) of the ILC Articles on State Responsibility, instead, provides that 'compensation shall cover any financially assessable damage including loss of profits insofar as it is established'.

482 See F. Capone 'Comparing and Discussing the Different Approach to Remedies for Child Victims before the European Court of Human Rights and the Inter-American Court of Human Rights', in D.M. Vicente (ed.), *Towards a Universal Justice? Putting International Courts and Jurisdictions into Perspective*, Brill, Leiden, 2016, 190, at 199–202. See, for example, Judgment of 20 March 2012, ECtHR, Application No. 26692/05. The case concerned a seven-year-old child, who was repeatedly raped by a man, eventually acquitted, who had forced his way into the family flat when the boy had come home alone from school. The Court awarded to the victim the sum of 15,000 euros in respect of non-pecuniary damages. See also Judgment of 18 June 2013, ECtHR, Application No. 48609/06. Due to the inactivity of the responsible public institutions, 15 children and young adults died between December 1996 and March 1997 in a home for physically and mentally disabled young people in the village of Dzhurkovo, from the effects of cold and shortages of food, medicines and basic necessities. The Court awarded to the applicants 10,000 euros in respect of non-pecuniary damages.

483 See Contreras-Garduño and Fraser, above note 89, at 195.

484 Judgment of 18 September 2003 (Merits, Reparations and Costs), IACtHR, Series C No. 100, §99.

At the domestic level the Victims' Law enacted by the Colombian government in 2011 contains a provision that enables child victims to receive compensation. Article 184 states that boys and girls are entitled to obtain compensation and their legal representatives can bring a claim for indemnification on their behalf.[485] Children formerly associated with armed forces or groups have also been the beneficiaries of DDR processes and in some countries the benefits have included monetary payments. For instance in Liberia ex-child soldiers, just like adult combatants, have received Transition Support Allowance ('TSA') for officially disarming and demobilising, intended to assist the children in the transition to civilian life and to provide an added incentive for reunification with their families and reintegration in home communities.[486] As reported by Aptel and Ladish, awarding compensation to former child soldiers is a delicate and complex choice, which may trigger jealousy and resentment among those affected by their role in the armed conflict, to the point where the payment of monetary compensation is wrongly interpreted as a prize for taking part in the hostilities.[487]

4.1.3. REHABILITATION

Rehabilitation is the third form of reparation listed in the UNBPG and it should include medical and psychological care as well as legal and social services. Article 39 of the CRC explicitly refers to this specific kind of reparation, which enshrines the whole set of appropriate measures to promote physical and psychological recovery and social reintegration. According to van Boven the scope of rehabilitation is wider than what is explicitly spelled out in the Basic Principles and Guidelines as it also includes 'medical and psychological care, legal and social services, education, housing, financing of paralegals, restoration of the good name of the victim, restoration of passports/travel documents and other elements'.[488] Rehabilitation must be tailored to the specific needs of the victims since it cannot be standardised in the same way as compensation.[489]

---

485 Art. 184, Ley [L.] 1448 DIARIO OFICIAL [D.O.].

486 Final Report of the Truth and Reconciliation Commission of Liberia, Volume Three: Appendices, Title II: Children, the Conflict and the TRC Children Agenda, June 2009, at 71.

487 See APTEL and LADISCH, above note 264.

488 This view was expressed by Professor T. van Boven, see T. van BOVEN, 'Rehabilitation as a Form of Reparation' (2010) Workshop Report, Redress and Essex University Transitional Justice Network, available at: www.redress.org/downloads/publications/Report_of_the_Expert_Seminar_on_Rehabilitation_October_2010.pdf.

489 See M. BRINTON LYKES and M. MERSKY, 'Reparations and Mental Health: Psychosocial Interventions towards Healing, Human Agency and Rethreading Social Realities', in de GREIFF, above note 22, at 593.

The IACtHR has ordered rehabilitation on several occasions, in particular for the victims and surviving relatives of mass human rights abuses. In the *Plan de Sánchez Massacre* case, for instance, the IACtHR imposed on the government of Guatemala, held responsible for the massacre of more than 250 people, the creation of a mental health treatment programme provided free of charge, 'with the special circumstances of each person taken into account for individual, family or collective treatment'.[490] Another relevant example of rehabilitation awarded as a form of reparation stems from the Reparation and Rehabilitation Committee of the South African TRC, which recommended that the State establish local treatment centres and provide rehabilitation for perpetrators and their families, mental health services, survivors' support groups, skills training, specialised trauma counselling services, family-based therapy and several other measures aimed at restoring the physical and psychological well-being of the victims as well as fostering dialogue and reconciliation within the affected communities.[491] Rehabilitation is also one of the key components of the ICC TFV's assistance mandate, which focuses mainly on physical and psychological rehabilitation. The former includes reconstructive surgery, general surgery, bullet and bomb fragment removal, prosthetic and orthopaedic devices, referrals to services like fistula repair and HIV and AIDS screening, treatment, care and support. The latter instead refers to both individual and group-based trauma counselling, music, dance and drama groups to promote social cohesion and healing, community sensitisation workshops and radio broadcasts on victims' rights, information sessions and large-scale community meetings.[492] The TFV started field operations related to its assistance mandate in northern Uganda and the DRC in 2008 and several projects were officially completed by August 2015. The rehabilitation of child victims, child mothers and vulnerable children affected by armed conflict has been the focus of many initiatives led by the TFV, which will be further discussed in the next part of this book. Rehabilitation has also been included in the forms of reparations envisaged for the victims of child recruitment in the *Lubanga* case. In fact the Appeals Chamber of the ICC in the amended Order for Reparations against Mr Lubanga stressed that

> [t]he rehabilitation measures ought to include the means of addressing the shame that child victims may feel, and they should be directed at avoiding further victimisation of the boys and girls who suffered harm as a consequence of their recruitment. The steps taken to rehabilitate and reintegrate former child soldiers may also include their local

---

490 See Judgment of 19 November 2004, (2004) IACtHR, Series C No. 116, §107.

491 B. Goldblatt, 'Evaluating the Gender Content of Reparations: Lessons from South Africa', in Rubio-Marín, above note 48, at 71.

492 K. Peschke, 'The Role and Mandates of the ICC Trust Fund for Victims', in Bonacker and Safferling, above note 43, 317, at 320.

communities, to the extent that the reparations programmes are implemented where their communities are located.[493]

4.1.4. SATISFACTION

Satisfaction, like restitution and compensation, is also envisaged in the ILC Articles on State Responsibility. However, it is considered as a subsidiary form of reparation as the responsible State must give satisfaction for the injury caused 'insofar as it cannot be made good by restitution or compensation'.[494] Satisfactory measures are not properly defined, but they generally consist of an acknowledgement of the breach, an expression of regret, a formal apology, or a declaratory judgment or another modality. Under international law in general, 'the line between satisfaction as a remedy and satisfaction as an expression of disapproval or sanction has not always been clear'.[495] In the IHRL framework, satisfaction refers also to the range of measures that may contribute to the broader and longer-term restorative aims of reparation. The UNBPG identify eight, non-exhaustive, measures to ensure satisfaction for gross violations of IHRL and serious violations of IHL. Such measures include the cessation of continuing violations and also the verification of historical facts and public disclosure of the truth and tributes to victims. Satisfactory measures may encompass the establishment of monuments, memorials and public buildings to commemorate the life of the victims. In the *Street Children* case, for example, the IACtHR ordered the State 'to designate an educational center with a name allusive to the young victims in this case and to place in this center a plaque with the names [of the victims]'.[496]

Satisfaction can also take the form of a public apology, as in the case of Canada where, from the 1870s until 1996, more than 150,000 First Nations, Métis and Inuit children were placed in residential schools, often against their parents' wishes. Eventually, on 11 June 2008, the Prime Minister, on behalf of the government of Canada, delivered a formal apology in the House of Commons to former students and their families and communities for Canada's role in the operation of the residential schools.[497]

---

493 Judgment of 3 March 2015, ICC, above note 50, Order for Reparations, Annex A, §67.

494 See Art. 37(2) of the ILC Articles on State Responsibility; see also Redress, above note 3, at 19.

495 See Shelton, above note 21, at 848.

496 Judgment of 26 May 2001 (Reparations and Costs), (2001) IACtHR, Series C No. 77, §103.

497 See the Canadian TRC Report 'They Came for the Children', 2012, available at: http://www.attendancemarketing.com/~attmk/TRC_jd/ResSchoolHistory_2012_02_24_Webposting.pdf.

Public apologies can also result from a criminal proceeding. In the *Lubanga* case the ICC stated that

> [t]he convicted person has been declared indigent and no assets or property have been identified that can be used for the purposes of reparations. The Chamber is, therefore, of the view that Mr Lubanga is only able to contribute to non-monetary reparations. Any participation on his part in symbolic reparations, such as a public or private apology to the victims, is only appropriate with his agreement. Accordingly, these measures will not form part of any Court order.[498]

Whereas the ICC put the accent on Mr Lubanga's voluntary agreement, in the *El Alemán* case the Superior Court for the District of Bogota (Justice and Peace Chamber) established that, in order to finally end former child soldiers' subjugation, the convicted person's involvement in the reparations discourse should be carefully pondered.[499] According to the Court, some forms of symbolic reparations, such as, for example, the construction of a monument, could restore the hierarchy that existed within the armed group. The Court also envisaged the organisation of a public event on the international day against the use of child soldiers and it established the modalities of Mr Rendón Herrera's participation, stressing that on such occasion he is expected to apologise to the victims, their families and communities, without trying to explain or justify the reasons behind the crimes committed.[500]

4.1.5. GUARANTEES OF NON-REPETITION

Guarantees of non-repetition are preventive measures that mainly seek to avoid relapses. Under international law, the duties of the infringing State consist of first ceasing the wrongful conduct, and then guaranteeing that it will not occur again ('assurances and guarantees of non-repetition').[501] Under the ILC Articles on State Responsibility,[502] assurances and guarantees of non-repetition 'are concerned with the restoration of confidence in a continuing relationship, although they involve much more flexibility than cessation and are not required in all cases'.[503]

498 Decision of 7 August 2012 (Decision Establishing the Principles and Procedures to be Applied to Reparations), above note 24, §269.

499 Judgment of 16 December 2011 (Sentencia), above note 432, §864.

500 Ibidem.

501 See A.J. Carrillo, 'The Relevance of the Inter-American Human Rights Law', in de Greiff, above note 22, 504, at 526.

502 Art. 30 of the ILC Articles on State Responsibility.

503 See ILC Articles on the Responsibility of States for Internationally Wrongful Acts, above note 17, at 89.

Within the IHRL framework, guarantees of non-repetition are also recognised as an essential component of reparation, in particular for continuing and systematic abuses.[504] As with satisfaction, the UNBPG also identifies eight, non-exhaustive, types of guarantees of non-repetition, which combine both redress and prevention. These include, *inter alia*, providing, on a priority and continued basis, human rights and IHL education to all sectors of society and training for law enforcement officials as well as military and security forces; promoting mechanisms for preventing and monitoring social conflicts and their resolution; and reviewing and reforming laws contributing to or allowing gross violations of IHRL and serious violations of IHL.[505]

As noted by the ICC TFV in its observations on the appeals against Trial Chamber I's decision establishing the principles and procedures to be applied to reparations in the *Lubanga* case, '[p]rinciples of non-discrimination, doing no/less harm and aiming at reconciliation, measures that include education on the root and underlying causes of the conflict, background of crimes and conflict, as well as measures that aim at guaranteeing non-repetition of the crimes, necessarily and genuinely need to include broader communities'.[506] In other words, guarantees of non-repetition, due to their nature and scope, target by default not only the victims, but the community at large. The Superior Court for the District of Bogota (Justice and Peace Chamber) in the *El Alemán* case stressed that guarantees of non-repetition should address the underlying factors which led to the unlawful recruitment and use of child soldiers.[507] Moreover the Court, making reference to the case law of the Colombian Constitutional Court, highlighted that the responsibility for redressing these factors lies with the State, which is called upon to implement institutional and economic reforms in order to tackle the situation of vulnerability and extreme poverty that affect many segments of the population, in particular the youngest.[508]

4.2. INDIVIDUAL AND COLLECTIVE REPARATIONS

The UNBPG, by affirming that 'victims are persons who individually or collectively suffered harm', has officially introduced the issue of collectiveness

504 See C. Ferstman, 'Reparation as Prevention: Considering the Law and Practice of Orders for Cessation and Guarantees of Non-repetition in Torture Cases', March 2012, available at: http://oxford.academia.edu/CarlaFerstman/Papers/143260/Reparation_as_Prevention_Considering_the_Law_and_Practice_of_Orders_for_Cessation_and_Guarantees_of_Non-Repetition_in_Torture_Casesat 21.

505 UNBPG, above note 2, §23.

506 Observations of the Trust Fund for Victims on the appeals against Trial Chamber I's 'Decision Establishing the Principles and Procedures to Be Applied to Reparations', ICC-01/04–01/06, 8 April 2013, §168.

507 Judgment of 16 December 2011 (Sentencia), above note 432, §848.

508 Ibidem.

in the reparations discourse.[509] As noted by Redress, the terms 'individual' and 'collective' forms of reparation are not terms of art and have been used and applied in a variety of ways.[510] 'Individual' reparation consists of awards that address the harms and suffering of individual persons, in particular

> [o]n one end of the spectrum, they are intended to respond to actual pecuniary and non-pecuniary losses suffered, and are determined following a process in which those harms and losses are scrutinised and assessed by decision-makers (both in terms of the quantum and quality of harm suffered). Such awards can relate to claims involving single, multiple or extremely large numbers of persons and may entail monetary or non-monetary elements ... or both. At the other end of the spectrum decision-makers have made individual awards to beneficiaries that have mainly consisted of lump-sum or standardised payments or, non-monetary benefits. This is typically for reasons such as a large number of claimants, the difficulties for individuals to prove the injuries to a sufficiently high standard and/or the high administrative costs for decision-makers to assess with precision on a case-by-case basis individuals' injuries, or because the parties to a reparation claim have agreed a specific settlement amount.[511]

Individual reparations, as stated by Magarrell, 'are important because international human rights standards are generally expressed in individual terms. Reparation to individuals therefore underscores the value of each human being and their place as rights holders.'[512] Despite not being legally defined, the term 'individual reparation' is rather straightforward and it is interpreted in a uniform way. On the contrary, as noted by the Special Rapporteur on the promotion of truth, justice, reparation and guarantees of non-recurrence, '[t]he term "collective reparation" is ambiguous, as "collective" refers to both *the nature* of the reparation (i.e. the types of goods distributed or the mode of distributing them) and the kind of *recipient* of such reparation (i.e. collectivities)'.[513] The term collective reparations[514] has been explained as 'the benefits conferred on collectives in order to undo the collective harm that has been caused as a

509 UNBPG, above note 2, §8.

510 Redress Trust Observations Pursuant to Article 75 of the Statute, Trial Chamber I, Situation in the Democratic Republic of the Congo in the Case of the *Prosecutor v Germain Katanga*, ICC-01/04-01/07, 15 May 2015, §12.

511 Ibidem.

512 See L. Magarrell, 'Reparations in Theory and Practice', ICTJ, 2007, available at: http://ictj.org/sites/default/files/ICTJ-Global-Reparations-Practice-2007-English.pdf.

513 P. de Greiff, Report to the General Assembly on Reparations for Gross Human Rights Violations and Serious Violations of International Humanitarian Law, UN doc. A/69/518, 14 October 2014, §38.

514 Decision of 7 August 2012 (Decision Establishing the Principles and Procedures to be Applied to Reparations), above note 24, §61. 'Women's Initiatives highlights the absence of a definition of collective reparations in international law. It submits that the term "collective reparations" encompasses reparations that are directed at specific groups of people, as well as the wider community.'

consequence of a violation of international law'.[515] According to Rosenfeld, the elements that qualify reparations as 'collective' are four: the benefits, a collective as beneficiary, a collective harm, and a violation of international law. The author defines collective reparation as the immediate corollary to collective harm, clarifying that 'the targeting of a collective can cause harm that differs from the harm caused by targeting the same number of individuals who are not part of a collective'.[516] The Rabat Report[517] provides an additional explanation, stating that 'collective reparation(s) are focused on delivering a benefit to groups of victims that suffered from human rights or humanitarian law violations, such groups may be bound by different factors, which include a common identity (cultural, religious, ethnic or tribal roots), gender, vulnerability, age etc. … '.[518]

During the process of drafting its first decision on reparations in the *Lubanga* case the ICC also took an active part in the discussion on collective reparations.[519] As the Office of the Public Council for Victims ('OPCV') underlined in its submission to the Trial Chamber I on the issue of reparations:

> [C]ollective reparations can be given a broad and a narrow interpretation. A narrow approach would include measures that cater for existing groups who are linked by cultural, ethnic, social, cultural or spiritual factors. Applying a broad interpretation, collective reparations would address the position of individual victims who are part of a community or other group, and the awards would complement any individual reparations measures.[520]

---

515 See also R.M. Letschert and T. van Boven, 'Providing Reparation in Situations of Mass Victimization: Key Challenges Involved', in R.M. Letschert, R. Haveman, A.M. de Brouwer and A. Pemberton (eds.), *Victimological Approaches of International Crimes*, Intersentia, Antwerp, 2011, 155. See F. Rosenfeld, 'Collective Reparations for Victims of Armed Conflicts', (2010) 92 *International Review of the Red Cross* 731, at 732–746.

516 Ibidem, at 734.

517 See ICTJ, 'The Rabat Report: The Concepts and Challenges of Collective Reparations', 2009, available at http://ictj.org/sites/default/files/ICTJ-Morocco-Reparations-Report-2009-English.pdf. See also Magarrell above note 512, at 5–6.

518 Ibidem, at 42. It is clearly impossible to list such factors exhaustively, nevertheless the Rabat Report provides some useful examples, in particular 'the Peruvian reparations process considers certain groups of people as beneficiaries of the collective reparations program. One category includes peasant communities, indigenous populations, and villages affected by the conflict. A second category refers to non-returning displaced people from affected communities. The criteria for identifying the first category consist of a combination of geographical circumstances and a certain level of direct harm, whether individual or collective.' See also the ILA Committee on the Right to Reparation for Victims of Armed Conflict, The Hague, August 2010. According to the commentary to Art. 6, 'the concept of collective reparation has been even less explored than the right to individual reparation. Still, there are some developments that indicate that international law endorses collective reparation.'

519 Decision of 7 August 2012 (Decision Establishing the Principles and Procedures to be Applied to Reparations), above note 24.

520 Ibidem, §§31–32.

Furthermore, as specified by the TFV, 'collective reparations shall be distinguished between collective reparations that are inherently collective and exclusive (such as specialised health services for a targeted group of victims), and those that are community oriented and not exclusive (such as schools that benefit the entire community)'.[521] In the *Lubanga* case Trial Chamber I found that collective measures were appropriate to repair the harm suffered as a result of child conscription, enlistment and use in hostilities, in light of 'the uncertainty as to the number of victims of the crimes in this case – save that a considerable number of people were affected – and the limited number of individuals who have applied for reparations'.[522] The Appeals Chamber in its judgment on the appeals against the Trial Chamber's decision establishing the principles and procedures to be applied to reparations in the case against Mr Lubanga Dyilo considered that, even if the award of individual reparations was not explicitly excluded, the Trial Chamber decided to award reparations only on a collective basis.[523] Despite the submission of individual applications claiming for individual reparation, the Appeals Chamber ultimately agreed with the Trust Fund's position that 'a community-based approach, using the [Trust Fund]'s voluntary contributions, would be more beneficial and have greater utility than individual awards, given the limited funds available and the fact that this approach does not require costly and resource-intensive verification procedures'.[524] Notably, even though it remained silent on the issue of individual reparations, the Appeals Chamber specifically reversed the generic use of the concept of 'community' reparations by the Trial Chamber. It thus clarified that collective reparations to the community as a whole require the establishment of a sufficient link between the harm suffered by community members and the crimes of the convicted person.[525]

In the *El Alemán* case the Superior Court for the District of Bogota (Justice and Peace Chamber) did not treat the victims as a 'collectivity' because it ultimately established that being recruited as child soldiers into the same paramilitary group was not enough to determine the existence of a unique history or project, or a community with shared values and traditions. The Court thus determined that considering the minors as a unique social group entitled solely to collective reparation on the basis of their age was inappropriate. According to the Court, implementing collective reparation measures could not be the right way to proceed as the minors would have realised that they did not share much

---

521 See Trust Fund for Victims, Observations on Reparations in Response to the Scheduling Order of 14 March 2012, ICC-01/04-01/06-2872, 25 April 2012, §174.

522 Decision of 7 August 2012 (Decision Establishing the Principles and Procedures to be Applied to Reparations), above note 24, §219.

523 Judgment of 3 March 2015, ICC, above note 50, §140.

524 Ibidem, §219 and §274.

525 Ibidem.

apart from age and would have felt dissatisfied and wished they had received individual reparation instead.[526] This reasoning departs significantly from the approach adopted by the ICC, which focused mainly on considerations about the feasibility of the reparations awarded rather than on the victims and their needs.

In other settings, e.g. before the IACtHR, individual and collective reparations have often been awarded 'in tandem'. For example in the *Moiwana Community v. Suriname* case, concerning the killing by the Suriname armed forces of over 40 men, women and children and the destruction of the Moiwana village, the IACtHR stated that since 'the victims of the present case are members of the N'djuka culture, ... the individual reparations to be awarded must be supplemented by communal measures ... to the community as a whole'.[527] As a result the Court ordered the government to establish a development fund for projects for the benefit of the displaced survivors.

Throughout the Court's jurisprudence the notion of collective reparation has been broadly interpreted by awarding a wide variety of collective measures, in particular in cases of mass victimisation.[528] In instances involving the rights of indigenous peoples the Court has adopted a far-reaching approach, considering that 'collective reparations for indigenous communities not only aim to repair the harm caused directly by the human rights violations asserted, but also attempt to improve the often destitute living conditions of these marginalised communities in the long term'.[529] For example, in the *Plan de Sánchez* case, regarding the attack of a village by members of the Guatemalan Army and civil collaborators during which around 268 people (most of them members of the Maya-Achí people) were killed and abused, the Court referred to the collective nature of the harm when awarding collective measures of reparation. Reparation included

---

526 Judgment of 16 December 2011 (Sentencia), above note 432, §§880–881.

527 Judgment of 15 June 2005 (Preliminary Objections, Merits, Reparations and Costs), (2005) IACtHR, Series C No. 124, §194.

528 See D. Contreras-Garduño, 'Defining Beneficiaries of Collective Reparations: The Experience of the Inter-American Court of Human Rights', (2012) 4 *Amsterdam Law Forum*, 41, at 42–50. Judgment of 15 September 2005 (Merits, Reparations and Costs), (2005) IACtHR, Series C No. 134, §316. See also Judgment of 19 November 2004 (Reparations and Costs), (2004) IACtHR, Series C No. 116, §§93–111. On this point see also T.M. Antkowiak, 'Remedial Approaches to Human Rights Violations: The Inter-American Court of Human Rights and Beyond', (2008) 46 *Columbia Journal of Transnational Law* 351, at 353. According to the author, 'the breadth and depth of the remedies ordered are impressive, in addition to monetary compensation, the Court required the State to take the following measures, among others: the investigation, prosecution, and punishment of the responsible parties; a public acceptance of responsibility for the case's facts; establishment of a village housing program; medical and psychological treatment for all surviving victims; implementation of educational and cultural programs; and translation of the judgment into the appropriate Mayan language'.

529 D. Contreras-Garduño and S. Rombouts, 'Collective Reparations for Indigenous Communities before the Inter-American Court of Human Rights', (2010) 27 *Utrecht Journal of International and European Law* 4, at 5–17.

not only material measures, but also symbolic ones. In particular the Court requested that the State provide funds to maintain and improve the chapel used by survivors to commemorate those who died, as well as the implementation of development programmes for the affected communities.[530]

In the *El Mozote v. El Salvador* case, which concerned the massacres committed between 11 and 13 December 1981 during a military operation led by the Atlacatl Battalion in seven places in the northern part of the department of Morazán, the IACtHR again dealt with a large number of victims, about 1,000 people, most of them children.[531] The reparations envisaged by the Court in this case took the form of restitution, compensation, rehabilitation, satisfaction and guarantees of non-repetition. All the measures were awarded following a community-based approach because the Court observed that, owing to the particular characteristics of the case, it was not possible to identify and individualise all the victims.[532] Regarding in particular the psychosocial impact and emotional consequences suffered by the victims, expert witness Yáñez de La Cruz explained that 'the massacre ... dissolved the social networks in which the life project of both the individual and the community was inserted ... There was a loss of the collective subject that identifies an individual with the community, and there was a significant impact on the collective dignity.'[533] Moreover, she pointed out that the violence took place in the village squares and churches and, just as it destroyed the land and the animals, it also destroyed 'the core of the collective way of life', 'the identity and symbols of the peasant universe'.[534] The Court ultimately found that the State must provide, free of charge, through its specialised health care institutions in El Salvador, adequately and effectively, medical, psychological or psychiatric, treatment to the surviving victims of the massacres and the next of kin of the victims who were executed. Furthermore, when providing the psychological or psychiatric treatment, the specific circumstances and needs of each victim must also be taken into consideration,

530 Judgment of 19 November 2004 (Reparations and Costs), (2004) IACtHR, Series C No. 116, §104 and §110.

531 The most recent lists of victims prepared by Tutela Legal del Arzobispado, based on the testimony of survivors and family members, contain 1,061 names of presumed victims who were executed; of these, approximately 54% were children, approximately 18% adult women and approximately 10% men and adult women over 60 years of age. Meanwhile, from the exhumations performed at 28 sites, mainly indicated by the survivors and other witnesses, remains have been recovered corresponding to a minimum of 281 individuals, of which approximately 74% correspond to children under 12 years of age. In particular, in Site 1, known as 'El Convento' in the village of El Mozote, of 143 individuals identified, 136 corresponded to children and adolescents, with an average age of 6 years. Judgment of 25 October 2012 (Merits, Reparations and Costs), (2012) IACtHR, Series C No. 252, §153.

532 Ibidem, §310.

533 Expert opinion provided by María Sol Yáñez De La Cruz before the Inter-American Court during the public hearing held on 23 April 2012.

534 Ibidem.

so that they may be provided with collective, family or individual treatments, as agreed with each of them and after individual evaluation. In other words, the measures to achieve rehabilitation, despite being essential for the collective healing of the community, must be tailored to the needs of the individual victims, thus reiterating how multifaceted and nuanced the issue of individual versus collective reparations can be.

As stressed by Redress and shown by the brief overview of cases above, there are two main ways to interpret and implement the notion of collective reparations. In the first place collective awards can address the breach of a right that is exercised collectively, or a harm or injury that is suffered collectively by a defined group of victims. It follows that collective reparation concerns those aspects of harm that are suffered by the group as such, which transcend or are different to the harms that members of the group may also have suffered in their individual capacities. Secondly, collective reparation measures have been awarded to benefit a large universe of individual victims (or potential victims). In such instances, the decision to award collective reparation stems mainly from practical considerations about how best to ensure that the widest array of persons who are understood to have suffered harm derive a benefit.[535]

4.3. DRAWING A LINE BETWEEN REPARATIONS AND OTHER ASSISTANCE MEASURES

In the aftermath of every war, the contours that define the notions of reparation and development aid (or 'relief', 'assistance') are often blurred. In order to distinguish among the different kinds of actions that can be put in place to restore, or rebuild, reconciliation and peace, a few clarifications are necessary. The strategies and plans elaborated to strengthen development and growth can be described as processes by which a war-torn society increases the general and individual prosperity and welfare of its citizens.[536] Reparation, on the other hand, is a legal remedy, which can be claimed, enforced and even waived by its legitimate holder. Development foremost pursues the aims of alleviating poverty, supporting post-conflict recovery and addressing the socio-economic needs of the population at large,while reparations, awarded through judicial and non-judicial mechanisms, aim to provide redress to the victims of human rights and humanitarian law violations.[537] Moreover, development assistance targets

535 Redress Trust Observations pursuant to Article 75 of the Statute, above note 510, §13.

536 N. Roht-Arriaza and K. Orlovsky, 'A Complementary Relationship: Development and Reparations', ICTJ Research Briefing, July 2009, available at http://ictj.org/sites/default/files/ICTJ-Development-Reparations-ResearchBrief-2009-English.pdf.

537 UN Women and UNDP Report of the Kampala workshop 'Reparations, Development and Gender', December 2010, available at: http://www.unrol.org/files/Kampala%20workshop%202011%20Reparations,%20Development%20and%20Gender.pdf.

members of the affected community, i.e. conflict-affected persons ('CAPs') in general,[538] while reparation is to the 'exclusive' benefit of the victims, recognised as those who suffered, either directly or indirectly, from the wrongful acts committed. As stressed by Carranza,

> [i]t is important to note the distinction between relief and reparations. Reparations recognise that rights have been violated and that the State is obligated to repair the consequences of the violation. Relief is the immediate assistance offered to those affected by man-made or natural disasters, where the goal is simply to relieve recipients of the extraordinary physical burdens brought on by an emergency or to help them deal with the immediate aftermath of the disaster. Relief is important and useful for victims but it cannot be a substitute for reparations.[539]

In other words the wrong, and the harm suffered therefrom, are the indispensable corollaries that qualify an individual or group as 'victims' and trigger the exercise of the right to reparation; the identification of the beneficiaries of a development strategy, however, does not depend on the occurrence of violations of IHRL or IHL. This does not interfere with the possibility of awarding reparations to an entire country, such as, for example, Israel, or to a very large number of victims, as occurred in the case of the UNCC, which since 1991 has received more than 2.6 million claims seeking a total of approximately US$352 billion in compensation.[540] The problem remains that in some instances, especially in poor or war-torn countries, reparations programmes risk concentrating on the production and provision of basic goods, to which individuals and groups should be entitled as citizens and not as victims.[541] For example, in the case of provisions that focus on education it is difficult to draw a line between the initiatives designed and implemented to foster the right to education of children affected by armed conflict and the redress measures specifically envisaged to provide redress to child victims. The Sierra Leonean TRC offered some guidance in this regard. In fact, whereas many of the recommendations of the Commission referred to all the children in Sierra Leone, some specific reparations measures were identified to tackle those children who suffered during the war or from its consequences. Consequently, the TRC recommended that the government

---

538 See R. Carranza, 'Relief, Reparations and the Root Causes of Conflict in Nepal', ICTJ 2012, footnote No. 5. Available at: http://www.ictj.org/sites/default/files/ICTJ-Nepal-Reparations-2012-English.pdf. According to the author, 'However, these ("CAPs" and "victims") are not equivalent terms since people can be affected by conflicts without having suffered a human rights or international humanitarian law violation.'

539 Ibidem, at 5.

540 See F. Wooldridge and O. Elias, 'Humanitarian Considerations in the Work of the United Nations Compensation Commission', (2003) 85 *International Review of the Red Cross* 555, at 560–581.

541 See de Greiff, above note 23, at 26.

provide access to primary education to all Sierra Leonean children and free education until senior secondary school level to the child victims belonging to the following categories:

> children who are amputees, 'other war-wounded' or victims of sexual violence; children who suffered abduction or forced conscription; orphans; children of amputees, other war wounded if their parents experienced a 50% or more reduction in earning capacity as a result of the violation committed against them, and victims of victims of sexual violence; and those children who have been through the DDR programme and are undergoing schooling or other training from that programme are excluded from this list.[542]

In sum, whenever collective reparations do not target victims specifically, it is almost impossible to unfold them from development programmes. The distinction between reparations and assistance can also become blurred if analysed against the backdrop of the two mandates of the TFV.[543] Whereas its 'reparations mandate' implements the awards ordered by the Court against a convicted person, through its 'assistance mandate' the TFV provides support to victims and their families in ICC situations. The assistance mandate serves as an immediate response to the urgent needs of 'victims and their communities' who have suffered harm from crimes within the jurisdiction of the ICC. The TFV so far has reached over 100,000 victims; as noted by Moffett a large percentage of these numbers refers to peace-building programmes implemented for the affected communities. If, on the one hand, the two functions seem easily distinguishable with regard to their scope and nature, on the other hand some confusion may stem from the adoption of the term 'victim'. The TFV in principle uses the same definition of 'victim' as the one set out in the Rome Statute and in the Court's RPE,[544] however in practice the TFV reaches a more extensive range of persons who are affected by the broader situations before the Court, regardless of whether the harm they suffered stems from particular crimes charged in a specific case and regardless of the conviction of the alleged perpetrator. The

---

542 See Truth and Reconciliation Commission Act 2000 Sierra Leone, Supplement to the Sierra Leone Gazette Vol. CXXXI, No. 9, dated 10 February 2000, Sierra Leone TRC Report, Volume 2, Chapter 4: Reparations, §§177–178.

543 On the two mandates of the TFV see H. Rombouts and S. Parmentier, 'The International Criminal Court and its Trust Fund are Coming of Age: Towards a Process Approach for the Reparation of Victims', (2009) 8 *International Review of Victimology* 149, at 160–182. See also A.L.M. de Brouwer, 'Reparation to Victims of Sexual Violence: Possibilities at the International Criminal Court and at the Trust Fund for Victims and Their Families', (2007) 20 *Leiden Journal of International Law* 207, at 210–237.

544 'The resources of the Trust Fund shall be for the benefit of victims of crimes within the jurisdiction of the Court, as defined in rule 85 of the Rules of Procedure and Evidence, and, where natural persons are concerned, their families'. Regulations of the Trust Fund for Victims, Resolution ICC-ASP/4/Res.3, §42.

obvious difference between the assistance and reparation mandates is, thus, that the reparation mandate is linked to accountability, springing from the individual criminal responsibility of a convicted person, whereas the assistance mandate is not. This seems to contradict the assumption that both mandates refer to the same concept of victims envisaged in Rule 85 of the RPE, which clearly links the harm suffered by the victims, direct or indirect, to the liability, ascertained in a criminal proceeding and, hence, beyond any reasonable doubt, of the perpetrator. Thus, the term 'victim' is not used to refer to victims of crimes within the TFV's assistance mandate, but it rather encompasses 'survivors' who benefit from measures that provide aid and support.

4.4. MATERIAL AND SYMBOLIC REPARATIONS

Reparation benefits can usually be 'material' or 'symbolic'. As explained by de Greiff:

> Material and symbolic reparations can take different forms. Material reparations may assume the form of compensation, i.e., payments in cash or negotiable instruments, or of service packages, which may in turn include provisions for education, health, housing, etc. Symbolic reparations may include official apologies, the change of names of public spaces, the establishment of days of commemoration, the creation of museums and parks dedicated to the memory of victims, or rehabilitation measures such as restoring the good name of victims.[545]

Symbolic benefits are gaining increasing attention and are very often envisaged in both judicial and non-judicial settings. In particular with regard to the latter it is worth noting that several national programmes are currently proposed by TCs, which have broader mandates and goals than typical judicial instances and therefore place a special emphasis on the need to reconcile the society at large.[546] In Sierra Leone, for example, the TRC recommended the implementation of both material and symbolic measures, emphasising the importance of placing individual reparations within the wider social and political context.[547] Similarly in Liberia the TRC stated that

> [r]eparations should aim at repairing the consequences of violations borne by children during the Liberian conflict. There should be symbolic and material reparations for

---

545 See de Greiff, above note 23, at 22.

546 Ibidem.

547 See Truth and Reconciliation Commission Act 2000 Sierra Leone, Supplement to the Sierra Leone Gazette Vol. CXXXI, No. 9, dated 10 February 2000, Sierra Leone TRC Report, Volume 2, Chapter 4: Reparations, §195.

> Liberia's children and young adults. Ideally, any reparation schemes will target entire communities and children as a group rather than single out individual children.[548]

Symbolic reparations have been regarded as important also to enhance the process of rehabilitation of former child soldiers, as stressed by the ICC in the *Lubanga* case.[549] In particular Trial Chamber I determined that the modalities of reparations other than restitution, compensation and rehabilitation, i.e. those with a symbolic, transformative and preventive value, should encompass measures to address the shame felt by some former child soldiers and held that reparations programmes should 'be directed at preventing future conflicts and raising awareness that the effective reintegration of these children requires eradicating the victimisation, discrimination and stigmatisation of young people in these circumstances'.[550]

Article 141 of the Colombian Victims' Law stresses that symbolic reparations refer to all the initiatives in favour of the victims or the whole community that aim at ensuring the preservation of the historical memory, the non-repetition of the victimising conducts, the public acceptance of responsibility for the acts committed and the restoration of victims' dignity. The choice of the objects or means through which symbolic reparations can be awarded is very complex and can have a deep impact on victims. To use Hamber's words:

> One could understand (symbolic) reparations objects (memorials and the like) as objects that assist in bridging the gaps between the interpersonal world and narrowing the micro and macro social world for victims and individuals in the society. Reparations objects of this kind bridge inner-directed grief and suffering, and mirror (to the world and individual) how that suffering is understood and accepted (or not) within the real socio-political world. Through the object the reactions of the real world are tested and messages are sent back (at a deep psychological level) to the victim about their personal value and psychological sense of belonging in society.[551]

Given the sacredness of the message conveyed, the identification of the vehicle is extremely important and this explains the rationale behind the decision made by the Superior Court for the District of Bogota (Justice and Peace Chamber) in the *El Alemán* case not to order the construction of a monument to remember child victims of unlawful recruitment. According to the Court, and in line with the recommendation of the expert witness, since the children in the ranks of an armed group are used to obeying and respecting their commander, a statue could

548 Final Report of the Truth and Reconciliation Commission of Liberia, Volume Three: Appendices, Title II: Children, the Conflict and the TRC Children Agenda, June 2009, at 107.

549 See Judgment of 3 March 2015, ICC, above note 50, Order for Reparations, Annex A, §67.

550 Ibidem, §202.

551 See Hamber, above note 460, at 571.

reiterate and reinvigorate those feelings rather than contributing to dissolving the hierarchy and the power structure.[552] The construction of monuments and memorials can also be problematic in relation to victims affected by sexual violence. Since part of the power of monuments lies in the individualisation and in the recognition of suffering, victims draw a certain sense of acknowledgement and satisfaction from seeing the name of a loved one, or their name, written in stone. However, in the case of victims of SGBV, the process of individualisation can exacerbate the stigma and ostracism that surround this type of crime and in particular those who have been affected by it.[553]

4.5. THE TRANSFORMATIVE POTENTIAL OF REPARATIONS

Although the ultimate goal of reparations is traditionally reckoned to be the restoration of the *status quo ante*, in the form of restitution, the current focus on victims other than States has led to a 'humanisation' of the field of remedies, which entails the effort to design reparations as a tool to adequately, effectively and promptly redress the harm suffered by the victims.[554] As discussed above, the steadily increasing number of violations that curtail the enjoyment of the most basic rights has led to the unavoidable question of whether restitution is feasible and advisable in cases where the victimisation is the obvious result of a disrupted and unjust social fabric. In response to this query, academics and practitioners have started to discuss the possibility of broadening the effective reach of reparations so as to target not only the consequences of a violation, but also its causes.

On 21 October 2009 Professor Rodrigo Uprimny Yepes delivered his inaugural lecture accepting the UNESCO Chair of Education for Peace, Human Rights and Democracy at the University of Utrecht in the Netherlands. During his speech Uprimny Yepes described the idea of 'transformative reparation' by explaining that 'the purpose of reparations of massive human rights violations in unequal societies should not be to restore poor victims to their previous situation of poverty and discrimination, but to change or "transform" the circumstances in which they lived … '.[555]

---

552 Judgment of 16 December 2011 (Sentencia), above note 432, §§855–858.

553 C. Duggan and R. Jacobson, 'Reparations of Sexual and Reproductive Violence: Moving from Codification to Implementation', in Rubio-Marin, above note 48, 121, at 151.

554 See UNBPG, above note 2, §15.

555 See R. Uprimny Yepes, 'Between Corrective and Distributive Justice: Reparations of Gross Human Rights Violations in Times of Transition', Inaugural Address of the UNESCO Chair in Education for Peace, Human Rights and Democracy, at 9, available at: http://www.uu.nl/university/research/EN/international_collaboration/latinamerica/Documents/OratieRodrigoUprimny.pdf.

This statement mirrors a number of declarations and other non-binding documents, which place the accent on the importance of overcoming the traditional and common understanding of the right to reparation and widen its scope so as to include the eradication of discriminatory practice. The Nairobi Declaration, for example, has stressed the need for reparations to go above and beyond the immediate reasons and consequences of the crimes and violations. In more detail the Nairobi Declaration explained that reparations must aim to address the political and structural inequalities responsible for negatively shaping women's and girl's lives and that reintegration and restitution by themselves are not sufficient goals of reparation, since the origins of violations of women's and girls' human rights pre-date the conflict situation.[556] Similarly the outcome document of the meeting on 'Reparations, Development and Gender' held by UN Women in Kampala in 2010 underlined the importance of recognising and investing in the transformative potential of reparations, stressing that reparations should be informed by principles of non-discrimination, gender equality, and victim participation and empowerment, and include efforts to provide remedy and redress for both the causes and consequences of serious violations and crimes.[557] In December 2012 the Committee Against Torture pointed out in its General Comment No. 3 that 'for restitution to be effective, efforts should be made to address structural causes to the violation, including any kind of discrimination related to, for example, gender, sexual orientation, disability, political or other opinion, ethnicity, age and religion, and all other grounds of discrimination'.[558] The CAT has thus broadened the scope of the precedent documents by making reference to discrimination based on all the grounds, not solely gender, which are likely to exacerbate the exposure of vulnerable individuals or groups to violations of their rights.

The UN Secretary-General in June 2014 released a Guidance Note to provide policy and operational guidance for United Nations engagement in the area of reparations for victims of conflict-related sexual violence, including activities to advocate for or support the establishment, monitoring and evaluation of reparation programmes and initiatives directed at victims of conflict-related sexual violence.[559] One of the principles for operational engagement enshrined in the Guidance Note spells out that reparations should strive to be transformative,

556 Nairobi Declaration on Women's and Girl's Right to a Remedy and Reparation, above note 34. See also Couillard, above note 192, at 445.

557 UN Women, 'Reparations, Development and Gender', October 2012, available at: http://www.unwomen.org/~/media/Headquarters/Attachments/Sections/Library/Publications/2012/10/06A-Development-Gender.pdf.

558 Committee Against Torture, General comment No. 3: Convention against Torture and Other Cruel, Inhuman or Degrading Treatment or Punishment: Implementation of article 14 by States Parties, 13 December 2012.

559 UN Secretary-General, Guidance Note: Reparations for Conflict-Related Sexual Violence, June 2014, available at:

including in design, implementation and impact. The Guidance Note stresses that this is true in particular with regard to sexual violence perpetrated in situations of armed conflict as this often results from and perpetuate patterns of pre-existing structural subordination and discrimination for both men and women. Reparations thus have the potential to trigger important changes, even if they alone cannot transform the root causes of conflict-related sexual violence or the structural conditions that made such violence possible. The Guidance Note also provides an example of what the term 'transformative reparations' should mean, by explaining that in certain settings women-centred economic compensation or access to productive resources or credit may help enhance women's economic empowerment and autonomy and *therefore be transformative*. What emerges from the Guidance Note, and more generally from all the documents that so far have made reference to the importance of broadening the traditional scope of reparations, is the fact that the 'transformation' envisaged shall take place by empowering the victims through measures that redress the consequences of the violations and at the same time tackle the underlying causes that placed them in an unfavourable situation. In other words reparations should combine measures of prevention with measures aimed at strengthening the victim's exercise of his/her rights.

However, the extent to which this 'transformative' component is inbuilt in reparations *tout court* or instead represents a new development has not yet been discussed thoroughly either in judicial or non-judicial settings. The empowering role of reparations has long been recognised in non-judicial settings, for example Sierra Leone's TRC recommended reparations that 'are comprehensive in nature and have the potential to make significant changes in women's and children's lives'.[560] The recommendations also included a number of gender-specific legal and institutional reforms, such as the repeal of all discriminatory legislation, enactment of gender-progressive laws, and ensuring that at least 30 per cent of candidates for public elections are women.[561] The recommendations do not, however, make explicit reference to 'transformative reparations' but rather refer to the twofold purposes of reparations, i.e. to provide redress to the victims and to accord 'a measure of social justice'.[562]

The ICC TFV in its Strategic Plan 2014–2017 has, instead, specifically mentioned the concept of 'transformation', by explaining that

> [i]t is often not appropriate to simply restore the *status quo* that gave rise to such crimes, in particular because the majority of victims of gross human rights violations will likely

560 Ibidem.

561 See Truth and Reconciliation Commission Act 2000 Sierra Leone, Supplement to the Sierra Leone Gazette Vol. CXXXI, No. 9, dated 10 February 2000, Sierra Leone Truth and Reconciliation Final Report 'Witness to Truth', Vol. 2 Chapter 4: Reparations.

562 Ibidem, at 229, §9.

> have been powerless and dispossessed at the time when the conflict erupted. Therefore, *combining reparations and assistance with structural transformative approaches* will be of particular importance to those who have suffered irreparable harm and are marginalized in their communities, especially for many women and girls, and victims of sexual and gender-based violence.[563]

Furthermore, the TFV has underlined how reparations can play a prominent role in empowering women and girls affected by historic patterns of subordination and social exclusion. The gender dimension of transformative reparations is thus stressed again to strengthen the link between reparations and empowerment.

The notion of transformative reparations is often associated with the case law of the IACtHR. In particular the *Cotton Field* case[564] is described as the first case in which the IACtHR 'articulated the need to provide reparations that do justice to women',[565] dealing with a situation of structural violence based on gender discrimination. In the section of the final judgment devoted to the reparations award for the injured parties, the IACtHR in a landmark passage stated:

> The Court recalls that the concept of 'integral reparation' (*restitutio in integrum*) entails the re-establishment of the previous situation and the elimination of the effects produced by the violation, as well as the payment of compensation for the damage caused. *However*, bearing in mind the context of structural discrimination in which the facts of this case occurred, which was acknowledged by the State, *the reparations must be designed to change this situation*, so that their effect is not only of restitution, but also of rectification. In this regard, reestablishment of the same structural context of violence and discrimination is not acceptable.[566]

The IACtHR has thus openly departed from the traditional notion of reparation which aimed at wiping out the consequences of a wrongful act in order to restore the *status quo*, clarifying the need to adopt a broader approach in those instances where the victims are 'targeted' because of existing inequalities that exacerbate vulnerability and are not duly prevented or addressed by the State. To this end the IACtHR has ordered Mexico to implement some measures as guarantees of non-repetition. In particular the Court has focused on the need to provide

563 The Trust Fund for Victims, Strategic Plan 2014–2017 as approved by the TFV board of Directors, August 2014, The Hague (emphasis added), available at: http://www.trustfundforvictims.org/sites/default/files/media_library/documents/pdf/TFV_Strategic_Plan_2014_2017__approved.pdf.

564 Judgment of 16 November 2009 (Preliminary Objection, Merits, Reparations and Costs), (2009) IACtHR, Series C No. 205.

565 R. Rubio-Marin and C. Sandoval, 'Engendering the Reparations Jurisprudence of the Inter-American Court of Human Rights: The Promise of the Cotton Field Judgment', (2011) 33 *Human Rights Quarterly* 1062, at 1090–1091.

566 Judgment of 16 November 2009, above note 564, §450 (emphasis added).

gender-sensitive training to the police, prosecutors, judges, military officials and public servants responsible for providing services and legal assistance to victims of crime, and any local or federal public officials who participate directly or indirectly in prevention, investigation, prosecution, punishment and reparation. Moreover, given the widespread and deep-rooted discrimination against women, the Mexican State has been requested also to offer a programme of education for the general public of the State of Chihuahua.[567] The Court has stressed that education and training initiatives with a gender perspective involve not only learning about laws and regulations, but also developing the capacity to recognise the discrimination to which women are exposed in their daily lives. In particular, training should enable all the participants to discern the effects on women of stereotyped ideas and opinions in relation to the meaning and scope of human rights. Notably, in the *Cotton Field* case the IACtHR did not make any explicit reference to the notion of transformative reparations, instead it underlined the importance of establishing reparative measures able to rectify a situation of impairment and discrimination. Consistently with this scope, the Court ordered the State to put in place guarantees of non-repetition, in the form of the above-mentioned education and training programmes, to prevent future violations and at the same time to tackle existing discriminatory practice and structural inequalities.

Trial Chamber I of the ICC made explicit mention of 'transformative values' and 'transformative objectives' that reparations should envisage in its first decision establishing the principles and procedures to be applied to reparations in the *Lubanga* case.[568] In identifying the key principles to adopt in the specific case Trial Chamber I took into account the observations on reparations submitted by various actors. In particular the TFV[569] and the Women's Initiatives[570] specifically referred to the transformative component of reparations. The Women's Initiatives in fact pointed out that

> [o]ne of the aims of reparations *is to be transformative*, in particular in addressing sexual violence and the conditions that existed prior to the conflict that may have contributed to these crimes and that may prevent the full rehabilitation and restoration of the rights of victims/survivors of sexual violence.

UNICEF in its submission instead put the accent on the importance of guarantees of non-repetition, highlighting that they represent one of the 'major components'

---

567 Ibidem. §540 et seq.

568 Decision of 7 August 2012 (Decision Establishing the Principles and Procedures to be Applied to Reparations), above note 24, §222 and §236.

569 TFV, 'Observations on Reparations in Response to the Scheduling Order of 14 March 2012', 25 February 2012, ICC-01/04-01/06-2872, §§72–77.

570 The Women's Initiatives for Gender Justice, 'Observations of the Women's Initiatives for Gender Justice on Reparations', 10 May 2012, ICC-01/04-01/06-2876, §17.

of transitional justice and reparations.[571] Therefore, UNICEF has argued that in the process of identifying the most effective and adequate reparations the ICC should take into account the 'underlying causes of the violations, which constantly point to structural failures in the communities of the victims'.[572] Consistently, UNICEF has recommended that the ICC include in its reparations plan preventive programmes aimed at eradicating social instability and endemic poverty.

The Appeals Chamber in the amended Order for Reparations against Mr Lubanga Dyilo identified the appropriate modalities of reparations, which include restitution, compensation and rehabilitation, as well as other types of reparations such as those with a symbolic, preventive or transformative value.[573] The Chamber ultimately recognised the transformative potential of reparations in two instances: first, in relation to rehabilitation, stressing that 'programmes that have transformative objectives, however limited, can help prevent future victimisation, and symbolic reparations, such as commemorations and tributes, may also contribute to the process of rehabilitation'; and secondly, in respect of 'other forms of reparation, such as establishing or assisting campaigns that are designed to improve the position of victims; by issuing certificates that acknowledge the harm particular individuals experienced; setting up outreach and promotional programmes that inform victims as to the outcome of the trial; and educational campaigns that aim at reducing the stigmatisation and marginalisation of the victims of the present crimes'.[574]

What emerges from the approach adopted by the ICC in the *Lubanga* case, and more generally from the overview provided in this section, is that reparations can have a transformative capability, but it is not correct to speak about 'transformative reparations' *per se*. Every form of reparation, from restitution to guarantees of non-repetition, is potentially able to have an impact also on the causes that led to the violation in the first place, but this possibility depends on various factors such as the threshold of vulnerability of the victims, the kind of harm experienced, the feasibility, and in order to avoid unrealistic expectations, the effectiveness and the breadth of the redress measures envisaged. Due to their nature and scope, guarantees of non-repetition represent the form of reparations more easily associated with the idea of 'transformation', but this does not exclude other kinds of measures from potentially achieving similar results. For example the Colombian Victims' Law, which focuses mainly on the restitution

571 UNICEF, 'Submission on the Principles to be Applied and the Procedures to be Followed by the Chamber with regard to Reparations', 10 May 2012, ICC-01/04-01/06-2878, §19.

572 Ibidem.

573 Judgment of 3 March 2015, ICC, above note 50, Order for Reparations, Annex A, §67.

574 Ibidem.

of the land unlawfully seized or abandoned as a result of protracted violence,[575] can have a transformative potential in terms of addressing the causes of child recruitment and sexual violence, which are crimes intimately entwined with the high rate of displacement within the country.[576] Provisions of education, such as, for example, full scholarships and vocational training, could also have a transformative impact on the lives of child victims whose vulnerability, and thus their risk of being disproportionately targeted in peace as well as in war time, has been exacerbated by living in the streets.[577] Also measures of satisfaction can carry a transformative potential. In the *Serrano Cruz Sisters* case the IACtHR ordered El Salvador to designate a day to honour the approximately 881 children who disappeared during the country's civil war.[578] The purpose of designating the national day was to raise awareness and also to enhance cooperation in the affected community. Awakening the public conscience and reminding people of the violations that occurred can contribute to preventing further relapses and trigger the community's interest in certain vulnerable victims, thus also carrying a transformative element.

4.6. CONCLUSIONS

Reparations are constantly adapting and adjusting to the changing world. Framing the discourse in terms which go beyond the inter-State dimension and drawing attention to the most vulnerable segments of the population, including child victims, triggers the need to rethink and challenge the traditional understanding of reparations.

---

575 Over the past 15 to 25 years alone, 1.8 million hectares of land have been abandoned or seized. See A.M. Ibanez and J.C. Munoz, 'The Persistence of Land Concentration in Colombia: What Happened between 2000 and 2010?', in M. Bergsmo, C. Rodriguez-Garavito, P. Kalmanovitz and M.P. Saffon (eds.) *Distributive Justice in Transitions*, Torkel Opsahl Academic EPublisher (TOAEP), 2010, 279, at 292.

576 UNHCR reports that according to official figures of 30 June 2014, more than 5.7 million people have been internally displaced in Colombia since the start of recording official cumulative registration figures; more than 64,500 people were officially declared displaced during the first half of 2014 and were awaiting registration; and almost 24,000 people were officially registered by the national Victims Unit; further information is available at: http://www.unhcr.org/pages/49e492ad6.html.

577 Consider, for instance, the case of Sierra Leone, where the majority of children abducted or recruited by armed forces and armed groups were 'raray boys'. See Zack-Williams, above note 474, at 92.

578 See Pasqualucci, above note 87, at 207.

Prior to completing the investigation of the theoretical foundations and moving on to its practical application, the forms and the scope of reparative measures have ultimately been analysed placing children at the centre of the discourse. As this chapter has shown, none of the forms of reparations enshrined in the UNBPG prevails over the others as each of them has a different scope and entails a number of benefits for the victims and/or for the community at large. The widespread commission of gross IHRL and serious IHL violations has destabilised the supremacy of restitution and also called for a more far-reaching and comprehensive approach to reparations, to include, when possible, both material and symbolic measures. The identification and the recognition of the victims, as individuals or groups, has been presented as crucial to drawing a line between reparations and other types of assistance, to which children are entitled as citizens and not in light of the harm suffered as a result of a violation of their rights. Finally, the question of whether reparations can address not only the consequences of victimisation, but also the factors that lead to it has been posed. Recognising that reparations can be instrumental in advancing social justice and preventing some recurring patterns of stigmatisation and discrimination is an important step forward that should be balanced with a thorough reflection, covering both the concrete circumstances as well as victims' expectations. Unpacking the often misused concept of transformative reparations has, thus, finally highlighted that all forms of reparations may have a transformative potential that needs to be endorsed and strengthened.

PART II

CURRENT APPLICATION OF THE PRINCIPLES AND NORMS

CHAPTER 5

CHILD VICTIMS' RIGHT TO REPARATION IN 'QUASI-JUDICIAL' AND JUDICIAL INTERNATIONAL SETTINGS

5.1. INTRODUCTION

The aim of this chapter is to analyse how child victims' right to reparation is exercised in international quasi-judicial and judicial settings. Since the focus of the present work is on child victims of armed conflict, this part will introduce and discuss only those bodies that have dealt (or are likely to deal in the future) with the consequences of gross human rights violations and serious violations of humanitarian law perpetrated against children during or in the aftermath of NIACs and IACs. The actors responsible for satisfying children's right to reparation are traditionally national and international criminal courts dealing with individual perpetrators, regional human rights bodies, States, TCs, trust funds and other transitional justice instruments. They can act in concert as components of a holistic justice process or they can behave independently when no such process of integral transition has been set up in the country.

The first part of the book served the purpose of laying down the theoretical framework that governs children's right to reparation, explaining *inter alia* which are the key developments under international law and their impact on child victims. The present part will deal with the concrete issues arising when children 'face' the actors entitled to award reparations as the outcomes of judicial proceedings or as the results of national strategies. This chapter, in particular, will discuss to what degree international bodies, quasi-judicial and judicial, comply with the demand to award reparations, which are adequate, prompt and effective.

5.2. COMPLAINT MECHANISMS OF UN TREATY BODIES AND THE THIRD OPTIONAL PROTOCOL TO THE CONVENTION ON THE RIGHTS OF THE CHILD ON A COMMUNICATIONS PROCEDURE

The UN has two different types of dedicated human rights mechanisms, namely those established under a human rights treaty and those set up under the Human

Rights Council. The latter are often described as 'Charter-based' mechanisms, 'non-conventional mechanisms' or 'non-treaty procedures'.[579] The mechanisms established under the Human Rights Council may be divided into procedures at the level of the Council itself and the 'special procedures', which include also the Special Rapporteur on the promotion of truth, justice, reparation and guarantees of non-recurrence. The IHRL mechanisms established under the core human rights treaties are invested with various tools to assist States parties' implementation of their treaty obligations, i.e. consideration of States' reports, the issuance of General Comments, the conduct of inquiries and individual communication procedures.[580] The UN treaty monitoring bodies, which are often described as 'Committees' and composed of between 10 and 23 independent experts, have competence to consider individual complaints or communications on human rights matters. These complaints are usually brought by any individual, a group of individuals, or by someone else on behalf of the individual(s), claiming a violation of a right under a particular treaty, depending on the terms of that treaty.[581] The perpetrator must be a State party to that treaty and it must have recognised the competence of the committee to consider such complaints. The treaty bodies do not examine complaints against private individuals or national or international organisations. In addition, the domestic remedies must have been exhausted, with the exception of local remedies that are not effective, not available or unduly prolonged. The complaints must be submitted in writing, with the facts and the alleged violations presented in chronological order and an indication of the exhausted domestic remedies. Complaints cannot be sent simultaneously to a different human rights mechanism. Furthermore, complainants do not need to be legally represented. Even though this would be advisable, at the moment there is no UN system of legal aid to help with the issue of legal representation.

As noted by several authors, the main weakness of the treaty body complaints procedures is that the final merit decisions are not binding upon States and thus there is no enforcement mechanism.[582] However in its General Comment No. 33 the HRC has clarified that, although its views are not binding, they 'exhibit some

---

579 See T. Karimova, G. Giacca and S. Casey-Maslen, *United Nations Human Rights Mechanisms and the Right to Education in Insecurity and Armed Conflict*, Geneva Academy of International Humanitarian Law and Human Rights/Protect Education in Insecurity and Conflict, 2013, at 35.

580 See J. Connors and M. Schmidt, 'United Nations', in Moeckli, Shah and Sivakumaran, above note 469, at 359.

581 See generally, S. Joseph, K. Mitchell and L. Gyorki, *Seeking Remedies for Torture Victims: A Handbook on the Individual Complaints Procedures of the UN Treaty Bodies'* OMCT Series, Volume 4, Geneva, 2006.

582 See T. Buergenthal, 'The UN Human Rights Committee', (2001) 5 *Max Planck Yearbook of United Nations Law*, 341, at 341–345; see also Connors and Schmidt, above note 580, at 383.

important characteristics of a judicial decision'.[583] Moreover the HRC stressed that its views are 'an authoritative interpretation of the ICCPR by a body entrusted by States parties to give such interpretations, and, as such the principle of good faith to treaty obligations requires that States cooperate with the Committee and inform it of actions to implement its views'.[584] The committees, in particular the HRC, which is most frequently resorted to, have also heard complaints for violations occurring in conjunction with armed conflict and awarded reparations for the harm suffered. For example, in the case of *Sharmila Tripathi et al.*,[585] which dealt with the arbitrary detention, torture and disappearance of the applicant's husband during the armed conflict that took place in Nepal in 2003, the HRC recognised the anguish and distress caused to the author and her minor daughter by the disappearance of Mr Tripathi and identified the kinds of reparations that Nepal should implement. In particular the HRC affirmed that the State party, which according to Article 2(3) of the ICCPR is under an obligation to provide the author with an effective remedy, was expected to: (a) conduct a thorough and effective investigation into the facts surrounding the detention of Mr Tripathi and the treatment he suffered; (b) release him if he was still alive; (c) in the event that Mr Tripathi was deceased, hand over his remains to his family; (d) prosecute, try and punish those responsible for the violations committed; (e) provide adequate compensation for the violations suffered, to the author, her daughter and Mr Tripathi, if he was still alive; (f) ensure that necessary and adequate psychological rehabilitation and medical treatment were provided to the author and her daughter; and (g) provide appropriate measures of satisfaction.[586]

In another similar proceeding brought before the HRC by Mrs Tija Hero and her children concerning a case of enforced disappearance that took place during the armed conflict surrounding the independence of Bosnia Herzegovina, the Committee issued a view that aimed at redressing the suffering of the victims, but also at addressing the current legal framework in order to simplify access to social benefits and measures of reparations for the family of the missing persons.[587] The authors based their complaint on the multi-offensive nature of enforced disappearance. In particular with regard to the son and daughter of the missing person it was argued that they had never received any compensation for the harm suffered as a result of the disappearance of their father. Instead of being granted the special measures of protection they would have been entitled

583 HRC, General Comment No. 33, The Obligations of States Parties under the Optional Protocol to the International Covenant on Civil and Political Rights, UN doc. CCPR/C/GC/33, 5 November 2008, §11.

584 Connors and Schmidt, above note 580, at 383.

585 Communication No. 2111/2011, CCPR/C/112/D/2111/2011, 25 November 2014.

586 Ibidem, §9.

587 Communication No. 1966/2010, CCPR/C/112/D/1966/2010, 27 November 2014.

to as minors, they had to grow up without the presence of their father, and were forced to live with the dreadful uncertainty as to what exactly had happened to him. As a result the Committee found that the State party is under an obligation to provide the authors with an effective remedy, including (a) continuing its efforts to establish the fate or whereabouts of the missing person, as required by the Law on Missing Persons 2004, and having its investigators contact the authors as soon as possible to obtain the information that they could contribute to the investigation; (b) continuing its efforts to bring to justice those responsible for his disappearance, without unnecessary delay, as required by the national war crimes strategy; and (c) ensuring adequate compensation for the authors. Furthermore, the Committee stressed that the State party is also under an obligation to prevent similar violations in the future and therefore it must ensure that investigations into allegations of enforced disappearances are accessible to the families of missing persons, and that the current legal framework is not applied in a manner that requires the relatives of victims of enforced disappearance to receive certification of the death of the victim as a condition for obtaining social benefits and measures of reparation. The existing provisions, in fact, oblige relatives of disappeared persons to have the family member declared dead in order to be eligible for compensation. This makes the availability of compensation dependent on a harmful process, which according to the Committee constitutes inhuman and degrading treatment and, therefore it should be promptly amended.[588] The views expressed by the HRC, despite their non-binding nature, are in line with a victims-centred understanding of reparations and also embrace the transformative potential that redress measures can have in relation to victims and society at large.

Like the other complaints procedures set up within the UN treaty bodies framework, the Optional Protocol to the Convention on the Rights of the Child on a Communications Procedure is a tool designed to strengthen access to international justice for victims seeking redress in the aftermath of human rights violations in cases where domestic remedies are grossly inadequate or absent.[589] Unlike the other complaints procedures, this one focuses specifically on children and provides them with a forum to resort to when the rights enshrined in the CRC and its Optional Protocols, i.e. the Optional Protocol to the Convention on the sale of children, child prostitution and child pornography and the Optional Protocol to the Convention on the involvement of children in armed conflict, are breached.[590] Remarkably, the Optional Protocol on Communications was

---

588 Ibidem, §9.7.

589 See S.C. Grover, *Children Defending their Human Rights Under the CRC Communications Procedure: On Strengthening the Convention on the Rights of the Child Complaints Mechanism*, Springer-Verlag, Berlin-Heidelberg, 2015.

590 At the time of writing 27 States have ratified the Optional Protocol on a Communications Procedure.

long awaited, reflecting many States' reluctance to provide children with better and potentially more child-friendly access to international justice remedies.[591]

Not surprisingly during the drafting process several aspects of the CRC-OP3 were considerably watered down. As a result the third Optional Protocol does not provide children with the greatest feasible and necessary degree of protection in making a communication or easy access to international justice through this mechanism.[592] In the first place it is worth noting that the CRC communications mechanism is embodied in an Optional Protocol to the Convention, which the States parties must accede to or ratify in order to be considered to have assumed the obligations it sets out. Furthermore, States parties are entitled to make reservations to the CRC-OP3, as well as to the Convention and its first two Optional Protocols. It therefore, as stressed by Grover,[593] undermines instead of promoting children's fundamental rights, including their right to participation, as outlined in Article 12 of the CRC.

The second major concern related to the CRC-OP3 is the denial of the opportunity to bring collective complaints. The current text of the Optional Protocol in fact establishes that 'communications may be submitted by or on behalf of an individual or group of individuals, within the jurisdiction of a State party, claiming to be victims of a violation by that State party of any of the rights set forth in any of the following instruments to which that State is a party'.[594] In order to be admissible, the communications cannot be anonymous and therefore collective complaints that report widespread violations without identifying the victims are not valid.[595] As explained by the former vice-chairperson of the Committee on the Rights of the Child, the Committee was unanimously in favour of the possibility to receive and consider collective complaints, in anonymous form. An earlier draft of the Optional Protocol included the collective communications procedure with an opt-in possibility. In the end, this procedure was simply taken out.[596] This means that under the CRC-OP3 the representatives of child victim complainants, namely reputable NGOs, the child victim's parents, other legal or kinship guardians, legal counsel or other vetted representatives, or the complainants themselves, will be blocked from

---

591 Grover, above note 589, at 7.

592 M. Langford and S. Clark, 'The New Kid on the Block: A Complaints Procedure for the Convention on the Rights of the Child', Working Paper No. 1. Socio-Economic Rights Programme, Norwegian Centre for Human Rights, University of Oslo, 2010, available at: http://www.jus.uio.no/smr/english/people/aca/malcolml/new-kid-on-the-block-langford-clark.pdf.

593 Grover, above note 589, at 9.

594 See Art. 5 of the CRC-OP3.

595 See Art. 7 of the CRC-OP3.

596 HRTD Newsletter No. 11 January–February, 2011, '"A Communication Procedure on Children's Rights". Mr. Jean Zermatten, Vice-Chairperson of the CRC, shares his thoughts on the draft CRC-OP3'.

bringing complaints as a group unless each and every one of the child victim complainants in the group is named and thus accurately identified alongside the group's representatives where the victims do not bring the complaints themselves. This restriction in the CRC-OP3 mechanism ultimately results in a potential denial of justice for innumerable child victims including those at risk of victimisation due to widespread, systemic and/or institutionalised forms of human rights violations.[597]

Newell noted that the inclusion of a collective procedure for child victims would have been beneficial on a number of levels. It could have helped reduce the risk of States' retaliation against children who file communications under CRC-OP3 and better ensure confidentiality. Furthermore the acceptance of this tool could have provided a potential remedy also to small and large collectives of victims of particular systemic and/or grave IHRL violations who were unable to come forward in the first instance for whatever reason. The admissibility of a collective procedure could also have increased the chances for States parties to the CRC communications protocol to undertake necessary systemic changes to better respect and promote children's fundamental rights. Finally, the use of collective complaints could have enhanced procedural efficiency as collective communications can reduce the workload of the Committee on the Rights of the Child and spare it from considering large numbers of similar communications from various individual child victims or disparate groups.[598]

An important shortcoming highlighted also by the members of the Committee on the Rights of the Child is the inadmissibility of non-written complaints, which will probably limit the possibility of the child to act directly. The Committee is of the view that the written procedure is not always the best one for children and therefore alternative modes for communications, such as video or audio recordings, video conferences and oral submissions, were originally included in the draft CRC-OP3, then deleted.[599] Moreover, it should be noted that the CRC-OP3 does not allow for consideration of cases where the victimised child has turned 18 or older by the time the communication reaches the Committee on the Rights of the Child. Langford and Clark pointed out that this limitation conflicts with the idea of an instrument capable of enhancing victims' access to remedies as

> [m]any children may only become aware in their adulthood that a violation has occurred when they were young or only as an adult do they have the capacity to set

597 Grover, above note 589, at 21.

598 See P. Newell, 'Expert Briefing to the First Session of the Working Group to Explore the Possibility of Elaborating an Optional Protocol to the Convention on the Rights of the Child', September 2010, at 5.

599 See HRTD Newsletter No. 11 January–February, 2011, 'A Communication Procedure on Children's Rights', at p. 3, in which Mr Jean Zermatten, Vice-Chairperson of the CRC, shared his thoughts on the draft Optional Protocol to the Convention on the Rights of the Child on a Communications Procedure.

> the litigious wheels in motion. By the time the slow-moving machinery of domestic and international remedies reaches its conclusion in the Committee, the complainant may very well be an adult. The low reported usage of the existing treaty-body system by children may be partly because they are adult by the time they register a case ... Such adult-inclusive jurisdiction would also potentially improve and expand the jurisprudence of the Committee and increase the deterrent effect of its rulings.[600]

Another main issue of concern under the CRC-OP3 regards the inquiries that, according to Article 13(7), the Committee can conduct only if the interested State party has not opted out in contrast with Article 45 of the ACRWC, which does not provide for an opt-out option regarding investigations or inquiries by the African Committee of Experts that monitors implementation of the African Charter.[601] A State party to the CRC-OP3, in fact, can decline to recognise the Committee's competence to conduct inquiries into that State's alleged systematic and/or grave violations of the CRC and/or of one or both of its two Optional Protocols. By allowing a possible declaration from the State party opting out of the inquiry procedure the CRC-OP3 fails to fully protect children from some of the most severe human rights violations. Furthermore, even if the State accepts the Committee's jurisdiction in relation to an inquiry procedure under the CRC-OP3, consent is required for representatives of the Committee to conduct an on-site visit as part of the inquiry. The suggestion has been made by some that a visit to the State as part of the inquiry, if deemed necessary by the Committee, should be compulsory and not dependent on State's consent.[602]

Finally, as stressed by Grover, the CRC-OP3 does not foresee the possibility of transferring to the ICC information regarding systematic and grave violations against children, where the communication enshrines facts relevant to determining the individual's liability. This appears to be a serious drawback as there is a need, and potentially the opportunity, to establish a cooperative working relationship between the Committee and the ICC.[603] At the time of writing the Committee has not issued any views yet. The provision of Article 11 concerning the follow-up procedure is, however, inadequate to guarantee that States will deliver the reparations recommended by the Committee.[604] Ultimately, the shortcomings highlighted above are likely to significantly downsize the role the CRC-OP3, whose scope, as originally envisaged, was to provide child victims

600 Langford and Clark, above note 592.

601 Art. 45 of the ACRWC.

602 Langford and Clark, above note 592, at 24.

603 Grover, above note 589, at 306.

604 Art. 11 of the CRC-OP3 reads 'The State party shall give due consideration to the views of the Committee, together with its recommendations, if any, and shall submit to the Committee a written response, including information on any action taken and envisaged in the light of the views and recommendations of the Committee. The State party shall submit its response as soon as possible and within six months'.

with an effective procedure and a child-friendly venue for reparations, which is still lacking under the existing international legal framework.

5.3. CHILDREN'S RIGHT TO REPARATION BEFORE INTERNATIONAL TRIBUNALS AND COURTS

With the emergence of the international criminal justice system, accountability for the crimes under international law has been sought through a number of judicial means.[605] As already stressed in the previous chapters, during the last decade the international community has had to cope with large-scale human rights and humanitarian law violations often perpetrated against children. The primary responsibility for prosecuting those crimes, which due to their gravity constitute a threat to international peace, is borne by national courts.[606] Nevertheless, since in many countries affected by armed conflicts the infrastructure of the judicial system is often non-existent or inadequate, the international community has been charged with assisting States to end the culture of impunity and pursue justice.

The work of the first international tribunals set up to deal with international crimes has already been referred to in Chapter 3, especially with regard to its legacy in terms of scant victim participation. Departing from the Nuremberg Trials, the international and hybrid courts subsequently tasked with ensuring accountability for individual perpetrators have started to gradually adopt a different approach to victims, slowly recognising their role, their suffering and ultimately their right to obtain reparations. The degree of compliance with victims' rights has significantly increased, marking an upward phase of its trajectory from the *ad hoc* tribunals to the ICC. Nonetheless, when it comes to child victims, the following paragraphs will show that further efforts are urgently needed and that adequate, prompt and effective reparations are still little more than ink on paper.

5.3.1. A GLANCE AT THE INTERNATIONAL CRIMINAL TRIBUNAL FOR THE FORMER YUGOSLAVIA AND THE INTERNATIONAL CRIMINAL TRIBUNAL FOR RWANDA

The ICTY and the ICTR, nowadays 'replaced' by the so-called residual mechanism for international criminal tribunals, were both created to determine

605 See No Peace without Justice and UNICEF Innocenti Research Centre, 'International Criminal Justice and Children', September 2002, available at: http://www.unicef.org/emerg/files/ICJC.pdf.

606 See in general M.C. Bassiouni, 'Universal Jurisdiction for International Crimes: Historical Perspectives and Contemporary Practice', (2001) 42 *Virginia Journal of International Law* 81, at 82–162.

responsibility for the crimes committed during armed conflicts.[607] They had jurisdiction over natural persons without references to their age, unlike the ICC, since Article 26 of the Rome Statute clearly states that the Court shall have no jurisdiction over people who were under the age of 18 years at the time of the alleged commission of the crimes.[608] Neither of the *ad hoc* tribunals considered prosecuting children as they both focused their resources and efforts on prosecuting 'the persons responsible for serious violations of humanitarian law' and their jurisdiction was not limited by reference to the degree of responsibility of the accused.[609]

Although, in theory, children could have been prosecuted by the ICTY and the ICTR, in practice neither of the tribunals ever indicted a minor. Therefore, children could only play a role as witnesses and victims. In the first place it is worth mentioning that all the international courts and tribunals have some form of victims and witnesses unit ('VWU'), though the level of support they are able to provide varies considerably. In the case of the ICTY and the ICTR the significance of those units has been defined as 'quite modest'.[610] They were established with delay and hesitation by including specific provisions in the tribunals' RPEs and their early functioning was fully based on voluntary contributions.[611] Only at a later stage was the expenditure for these units finally incorporated into the overall regular budget, although voluntary contributions were still the most relevant source of funding. The limited role played by the VWUs of the ICTY and the ICTR reflects what was made clear in the majority of sentences issued by the *ad hoc* tribunals, namely that their primary scope is 'deterrence and punishment'. This approach is consistent with the scant

---

607 It does not fall within the purpose of the present work to explore the effectiveness of the *ad hoc* tribunals in fulfilling their mandate. For further reference, see L.A. Barria and S.D. Roper, 'How Effective are International Criminal Tribunals? An Analysis of the ICTY and the ICTR', (2005) 9 *The International Journal of Human Rights* 349; and also M.A. Drumbl, 'Punishment Post-Genocide: From Guilt to Shame to Civis in Rwanda', (2000) 75 *New York University Law Review* 1221, at 1222–1236.

608 C. van de Voorde and R. Barberet, 'Children and International Criminal Justice', in M. Natarajan (ed.), *International Crime and Justice*, Cambridge University Press, Cambridge, 2011, 41.

609 The Special Court for Sierra Leone instead only tried those who bore the greatest responsibility and since children usually did not occupy a position of leadership such a limitation can effectively prevent the prosecution of child perpetrators.

610 T. Ingadottir, F. Ngendahayo and P. Sellers, 'The Victims and Witnesses Unit', in T. Ingadottir (ed.), *The International Criminal Court: Recommendations on Policy and Practice*, Transnational Publishers, New York, 2003, 5.

611 'The VWU at the ICTR was established from resources available in the Tribunal's Voluntary Trust Fund ..., the ICTY's VWU was financially and professionally supported by the European Union and the Danish Rehabilitation and Research Centre for Torture Victims from 1995 to 1998, when the Tribunal assumed financial responsibility for the salaries of the staff participants. The ICTY and the ICTR's VWUs relied heavily on gratis staff on their early years.' Ibidem at 10.

attention paid to the implementation of the VWUs and victims' needs in general. Nevertheless, as noted by Evans 'the experiences of victims in the *ad hoc* tribunals have provided an impetus for advocacy towards recognition of victims' rights'.[612]

5.3.1.1. *Children as Witnesses before the* Ad Hoc *Tribunals*

Children's participation in the proceedings as witnesses was regulated by the RPE of the ICTY and ICTR. According to Rule 90 of the RPE of the two *ad hoc* tribunals,[613] a child witness who did not understand the significance of the solemn oath declared before giving evidence was allowed to testify without taking the oath if the Chamber believed the child sufficiently mature to report the facts within his/her knowledge.[614] Nevertheless, the judgment could not be based only on the unsworn testimony of the child. As it had to comply with the human rights standard on the right to a fair trial, the child's testimony needed to be further corroborated in order to be considered reliable. Notably, no corroboration was required in case of child victims of sexual assault.[615]

Besides Rule 90, the RPE of both tribunals did not contain any child-specific provisions, hence, in cases of child witnesses willing to testify before the ICTY or the ICTR the general provisions regarding the protection of witnesses and victims applied. Children did not testify before either of the *ad hoc* tribunals,[616] neither of the *ad hoc* tribunals was statutorily required to hire staff with proper expertise on child protection and children's rights as they generally referred to 'qualified staff'. However, both tribunals have dealt with cases involving crimes committed against children. In particular with regard to crimes of sexual violence that targeted also children and that were discussed before either the ICTY or the ICTR, the testimonies of the adult witnesses were considered sufficient and minors were not heard.[617] Nevertheless, in the *Krstìc* case held before the ICTY a witness aged 22 gave evidence of what occurred in Srebrenica when he was

---

612 Evans above note 47, at 89. On this point see Judgement of 10 December 1998, (1998) ICTY Case No. IT-95-17/1-T, §288; and also Judgment of 2 December 2003, (2003) ICTY, Case No. IT-02-60/1, §. 86.

613 Rule 90(b) of the ICTY RPE, and Rule 90(c) of the ICTR RPE.

614 There is no reference to the way such maturity was actually assessed by the Chamber.

615 See Rule 96 of the ICTY RPE and ICTR RPE.

616 The UN SC on 22 December 2010 established the Mechanism for International Criminal Tribunals ('MICT') to carry out a number of essential functions of the ICTY and ICTR after the completion of their respective mandates. The MICT branch of the ICTR is in Arusha and commenced functioning on 1 July 2012. The other branch is located in The Hague and has already inherited some functions from the ICTY. It commenced functioning on 1 July 2013; the ICTR was officially closed on 31 December 2015, whereas the ICTY is currently completing the pending appeals proceedings.

617 See Office of the Special Representative of the Secretary-General for Children and Armed conflict, Working Paper No 3, above note 152, at 14.

17 years old and in the *Foča* trials two girls, who were minors when they suffered from mass rape, also testified.[618] According to Bakker, in the ICTY jurisprudence the age and sex of the victims of crimes against humanity were specifically taken into account as an aggravating factor in the process of sentencing. The author referred in particular to the tribunal's judgment in the *Kunarac* case, where the Trial Chamber stated that the relatively youthful age of one victim, who was 20 years old, and the very young age of another, who was 12 years old, when the offences of rape and sexual enslavement were committed against them, were considered as an aggravating circumstance.[619]

5.3.1.2. *The Right to Reparation before the International Criminal Tribunal for the former Yugoslavia and the International Criminal Tribunal for Rwanda*

The primary concern of the drafters of the Statute and the RPE of the ICTY and the ICTR was to punish the individuals who had committed serious violations of international law.[620] To this end, while in some civil law jurisdictions the victims have *locus standi* to initiate civil claims within criminal proceedings, the *ad hoc* tribunals were mainly based on the adversarial system, where the victims were represented by the prosecution at any stage of the trial and their role was solely to appear as witnesses.[621]

The forms of reparations, mentioned in the Statute and its RPE, were compensation, restitution and rehabilitation. As for the first kind of reparation, according to Rule 106 victims should seek compensation before the national courts or other competent body, meaning that the *ad hoc* tribunals left to municipal fora the task of dealing with victims' requests.[622] The same approach was followed by

---

618 Before the ICTY approximately 4% of witnesses were in the age range of 18 to 30.

619 C. Bakker, 'Prosecuting International Crimes against Children: the Legal Framework', UNICEF Innocenti Research Centre, Innocenti Working Paper No. 2010-13, Florence, at 6: 'The Trial Chamber also held that "The fact that his offences were committed against particularly vulnerable and defenceless girls and a woman is a matter considered in aggravation". These considerations were confirmed on appeal. The Appeals Chamber also held that the Trial Chamber has "*an inherent discretion* to consider the victim's age as an aggravating factor"'.

620 This is clear from the words used in UNSC Resolution 827 (1993), which established the ICTY and stated that this tribunal was set up 'for the sole purpose of prosecuting persons responsible for serious violations of international law'. UN doc. S/RES/827 (1993).

621 See Chapter 3, Section 3.2.3 above.

622 Rule 106(b) states that 'pursuant to the relevant national legislation, a victim or persons claiming through the victim may bring an action in a national court or other competent body to obtain compensation'. In the drafting process of the RPE of the Tribunals, some attempt was made to address the issue of compensation. However, as noted by Cassese, this possibility was compromised due to the absence of a corresponding provision in the Statutes. See Cassese, above note 335, at 429.

the STL, which has incorporated in its Statute a similar provision.[623] Restitution instead could be provided directly by the ICTY and the ICTR in a special hearing, as stated in Rule 105.[624] According to de Brouwer, 'the most direct and accessible way for victims to receive restitution of property or the proceeds thereof seems to be by order of the Trial Chamber upon the determination of the rightful owner on the balance of the probabilities'.[625] Such a determination could be made by the Chamber only through a proper level of investigation, conducted mostly by the prosecution, during the pre-trial or the trial stages. If the Chamber failed to determine the legitimate ownership, the competent national authorities were required to take over the identification of the owner, upon which the Trial Chamber would order the restitution of the property. In both cases the Registrar was responsible for the transmission to the competent national authority of the orders for the restitution of the property and its proceeds, since the national authority was the one in charge of enforcing the orders. With regard to the third and last form of reparation, namely rehabilitation, it was enshrined in Rule 34 of the ICTR's RPE; while in the case of the ICTY the correspondent Rule 34 merely alluded to the mandate to provide 'counselling and support for them (the victims), in particular in cases of rape and sexual assault'. According to Rule 34 of the ICTR the establishment of the Victims and Witnesses Support Unit served the purpose of ensuring that victims received relevant support, including physical and psychological rehabilitation.[626]

Unlike the ICTY, the ICTR tried to address at least the most immediate and concrete necessities of the victims, in particular of those who suffered from sexual violence and found themselves in need of rehabilitative measures. In fact, some of the victims who appeared as witnesses before the ICTR were provided with medical assistance, including antiretroviral treatment in the case of HIV positive persons. The assistance, also provided after a trial, was granted only and exclusively to the victims who testified before the tribunal, stressing again that the ICTR, and the ICTY, were not capable of separating the concepts of 'victim' and 'witness'.[627]

It is noteworthy that there were a few attempts to change the victims' situation before the *ad hoc* tribunals. In particular, in November 2000 the ICTY and ICTR Prosecutor, Ms Carla del Ponte, addressing the UNSC, advocated the creation of

---

623 Art. 25 of the STL Statute.

624 See also Art. 24(3) of the ICTY Statute, mirrored by Art. 23(3) of the ICTR Statute, '[I]n addition to imprisonment, the Trial Chamber may order the return of any property and proceeds acquired by criminal conduct, including by means of duress, the rightful owner'.

625 See de Brouwer, above note 193, at 396.

626 Rule 34 of the ICTR RPE.

627 See Evans, above note 47, at 89 'As recognised by the former President Jorda of the ICTY, victims have largely been considered as "object-matter or an instrument" in the proceedings of the ad hoc Tribunals'.

a Claims Commission to compensate the victims.[628] At the same time, to endorse and enforce the request of the Prosecutor, the judges of the ICTY submitted a report to the UNSC. This report underlined the existence of a general trend under international law towards the recognition of an individual right to demand reparations and it recommended the creation of a body that could operate as an international compensation commission.[629] Moreover, the report affirmed that the victims of the crimes under the ICTY jurisdiction were clearly entitled to compensation and that, to avoid further delays in the proceedings, the best solution would not be to amend the tribunal's mandate, but rather to set up an external mechanism. The 'appeals' launched by the Prosecutor and the judges simply remained unheard as no official reply from the Security Council was ever issued. Nevertheless, these initiatives demonstrated a growing awareness of a strong necessity to broaden the scope of ICL and to create room for the exercise of victims' rights, especially their right to participate in the proceedings and ask for reparations.

Although not classifiable as either reparations or redress measures, both tribunals, years after their establishment, set up an outreach programme. The outreach programmes were created as trust funds outside the main tribunal budgets, which put them 'in a situation where they must constantly fight for their financial survival and divert resources to fundraising rather than outreaching'.[630] The ICTR outreach programme started in 1998 and the activities carried out included broadcasting proceedings of the tribunal on Rwandan national television and radio, arranging travel facilities to the tribunal and a monthly newsletter. The ICTY outreach programme began its work in 1999, by translating the tribunal's website and documents into Bosnian, Croatian and Serbian. Its range of activities appeared to be much wider than that accomplished by the ICTR outreach programme, as it encompassed also the organisation of conferences, roundtables and training seminars across the former Yugoslavia, including events specially crafted for high school and university students meant

---

628 Address by the Prosecutor of the ICTY/ICTR, Carla del Ponte, to the Security Council on 21 November 2000, ICTY Press Release JL/P.I.S./542-e, '[I]t is regrettable that the Tribunals' statutes ... make only a minimum of provision for compensation and restitution to people whose lives have been destroyed ... my office is having considerable success in tracing and freezing large amounts of money in the personal accounts of the accused. Money that could very properly be applied by the courts to the compensation of the citizens who deserve it ... I would therefore respectfully suggest to the Council that the present system falls short of delivering justice to the people of Rwanda and the former Yugoslavia, and I would invite you to give serious and urgent consideration to any change that would remove this lacuna', available at: www.un.org/icty/pressreal/p542-e.htm.

629 See generally Evans above note 47, at 207.

630 See Lawyers Committee for Human Rights, 'Effective Public Outreach for the International Criminal Court, Lawyers Committee for Human Rights', January 2004, available at: https://www.humanrightsfirst.org/wp-content/uploads/pdf/outreach_brief_paper011404.pdf.

to fulfil the tribunal's mandate to contribute to achieving lasting peace as well as reconciliation.[631] The ICTY outreach programme's activities with a focus on education and information represented the only concrete effort made to assist, although to a very limited extent, young people raised in a country deeply affected by war and ethnic conflicts.

5.3.2. THE SPECIAL COURT FOR SIERRA LEONE AND CHILD VICTIMS

The armed conflict in Sierra Leone lasted from 1991 to 2002. The Sierra Leonean war was marked, probably more than any other conflict, by the brutality and over-abundance of the crimes committed against children. The SCSL was set up in 2002 as part of the international agreement between the government and the UN, and found itself in the difficult position of dealing with the prosecution of crimes that most of all affected the civilian population. The SCSL completed its mandate in 2013 and since then has transitioned to a residual mechanism.[632]

In response to the escalation of violence and terror perpetrated throughout the country for more than ten years, a complex transitional justice process was established, which included the TRC, charged with investigating the roots of the conflict and making recommendations for the future, and the SCSL, a so-called 'hybrid' retributive judicial body, characterised by extensive national involvement, both in substantive and in practical terms. Unlike the ICTY and the ICTR, the efforts of the SCSL were explicitly directed towards the people who bore the greatest responsibility for the crimes committed during the war. Nevertheless, due to the significant number of child perpetrators involved in the hostilities,[633] the SCSL had jurisdiction over persons aged 15 years at the time of the alleged commission of the crimes.[634] Notwithstanding the provision

---

631 For further details on the ICTY outreach activities, see http://www.icty.org/sections/Outreach/OutreachActivities.

632 On the legacy of the SCSL see C. Chernor Jalloh (ed.), *The Sierra Leone Special Court and its Legacy: The Impact for Africa and International Criminal Law*, Cambridge University Press, Cambridge, 2015.

633 'UNICEF estimates that 15,000 to 30,000 children were involved in combat activities during the conflict in Sierra Leone. While some of these children may have been used as spies, labourers or sex slaves, many of them played a key role in combat as well.' See K. Sanin and A. Stirneman, *Child Witnesses at the Special Court for Sierra Leone*, War Crimes Study Centre University of Berkeley, March 2006, at 6, available at: http://wcsc.berkeley.edu/wp-content/uploads/documents/ChildWitnessReport_000.pdf.

634 See Art. 7(1) of the Statute of the SCSL: 'The Special Court shall have no jurisdiction over any person who was under the age of 15 at the time of the alleged commission of the crime. Should any person who was at the time of the alleged commission of the crime between

enshrined in its Statute, the Court never contemplated prosecuting people who were minors when the conflict occurred, partly because its mandate targeted unequivocally the 'leaders', and partly because of the complexity of a child soldier's status as, first and foremost, a 'victim'.[635] Therefore the Statute specifically set out two crimes for which the victimisation of a child is a material element, namely conscription and enlistment of children younger than 15 into armed forces or their use as active participants in the hostilities and the abuse of girls under the 1926 Prevention of Cruelty to Children Act, including abuse of girls younger than 14 and abduction of girls for immoral purposes.[636]

With regard to the conscription, enlistment and use of children, the Court was extensively questioned about its authority and jurisdiction to prosecute the accused of this crime. The issue immediately arose during the first trial held before the SCSL, the *Hinga Norman* case, which started in June 2004. Prior to the beginning of the proceedings the defence team argued that the recruitment of child soldiers was not a crime under international law at the time of the alleged commission of the offence, and, since Article 1(1) limits the Court's authority to deal only with the crimes committed in the territory of Sierra Leone since 30 November 1996, the indictment violated the principle of non-retroactivity of criminal law, traditionally expressed with the Latin maxim *nullum crimen sine lege*.[637] In particular in the Preliminary Motion, the defence for Mr Hinga Norman claimed that child soldiers' enlistment did not attain the status of a war crime until the entry into force of the Rome Statute and the Optional Protocol to the CRC on the involvement of children in armed conflict. Furthermore, the defence claimed that there was not adequate State practice condemning the enlistment of children under 15 years of age prior to the enactment of these two treaties to justify the existence of customary international law.[638] The Appeals Chamber, in response, stated that the prohibition on recruiting children to take part in hostilities had become part of customary international law even before 1996. To support this statement the Court cited the CRC, the Geneva Conventions and the ACRWC, and it stressed that child recruitment was criminalised before it was outlined as a criminal prohibition in treaty law because in any case 'a norm

---

15 and 18 years of age come before the Court, he or she shall be treated with dignity and a sense of worth, taking into account his or her young age and the desirability of promoting his or her rehabilitation, reintegration into and assumption of a constructive role in society, and in accordance with international human rights standards, in particular the rights of the child.'

635 See McDonald, above note 267, at 591.

636 See Art. 4(c) and Art. 5(a) of the Statute of the SCSL. See V. Oosterveld, 'The Special Court for Sierra Leone's Consideration of Gender-based Violence: Contributing to Transitional Justice?', (2009) 10 *Human Rights Review* 73, at 74. According to the author an estimated 215,000–275,000 women and girls may have been subjected to at least one form of gender-based violence during the Sierra Leonean conflict.

637 See Judgment of 26 June 2003, (2003) SCSL, Case No. SCSL-2003-08-PT.

638 See McBride, above note 195, at 95.

does not need to be explicitly stated in an international treaty for it to crystallise as a crime under customary international law'.[639] The Appeals Chamber further determined that effective criminalisation had occurred sometime between 1994 and 1996, as this was the period during which the majority of States criminalised this conduct.

5.3.2.1. *Children's Participation in the Trials before the Special Court for Sierra Leone*

Thus far only a few children have appeared as witnesses before international and hybrid tribunals, nevertheless the SCSL distinguished itself in this field by adopting several procedures and measures to ensure witness protection for young people in an attempt to avoid re-traumatisation. The issue of balancing fair trial standards with the need to give voice to the most vulnerable victims, who are often accused of giving tainted evidence and of being influenced by adults, has also emerged with regard to the work of the SCSL. In the first place it is interesting to note that the Court conferred a broad meaning on the notion of 'child witness'. The prosecution's principal criterion to determine whether or not a witness could be regarded as a 'child witness' was his/her past as child soldier. Therefore the individual's current age did not appear in the equation, meaning that the Court mostly focused on the personal history and vulnerability of the witness.[640] The prosecution teams could decide to include a witness in the child witnesses' category (named category B) if one of the following circumstances occurred: when the witness him/herself claimed to know his/her age; the age had been determined during the demobilisation process; the legal guardian knew the age of the alleged child witness; or, as already mentioned, the person was a child soldier.

Once a witness was classified as a child witness he/she was entitled to benefit from the special measures set up by the SCSL. Article 16(4) of the Statute established the Witnesses and Victims Services Unit ('WVSU') within the Registry. According to this provision the WVSU provided counselling and assistance to all the witnesses, including children. Rule 34 of the RPE further stated that the WVSU was in charge of developing both short- and long-term plans for witnesses' protection and support. According to Rule 69(b) the Trial

639 Judgment of 31 May 2004 (Decision on Preliminary Motion Based on Lack of Jurisdiction (Child Recruitment)), (2004) SCSL, Case No. SCSL-2004-14-AR72(E). The assumption that individual criminal responsibility can exist notwithstanding lack of treaty provisions specifically referring to criminal liability had already been made clear in the *Tadic* case before the ICTY; see Judgment of 2 October 1995 (Jurisdiction Decision), (1995) ICTY, Case No. IT-94-1-AR72, §94.

640 As noted in Section 5.2 above, the CRC-OP3 instead considers 'child victims' only those who are still minors when they submit a complaint to the Committee on the Rights of the Child.

Chamber should consult the WVSU with regard to the protective measures needed during the trial, which encompassed, for example, the non-disclosure of a victim's identity and testimony via videolink from a different room.[641]

In order to enhance and guarantee child witnesses' protection, the SCSL had to design, relying on UNICEF's expertise, a set of guidelines able to promote children's active participation without jeopardising their efforts to overcome the traumatic events that had occurred. In the first place the WVSU, the Office of the Prosecution and the experts from UNICEF identified suitable child witnesses among those who were more resilient and already resettled with their families or communities. Secondly, UNICEF provided special training to both prosecution and defence investigators in order to make them able to interrogate the child witnesses, taking into account their best interests, and accordingly the guidelines developed. The exercise of children's right to participation, as enshrined in Article 12 of the CRC, was subjected to the full consent of the child and his/her parents or legal guardian. Since many children were still displaced when the Court started its work and the first witnesses were selected, the consent was often given by the child and the child protection agency responsible for taking care of him/her during the process of demobilisation. Upon confirmation of the child witness, he/she was then brought to Freetown and placed under the care of the WVSU. Child witnesses, although separated from adult witnesses, were accommodated in the so-called 'safe houses', assigned also to adult witnesses who, according to the investigators, were threatened and could not remain within their own community.[642] Immediately after arrival, the qualified staff of the WVSU used to provide children with psychosocial support and relevant information about the process and its procedures.[643] Children, exactly like adult witnesses, received an allowance for their service before the Court, an allowance that corresponded to 16,000 Leones per day, the equivalent of US$5.25.[644] Notwithstanding the fact

641 See also Rules 75 and 85 of the SCSL RPE, amended in May 2005. The option to testify in camera or via videolink was available for all vulnerable witnesses, including children, nevertheless neither the Statute nor the RPE specified children's vulnerability. However the Trial Chambers have ruled that child witnesses under 18 always had the opportunity to testify using these methods rather than appearing in the courtroom.

642 R. Horn, S. Vahidy and S. Charters, 'Testifying in the Special Court for Sierra Leone: Witness Perceptions of Safety and Emotional Welfare', (2011) 17 *Psychology, Crime & Law* 435, at 443. According to the authors, 'the witness remains in the safe house until after they have testified. Following their testimony, some are relocated within Sierra Leone, and others are relocated abroad within the West Africa region. WVS covers the expenses of relocation and provides the witness with a one-off "start-up" payment. In practice, the vast majority of witnesses are not deemed as being under a high "perceived threat", although their security status is always open to review. Most witnesses receive no services until the testimony date is imminent.'

643 Ibidem, at 444.

644 The allowance corresponds to the daily salary of a UN General Service 1, step 1 level employee in Sierra Leone.

that the amount of the allowance was in line with the witness compensation scheme adopted also by the ICTY and the ICTR, the payments made by the SCSL to its witnesses have attracted much criticism, mostly due to the chronic poverty of the country and the huge gap existing between the allowance and the average salary received by workers in the public and private sectors. In particular with regard to children, one of the main concerns expressed by UNICEF pertained to the individualistic approach followed by the Court, which privileged the payment of benefits to each child witness rather than the development of a comprehensive strategic plan able to trigger the reintegration and rehabilitation of many child witnesses. In commenting on the procedure adopted by the SCSL, UNICEF also raised another important point, namely that child witnesses after the trial appeared 'ill-equipped for the reality of the life in Sierra Leone', as they normally went back to school with clothes and supplies that prompted the classmates to think that the child in question was a former child soldier.[645]

The benefits awarded to child witnesses were not considered as redress measures for the harm suffered during the war, but simply as benefits stemming from the cooperation with the Court. In fact, the issue of reparation was not raised at all during the discussion on the establishment of the SCSL and it seems that it was not even remotely contemplated that the Court could play a role in this respect.[646]

5.3.2.2. *Assessing Children's (Lack of) Right to Reparation before the Special Court for Sierra Leone*

As underlined in the previous paragraph, children's participation was not only allowed by the SCSL, but to some extent the Court even boosted children's active involvement, marking a new path subsequently followed by the ICC. Nevertheless, unlike the ICC, the SCSL did not seek to fulfil victims' right to reparation. Instead the SCSL focused on the prosecution of the people who bore the greatest responsibilities for the crimes committed during the civil war and, incidentally, it strengthened the participation of witnesses, including children, who were finally able to confront their perpetrators before an international judicial forum in order make their voice heard. Children's rights in international proceedings cannot be satisfied solely by providing them with the possibility to take part in the trials as witnesses. Nor can the allowance lavished upon them by the SCSL be regarded as a compensation for the suffering experienced. As stressed above, the Statute of the Special Court for Sierra Leone did not contain any provision that

645 Ibidem.

646 See W. Schabas, 'Reparation Practice in Sierra Leone and the Truth and Reconciliation Commission', in De Feyter et al, above note 22, 289, at 295.

entitled the victims to claim for reparations. The only exception is represented by Article 19(3) of the Statute, affirming that '[I]n addition to imprisonment, the Trial Chamber may order the forfeiture of the property, proceeds and any assets acquired unlawfully or by criminal conduct, and their return to their rightful owner or to the State of Sierra Leone'.[647] However, the Court did not exercise this ability.[648] As noted by Clark, the diamond industry funded and fuelled the armed conflict in Sierra Leone, but the SCSL did not indict any of the businessmen who benefitted from the crimes committed and who, arguably, possessed assets that could have been used by the State to provide reparations to the victims.[649] Moreover, the Court in the *Taylor* case missed an excellent opportunity to apply Article 19(3),[650] as the former Liberian President is one of the very few wealthy people among those convicted of genocide, war crimes and crimes against humanity in the modern international criminal courts and tribunals. In fact, as will emerge in relation to the ICC jurisprudence, one of the main obstacles to reparations within the ICL framework is represented by the indigence of the perpetrators, who are often not able to contribute to victims' redress.

Mr Taylor was convicted on 11 counts. In five counts he was charged with crimes against humanity, in five counts with violations of Article 3 Common to the Geneva Conventions, and in one count he was charged with other serious violations of IHL, namely conscripting, enlisting or using children under the age of 15 years to participate in hostilities.[651] In the *Taylor* case both the Trial and the Appeals Chamber found that the RUF/AFRC leadership, which Mr Taylor aided and abetted, had instituted an organised system for the abduction, conscription, training and use of child soldiers, and further engaged in the abduction, military training, and use of children.[652] There was a consistent pattern of abducting children and forcing them into Small Boys Units ('SBUs') and Small Girls Units ('SGUs'), which were made up of children generally in the range of 5 to 17 years. The existence of specific combat units designated for children further demonstrated the institutionalised nature of conscription and use of children by the RUF/AFRC. Nonetheless, the age of the victims of the crime of conscription,

---

647 Art. 19(3) of the Statute of the SCSL.

648 See T. Clark, 'Assessing the Special Court's Contribution to Achieving Transitional Justice', in Chernor Jalloh, above note 632, 746, at 765.

649 Ibidem.

650 On the *Taylor* trial see M. Frulli, 'Piercing the Veil of Head-of-State Immunity: The Taylor Trial and Beyond', in Chernor Jalloh above note 632, 325, at 326–330. See also K. Ambos and O. Njikam, 'Charles Taylor's Criminal Responsibility', (2013) 11 *Journal of International Criminal Justice* 789, at 790–791; M. Glasius and T. Meijers, 'Constructions of Legitimacy: The Charles Taylor Trial', (2012) 6 *International Journal of Transitional Justice* 229, at 233–237; and O. Njikam, *The Contribution of the Special Court for Sierra Leone to the Development of International Humanitarian Law*, Duncker & Humblot, Berlin, 2013.

651 Art. 4 of the Statute of the SCSL.

652 Judgment of 26 September 2013 (Trial Judgment), (2013) SCSL, Case No. SCSL-03-01-A, §1603.

enlistment and use in hostilities was not included among the aggravating factors identified by the Trial Chamber and endorsed by the Appeals Chamber.[653] In particular it is a pity that neither Mr Taylor's special status and responsibility at the highest level nor his exploitation of the Sierra Leonean conflict for financial gain were analysed against the backdrop of crimes committed against children; such analysis could have resulted in the determination of a further aggravating factor and it could have drawn more attention to the issue of reparations.

5.3.3. THE INTERNATIONAL CRIMINAL COURT: PRELIMINARY CAVEATS

According to its Statute the ICC has jurisdiction over the most serious crimes of concern to the international community as a whole, namely genocide, war crimes, crimes against humanity and, from 2017, the crime of aggression.[654] Like the SCSL Statute, the Rome Statute explicitly includes and outlines crimes committed *against* children.

The concept of child victim, read in light of the definition enshrined in Rule 85(a) of the ICC RPE, applies to every human being under the age of 18 years who has suffered from genocide, crimes against humanity and war crimes.[655] The Rome Statute encompasses all the typologies of crimes against children introduced in Chapter 2, namely child-specific crimes, crimes which target children in such a way that they are disproportionally victimised in comparison to the adult population and crimes with particularly serious effects on children.[656] Article 6(e) criminalises as genocide the forcible transfer of children from one group to another with the intent to destroy, in whole or in part, a national, ethnic or racial group as such; Article 7(1)(c) outlaws widespread or systematic enslavement, including trafficking in children, while Article 8(2)(b)(xxvi), (e)(vii) lists as war crimes the conscription, enlistment or use to actively participate in hostilities of child soldiers under the age of 15 years, both in international and non-international armed conflicts. As for the second category of crimes, those which affect children disproportionally, the Rome Statute condemns intentional attacks against non-military objectives such as buildings dedicated to religion, education, art, science or charitable purposes (Article 8(2)(b)(xxiv), (e)(ii)) and also attacks against personnel, installations, material, units or vehicles involved

653 Ibidem, §667.

654 M. Politi, 'The ICC and the Crime of Aggression: A Dream that Came Through and the Reality Ahead', (2012) 10 *Journal of International Criminal Justice* 267, 270–278. See also C. McDougall, *The Crime of Aggression under the Rome Statute of the International Criminal Court*, Cambridge University Press, Cambridge, 2013.

655 See also Rule 85(b).

656 See Chapter 2, Section 2.1 above.

in a humanitarian assistance or UN peacekeeping missions (Article 8(2)(b)(iii), (e)(iii)). Finally, the wrongful conduct which falls within the third category of crimes, is criminalised under Articles 7(1)(g) and 8(2)(b)(xxii), (e)(vi), according to which rape, sexual slavery, enforced prostitution, forced pregnancy, enforced sterilisation and other forms of sexual violence amount to both war crimes and crimes against humanity.

With regard to the ICC jurisdiction *ratione personae*, the Rome Statute provides that the Court only has jurisdiction over natural persons.[657] The question of pursuing non-natural persons was raised during the treaty's negotiations. However, the discussion on this subject raised disagreements among many States and in the end it was decided not to integrate this competence into the Rome Statute.[658] The Court operates in accordance with the principle of complementarity, meaning that it intervenes only if the State that has jurisdiction is genuinely unwilling or unable to carry out the investigation or prosecution.[659] This distinguishes the ICC from other ICL mechanisms, including the ICTY and the ICTR.[660] The Rome Statute recognises that States have the first responsibility and right to prosecute international crimes and that domestic courts shall act as the primary vehicle to implement ICL.[661] The principle of complementarity is based both on respect for the primary jurisdiction of States and on considerations of efficiency and effectiveness because States will generally have the best access to evidence and witnesses and the resources to carry out investigations and prosecutions. As a result the ICC may only exercise jurisdiction as a court of last resort, where national legal systems fail to do so, including where they manifest the intention to act but in reality are unwilling or unable to genuinely carry out proceedings.[662] Pursuant to the Rome Statute, the Prosecutor can initiate an investigation on the basis of a referral from any State party or from the UNSC.[663] In addition, the Prosecutor can initiate investigations *proprio motu* on the basis of information on crimes within the jurisdiction of the Court received from

---

657 Art. 25(1) of the Rome Statute.

658 On this point Clapham, above note 84, at 919.

659 On the functioning of the ICC, see generally A. Cassese, P. Gaeta and J.R.W.D. Jones (eds.), *The Rome Statute of the International Criminal Court: A Commentary*, vol. I, Oxford University Press, Oxford, 2002.

660 On the difference between the principle of primacy and the principle of complementarity, see M.M. El Zeidy, 'From Primacy to Complementarity and Backwards: (Re)-Visiting Rule 11 *Bis* of the *Ad Hoc* Tribunals', (2008) 57 *International and Comparative Law Quarterly* 403, 405–415.

661 The Preamble of the Rome Statute reiterates the essential duty of every State to exercise its criminal jurisdiction over those responsible for international crimes and emphasises that the ICC jurisdiction 'shall be complementary to national criminal jurisdictions'. See also M.S. Ellis, 'International Justice and the Rule of Law: Strengthening the ICC through Domestic Prosecutions', (2009) 1 *Hague Journal on the Rule of Law* 79, at 81.

662 Art. 17 of the Rome Statute.

663 See Art. 13 and Art. 14 of the Rome Statute.

individuals or organisations.[664] To date, four States parties to the Rome Statute, namely Uganda, the DRC, the Central African Republic and Mali, have referred situations on their territories to the Court. In addition, the Security Council has referred the situation in Darfur, Sudan, and the situation in Libya, which are both non-parties to the Rome Statute.

At the time of writing the ICC has convicted two perpetrators, Mr Lubanga Dyilo and Mr Katanga. In the *Lubanga* case the decision on reparations was issued by Trial Chamber I and subsequently modified by the Appeals Chamber; in the *Katanga* case a decision on possible reparations to victims has not been rendered yet. In particular, with regard to the *Katanga* case it should be noted that Trial Chamber II ultimately found Mr Germain Katanga guilty, as an accessory, within the meaning of Article 25(3)(d) of the Rome Statute, of one count of crimes against humanity, i.e. murder, and four counts of war crimes, i.e. murder, attacking a civilian population, destruction of property and pillaging committed on 24 February 2003 during the attack on the village of Bogoro, in the Ituri district of the DRC. Trial Chamber II thus acquitted Mr Katanga of the other charges that he was facing, also which included the use of children under the age of 15 years to take part in hostilities.

Pre-Trial Chamber I found that there was sufficient evidence to establish substantial grounds to believe that the war crime under Article 8(2)(b)(xxvi) was committed by Germain Katanga, who had consistently used children under the age of 15 years to participate actively in hostilities prior to, during and following the 24 February 2003 attack on the village of Bogoro.[665] Pre-Trial Chamber I stated that children were not only fully integrated into the militias during the fighting on 24 February 2003 but were also used by Mr Katanga and other Front for Patriotic Resistance in Ituri's commanders as part of an escort or personal bodyguards. Trial Chamber II, however, reached a different conclusion.

The Chamber agreed with the findings of Pre-Trial I that children were present in the armed forces operating in Ituri, including in the ranks of the Ngiti militia, as of 2002 and also during the period of hostilities in which the 24 February 2003 battle of Bogoro took place. Furthermore, Trial Chamber II was able to establish that children, who were referred to locally as 'kadogos' and who, in some cases, were estimated to be under the age of 15 years, were among the Ngiti combatants at the attack on Bogoro and participated not only in the fighting, but also in certain acts of violence meted out to the local population and its property. Moreover, Trial Chamber II found that, shortly after 24 February 2003, there were children among the militia members at the camp where an eyewitness was, although it was impossible to determine whether they were under the age of

664 Art. 15 of the Rome Statute.

665 Judgment of 30 September 2008 (Pre-Trial Chamber Decision on the confirmation of charges), (2008) ICC, Case No. ICC-01/04-01/07, §§253–258.

15 years. Thus, Trial Chamber II ultimately concluded that it was not in a position to establish a direct nexus between Mr Katanga and the children under the age of 15 who participated in the hostilities connected to the battle of Bogoro that would demonstrate that he used them for military purposes.[666]

In the *Lubanga* case, on the contrary, the entire prosecutorial strategy was built on the crime of recruitment, conscription and use of child soldiers to participate in hostilities. The decision on reparations issued by the ICC in the *Lubanga* case represents a milestone in the history of victims within the ICL framework and it is also clear evidence of the Court's growing interest in child victims.[667]

Just like the SCSL, the ICC has fully recognised the abhorrence of the crimes committed against children, but differently from the other international tribunals the ICC has also stressed the need to *empower* the children affected by those offences, making them not only able to testify, but also to apply for so-called 'victim status' and to claim for reparations.

5.3.3.1. *Children as 'Victims' before the International Criminal Court*

The ICC recognises as 'vulnerable victims' children, elderly persons, persons with disabilities and victims of sexual or gender violence.[668] Article 68 of the Rome Statute specifies that

> [t]he Court shall take appropriate measures to protect the safety, physical and psychological wellbeing, dignity and privacy of victims and witnesses. In so doing, the Court shall have regard to all relevant factors, including age, gender as defined in article 7(3),[669] and health, and the nature of the crime, in particular, but not limited to, where the crime involves sexual or gender violence or violence against children.

In line with the general definition of vulnerability adopted in this book,[670] this provision recognises that some factors may lead to the exposure to uninsured risks, both biological and environmental, the latter encompassing also the risk of being re-traumatised following the participation in a judicial proceeding.[671]

---

666 Judgment of 7 March 2014 (Judgment Pursuant to Article 74 of the Statute), (2014) ICC (Trial Chamber II), Case No. ICC-01/04-01/07, §§1074–1085.

667 See C. Chamberlain, *Children and the International Criminal Court, Analysis of the Rome Statute through a Children's Rights Perspective*, Intersentia, Antwerp, 2015, 145.

668 Art. 68 of the Rome Statute and Rule 86 of the RPE.

669 Art. 7(3) of the Rome Statute clarifies that 'For the purpose of this Statute, it is understood that the term "gender" refers to the two sexes, male and female, within the context of society. The term gender does not indicate any meaning different from the above.'

670 On the definition of vulnerability see Chapter 2, Section 2.4 above.

671 See H. Hamzei, 'Child Victims before the International Criminal Court: Avenue to Justice for the Most Vulnerable?', in L. Hopkins, M. Macleod and W.C. Turgeon (eds.) *Negotiating Childhoods*, Inter-Disciplinary Press, Oxford, 2011, at 115.

Bearing this caveat in mind, through the conferring of 'victim status' the ICC offers an 'alternative and innovative mechanism, which may be less stressful for a child and is less likely to cause re-traumatisation'.[672] Nevertheless, to be granted victim status, which permits participation in the trial without being a witness, some requirements need to be met. In the first place child victims, like adult victims, must have suffered harm, including physical or mental injury, emotional suffering, economic loss, or substantial impairment of fundamental rights through acts or omissions that constitute gross violations of human rights law or serious violations of humanitarian law.[673] Secondly, according to Article 68(3) of the Rome Statute, in order for the views and concerns of the victim to be legitimately presented and considered, at stages of the proceedings determined to be 'appropriate' by the Court, his/her personal interests have to be affected.[674] The way the provision was formulated during the negotiations phase, which led to the adoption of the Rome Statute, has left the concept of 'personal interests' undefined and therefore the task of shedding light on the scope of victims' participation has been entirely deferred to the bench's decisions.[675]

The findings of the Court can be summarised by affirming that the procedural status of victims, in the case of natural persons, may be assigned to those applicants who have suffered harm if two conditions are satisfied, namely that the crime from which the harm resulted must fall within the jurisdiction of the Court and that it must be included in the charges being tried.[676] In particular with regard to the latter point, namely the necessary existence of a link between the harm alleged by the victims and the charges against the accused person, it is noteworthy that the ICC in its first case had originally adopted a broader approach, allowing the potential participation of all the victims of the crimes under the Court's jurisdiction perpetrated in the DRC and not only of those crimes contained in the charges brought against Mr Lubanga. Writing in dissent, Judge René Blattmann stressed how such a ploy transgressed the fundamental

672 See UNICEF and No Peace without Justice, above note 605, at 18.

673 Ibidem.

674 See A. Zammit Borda, 'The Role of Victims in the First Trial of the International Criminal Court', (2010) 9 *Trinity College Dublin Journal of Postgraduate Studies* 20, at 24–34. According to the author the configuration of Art. 68(3) is based on paragraph 6(b) of the Declaration of Basic Principles of Justice for Victims of Crime and Abuse of Power, adopted by the UNGA in November 1985.

675 See on this point C.H. Chung, 'Victims' Participation at the International Criminal Court: Are Concessions of the Court Clouding the Promise?' (2008) 6 *Northwestern Journal of International Human Rights* 459, at 465–545. See with regard to the *Lubanga* case, Decision of 18 January 2008 (Decision on Victims' Participation), (2008) ICC, Doc. ICC-01/04-01/06-1119, §58.

676 On the ICC reparations regime see Redress, 'Justice for Victims: the ICC's Reparations Mandate', May 2011, available at: http://www.redress.org/downloads/publications/REDRESS_ICC_Reparations_May2011.pdf.

principles of ICL, in particular the principle of legality according to which the status of 'victim' and the consequent rights of participation and reparation have to be linked to the charges confirmed against the accused person. In his view the full respect of the principles of criminal justice is instrumental to the recognition of victims as right holders rather than as mere beneficiaries of the Court's concession and in order for victims' participation to be meaningful this must be strictly regulated in accordance with the Rome Statute.[677] The ICC's current orientation, corroborated by the Appeals Chamber, has definitely leant towards a restricted interpretation of Rule 85(a), which, read together with Article 68(3) of the Rome Statute, admits exclusively the participation of the victims, direct or indirect, who can demonstrate a nexus between the harm experienced and the particular crimes charged.[678] If this criterion is met, a child, *or* someone acting on his/her behalf, can finally apply.[679] The status of victim bestows on the child the right to have a highly qualified legal representative who advocates for him/her before the ICC, to benefit from the same protective measures prescribed for child witnesses and to claim for reparations. The procedure to attain victim status requires the completion of the paperwork and proof of the child's identity. According to Regulation 86 of the Court's Regulations all the victims have to submit a written application to the Registrar. If the application is successful, in the sense that the applicant has been acknowledged as a victim, then he/she can participate in the trial and/or claim for reparations. The acquisition of victim status, which can be relatively easy for an adult, is still very complicated in the case of child victims. The first difficulty, in fact, arises when the child has to prove his/her identity. In some countries obtaining such a document is similar to an obstacle race, which goes far beyond the efforts sustainable by a child. Pre-Trial Chamber II in the Situation of Uganda asked the Victims Participation and Reparation Section ('VPRS') to carefully examine the concrete availability of identification documents under the Ugandan law. The results are enshrined in a report that addresses all the main concerns, especially with regard to children who are unable to travel on their own and to bear the expenses related to the

677 See Decision of 18 January 2008 (Decision on Victims' Participation), Separate and Dissenting Opinion of Judge René Blattman to Decision on Victims' Participation (2008) ICC, Doc. ICC-01/04-01/06-1119, §21.

678 See ICC, Judgment of 11 July 2008 (the Appeals of the Prosecutor and the Defence against Trial Chamber I's Decision on Victims' Participation of 18 January 2008), (2008) ICC, Doc. ICC-01/04-01/06-1432.

679 In the *Lubanga* case the ICC has accepted applications submitted on behalf of the child victims by community leaders, civil society organisations and teachers. Whoever acts on behalf of the child needs to obtain the child's informed consent and, due to the fact that children during the conflicts are often separated from their families or left orphans, in the Rome Statute there is no requirement that the legal representative has to be a parent or the legal guardian. See Decision of 15 December 2008 (Decision on the Applications by Victims to Participate in the Proceedings) (2008) ICC, Doc. ICC-01/04-01/06 21/41, §67.

document's release.[680] According to the wording of the application form, the proof of identity can generally be established through the submission of different documents such as passport, driving licence, a letter from a local authority or even tax document. Since for many children it may be really difficult, or even impossible, to obtain one of the documents listed above, the ICC's Chambers have decided to admit as proof of identity also family registration booklets, pupil identity cards, school documents and documents issued in rehabilitation centres for children associated with armed groups.[681]

The ICC has ultimately interpreted victims' participation as to include the following activities: attend hearings; make oral motions, responses, and submissions; file written submissions; access evidence; ask questions; submit evidence; call witnesses; and to be notified of issues or proceedings which affect them.[682]

5.3.3.2. *Children as Witnesses before the International Criminal Court*

As stated in the Manual for Legal Representatives redacted by the OPCV of the ICC, victims who participate in the proceedings and witnesses are entitled to enjoy protective measures, which are of primary importance in order to encourage them to communicate with the Court and to testify without endangering their security. However, these measures cannot be applied in a manner which is prejudicial to or inconsistent with the rights of the suspect or accused and a fair and impartial trial.[683] Article 43(6) of the Rome Statute provided for the creation of a VWU within the Registry in order to assist and advise victims and witnesses, as well as Chambers and participants, on protective measures and security arrangements.[684] The protection also extends to persons who are at risk

---

680 See the Victims Participation and Reparations Section, 'Report on the Identity Documents Available in the Ugandan Legal and Administrative System and other Supporting Documentation for Applications for Participation in Proceedings in Uganda', 12 October 2007, ICC-02/04-125-Anx, at 10.

681 Decision of 3 July 2008 (Decision on the applications for participation filed in connection with the investigation in the Democratic Republic of Congo by Applicants a/0047/06 to a/0052/06, a/0163/06 to a/0187/06, a/0221/06, a/0226/06, a/0231/06 to a/0233/06, a/0237/06 to a/0239/06, and a/0241/06 to a/0250/06) (2008) ICC, Decision no. ICC-01/04-505, §18.

682 Rules 91–92 and 144 RPE. See Decision of 22 January 2010 (Decision on the Modalities of Victim Participation at Trial), (2010) *ICC*, Decision No. ICC-01/04-01/07-1788; Decision of 12 December 2008 (Fourth Decision on Victim's Participation), (2008) *ICC*, Decision No. ICC-01/05-01/08-320.

683 The Office of Public Counsel for Victims, 'Representing Victims before the International Criminal Court: A Manual for Legal Representatives', 2nd edn. December 2012, at 31 (hereinafter 'the Manual for Legal Representatives').

684 This Unit is the only one expressly mentioned in the Rome Statute with regard to the protection of victims and witnesses.

on account of testimony given by someone else, for example the family members of the witnesses, and generally to persons at risk because of their interaction with the Court.

Concerning the protective and special measures, in line with the general principle enshrined in Rule 86 of the RPE, the ICC has recognised that there are particular special needs to be taken into account for some categories of victims participating in the proceedings, namely children and elderly victims, victims with disabilities, and victims of sexual and gender violence. As stated in Rule 88 of the RPE, the Chambers may order special measures to assist victims and witnesses, including measures to facilitate the testimony of a traumatised victim or witness, again children, the elderly, disabled persons and victims of sexual and gender violence.[685] In addition to internal structural arrangements to protect witnesses, the ICC is mandated to apply in-court protective measures to protect vulnerable witnesses under the Statute and RPE. Furthermore, according to Rule 88(5) of the RPE, Judges may also apply 'special measures' to protect vulnerable witnesses, including by 'vigilantly' controlling the manner of questioning of a witness or victim so as to avoid any harassment or intimidation.[686] Such measures have been implemented, to different extents, in all ICC trials. As reported by the International Bar Association:

> During the Lubanga trial for example, the Trial Chamber ordered a variety of protective measures including withholding witnesses' identities from the public; use of pseudonyms; and conducting parts of the proceedings in closed session. Face and voice distortion was in place for all alleged former child soldiers, and screens were used so that witnesses did not have to see the accused while testifying. Furthermore, testimony via electronic means was permitted, and the Chamber allowed some child witnesses to be accompanied during testimony by a family member, psychologist or legal representative.[687]

All these measures began to be adopted after the first former child soldier who served as a witness in the *Lubanga* case recanted his testimony, most likely due

685 See the 'Manual for Legal Representatives', above note 683, at 68.

686 See Rule 88(5) of the ICC RPE.

687 See International Bar Association, 'Witnesses before the ICC: International Criminal Court Programme Report on the ICC's Efforts and Challenges to Protect, Support and Ensure the Rights of Witnesses', July 2013, available at: http://www.ibanet.org/ICC_ICL_Programme/Reports.aspx. The Report also specifies that in the *Katanga Ngudjolo* trial the Court made use of pseudonyms, and facial and voice distortions. However, there were reportedly fewer closed sessions during that trial in comparison to the *Lubanga* case. Moreover, given its high numbers of victim-witnesses who allegedly suffered sexual violence, other vulnerable witnesses and high-profile defence witnesses, the *Bemba* trial has perhaps employed the most frequent use of in-court protective measures, mostly in the form of pseudonyms, face and voice distortion during testimony and closed-session hearings.

the fact that at the beginning of the trial he sat in clear view of Mr Lubanga and was able to make eye contact with his persecutor. As a result, additional precautions were put in place, in particular all child soldiers were shielded from Mr Lubanga's direct view when providing testimony to the Court through the use of curtains pulled across the sides of the witness box.[688] Significantly, some of the former child soldiers who took part in the *Lubanga* case enjoyed a 'dual status', which entailed that a victim could also be called as a witness by the prosecution, the defence or a legal representative.[689] In the case at hand, however, conferring the dual status did not produce the expected results, namely enhancing child victims' participation; on the contrary, it demonstrated how little children's special vulnerability and needs are taken into consideration.

As explained in the judgment pursuant to Article 74 of the Statute, due to inconsistencies within and between the accounts of the alleged former child soldiers, Trial Chamber I ultimately deemed their testimonies unreliable as regards the matters that were relevant to the charges in the *Lubanga* case.[690] In addition to discharging the testimonies, the majority of the judges, given the Chamber's conclusions as to the reliability and accuracy of the witnesses, decided that it was necessary to withdraw the victims' right to participate on the account that 'it would be unsustainable to allow victims to continue participating if a more detailed understanding of the evidence has demonstrated they no longer meet the relevant criteria'.[691] This episode sheds light on the fact that despite the crucial efforts made, the ICC is still far from striking a balance between the best interests of child victims and the implementation of fair trial standards.[692] In fact, as stressed by Judge Odio Benito in her separate and dissenting opinion:

> These witnesses were subject to multiple interviews and strenuous examination and cross-examination, which took place on numerous occasions, during a period of time ranging from 2005 to 2009–2010. In all of these interviews and interrogatories they were asked to recall events that occurred between 2002 and 2003 ... although I agree with the Majority of the Trial Chamber that the testimonies of these young individuals should

[688] See C.E. Lara, 'Child Soldier Testimony Used in Prosecuting War Crimes in the International Criminal Court: Preventing Further Victimisation', (2011) 17 *Southwestern Journal of International Law* 101, at 110–121.

[689] Decision of 5 June 2008 (Decision on Certain Practicalities Regarding Individuals who have the Dual Status of Witness and Victims), (2008) ICC, Decision No. ICC-01/04-01/06-1379, §52, principle b: 'The fact that an individual has dual status does not grant him or her rights in addition to those of someone who is only a victim or a witness.'

[690] See Judgment of 14 March 2012, (Judgment pursuant to Article 74 of the Statute), (2012) ICC, above note 235, §478 et seq.

[691] Ibidem, §484.

[692] See Preamble of the Guidelines on Matters Involving Child Victims and Witnesses of Crime, ECOSOC Resolution 2005/20 of 22 July 2005. According to the Guidelines 'justice for child victims and witnesses of crimes must be assured while safeguarding the rights of the accused persons'.

not be used for the purposes of determining the individual criminal responsibility of Mr Lubanga, their victims' status should remain unaffected.[693]

In withdrawing the former child soldiers' right to participate in the proceedings as victims the Trial Chamber failed to consider the extent of the trauma suffered and its impact on the witnesses' capability to provide a lucid and precise account of their experiences. In particular the Chamber ignored the fact that, as stated by the expert witness Ms Elisabeth Schauer, recalling traumatic events entails extraordinary hurdles for the victims affected by post-traumatic stress disorder:

> Once posttraumatic stress disorder has developed, we see victims, including child soldiers, experience immense suffering due to involuntary sensory, visual or other recall of the most horrific moments of their lives, whereby their autobiographic memory is fragmented and their ability to willingly focus their mind and concentrate is reduced. Much of the daily and nightly energy is spent avoiding to get reminded, since remembering the traumatic experience brings up painful emotions and panic like physical arousal and distress. The severity of trauma symptoms and distress of talking about the event are tightly linked to each other. We have observed, that with increasing severity of symptoms, the distress felt in people, when asked to disclose their traumatic scene increases.[694]

Moreover, it should be borne in mind that former child soldiers, when called to testify, relive their experiences both as victims and as perpetrators, meaning that, although the Rome Statute clearly excludes from its jurisdiction *ratione personae* those who committed crimes while under the age of 18 years old, child soldiers can be influenced by the irrational, but yet understandable, fear that telling their stories in a court room can lead to unforeseen repercussions, such as being indicted and detained.

5.3.3.3. *Child Victims' Right to Reparation before the International Criminal Court*

The ICC reparations regime is laid down in Articles 75 and 79 of the Rome Statute and is further elaborated in Rules 94–99 of the Court's RPE. According to Article 75, which can be regarded as the key provision on reparations within the ICC Statute:

> The Court shall establish principles relating to reparations or in respect of, victims, including restitution, compensation and rehabilitation. On this basis, in its decision the Court may, either upon request or on its own motion in exceptional circumstances,

---

693 See Judgment of 14 March 2012 (Separate and Dissenting Opinion Judge Elizabeth Odio Benito), (2012) ICC, Case No. ICC-01/04-01/06-2842, §§30–34.

694 This condition is known as 'speechless terror', see Expert Report of Ms Schauer, above note 173, at 34.

determine the scope and the extent of any damage, loss and injury to, or in respect of, victims and will state the principles on which it is acting.[695]

As noted by McCarthy, under international law there are no secondary rules that require the individual perpetrators to remedy the harms caused by their unlawful conduct, meaning that there is no existing body of international legal principles upon which the Court can rely on when imposing reparations.[696] Article 75 thus attributes to the ICC itself the challenging task of establishing reparations principles and implementing a significant change in the way ICL has been perceived so far. The ICC can only order reparations, after conviction, either directly against the convicted person or through the TFV. Either way, the case built by the Prosecutor and the charges tried provide the framework for future reparations. Article 75, moreover, confers on the Court a high degree of discretion as it establishes that reparations shall include, but are not limited to, restitution, compensation and rehabilitation. In May 2011, the Court's President Sang-Hyun Son, officially announced that the reparations principles will be developed through the ICC's jurisprudence rather than prepared and agreed on in advance, as expected and suggested by many actors, in particular NGOs.[697] In crafting its own principles on reparations the Court is encouraged to look at both international public law and IHRL; nevertheless as it deals with the liability of individual perpetrators and not with States' international responsibility, the ICC is 'required to fashion a range of reparation principles that are appropriate for the distinctive legal context in which it operates'.[698]

As the ICC's Pre-Trial Chamber stated when called to decide on the arrest warrant against Mr Lubanga Dyilo, '[t]he success of the Court is to some extent, linked to the success of its reparation regime'.[699] It follows that the recognition of victims' rights and needs is not just one of the ICC's characteristics, but it represents a unique and unprecedented feature that distinguishes the Court from the other international criminal justice bodies.

5.3.3.3.1. Trial Chamber I Decision on Reparations Principles and Procedures in the *Lubanga* Case

Following Mr Lubanga's conviction on 10 July 2012, the ICC's first decision on reparations was eagerly awaited. The decision on reparations' principles and procedures was issued on 7 August 2012 and subsequently modified by the

---

695 See Art. 75 of the Rome Statute.

696 See McCarthy, above note 67, at 54–65.

697 See Redress, above note 676, at 24, footnote 120. See also Opening Address, 'Reparations before the ICC: Issues and Challenges', Conference organised by Redress and Leiden University/Grotius Centre, Peace Palace, The Hague, 12 May 2011, report available at: http://www.redress.org/downloads/publications/SUMMARYreport.pdf.

698 See McCarthy, above note 67, at 256.

699 Decision of 10 February 2006 (Decision on the Prosecutor's Application for a Warrant of Arrest, ex Article 58 of the Rome Statute), (2006) ICC, Case No. ICC-01/04-01/06, §136.

Appeals Chamber on 3 March 2015. The first decision drafted by Trial Chamber I relied extensively on the submissions received by the TFV, the Registrar, UNICEF, the International Centre for Transitional Justice ('ICTJ'), Women's Initiatives and other NGOs. It was emphasised that the principles enunciated within the first decision had been circumscribed to the specific case and therefore they did not represent the principles that would guide the future decisions of the Court on reparations.[700] With regard in particular to children, Trial Chamber I underlined that the age of the victims should be one of the key factors to be taken into consideration, in particular '[i]n reparations decisions concerning children, the Court should be guided, inter alia, by the Convention on the Rights of the Child and the fundamental principle of the "best interests of the child" that is enshrined therein. Further, the decisions in this context should reflect a gender-inclusive perspective.'[701]

The Chamber also made explicit reference to Article 39 of the CRC, which requires States parties to promote the recovery and reintegration of child victims, including child victims of war. In the decision under consideration the Court also stressed the importance of taking into account the views of the child victims, as they necessarily 'are to be considered when decisions are made about individual or collective reparations that concern them, bearing in mind their circumstances, age and level of maturity'.[702] As for the procedural issues, which are dealt with in the second part of the decision, Trial Chamber I affirmed that reparations are an integral part of the overall trial process and, since the Rome Statute does not specify which body of the Court is in charge of monitoring and supervising the reparation order, the Chamber explained that such tasks fall within the responsibilities of the judiciary. Thus, Trial Chamber I clarified that during the reparations proceedings new judges will be appointed to substitute the current bench,[703] giving rise to the legitimate, but unanswered, question of what impact the replacement of the judges will have on the victims. The core of the decision lies, though, in the central role assigned to the TFV, which has been appointed by the Chamber as the designated body to deal with the overarching implementation of a five-step reparations plan.[704] In fact, the indigence of the

---

700 See, for instance, Carla Ferstman, Director of Redress, speaker at the rapid response seminar on 'Reparations to Victims: the Recent international Criminal Court Decision and beyond', hosted by the British Institute of International and Comparative Law in London on 12 September 2012, available at http://www.biicl.org/files/6103_icc_7_august_2012_decision_-_rapid_response_seminar_report.pdf.

701 Decision of 7 August 2012, (Decision Establishing the Principles and Procedures to be Applied to Reparations), ICC, above note 24, §211.

702 Ibidem, §215.

703 Ibidem, §§262–263.

704 According to Swart, 'it is unclear whether the Court did so because it felt the TFV had greater expertise in this regard, or whether the Court lacks the confidence and expertise to specify reparation awards'. See M. Swart, 'The Lubanga Reparations Decision: A Missed Opportunity?', (2013) 32 *Polish Yearbook of International Law* 169, at 182.

convicted person and his lack of private assets pushed the Court to rely solely on the logistical and financial resources of the TFV, in particular

> the Chamber is of the view that when the convicted person has no assets, if a reparations award is made 'through' the Trust Fund, the award is not limited to the funds and assets seized and deposited with the Trust Fund, but the award can, at least potentially, be supported by the Trust Fund's own resources. This interpretation is consistent with Rule 98(5) of the Rules and Regulation 56 of the Regulations of the TFV. Rule 98(5) of the Rules provides that the Trust Fund *may* use 'other resources' for the benefit of victims.[705]

Concerning the identification of the beneficiaries and the distribution of the benefits, the Chamber adopted a broader approach by affirming that reparations should be awarded to those who suffered personal harm as the result of the offences, *regardless of whether they participated in the trial.*[706] Notably the Court has included also victims of gender violence among those who can have access to reparations,[707] showing that the decision went beyond the restricted notion of 'victim' inferred by the prosecutorial strategy and the limited charges tried. In a nutshell the difference in the Chamber's approach regarding the issue of sexual violence for the purpose of sentencing and consideration of such evidence for the purpose of a reparations award can be explained by the fact that the standard of proof is different in each of these phases. In fact, while the prosecution must establish aggravating circumstances beyond a reasonable doubt for the purpose of sentencing, a less exacting standard, 'the but for test', has been used to determine the issue of causation in the reparation phase. This is in principle correct as a less exacting standard should apply to reparations proceedings because they are fundamentally different from trial proceedings. However, the adoption of a different standard of proof does not entail that reparations can depart from the charges as erroneously sustained by the Trial Chamber; on the contrary, as clarified by the Appeals Chamber, reparation orders are intrinsically linked to the individual whose criminal responsibility is established in a conviction and whose culpability for these criminal acts is determined in a sentence.[708]

As for the distribution of the reparations, Trial Chamber I has not excluded *tout court* the possibility of individual reparations, but it has made clear that

---

705 Decision of 7 August 2012, (Decision Establishing the Principles and Procedures to be Applied to Reparations), ICC, above note 24, §271.

706 Ibidem, §194 'pursuant to Rule 85 of the Rules, reparations may be granted to direct and indirect victims, including the family members of direct victims; anyone who attempted to prevent the commission of one or more of the crimes under consideration; and those who suffered personal harm as a result of these offences, regardless of whether they participated in the trial proceedings'.

707 Ibidem, §207 et seq.

708 Judgment of 3 March 2015, ICC, above note 50, Order for Reparations, Annex A §65.

a collective approach will be implemented.[709] In relation to the individual applications submitted, the decision established that the TFV should receive them from the Registry. The Trial Chamber did not include in the order any confidentiality clause to protect the identity of the victims who applied for individuals' reparations. Furthermore, Trial Chamber I determined that 'if the TFV considers it appropriate, victims who have applied for reparations *could be included* in any reparations programme that is to be implemented by the TFV', thus leaving to the TFV the duty to examine individual applications and evaluate whether to somehow 'absorb' their claims into the collective measures to be envisaged within the future reparations plan.[710] Trial Chamber I also entrusted the TFV with the assessment of the harm, to be carried out during the consultations phase in the different localities identified,[711] thus avoiding defining the harm to victims caused by the crimes for which Mr Lubanga was convicted and assigning this task to a non-judicial body. The Chamber simply stated that the concept of harm denotes 'hurt, injury and damage' and it can be direct or indirect, as long as it is 'personal' to the victim.[712] Ultimately, Trial Chamber I did not provide a sufficiently comprehensive definition and discussion of the 'harm' requirement, which in a criminal justice context is crucial to reconcile the idea of accountability towards victims with the need for specificity and the protection of the rights of the convicted persons.

5.3.3.3.2. The Appeals Chamber Judgment on Reparations' Principles and Procedures in the *Lubanga* Case

The Trial Chamber I decision on principles and procedures on reparations mainly outsourced the reparations regime to the TFV and left several questions unanswered, thus fuelling, instead of finally quelling, the discussion on whether the ICC can truly provide a forum to strike a balance between fair trial standards and victims' rights.[713] The Appeals Chamber significantly amended the decision by Trial Chamber I and issued a newly drafted Order for Reparations.[714] Finally shedding light on what 'reparations' means in an international judicial setting, the Appeals Chamber has determined that:

> An order for reparations under Article 75 of the Statute must contain, at a minimum, five essential elements: 1) it must be directed against the convicted person; 2) it must

709 Decision of 7 August 2012, (Decision Establishing the Principles and Procedures to be Applied to Reparations), ICC, above note 24, §§219–221.

710 Ibidem, §289.

711 Ibidem, §283.

712 Ibidem, §228.

713 See in general L. Moffett, *Justice for Victims before the International Criminal Court*, Routledge, Abingdon, 2014, 281; J.O. Wemmers, 'Where Do They Belong? Giving Victims a Place in the Criminal Justice Process', (2009) 20 *Criminal Law Forum* 395, at 396–416.

714 Judgment of 3 March 2015, ICC, above note 50, Order for Reparations, Annex A.

> establish and inform the convicted person of his or her liability with respect to the reparations awarded in the order; 3) it must specify, and provide reasons for, the type of reparations ordered, either collective, individual or both, pursuant to rules 97 (1) and 98 of the Rules of Procedure and Evidence; 4) it must define the harm caused to direct and indirect victims as a result of the crimes for which the person was convicted, as well as identify the modalities of reparations that the Trial Chamber considers appropriate based on the circumstances of the specific case before it; and 5) it must identify the victims eligible to benefit from the awards for reparations or set out the criteria of eligibility based on the link between the harm suffered by the victims and the crimes for which the person was convicted.[715]

These elements have thus been described as the cornerstone of every Order for Reparations and have been used by the Appeals Chamber to assess the decision issued by Trial Chamber I. The five elements must be kept separate from the principles, i.e. general concepts that can be formulated in light of the circumstances of a specific case, but nonetheless be applied, adapted, expanded upon, or added to by future Trial Chambers. In relation to the first element identified in the Appeals Chamber's judgment, the ICC legal framework clearly establishes that an Order for Reparations has to be issued in all circumstances *against* the convicted person.[716] When appropriate, such an Order for Reparations can, in addition, be made *through* the TFV, meaning that the person who is individually responsible for reparations remains the convicted perpetrator, but, in cases where he/she is unable to immediately comply for reasons of indigence, the TFV may advance its other resources pursuant to Regulation 56 of the Regulations of the Trust Fund. Contrary to the interpretation given by Trial Chamber I, such intervention does not exonerate the convicted person from liability as he/she remains liable and in principle must reimburse the TFV.[717] The Appeals Chamber also determined that the Trial Chamber's adoption of two different standards of proof with regard to reparations made through the TFV, i.e. 'wholly flexible approach', versus reparations ordered against the convicted person, i.e. 'balance of probabilities', is legally incorrect, because an Order for Reparations must always be made against the convicted person. The Appeals Chamber did not address this issue further since Mr Lubanga's Defence argued that the standard of 'preponderance of probabilities' should apply, but it did not appeal the Trial Chamber's decision in respect of the other standard of proof adopted.[718]

---

715 Ibidem, §35.

716 The Appeals Chamber considered that reparations awarded through the TFV pursuant to Article 75(2) of the Statute were not an alternative to reparation orders made against a convicted person. Ibidem, §74.

717 Ibidem, §§83–84.

718 Ibidem, §86.

The second crucial point clarified by the Appeals Chamber concerns the nexus between criminal conviction and reparations. The Appeals Chamber stressed that the scope of a convicted person's liability for reparations may differ depending on, for example, the mode of individual criminal responsibility established with respect to that person and on the specific elements of that responsibility. Accordingly, the Appeals Chamber found it necessary and appropriate to be guided by a principle not previously articulated by the Trial Chamber, namely that 'a convicted person's liability for reparations must be proportionate to the harm caused and, inter alia, his or her participation in the commission of the crimes for which he or she was found guilty, in the specific circumstances of the case'.[719] The standard adopted by the Trial Chamber to reach this determination was indicated as the 'proximate cause', which is satisfied whenever there exists a 'but for' relationship between the crime and the harm.[720] Since the defence failed to demonstrate that this standard could negatively impact on the rights of the convicted person, the Appeals Chamber rejected this ground of appeal.

The third element upon which the Appeals Chamber shed light is the determination of the types of reparations ordered. In this regard the Chamber clarified that despite a certain ambiguity in the Trial Chamber's decision, collective reparations ought to be the only kind of award implemented. The Appeals Chamber considered that the Court's legal texts provide for two distinct procedures for awards for reparations. The first, which relates to individual reparation awards, is primarily based on the applications submitted by the individual victims and is regulated by Rules 94 and 95 of the RPE. The second, instead, relates to collective reparation awards and is regulated by Rules 97(1) and 98(3) of the RPE.[721] With respect to the latter, Trial Chamber I held that a decision ordering only collective reparations awards did not require a ruling on the merits of individual applications and therefore it rejected the argument brought by the participants, i.e. the legal representatives of victims and the OPCV, according to which the Court had in any case the obligation not to dismiss them without due consideration and adjudication.[722] Moreover, the Trial Chamber made individual victims' participation in collective reparations programmes dependent on whether the TFV considers it 'appropriate'.[723]

---

719 Ibidem, §118.

720 Decision of 7 August 2012, (Decision Establishing the Principles and Procedures to be Applied to Reparations), ICC, above note 24, §§247–250.

721 Judgment of 3 March 2015, *ICC*, above note 50, Order for Reparations, Annex A, §149.

722 Représentants légaux du groupe de victimes V01, 'Document à l'Appui de l'Appel contre la Decision Establishing the Principles and Procedures to Be Applied to Reparations du 7 août 2012', ICC-01/04-01/06, 5 février 2013, §14. See also Office of Public Counsel for Victims and V02 team of legal representatives, 'Document in support of the appeal against Trial Chamber I's 7 August 2012 Decision Establishing the Principles and Procedures to Be Applied to Reparation', ICC-01/04-01/06, 5 February 2013, §§23–26.

723 Decision of 7 August 2012, (Decision Establishing the Principles and Procedures to be Applied to Reparations), ICC, above note 24, §204.

The Appeals Chamber noted that, at the time of making applications for reparations, the victims have either applied for individual awards or applied for a collective award, without knowledge of the kind of collective programme that would be ultimately be adopted. Therefore the Appeals Chamber found it necessary to seek the victims' consent when a collective award is made, consistently with the principle that reparations are entirely voluntary and victims are free to decide whether they would like to benefit from a type of reparation different from the one they had originally applied for.

After considering the issue of individual versus collective reparations, the Appeals Chamber focused on the fourth element, namely the determination of the harm caused to direct and indirect victims as a result of the crimes for which the person was convicted, as well as the identification of the modalities of reparations that the Trial Chamber considered appropriate. Concerning the former aspect the Appeals Chamber found that the Trial Chamber had 'erred in delegating to the TFV the task of defining the harms caused to direct and indirect victims as a result of the crimes for which Mr Lubanga was convicted'.[724] The Chamber emphasised that the identification of the harm to victims must be determined by the Trial Chamber, considering that the victims and the convicted person must be informed of this critical aspect of reparations orders and be able to meaningfully challenge it. In other words the Trial Chamber is expected to enter into separate evidentiary analysis before making an Order for Reparations, entailing reparations hearings to assess harm specifically for the purposes of reparation.[725] The Appeals Chamber left the possibility open for a 'future Trial Chamber' to address harm not mentioned in the sentencing decision.[726] According to Stahn, the 'approach of the Appeals Chamber might ultimately point towards the need for a specialised "Reparations Chamber" at the Court'.[727] This solution would be in line with several aspects discussed so far, all stemming from the reality that, as stressed above, reparations proceedings are different from trial proceedings. In the case under scrutiny the Appeals Chamber had to ultimately amend the impugned decision and determine the harm by itself.

Taking into account decisions relevant to victims' participation and findings in the Conviction Decision the Appeals Chamber has defined the harm attached to direct victims as

i. physical injury and trauma;
ii. psychological trauma and the development of psychological disorders, such as, inter alia, suicidal tendencies, depression, and dissociative behaviour;

---

724 Judgment of 3 March 2015, ICC, above note 50, Order for Reparations, Annex A, §184.

725 Ibidem, §187.

726 Ibidem.

727 C. Stahn, 'Reparative Justice after the Lubanga Appeals Judgment: New Prospects for Expressivism and Participatory Justice or "Juridified Victimhood" by Other Means?', (2015) 13 *Journal of International Criminal Justice* 801, at 805–813.

iii. interruption and loss of schooling;
iv. separation from families;
v. exposure to an environment of violence and fear;
vi. difficulties socialising within their families and communities;
vii. difficulties in controlling aggressive impulses; and
viii. the non-development of 'civilian life skills' resulting in the victim being at a disadvantage, particularly as regards employment.[728]

With regard to indirect victims:

i. psychological suffering experienced as a result of the sudden loss of a family member;
ii. material deprivation that accompanies the loss of the family members' contributions;
iii. loss, injury or damage suffered by the intervening person from attempting to prevent the child from being further harmed as a result of a relevant crime; and
iv. psychological and/or material suffering as a result of aggressiveness on the part of former child soldiers relocated to their families and communities.[729]

The identification of the harm suffered by direct and indirect victims is crucial to determining the beneficiaries of the reparations award, which according to Trial Chamber I must also encompass victims of SGBV.[730] Trial Chamber I thus sought to broaden the scope of reparations and include among the beneficiaries also those persons who did not fall within the definition of victims enshrined in Rule 85 because the harm suffered was not sufficiently linked to the charges tried.[731] As a result, whereas Trial Chamber I decided to adopt a 'wholly flexible approach' to the determination of harm in cases where reparations are made through the Trust Fund and, thus, justify Mr Lubanga's liability also for SGBV, the Appeals Chamber amended the impugned decision in this respect and suggested instead that the Board of Directors of the Trust Fund consider, in its discretion, the possibility of including such victims in the assistance activities undertaken according to its mandate.[732] The Appeals Chamber evidently strove to avoid any overlapping and confusion with regard to the TFV's two different mandates as this may result in a significant prejudice to the rights of the convicted person.

Concerning the modalities of reparations identified by the Trial Chamber and endorsed by the Appeals Chamber, these include restitution, compensation and

728 Judgment of 3 March 2015, ICC, above note 50, Order for Reparations, Annex A, §191.
729 Ibidem.
730 Decision of 7 August 2012, (Decision Establishing the Principles and Procedures to be Applied to Reparations), ICC, above note 24, §§207–208.
731 See A. Wiersing, 'Lubanga and its Implications for Victims Seeking Reparations at the International Criminal Court', (2012) 4 *Amsterdam Law Forum* 21, at 21–23.
732 Judgment of 3 March 2015, ICC, above note 50, Order for Reparations, Annex A, §199.

rehabilitation, as well as other types of reparations such as those with a symbolic, preventive or transformative value. According to the Appeals Chamber the definition of the harm caused to direct and indirect victims as a result of the crimes for which a person is convicted is interlinked with the designation of the appropriate modalities of reparations in that specific case.[733] In this sense, the appropriateness of a modality of reparation can only be determined by reference to the harms that were caused and which the reparations seek to remedy. In designing the awards for reparations, which shall be informed by the views received during the consultation stage with victims, members of the affected communities and experts, the Trust Fund should endeavour to implement all the identified modalities of reparations contained in the judgment. In particular the Appeals Chamber has noted that restitution will probably be 'unachievable' for victims of the crimes at stake, however it did not exclude the possibility for the TFV to reach a different conclusion, subject to providing a detailed account of the reasons that informed this finding.[734]

As the fifth element of an Order for Reparations the Appeals Chamber listed the identification of the victims eligible for reparations or in the alternative the criteria of eligibility. The Trial Chamber did not identify eligible victims. However, in order to enable their identification by the TFV, Trial Chamber I indicated certain characteristics of groups of eligible victims[735] by stating that 'the measures put in place for awarding compensation should take into account the gender and age-specific impact that the crimes of enlisting and conscripting children under the age of 15 and using them to participate actively in the hostilities can have on direct victims, their families and communities'.[736] With regard to the community-based approach promoted by the Trial Chamber, the Appeals Chamber decided to amend the decision to the extent to which it was inconsistent with the applicable provisions regarding reparations (in the legal meaning of the term). In fact, the Appeals Chamber noted that a distinction must be drawn between the members of the community directly or indirectly *victimised* by the crimes of which Mr Lubanga was found guilty and other members of the community who were also *affected* by Mr Lubanga's conduct, but did not fall into the previous category. The former are entitled to receive reparations, whereas the latter could possibly be included in the programmes operated by the TFV through its assistance mandate.[737] Ultimately, concerning the inclusion in the Trial Chamber's decision of localities mentioned in the

733 Ibidem, §200.

734 Ibidem, §204.

735 Ibidem, §205.

736 Decision of 7 August 2012, (Decision Establishing the Principles and Procedures to be Applied to Reparations), ICC, above note 24, §231.

737 Judgment of 3 March 2015, ICC, above note 50, Order for Reparations, Annex A, §215.

evidence and not only in the Conviction Decision, the Appeals Chamber found no error and thus rejected Mr Lubanga's argument in this regard.

Finally, the Appeals Chamber shed light on the draft implementation plan that the Trust Fund should design in accordance with the amended Order for Reparations and then submit to the newly constituted Trial Chamber. The newly composed Trial Chamber should monitor and oversee the implementation stage of the amended Order for Reparations, including having the authority to approve the draft implementation plan submitted by the Trust Fund. The Chamber may be seized of any contested issues arising out of the work and the decisions of the Trust Fund.[738] In particular, prior to the Trial Chamber setting the amount of Mr Lubanga's liability, the parties should have the opportunity to appear before the Trial Chamber or make submissions in writing on the scope of Mr Lubanga's liability, in light of the information provided by the Trust Fund in its draft implementation plan, within a time limit to be set by the Trial Chamber.[739]

The judgment and the amended Order for Reparations have, at last, clarified a number of important points, including the relationship between the conviction and the reparations phase, the role of the TFV and its interplay with the ICC, the scope of reparations awarded in an international judicial setting and the practical hurdles that inevitably downsize the Court's ambition to act as a body able to successfully combine retributive and restorative justice. In the Order for Reparations the Appeals Chamber has crystallised the arguments expressed in the judgment and outlined the principles and the procedures to apply in the *Lubanga* case. In particular, since the case dealt with child victims, i.e. former child soldiers, the Chamber has clarified the importance of duly taking into account the age-related harm experience of the victims, in line with Article 68 of the Rome Statute, and of differentiating between the impact of the crimes on boys and girls.[740] Furthermore the Appeals Chamber has referred to the key CRC principles that must guide and inform every reparations award for child victims, namely the best interests of the child; the promotion of children's recovery and reintegration; and children's right to participation.[741]

The Appeals Chamber has also acknowledged that reparations orders must result in adequate, prompt and effective reparations, as stated in the UNBPG. To this end, reparations must aim at relieving the suffering caused by the serious crimes committed; affording justice to the victims by alleviating the consequences of the wrongful acts; deterring future violations; and contributing to the effective reintegration of former child soldiers.[742] Remarkably these goals

738 Ibidem, §76.
739 Ibidem, §241.
740 Ibidem, §23–28.
741 See Chapter 2, Section 2.3.3 above.
742 Judgment of 3 March 2015, ICC, above note 50, Order for Reparations, Annex A, §71.

should be pursued *to the extent achievable*,[743] thus highlighting that the ICC has limited capacity to actually enforce a reparations regime able to significantly address the harm suffered by the victims. This point emerged quite strongly since, as discussed at length in the judgment, the Order for Reparations ultimately focused solely on collective reparations against Mr Lubanga to be made through the Trust Fund pursuant to Rule 97(1) and Rule 98(3) of the RPE.[744] In the end the Appeals Chamber has not narrowed the scope of reparations by abruptly excluding victims of SGBV, but it has redirected the Trial Chamber's efforts to expand it in a way that complies with the legal requirements of reparations awards that stem from a criminal proceeding. It has done so first by unpacking the concept of harm and defining it in relation to both direct victims (i.e. the former child soldiers) and indirect victims (i.e. victims' relatives, the persons who tried to prevent the commission of the crime *and* those who experienced psychological and/or material suffering as a result of aggressiveness on the part of former child soldiers relocated to their families and communities),[745] and secondly by explaining that Mr Lubanga's liability for reparations extends to localities not mentioned in the Conviction Decision, but in the evidence of the witnesses listed in that sentence.[746]

5.4. CONCLUSIONS

The present chapter has summarised the main shortcomings and achievements of the international bodies analysed. The overview provided was not limited to the case law, but encompassed the 'functioning' of the relevant fora against the backdrop of child victims' needs and rights. What emerged is that the international community is finally recognising the existence of children affected by IHRL and IHL violations and it is, at least to some extent, striving to identify principles and procedures able to take into account and, whenever possible, address their peculiarities.

The issue remains as to what level of compromise is required to enhance child victims' rights without curtailing States' sovereignty or fair trial standards and to what degree the trade-off is still able to result in adequate, prompt and effective reparations. The potentialities of the CRC-OP3, which provides a justice venue also to child victims of armed conflict, have been significantly watered down and the final draft endorsed by States presents a number of limitations that are likely to affect children's access to remedies. For example, despite the conceivable benefits stemming from the cooperation between the CRC-OP3 and the ICC,

743 Ibidem.
744 Ibidem, §73.
745 Ibidem, §58.
746 Ibidem, §56.

this option has not been explored by the drafters, creating a potential loophole in child victims' protection.

With regard to the ICC it is easy to observe that the establishment of the Court marked a crucial achievement within the ICL framework. The inclusion and enforcement of provisions devoted to first recognising and then even enhancing the role of victims in the proceedings represents a long-awaited novelty, which helped in rethinking international crimes and adopting an unspoiled perspective. Nonetheless, the challenges to develop and implement a successful reparations scheme are still difficult to overcome. As a result, while the different Chambers struggled to achieve some legal clarity in an under-explored field, the victims are still waiting even though the trial of Mr Lubanga Dyilo officially commenced in 2009 and the crimes committed date back to 2002–2003. The Appeals Chamber's decision has certainly contributed to shaping the reparations regime of the ICC in a way that, in comparison with the earlier decision, is more in line with the underlying principles of an international criminal proceeding. If on the one hand the establishment of a Reparations Chamber to deal separately with issues related to victims' redress were to be a significant step towards an International Criminal Court that incorporates 'expertise and skills differing from criminal adjudications',[747] on the other hand it is legitimate to wonder how much such a change would actually benefit the victims, especially children, if the trials keep lasting so long and the capability to award meaningful reparations remains inadequate or in any case utterly subordinate to achieving accountability and deterrence. The latter point has not been raised as a criticism, but rather as a direct and logical consequence of the fact that we are navigating in the ICL realm and the ICC acts first and foremost as a specialised criminal tribunal. The extent to which the Court will be able and willing to renegotiate its priorities is as yet impossible to determine.

---

747 See Stahn, above note 727.

CHAPTER 6
CHILD VICTIMS' RIGHT TO REPARATION IN 'QUASI-JUDICIAL' AND JUDICIAL REGIONAL SETTINGS

6.1. INTRODUCTION

Regional human rights systems play a crucial role in strengthening IHRL. Initial concerns that regional systems could undermine the universality of human rights law have been surmounted in light of the important results achieved. In particular regional human rights systems provide a significant layer of protection, they can be more effective than UN bodies as they are closely connected to political regional developments and they have largely contributed, especially through their jurisprudence, to the enhancement of IHRL.[748] In the field of reparations the Inter-American Commission and the Inter-American Court have paved the way to all the major developments, also in cases affecting children. The African human rights system, and in particular the African Committee of Experts on the Rights of the Child, the African Commission and Court on Human Rights and People's Rights, will be also analysed as the African continent is the most affected by violations of children's rights in armed conflict.[749] The European human rights system will not be included in this overview because it has not dealt with the impact of armed conflict on children.

6.2. THE AFRICAN HUMAN RIGHTS SYSTEM

The protection of human rights in Africa is monitored not only by the UN system, but also by a complex framework of regional instruments adopted by the

---

748 See I. Bantekas and L. Oette, *International Human Rights Law and Practice*, Cambridge University, Cambridge, 2013, at 219.

749 See Annual Report of the Secretary-General on Children and Armed Conflict, above note 11.

Organisation of African Unity and its successor, i.e. the African Union ('AU').[750] The African human rights system includes not only the regional framework with the ACtHPR and the African Commission on Human and Peoples' Rights, but also sub-regional organisations like the Economic Community of West African States ('ECOWAS'), the East Africa Community ('EAC') and the Southern African Development Community ('SADC'). The African Charter on Human and People's Rights entered into force in 1986 and has now been ratified by all 53 Member States of the AU, except for South Sudan.[751] The African Commission on Human and People's Rights was the sole human rights body of the continent from its establishment in 1986 until January 2004, when the Protocol to the African Charter on Human and Peoples' Rights on the Establishment of an African Court on Human and Peoples' Rights came into force.[752] The AU Assembly decided in July 2004, only a few months after the entry into force of the Protocol, to merge the ACtHPR with the African Court of Justice, originally intended to be the principal judicial organ of the AU. The reason for this sudden change of mind was attributed to the need to rationalise the expenses and make the most out of the already existing structures. To this end in July 2008 the AU adopted the Protocol on the Statute of the African Court of Justice and Human Rights ('ACJHR').[753] The Protocol, and the Statute annexed to it, will enter into force 30 days after the deposit of the instruments of ratification by 15 Member States. In June 2014, the AU adopted a new protocol at its 23rd Ordinary Session summit in Malabo, Equatorial Guinea, to further expand the jurisdiction of the ACJHR and also cover individual liability for serious crimes committed in violation of international law. Once established, the new Court will have a tripartite function, encompassing a human rights section, a general affairs section and an ICL section.[754]

---

750 See C. Heyns and M. Killander, 'Africa' in Moeckli, Shah and Sivakumaran, above note 469, 441, at 445–457. See also J. Sarkin, 'The Role of Regional Systems in Enforcing State Human Rights Compliance: Evaluating the African Commission on Human and Peoples' Rights and the New African Court of Justice and Human Rights with Comparative Lessons from the Council of Europe and the Organisation of American States', (2008) 2 *Inter-American and European Human Rights Journal* 199, at 200–242.

751 Organisation of African Unity (OAU), ACHPR ('Banjul Charter'), 27 June 1981, entered into force on 21 October 1986, CAB/LEG/67/3 rev. 5, 21 ILM 58 (1982).

752 OAU, Protocol to the African Charter on Human and People's Rights on the Establishment of an African Court on Human and People's Rights, 10 June 1998, entered into force on 25 January 2005, Doc. OAU/LEG/EXP/AFCHPR/PROT (III).

753 AU, Protocol on the Statute of the African Court of Justice and Human Rights, 1 July 2008.

754 AU, Decision on the Draft Legal Instruments, Assembly/AU/Dec. 529(XXIII), Decisions, Declarations and Resolution of the Assembly of the Union, Twenty-Third Ordinary Session, 26–27 June 2014.

6.2.1. THE 'QUASI-JUDICIAL' BODIES OF THE AFRICAN HUMAN RIGHTS SYSTEM

Article 30 of the ACHPR provides for the establishment of the African Commission on Human and Peoples' Rights. The mandate of the Commission focuses on the promotion of human rights through research, dissemination of information and cooperation with other human rights bodies.[755] The Commission considers States' reports on the implementation of the African Charter, interprets its provisions and receives complaints against alleged violations of the ACHPR committed by States parties. The Charter is silent with regard to who can actually bring an individual complaint, however from the Commission's jurisprudence it is evident that complaints can be submitted by both individuals and NGOs.[756] The African Commission has recognised that 'the main goal of the communications procedure before the Commission is to initiate a positive dialogue, resulting in an amicable resolution between the complainant and the State concerned, which remedies the prejudice complained of'.[757] If the Commission ultimately finds a violation it may make non-binding recommendations to the State. These often include the cessation of the continuing violation, restitution, compensation,[758] and amendment of a specific law. The latter recommendation has been made, for example, in relation to a complaint brought against Sudan by a group of female students who were sentenced to 25–40 lashes for public order offences resulting from their participation in a picnic with boys. The Commission recognised a violation of Article 5 of the African Charter, which prohibits inhuman and degrading treatment, and requested that the government of Sudan immediately amend the Criminal Law of 1991, in conformity with its obligations under the African Charter and other relevant international human rights instruments; abolish the penalty of lashes; and take appropriate measures to ensure compensation to the victims.[759]

Since the African regional system is the only one that includes a Committee on the Rights and Welfare of the Child,[760] communications related to children's rights violations should, in principle, be directed to this specific body. Article 44

755 Art. 45 of the ACHPR.

756 See Heyns and Killander, above note 750, at 449.

757 Communication No. 25/89, *Free Legal Assistance Group v. Zaire*, 1997, 4 International Human Rights Reports 89, §39.

758 Communication No. 276/03, *Centre for Minority Rights Development (Kenya) and Minority Rights Group (on behalf of Endorois Welfare Council) v. Kenya*, 25 November 2009.

759 Communication No. 236/2000. *Curtis Francis Doebbler v. Sudan*, 29 May 2003.

760 The mandate of the African Committee on the Rights and Welfare of the Child is outlined in Arts. 32–46 of the ACRWC.

of the ACRWC empowers the Committee to consider individual communications alleging a violation of any of the rights enshrined in the Charter.[761]

The Committee's guidelines explain that where a child is capable of expressing his/her opinions, they should be heard by a Committee member, stressing that whenever feasible, children's participation should be ensured and encouraged.[762] Remarkably, unlike the CRC-OP3 the African Committee can accept collective communications[763] and also admit communications from a State non-signatory to the Charter in the overall best interests of the child.[764]

The Committee, although it became operational in 2002, only handed down its first decision on a communication procedure in 2011. The case in question dealt with the right to nationality of Nubian children in Kenya and the Committee recommended systemic remedial steps to be taken by the Kenyan government to rectify the unjustifiable denial of Kenyan citizenship to the complainants.[765] In particular the Committee found that the government of Kenya should take all necessary legislative, administrative and other measures in order to ensure that children of Nubian descent in Kenya, who are otherwise stateless, can acquire Kenyan nationality and the proof of such nationality at birth; it should take measures to ensure that existing children of Nubian descent whose Kenyan nationality is not recognised are systematically afforded the benefit of these new measures as a matter of priority; it should implement its birth registration system in a non-discriminatory manner; and it should adopt a short-term, medium-term and long-term plan to ensure the fulfilment of the right to the highest attainable standard of health and of the right to education, preferably in consultation with the affected beneficiary communities.[766]

The Committee has so far not heard any complaints concerning violations of children's rights committed in conjunction with an armed conflict. On 30 June 2015 the Committee concluded its first study on the impact of war on children.

---

761 Art. 44 of the ACRWC. (1) The Committee may receive communication, from any person, group or non-governmental organisation recognised by the Organisation of African Unity, by a Member State, or the United Nations relating to any matter covered by this Charter. (2) Every communication to the Committee shall contain the name and address of the author and shall be treated in confidence.

762 See Grover, above note 589, at 54. The author noted how, in contrast with the approach followed by the Committee on the Rights and Welfare of the Child, the rules of procedure for the administration of the CRC-OP3 refer only to (i) the child or children's possible participation in an oral hearing (and if not contrary to the child's best interest) where clarification of facts may be gleaned and questions raised relevant to the Committee's merit determination and (ii) possible participation of the child victim(s) in hearings held during an on-site visit as part of an inquiry procedure.

763 See, for example, Communication No. 002/2009, *Institute of Human Rights and Open Society Justice Initiative v. Kenya*, Decision on the Merits, 22 March 2011.

764 Guidelines for Consideration of Communications Provided for in Art. 44 of the ACRWC, Conditions of Admissibility of Communications Article 1 (Part 2)(2): Conditions of Form.

765 Communication No. 002/2009, above note 763, §69.

766 Ibidem.

As a result of the workshop 14 States were selected to assess the consequences of armed conflict on minors. Field visits will be organised in four countries, while desk-based research will analyse the situation of the remaining ten.

6.2.2. THE AFRICAN COURT ON HUMAN AND PEOPLES' RIGHTS

The ACtHPR, exactly like its American and European counterparts, provides individuals affected by violations of the rights enshrined in the ACHPR with a right to remedy.[767] According to Article 27 of the Protocol to the ACHPR, '[i]f the Court finds that there has been violation of a human or peoples' right, it shall make appropriate orders to remedy the violation, including the payment of fair compensation or reparation'.

Article 5 of the Protocol to the ACHPR further establishes that cases can be brought before the ACtHPR by the African Commission, the State party which has lodged a complaint to the Commission, the State party against which the complaint has been lodged, the State party whose citizen is a victim of the human rights violation and African Intergovernmental Organisations. In December 2014 the ACtHPR issued a decision affirming that the Committee on the Rights and Welfare of the Child is not an intergovernmental organisation and therefore it is not entitled to seek the right to access the Court in contentious matters,[768] but it can request advisory opinions in accordance with Article 4(1) of the Protocol.[769]

Moreover, Article 5(3) specifies that the Court may allow relevant 'non-governmental organisations with observer status before the Commission, and individuals to institute cases directly before it, in accordance with Article 34(6) of this Protocol', according to which

> at the time of the ratification [of this Protocol] or any time thereafter, the State shall make a declaration accepting the competence of the Court to receive cases under Article 5(3). The Court shall not receive any petition under Article 5(3) involving a State party which has not made such a declaration.

---

767 See Capone et al., above note 161, at 83.

768 The Court noted that while the Committee had not been mentioned among institutions that can bring cases to the Court under Art. 5(1) of the Protocol, it had been specifically authorised to do so in the subsequent 2008 Protocol on the merger of the current Court with the Court of Justice of the African Union to create the African Court of Justice and Human Rights.

769 See 'Request for Advisory Opinion by the African Committee of Experts on the Rights and Welfare of the Child on the Standing of the African Committee of Experts on the Rights and Welfare of the Child before the African Court of Human and Peoples' Rights', Request No 002/2013, 20 December 2014.

Remarkably, this opt-in procedure was introduced at a very late stage of the negotiations that led to the drafting of the Protocol.

Whereas NGOs play a crucial role in cases brought before the quasi-judicial bodies of the African human rights system, their access to the ACtHPR is significantly curtailed by the procedural hurdles enshrined in the Protocol. This has a ripple effect on victims as, due to widespread illiteracy and lack of means, NGOs remain the main champions of human rights in the continent. In December 2009 the African Court issued its first judgment, in which it declared that it had no jurisdiction in the case because Senegal did not allow individuals direct access to the Court. Since then the Court has received 40 applications, the majority of which were struck out or are still pending. It follows that the ACtHPR contribution in the field of reparations has so far been almost non-existent[770] and it is still too soon to determine what role it will play with regard to child victims.

6.3. THE INTER-AMERICAN HUMAN RIGHTS SYSTEM

The Inter-American human rights system was created by the Organisation of American States ('OAS'). The 1948 conference that approved the OAS Charter also adopted the American Declaration of the Rights and Duties of Man ('American Declaration').[771] Both the Inter-American Court and Commission have held that even though the American Declaration was not conceived as a binding treaty, nowadays it represents a source of obligations for the OAS Member States.[772] In 1969 the OAS promulgated the American Convention on Human Rights, which has been ratified by 23 of the 35 States parties to the OAS.

The two enforcement bodies are the IACHR and the IACtHR. They have different but complementary functions and a primary role played by both organs

770 In June 2013 the ACtHPR issued its first ruling on reparations in *Mtikila v. United Republic of Tanzania*. In its ruling the Court found that there exists a fundamental principle of international law that where a violation of an 'international obligation' causes harm, there is an obligation to provide adequate reparation which the Court should follow and is reflected in Art. 27(1) of the Court's Protocol. The Court found that applying this principle, pecuniary and non-pecuniary damages and legal expenses were capable of being awarded by the Court, but that the Applicant had failed to provide evidence of a link between the damages and expenses claimed and the claim itself. See Judgment of 15 June 2013 (Merits), (2013) ACtHPR, Application No. 011/2011.

771 Charter of the Organisation of American States, 30 April 1948, entered into force on 13 December 1951, 119 UNTS 3; American Declaration of the Rights and Duties of Man, OAS Res. XXX, reprinted in Basic Documents Pertaining to Human Rights in the Inter-American System, OAS/Ser.L/V/I.4 Rev. 9 (2003).

772 See J. Pasqualucci, 'The Americas', in Moeckli, Shah and Sivakumaran, above note 469, at 398–399.

is the processing of individual complaints that allege that an American State is liable for the violation of protected human rights.[773] Within the Inter-American human rights system it is important to clarify from the outset that child victims, and victims in general, cannot directly access the IACtHR. According to the provisions enshrined in the ACHR[774] only the Inter-American Commission and States parties to the American Convention may submit complaints directly to the Court,[775] while individuals, groups and organisations can resort to the Inter-American Commission.[776] Unlike the European Convention on Human Rights, the American Convention contains a specific provision for the protection of children, which is enshrined in Article 19. The norm promotes children's special protection on the basis of their peculiar condition as minors and it imposes on the family, society and the State the duty to guarantee it. What makes Article 19 so relevant in the field of children's rights is not the text itself, but rather the way the Commission and the Court have been applying and interpreting its wording.

6.3.1. THE INTER-AMERICAN COMMISSION ON HUMAN RIGHTS AND ITS ROLE IN RELATION TO CHILD VICTIMS

Since its establishment, the Inter-American Commission on Human Rights ('IACHR') has referred to children's rights both in general reports and in several decisions on petitions and cases. During the 1960s, 1970s and 1980s, the Commission mainly focused on the situation of human rights violations or decided whether or not the human rights of a child were violated, without proceeding to substantive development of the content of the law. During that time, the IACHR relied exclusively on the legal framework the American Declaration of the Rights and Duties of Man, which enshrines two provisions on children's rights.[777] Both provisions depict children as human beings that deserve assistance and care due to their status as minors and neither of them manages to go beyond a restricted view of children's rights. The entry into force of the ACHR marked a turning point for the Inter-American human rights system and has significantly contributed to enhancing children's rights in the region. When the CRC came into effect the IACHR further increased its recognition of children as legal subjects entitled to human rights and in the past 25 years it has heard cases involving street children, use of children in armed conflicts and recruitment of

773 Ibidem.
774 Ibidem.
775 Art. 61(1) of the ACHR.
776 M. Pinto, 'The Role of the Inter-American Commission and Court of Human Rights in the Protection of Human Rights: Achievements and Contemporary Challenges', (2013) 20 *Human Rights Brief* 34.
777 See Art. VII and Art. XXX of the American Declaration.

children into compulsory military service, imprisonment of children with their parents, the situation of displaced children, abusive treatment and deplorable conditions in detention centres for children, sexual exploitation, and labour exploitation.[778]

Before giving some examples of the IACHR's approach to child victims, a few general caveats are needed with regard to the IACHR's capability to issue decisions on IHRL violations. When the IACHR processes individual petitions it must abide by the American Convention as well as the Commission's Statute and Rules of Procedure. Article 23 of the IACHR's Rules of Procedure states that any person or group of persons or non-governmental entities legally recognised in one or more of the Member States of the OAS may submit petitions to the Commission, on their behalf or on behalf of third persons.[779]

With regard to individual complaints, in addition to the details of the person or organisation submitting it, the petition must also include information about the alleged human rights violation, the alleged victim(s) and the alleged perpetrators (when feasible). In particular, the petition must include an accurate description of the government's responsibilities for the human rights abuse in question. The State may be involved in the violation directly by committing the abuse, or indirectly, by failing to prohibit, prevent, or stop the human rights violation in question.[780] In order for the petition to be admissible, the remedies available at the domestic level must have been exhausted, the petition must have been lodged within the prescribed time and must not duplicate another petition. When the petition is regarded as admissible, the petitioner is given two months to submit additional information on the merits. This information is then transferred to the State, which then also has two months to respond. Prior to deciding on the merits of the case, the IACHR sets a time period for the parties to consider the possibility of reaching a friendly settlement.[781] When no friendly settlement is pursued, the IACHR deliberates on the merits of the case. If it is established that there have been one or more violations of the ACHR, the IACHR drafts a preliminary report with recommendations. The concerned State must then

[778] *The Rights of the Child in the Inter-American Human Rights System*, 2nd edn., Chapter II, Summary on Jurisprudence of the Inter-American System Of Human Rights Pertaining to Children, OEA/Ser.L/V/II.133, doc. 34, 29 October 2008.

[779] See Rules of Procedure of the Inter-American Commission on Human Rights (Approved by the Commission at its 109th special session held 4–8 Dec 2000 and amended at its 116th regular period of sessions, held 7–25 Oct 2002). Art. 23 of the Rules of Procedure mirrors Art. 44 of the ACHR. According to Art. 24 of the Rules of Procedure, '[T]he Commission may also, *motu proprio*, initiate the processing of a petition which, in its view, meets the necessary requirements'.

[780] See Art. 28(f) of the Rules of Procedure.

[781] See Art. 41 of the Rules of Procedure. See generally R.K. Goldman, 'History and Action: The Inter-American Human Rights System and the Role of the Inter-American Commission on Human Rights', (2009) 31 *Human Rights Quarterly* 856, at 856–860.

report on the measures adopted to comply with the recommendations within a certain time frame. Although non-binding, these recommendations are influential. If a State does not comply with the recommendations, the IACHR can bring the case to the IACtHR. To do so, the State must have ratified the ACHR and voluntarily accepted the IACtHR's jurisdiction, either on a blanket basis or for a specific case. The ACHR specifies that there is a three-month deadline to submit a case to the Court if the matter has not been settled.[782] It is worth noting that in 1998, pursuant to Article 15 of the Rules of Procedure, which enable the Commission to establish rapporteurships to better fulfil its functions, the Office of the Rapporteur of the Rights of the Child was set up within the Inter-American Commission. The Office provides advice to the IACHR in the proceedings of individual petitions, cases and requests for precautionary and provisional measures, which address the rights of the child.[783]

The IACHR has heard many cases related to violations against children and it has used its powers to strengthen, to the maximum extent possible, respect and promotion of children's rights. For example, in the *Jailton Neri da Fonseca v. Brazil* case, which involved the arbitrary detention and extra-judicial execution by the military police of a 14-year-old child,[784] the IACHR established that, in light of Article 19 of the ACHR,

> respect for the rights of the child constitutes a fundamental value in a society that claims to ensure social justice and human rights. This not only entails providing children care and protection, basic parameters that have traditionally guided the legal and theoretical concept of the content of such rights, but also means recognizing, respecting, and guaranteeing the individual personality of the child, as a holder of rights and obligations.[785]

According to the IACHR, 'it is reasonable to infer that Jailton was perfectly aware that his life was in serious and imminent danger and that such circumstance caused extreme fear and psychological and moral suffering in him'. The Commission considered that these acts constitute torture, as defined in Article 2 of the Inter-American Convention to Prevent and Punish Torture, according to which '... torture shall also be understood to be the use of methods upon a person intended to obliterate the personality of the victim or to diminish his physical or mental capacities, even if they do not cause physical pain or mental anguish'. In particular the IACHR noted that 'in the case of children the highest standard must be applied in determining the degree of suffering, taking into

---

782 See Art. 51(1) of the ACHR.

783 Further information about the mandate of the Rapporteurship on the Rights of the Child is available at: http://www.oas.org/en/iachr/children/mandate/Functions.asp.

784 Case of 11 March 2004, (2004), IACHR, Report No. 33/04, Case No. 11.634.

785 Ibidem, §80.

account factors such as age, sex, the effect of the tension and fear experienced, the status of the victim's health, and his maturity, for instance'.[786] Significantly the Commission stated that extra-judicial executions amount to psychological torture and in cases involving children, due to their vulnerability, this results in the victim experiencing extreme fear and terror. The IACHR recommended that the State make full reparations to the next of kin of Jailton Neri da Fonseca. Further the Commission asked the State to: ensure a full, impartial, and effective investigation into the crime conducted by non-military organs, with a view to establishing responsibility for the acts related to the detention and murder of Jailton Neri da Fonseca and punishing the responsible parties; pay compensation to the next of kin of the victims in an amount sufficient to make up for both the material damages and the moral damages suffered on the occasion of his murder; amend Article 9 of the Military Criminal Code and Article 82 of the Code of Military Criminal Procedure, in addition to any other domestic legal provisions that need to be amended to abolish the competence of the military police to investigate human rights violations committed by members of the military police, and transfer that competence to the civilian police; adopt and implement measures to educate officers of the justice system and members of the police to prevent acts involving racial discrimination in police operations, and in criminal investigations, proceedings, or sentencing; and adopt and implement immediate measures to ensure observance of the rights established in the American Convention, the CRC, and the other national and international standards on the matter, in order to ensure that the right to special protection of children is enforced in Brazil.[787] Even though the State did not fully comply with the recommendations made by the IACHR, the case has not been brought before the IACtHR because the event, as well as the investigations and the rest of the proceedings, occurred prior to the date on which Brazil accepted the jurisdiction of the Inter-American Court of Human Rights.[788]

In another landmark case, *Gerardo Vargas Areco v. Paraguay*,[789] the IACHR dealt with the recruitment of a 15-year-old boy arrested for failing to make a voluntary and timely return to his military post after a leave of absence and who was ultimately killed while allegedly trying to escape the punishment. In its Merits Report No. 76/04 of 19 October 2004, the Commission stated that

> the lack of the obligation to prevent consists in allowing, against what is stated in its Constitution and its domestic laws, that children under 18 years old, such as Geraldo

786 Ibidem, §64.
787 Ibidem, §155.
788 Ibidem, §154.
789 Case of 11 October 2004, (2004) IACHR, Report No. 76/04, Case No. 12.300.

> Vargas Areco, are recruited into military service. To place a child under that situation implies a breach of the obligation to ensure the right to life.[790]

Furthermore the IACHR stressed that

> the integral protection recognised in Article 19 of the Convention demands in the present case, that the State enforces its Constitution and its domestic laws. It implied that the armed forces do not recruited [*sic*] Vargas Areco into compulsory military service ... The integral protection that required Vargas Areco [*sic*] also demanded that he was not treated as an adult, instead of being treated as a child. It also meant not to torture or to subject him to cruel, inhuman and degrading treatment, as it happened.[791]

Since the State did not implement the recommendations issued by the IACHR, the case has been brought before the IACtHR. As Paraguay did not accept the jurisdiction of the Court until after Vargas Areco's recruitment and death, the Court could not hear violations of the victim's right to life directly, but it had to focus on the impact that his death had on his family. The Court also found that it could not hear claims surrounding the systematic recruitment of children in Paraguay as other child recruits were not party to the case. The Court did, however, note Paraguay's obligations to cease recruiting children under both the Optional Protocol to the CRC on the involvement of children in armed conflict and the CRC itself.[792] The Court ordered Paraguay to pay compensation to the family, to offer public apologies, to train military members in human rights, and to reform the national laws so that they were in line with the international regulations against recruiting child soldiers.[793]

It is worth recalling that the issue of children's involvement in armed conflict was the object of a specific recommendation issued by the IACHR in 1999.[794] According to it:

> Although laws in most member countries establish a minimum age of 18 for conscription, practices violating the human rights of children persist. The Commission finds such practices comparable to slavery and forced servitude. One example is the forced 'drafting' by state military forces, which generally recruit young people from poor and/or indigenous families. Armed dissident groups also recruit minors, often through kidnapping, or by forcing families to surrender them as contributions to the

790 Ibidem, §144.

791 Ibidem, §70.

792 Judgment of 26 September 2006 (Merits, Reparations and Costs), (2006) IACtHR, Series C No. 155, §§84–87 and §§111–134.

793 Ibidem, §136 et seq.

794 IACHR, Annual Report of the Inter-American Commission on Human Rights 1999, Chapter 6, Recommendation for eradicating the recruitment of children and their participation in armed conflicts, OEA/Ser.L/V/II.106Doc. 3, 13 April 2000, at 1619.

> war. The use of children and adolescents in armed conflicts places their lives, well-being, and education at great risk. They are forced to use high-caliber weapons. They are required to lay explosives, to kill other children who are considered 'traitors' or change their minds, and to participate in kidnappings, surveillance, and bomb intelligence work. In some cases, children as young as eight are used for these perilous tasks. These illegal, perverse practices subject boys, girls, and youths to the inherent risks of combat, to sexual abuse, and to other forms of abusive, brutal, and humiliating treatment. They are drawn into a culture of violence, and their rights to education and to ordinary participation in society are curtailed.[795]

In line with this statement the IACHR has drafted a set of recommendations to the States as well as the other parties involved in armed conflicts (paramilitary groups and armed dissident groups). With regard to the latter the IACHR has recommended they observe, implement and enforce humanitarian and international law on the rights of children and refrain from any form of violence, pressure or monetary incentive designed to persuade families to facilitate access to or surrender their minor children for participation in armed or war activities. Concerning the former, the Commission identified as crucial the following actions: repealing any laws or regulations that permit conscription or voluntary enlistment of adolescents under the minimum age allowed by international instruments; urging States to sign and eventually ratify the Optional Protocol to the CRC on the involvement of children in armed conflict; enacting severe legislative, judicial or other measures to identify, prosecute and punish State agents or civilians who carry out, authorise, assist in or facilitate the recruitment of minors or their use in armed conflicts; establishing special policies, mechanisms and institutions for the recovery, re-education and social rehabilitation of children and youths who have participated in armed organisations, whether State or non-governmental; implementing policies for redressing damage to children and adolescents wounded or disabled by armed conflicts, indemnifying them and providing them with proper physical and psychological care and remedial education; and setting up mechanisms to compensate for the negative effects of armed conflicts on children and adolescents from refugee or internally displaced families.[796]

It is important to highlight that the IACHR has been playing a proactive role in promoting not only the development of the contentious jurisprudence of the Inter-American Court, but also the exercise of its advisory capacity in cases related to children. The most significant example is the request for an Advisory Opinion on the Juridical Status and Human Rights of the Child that the IACHR

795 Ibidem.

796 Ibidem.

submitted in 2001 pursuant to Article 64(1) of the ACHR.[797] The reasoning of the Court ultimately resulted in the recognition that

> ... it is undeniable that the international juridical subjectivity of the human being has been affirmed and expanded in the last decades ..., and that the child (as *titulaire* of rights) is no exception to that. In the face of the limitations of the juridical capacity of the child (to exercise his rights for himself), a legal representative is recognised to him. But independently of such limitations, the juridical personality of the child, – as of every human being, – projects itself at international level. As it is not possible to conceive rights – emanated directly from International Law – without the prerogative of vindicating them, the whole evolution of the matter has oriented itself towards the crystallization of the right of the individual – including the child – to resort directly to the international jurisdictions.[798]

Moreover, in cases affecting minors, the legal framework set to protect their human rights is not confined to the provisions enshrined in Article 19 of the ACHR. In fact, it also includes (for purposes of interpretation and not of direct application and in addition to other international instruments on human rights in general) the terms of the Declarations on the Rights of the Child of 1924 and 1959, the CRC, the United Nations Standard Minimum Rules for the Administration of Juvenile Justice, known as the 1985 Beijing Rules, the Standard Minimum Rules for Non-Custodial Measures, known as the 1990 Tokyo Rules, and the United Nations Guidelines for the Prevention of Juvenile Delinquency, known as the 1990 Riyadh Guidelines.[799] All these instruments are parts of a comprehensive 'international *corpus juris*' for the protection of the child, which should be used as a source of law by the Court to establish 'the content and scope' of the obligations undertaken by the State through Article 19 of the ACHR.[800]

6.3.2. CHILD VICTIMS BEFORE THE INTER-AMERICAN COURT OF HUMAN RIGHTS: PRELIMINARY REMARKS ON THE REPARATIONS AWARDED IN CASES CONCERNING CHILD VICTIMS

Since the recommendations issued by the Commission in its reports on the merits are not binding and therefore also the remedial measures identified are

797 Advisory Opinion of 28 August 2002 (Juridical Condition and Human Rights of the Child), above note 65.

798 Ibidem, §55.

799 Ibidem, §26. According to the IACtHR, 'at least 80 international instruments adopted during the 20th century are applicable to children in various degrees. Among them, the ones mentioned stand out.'

800 Ibidem.

not always punctually implemented, the interest of the petitioner in pursuing a lawsuit before the Inter-American Court is evident. According to Article 43 of the Rules of Procedure of the IACHR, the petitioner interested in resorting to the Court's jurisdiction, as stated in Article 43(3) of the Rules of Procedure, has to provide the IACHR with the following information:

> the position of the victim or the victim's family members, if different from that of the petitioner; the personal data relative to the victim and the victim's family members; the reasons he or she considers that the case should be referred to the Court; the documentary, testimonial, and expert evidence available; and the claims concerning reparations and costs.

So far violations of children's rights brought before the IACtHR have encompassed, *inter alia*, breaches of the right to life, prohibition of torture, extra-judicial executions, illegal detention and the right to nationality and to equal protection.[801] Child victims cannot be the applicants in cases concerning them, which have instead been referred to the Inter-American Court by the IACHR. In turn, most of the cases brought before the IACHR have been initiated by national and regional NGOs or by the children's relatives.[802] Article 8 of the ACHR provides that every person has the right to be heard by a tribunal in the determination of his or her legal rights. Article 25 completes the provision guaranteeing the right to a simple and prompt judicial remedy for violations of rights.[803] As already stressed, victims must resort to the IACHR to have their claims heard within the inter-American human rights system.[804] Whereas the Commission performs quasi-judicial tasks in the initial stages of an individual petition, its role changes before the IACtHR's proceedings and it can be described as being similar to that of a prosecutor since the Commission maintains an active function defending the public interest against the State.[805]

Originally, the Rules of Procedure of the Inter-American Court limited victims' participation only to the reparation phase. Nevertheless, since 2001 when the Rules were amended, victims have been granted the power to actively

---

801 See generally Feria Tinta, above note 6.

802 In particular Casa Alianza and the Center for Justice and International Law ('CEJIL').

803 See D. Cassel, 'The Inter-American Court of Human Rights', in Due Process of Law Foundation, *Victims Un-silenced: The Inter-American Human Rights System and Transitional Justice in Latin America*, July 2007, available at: http://www.dplf.org/uploads/1190403828.pdf.

804 See Arts. 48, 50 and 61 of the ACHR.

805 On the role of the Commission, see A.A. Cançado Trindade, *The Access of Individuals to International Justice*, Oxford University Press, Oxford, 2011. According to the author, in the proceedings before the IACtHR the Commission is reserved the role of defender of the public interest and an undesirable ambiguity is created if the Commission has the additional function of defending the interests of the alleged victims.

participate, along with the Commission, during all the phases of the trial, namely admissibility, merits and reparations. In order to effectuate the full participation of the victims, including those who cannot afford the legal expenses related to the proceedings, in 2008 the OAS's General Assembly established a Fund for Legal Assistance. In June 2010 the Court approved a document to regulate access to the fund for victims interested in bringing a case before the IACtHR.[806]

According to Article 40 of the Court's Rules of Procedure, from the day when notice of the case's presentation has occurred, the alleged victim(s) or their representatives have a non-renewable term of two months to submit to the Court a brief containing pleadings, motions and evidence, including all the claims and also those relating to reparations and costs. As stated by the Court itself in the *Goiburú et al v. Paraguay* case:

> [D]uring the investigation and judicial proceedings, the victims or their next of kin must have *ample opportunity to take part and be heard*, both in the elucidation of the facts and the punishment of those responsible, and in the quest for fair compensation, in accordance with domestic law and the American Convention.[807]

Alleged victims can be heard during the proceedings before the Court, alongside witnesses and expert witnesses. According to Article 51(5) unlike the witnesses and the expert witnesses the alleged victims shall not take the solemn oath before rendering their statements. Moreover, as stated in Article 51(11), 'the Court may receive the statements of witnesses, expert witnesses, or alleged victims through the use of electronic audio-visual means'; this provision may apply to all the people called to testify and there is no special provision for children.

With regard to reparations, the most relevant provision to take into consideration is Article 63 of the ACHR.[808] Shelton reported that the drafting history of the American Convention reveals no debate about conferring broad remedial competence to Article 63.[809] The IACHR was in charge of preparing the first draft of the American Convention and originally the power to award reparations was enshrined in Article 52(1). The Commission used as basis three documents submitted by the Inter-American Council of Jurists, the government of Chile and the government of Uruguay. These earlier drafts mirrored Article 50

806 See Resolución de la Asamblea General de la Organización de Estados Americanos (OEA), AG/RES/ 2426 de 3 de junio de 2008.

807 Judgment of 22 September 2006 (Merits, Reparations and Costs), (2006) IACtHR, Series C, No. 153, §117 (emphasis added).

808 Art. 63(1) of the ACHR states: '[T]hat if the Court finds that there has been a violation of a right or freedom protected by this Convention, the Court shall rule that the injured party be ensured the enjoyment of his right or freedom that was violated. It shall also rule, if appropriate, that the consequences of the measure or situation that constituted the breach of such right or freedom be remedied and that fair compensation be paid to the injured party.'

809 See Shelton, above note 21, at 217.

of the European Convention and thus conferred on the IACtHR a more restricted power. In the end the Commission adopted a text which is broader and more focused on defence of the injured party as it enables the Court to order measures that ensure the victim's enjoyment of future respect for the rights and freedoms that have been violated, remedy the consequences of the violations that occurred and compensate the harm suffered.[810] According to the Court itself, Article 63(1) expresses a principle of customary international law as regards States' responsibility for the commission of an unlawful act against individuals.[811] In a famous passage the Court further explained that

> reparation for damages caused by a violation of an international obligation requires, whenever possible, full restitution (*restitutio in integrum*), which is to reinstate the situation that existed prior to the commission of the violation. If, as in the instant case, full restitution is not possible, an international court must order a series of measures that will safeguard the violated rights, redress the consequences that the violations engendered, and order payment of compensation for the damages caused.[812]

The series of measures to which the Court referred encompass both pecuniary and non-pecuniary reparations and, although the IACtHR initially refrained from awarding non-monetary remedies, over the years it has fully exploited Article 63's potential to develop an extensive interpretation as to what can legitimately be considered a remedy under international law.[813]

The Court's dynamic and expansive application of Article 63(1) has also had an impact on the identification of the 'injured party'. The term refers to both the victim and his/her next of kin, who can also be considered as victims of the violation that occurred. As the Court stressed in the *Myrna Mack Chang* case, the notion of kinship enshrined in Article 2 of the Rules of Procedure applies to the immediate family, i.e. the direct ascendants and descendants, siblings, spouses or permanent companions, but it can be interpreted also in a broader way since the judges had assimilated the victim's first cousin to her siblings as there was evidence of a close and intimate relationship existing between them.[814]

---

810 Ibidem.

811 Judgment of 3 December 2001 (Reparations), (2001) IACtHR, Series C No. 88, §40, 'The Court has held that Article 63(1) of the American Convention embodies a rule of customary law that is one of the basic principles of contemporary international law as regards the responsibility of States. When an unlawful act imputable to a State occurs, that State immediately becomes responsible in law for violation of an international norm, which carries with it the obligation to make reparation and to put an end to the consequences of the violation.'

812 Ibidem, §41.

813 See B. Mayeux and J. Mirabal, 'Collective and Moral Reparations in the Inter-American Court of Human Rights', Report Human Rights Clinic, The University of Texas School of Law, November 2009, at 9, available at: https://law.utexas.edu/wp-content/uploads/sites/11/2015/04/2009-HRC-Cambodia-CollectiveReparations.pdf.

814 Judgment of 25 November 2003 (Merits, Reparations and Costs), (2003) IACtHR, Series C No. 101, §243, 'The provision of Article 2(15) of the Rules of Procedure should be underlined,

The criteria employed by the IACtHR to establish the next of kin are based on presumptions regarding the 'closeness of the family relationship, the particular circumstances of the relationship with the victim, the degree to which the family member was a witness of the events related to the [violation], the way in which the family member was involved in attempts to obtain information about the [violation] and the State's response to the steps undertaken'.[815]

As clarified by the President of the Court in the *Ituango Massacres v. Colombia* case, 'the victim or injured party is the possessor of the legally protected interest safeguarded by the rights established in the American Convention: life, liberty, safety, property, integrity etcetera. Thus the victim is who suffers the harm of the respective right'.[816] Furthermore, the President of the Court shed light on the distinction between 'direct victim', namely the individual against whom the illegal conduct of the State agent is directed immediately, explicitly and deliberately, and 'indirect victim', the individual who does not suffer this illegal conduct in the same way (i.e. *immediately, directly and deliberately*) but who also sees his own rights affected or violated by the impact on the so-called direct victim.[817] Although the distinction preserves its importance, both direct and indirect victims flow together into the notion of injured party and, therefore, are entitled to participate in the proceedings and claim for reparations. As established under Article 51(5) of the Rules of Procedure, during the first hearing the identities of the alleged victims must be determined, hence it follows that the injured party has to stand before the Court in order to take part in the trial and demand reparations. Nevertheless, the IACtHR has been flexible regarding both the idea of 'standing before the Court' and the issue of victims' identification. Concerning the first point, in *Bámaca-Velásquez v. Guatemala* the Court allowed one of the beneficiaries of the non-pecuniary damages, namely the victim's sister, to be added later in the judgment as complex circumstances delayed her inclusion in the case.[818] Also in the *Mack Chang* case the victim's sister did not participate in the proceedings, but nonetheless was recognised as a beneficiary of reparations.[819]

---

as regards the necessary breadth of the concept of "next of kin of the victim". Said concept includes all persons linked by close kinship, including the parents, children and siblings, who might have the right to compensation, insofar as they fulfil the requirements set forth in the case law of this Court. Regarding this point, we must highlight the criterion followed by the Court of assuming that the death of an individual causes non-pecuniary damage to the closest members of the family, especially those who were *in close emotional contact with the victim*' (emphasis added).

815 Judgment of 25 November 2000 (Judgment), (2000) IACtHR, Series C No. 70, §163.

816 Judgment of 1 July 2006 (Preliminary Objections, Merits, Reparations and Costs), (2006) IACtHR, Series C No. 148, Separate Concurring Opinion of Judge S. Garcia Ramirez, §10.

817 Ibidem, §11.

818 See Judgment of 22 February 2002 (Reparations and Costs), (2002) IACtHR, Series C No. 91, §36.

819 Judgment of 25 November 2003, above note 814, §245.

As for the second point, which concerns victims' identification, in the *Mapiripàn Massacre v. Colombia* case the IACtHR did not exclude the possibility of obtaining justice and reparations for the unidentified victims and their next of kin.[820] The same approach was followed in the *Moiwana Community v. Suriname* case where individuals already listed as beneficiaries in the proceedings were granted the possibility to prove their identity by providing birth certificates and family books. Moreover, the victims of the case who had not been properly identified through the submission before the Court of birth certificates or family books could appear within 24 months following the notification of the instant judgment and provide 'sufficient means' of identification, which entailed either an official document attesting the person's identity or a statement before a competent State official by a recognised leader of the Moiwana Community members, as well as the declarations of two additional persons.[821]

These examples provided an account of the Court's strong concern for victims and its attitude towards the definition of the 'injured party'. Such factors clearly have an impact also on child victims, especially when they are identified as injured parties in cases brought before the IACtHR.

6.3.2.1. *Reparations Awarded to Children as Indirect Victims*

Many of the judgments issued by the IACtHR have dealt with violations of the right to life, enshrined in Article 4 of the ACHR, or cases of forced disappearance. Therefore, when the direct victims have not survived the breaches or are still missing, complaints have been brought forward by their family members. The family members, who are injured parties according to Article 63(1) of the American Convention, have sought remedies for the harm experienced by the deceased prior to death, for the death itself and for the consequential damages suffered in their own right.[822]

The Court has consistently held that both pecuniary and non-pecuniary claims survive and pass to the victims' heirs. Pecuniary damages, or material damages, refer to economic loss, while non-pecuniary, or moral, damages clearly

[820] 'The Court will apply the provision set forth in the Chapter on beneficiaries to the next of kin of the victims who have not been individually identified in this proceeding, which is that to receive the respective payments they must appear before the officials in charge of the official mechanism established for that purpose within 24 months of the date when the State notifies them that their next of kin has been individually identified, and they must prove their relationship to or kinship with the victim, by means of adequate identification or of two attesting witnesses, as were the case'. See Judgment of 15 September 2005 (Merits, Reparations and Costs), (2005) IACtHR, Series C No. 134, §257 and §287.

[821] See Judgment of 15 June 2005 (Merits), (2005) IACtHR, Series C No. 124, §178.

[822] See Shelton, above note 21, at 212.

encompass the intangible injuries, such as the pain and suffering experienced.[823] Remarkably, rather than applying the national law of the State concerned or relying on the victim's testimony, the IACtHR has developed 'its own' law on succession and, thus, in the case of human rights violations the beneficiaries of the reparations do not need to also be regarded as the legitimate heirs under the municipal law of the State involved in the proceeding.[824] Both pecuniary and non-pecuniary damages, pursuant to the Court's succession law, are divided between the spouse and the children of the victim. According to Shelton the awards are usually distributed in a way that provides less to the spouse than would be the case in many national legal systems, and consequently the offspring receive a larger sum.[825] In the first case heard before the IACtHR, *Velásquez-Rodríguez v. Honduras*, great attention was paid to the future of the victim's children. With regard to pecuniary damages the Court drew a clear distinction between the calculation of loss of earnings in the case of a victim who is totally and permanently disabled and the calculation of compensation made in cases where the victim is deceased or disappeared and the beneficiaries are the family members. The case in question fell within the second scenario and therefore the IACtHR decided not to adhere to rigid criteria to establish the amount of damages, but rather to provide a 'prudent estimation' of the sum.[826] Through such estimation the Court assigned three-quarters of the indemnity to the victim's children and only the remaining one-quarter to his wife. In particular, the Court deemed it appropriate to order the institution of a trust fund, under the most favourable conditions permitted by Honduran banking practice, with the purpose of distributing to each child a monthly payment until the age of 25 years.[827]

---

823 See D. Cassel, 'The Expanding Scope and Impact of the Inter-American Court of Human Rights', in De Feyter et al. above note 22, at 198.

824 The Court had clarified this point already in its first case, see Judgment of 17 August 1990 (Interpretation of Compensatory Damages), (1990), IACtHR, Series C No. 4, §54.

825 See Shelton, above note 21, at 244.

826 See Judgment of 17 August 1990 (Interpretation of Compensatory Damages), above note 824, §§47–48. '[In that case] the compensation should include all he failed to receive, together with appropriate adjustments based upon his probable life expectancy. In that circumstance, the only income for the victim is what he would have received, but will not receive, as earnings. If the beneficiaries of the compensation are the family members, the situation is different. In principle, the family members have an actual or future possibility of working or receiving income on their own. The children, who should be guaranteed the possibility of an education which might extend to the age of twenty-five, could, for example, begin to work at that time. It is not correct, then, in these cases, to adhere to rigid criteria, more appropriate to the situation described in the above paragraph, but rather to arrive at a prudent estimate of the damages, given the circumstances of each case.'

827 Ibidem, §58.

This approach has been consistently followed by the Court with regard to cases which involved a relevant number of indirect victims. For instance in the *Aloeboetoe v. Suriname* case the IACtHR specified that

> the compensation fixed for the victims' heirs includes an amount that will enable the minor children to continue their education until they reach a certain age. Nevertheless, these goals will not be met merely by granting compensatory damages; it is also essential that the children be offered a school where they can receive adequate education and basic medical attention.[828]

Concerning symbolic reparations, the Court has further shown its creative attitude and its deep understanding of cultural differences. The principles which govern the Court's symbolic reparations are mainly 'the restoration of the victim's dignity' and the 'prevention of future violations'.[829] According to the IACtHR the judgment *per se* constitutes a form of reparations for the victims, nevertheless the Court has clarified that the victims cannot be entirely satisfied by the issuing of a judicial decision which acknowledges their sufferance and recognises them as the party injured by the State's misconduct.[830] The same reasoning has been applied to the State's admission of responsibility for the human rights violations concerned. As stressed by Antkowiak, since 1991 States have begun to recognise their legal responsibility for the violations attributed to them before the Inter-American Court.[831] Depending on the characteristics of the declaration made by the State, the Court can either examine the merits of the case or move directly to the reparations phase. Commonly the Court opts for the first solution since the discussion on the merits represents a form of reparation for the victims, although, as mentioned above, this is far from being an exhaustive remedy.[832] The most significant moral reparations issued by the Court include public ceremonies performed with the participation of local leaders and State authorities; the construction of memorials; the duty to publicise the Inter-American Court's judgments in national newspapers; and the imposition on the state of structural changes to domestic law.[833] Children, as indirect victims or simple members of

---

828 Judgment of 10 September 1993 (Reparations), (1993) IACtHR, Series C No. 15, §96. See also S. Davidson, 'Remedies for Violations of the American Convention on Human Rights', (1995) 44 *International and Comparative Law Quarterly* 405, at 410–414.

829 See Mayeux and Mirabal above note 813, at 13.

830 See for instance Judgment of 17 August 1990 (Interpretation of Compensatory Damages), above note 824, §260.

831 See Antkowiak, above note 528, at 64.

832 Ibidem, at 78.

833 See Judgment of 15 June 2005 (Merits), above note 527; Judgment of 25 November 2003, above note 814, Judgment of 1 March 2005 (Merits, Reparations and Costs), (2005) IACtHR, Series C No. 120; Judgment of 27 November 2008 (Merits, Reparations and Costs), (2008) IACtHR, Series C No. 191.

the community where the remedies are enforced, are among the beneficiaries of these collective and moral forms of reparations awarded by the Court.

6.3.2.2. *Reparations Awarded to Children as Direct Victims*

In some landmark judgments, e.g. *El Mozote v. El Salvador*, the IACtHR has stressed that cases in which children are victims of human rights violations are especially serious,[834] because children are holders of the rights established in the American Convention, and also possess the special measures of protection established in Article 19, which must be defined according to the particular circumstances of each specific case. The adoption of special measures for the protection of children corresponds to both the State and also the family, the community and the society to which they belong, and these include the measures relating to non-discrimination, the prohibition of torture, and the conditions that must be observed in cases in which children are deprived of liberty.[835]

Bearing this caveat in mind, the current section considers the most relevant developments achieved by the Court's jurisprudence on children's rights in cases where child victims have been affected by gross human rights violations perpetrated in the context of an internal armed conflict; it does not matter whether such violations were directly related to the conflict or not.

In the *Villagrán-Morales et al. v. Guatemala* case, where five young men, among whom three were still minors, were extra-legally executed by members of the Guatemalan National Police as part of a systematic pattern of violence carried out against so-called 'street children', the Court elaborated some fundamental concepts with regard to the enhancement of children's rights.[836] In this judgment the Inter-American Court referred to the notion of an international *corpus iuris* for the protection of the rights of children,[837] specifying that States are obliged to set special protective measures in order to guarantee not only the child's survival and development, but also the social rehabilitation or reinsertion of all children who are victims of abandonment or exploitation.[838] In particular in this case the State violated its duties to children by exposing them to a situation of double

834 Judgment of 31 August 2012 (Preliminary Objections, Merits, Reparations and Costs), (2012) IACtHR, Series C No. 246, §123.

835 Judgment of 25 October 2012 (Merits, Reparations and Costs), (2012) IACtHR, Series C No. 252, §150.

836 The crimes were committed in 1990; the civil war that affected the country for 36 years officially ended in 1996.

837 On the international *corpus iuris* for the protection of children's rights see Section 6.3.1 above.

838 See IACHR report, 'The Rights of the Child in the Inter-American Human Rights System', above note 794, at 471.

violation; in the first place because Guatemala did not prevent the children from living on the streets and secondly because, through its policies of neglect, it deprived them of the minimal conditions for a decent life.[839] Moreover, the children were denied the possibility of realising their 'project of life' (or 'life plan'), which, according to the Court, can be described as 'the victim's reasonable expectation for the future'.[840] In the judgment on reparations the IACtHR took into account the concept of 'life plan' for the calculation of the compensation due to the victims' families and imposed on the government of Guatemala the duties to adopt in its domestic legislation, legislative, administrative and any other measures that are necessary in order to adapt Guatemalan legislation to Article 19 of the Convention and to designate an educational centre with a name allusive to the young victims in this case and place in it a commemorative plaque with their names.[841] With regard to the victim's life plan, as noted by Pasqualucci, whereas in its earlier cases the IACtHR tried to lay down the framework for the institution of this innovative category of damages, more recently the Court seems to have abandoned this path.[842] The Court has explained that the all victims of gross IHRL violations suffer in the future as a result of the harm experienced and that 'no reparations could return the options of personal fulfilment of which the victim has been unfairly deprived'.[843] Consistently the Court has determined

839 See Judgment of 19 November 1999 (Merits), (1999) IACtHR, Series C No. 63, §184: 'The Commission described the three child victims of the facts of this case as persons who lived in extremely precarious socio-economic conditions and who fought to survive alone and fearful of a society that did not include them, but rather excluded them. Furthermore, it stated that, as the State abstained from taking effective measures to investigate and prosecute the perpetrators, it exacerbated the risk of violations of the rights of "street children" in general, and the victims of this case, in particular.'

840 The notion of project of life was first introduced in the Court's jurisprudence during the *Loyaza Tamayo v. Peru* case as the victim petitioned the Court for a ruling on the compensation which might be due to her in the form of damage to her 'life plan' and enumerated a number of factors that, in her judgement, should be taken into account to establish the scope of this head of damages and measure its consequences. The Court accepted the claim in principle and agreed that the applicant had suffered harm to her project of life, nevertheless the Court did not make an award under this head and, instead, invited the future victims and their representatives to elaborate a methodology capable of calculating this new kind of damage. See Judgment of 27 November 1998 (Reparations), (1998) IACtHR, Series C No. 42, §147: 'The head of damages to a victim's life plan has been examined both in recent doctrine and case law. This notion is different from the notions of special damages and loss of earnings. It is definitely not the same as the immediate and direct harm to a victim's assets, as in the case of "indirect or consequential damages". The concept of lost earnings refers solely to the loss of future economic earnings that can be quantified by certain measurable and objective indicators. The so-called "life plan" deals with the full self-actualisation of the person concerned and takes account of her calling in life, her particular circumstances, her potentialities, and her ambitions, thus permitting her to set for herself, in a reasonable manner, specific goals, and to attain those goals.'

841 Judgment of 19 November 1999 (Merits), above note 839, §123(5), (7).

842 See Pasqualucci, above note 87, at 246.

843 Judgment of 12 September 2005 (Merits, Reparations and Costs), (2005) IACtHR, Series C no 132, §189.

that considerations pertaining to the victim's life plan shall no longer be made in relation to the calculation of damages, instead the complex and comprehensive nature of this concept is better addressed through measures of satisfaction and guarantees of non-repetition.[844] An example of this trend can be found in the *Bulacio v. Argentina* case, which dealt with a 17-year-old boy who died from the violence suffered while at the hands of the Federal Argentinean Police.[845] In this case, the Court decided that there were insufficient grounds to assess the amount of loss of a definite chance, 'which must be estimated on the basis of certain damage with sufficient grounds to establish the probable realization of said damage'.[846]

In the *Molina Theissen v. Guatemala* case the Court dealt with the forced disappearance of Marco Antonio Molina Theissen, a 14-year-old boy kidnapped from his father's home by members of the Guatemalan Army. The IACtHR in its judgment reasserted the State's duty of special protection towards children, specifying that the State's responsibility for the breaches that occurred is 'compounded because what happened to the child Marco Antonio Molina Theissen was part of a practice of forced disappearance of persons, carried out by the State during the domestic armed conflict and carried out primarily by agents of its security forces, and children were also victims of this practice, as a means of torturing and frightening their families'.[847] In awarding collective reparations the Court in this case was particularly creative as it ordered the creation of a 'Hall of the Rights of the Child: Marco Antonio Molina Theissen' with the aim of honouring the memory of the boys and the girls who suffered violence during the armed conflict, and specifically that there should be a constant exhibit in remembrance of the victim; the establishment of a radio programme on the national radio station to discuss issues pertaining to children's rights; the dedication of a national day to the missing children who were victims of the domestic armed conflict in Guatemala; the granting of a scholarship for children's development and, specifically, one named after Marco Antonio Molina Theissen to provide access to a career in engineering for low-income youths since the victim was about to conclude his third year of secondary school and was therefore only two years away from obtaining his high school diploma and he planned to study civil engineering.[848]

In the judgment in the *Gómez Paquiyauri v. Peru* case the Court finally crystallised the concept of 'aggravated State responsibility'. The responsibility of

844 Ibidem.

845 Judgment of 18 September 2003 (Merits, Reparations and Costs), (2003) IACtHR, Series C No. 100. During the proceedings before the IACtHR an amicable settlement was reached and was validated by the Court itself.

846 Ibidem, §84. Judgment of 27 November 1998. Series C No. 43, §74.

847 See Judgment of 3 July 2004 (Reparations and Costs), (2004) IACtHR, Series C No. 108, §41.

848 Ibidem, §76 (d, e, f, g).

the Peruvian government for the systematic practice of human rights violations and extra-legal executions conducted by the State's agents against persons suspected of belonging to armed groups, in this case amounted to aggravated responsibility because the victims, two brothers, were children.[849] The aggravated responsibility of the State had a quantitative impact on the reparations awarded by the Court.[850] In the same case the Court also applied its own law on succession determining that the State should facilitate the registration of the name of the victim's daughter, who was born outside wedlock after the death of her father and therefore could not be recognised by him as required under the Peruvian domestic legislation.[851] As a symbolic form of reparation, the Inter-American Court imposed on the State the obligation to officially name a school in the province of El Callao after Rafael Samuel Gómez Paquiyauri and Emilio Moisés Gómez Paquiyauri, in a public ceremony and in the presence of the next of kin of the victims.[852]

The *Serrano Cruz Sisters v. El Salvador* case, concerning the kidnapping and forced disappearance of Ernestina and Erlinda Serrano Cruz (aged 7 and 3 years) perpetrated in 1982 by members of the Salvadoran Army Batallion during a military operation known as 'Operation Clean Up', is another landmark judgment in the jurisprudence of the IACtHR.[853] In this case the Court did more than establish the State's aggravated responsibility for the violations. Noting that under the domestic law of El Salvador forced disappearance was not classified as a crime, the Inter-American Court considered that El Salvador should include this crime appropriately in its national legislation and should adopt the necessary measures to ratify the Inter-American Convention on the Forced Disappearance of Persons.[854] The Court indicated further measures to be taken in order to find the two sisters and many other missing children. In particular the Court ordered the establishment of a National Commission to trace, with the active participation of civil society, the 'young people who disappeared when they were children during the armed conflict', the creation of a search web page and the

---

849 See Judgment of 8 July 2004 (Merits, Reparations and Costs), (2004) IACtHR, Series C No. 110, §76.

850 See Feria Tinta, above note 6, at 427, 'Nevertheless the award in the *Gomez Paquiyauri* case amounted to $740,500.00 in total. Whilst the Court awarded $240,500.00 for pecuniary damages, it was the award for moral damages that reflected more evidently the Court's view of the gravity of the violations incurred by the State of Peru in the said case.'

851 See above note 849, §253(13): 'The State must establish a scholarship up to university level, in favour of Nora Emely Gómez Peralta, and facilitate her registry as the daughter of Rafael Samuel Gómez Paquiyauri, under the terms set forth in paragraphs 237 and 238 of the instant Judgment.' See also §253(17).

852 Ibidem, §253(12).

853 See Judgment of 23 November 2004 (Merits, Reparations and Costs), (2004) IACtHR, Series C No. 118, §173.

854 Ibidem, §174.

setting up of a genetic information system to contribute to the identification of disappeared children.[855] In addition to that the Inter-American Court requested that the State designate a day dedicated to the children who had, for different reasons, disappeared during the internal armed conflict 'in order to make society aware of the need for all Salvadorans ... to work together to find the best solutions ... leading to the truth about the whereabouts of the children'.[856]

What emerges quite strongly from this overview of reparations awards issued by the IACtHR is that in the Court's view reparations should be understood always in an integral and holistic perspective,[857] in order to grasp the full complexity of the individual and collective damages produced by violence, also, if not especially, in cases involving child victims.

6.4. CONCLUSIONS

There is an important distinction to draw between international criminal courts and tribunals on the one hand and regional human rights bodies on the other. Traditionally, the former deal with individual criminal responsibility and focus on the punishment of the perpetrators rather than on the victims, whereas the latter, as demonstrated in the present chapter, aim to redress the misconduct of the States that have neglected or consciously breached their obligations under international law. The Annual Report of the Secretary-General on Children and Armed Conflict stressed that in 2014 the violations perpetrated against children increased, in particular in African countries, which are most affected by armed conflict, poverty and instability.[858] This situation further highlights the importance of an effective human rights system on that continent and it stresses the need to promote to the maximum extent possible compliance with children's rights. The hurdles that prevent victims from resorting to the 'transitory' ACtHPR and the State's discretion, which hampers the role traditionally played by NGOs in other settings, are crucial factors which significantly limit victims' access to remedies, including reparations. Whereas it is true that the African regional system is the only one that includes a Committee on the Rights and Welfare of the Child, it is also worth noting that it took the Committee nine years to hand down its first decision on a communication procedure and its 'jurisprudence' is

---

855 Ibidem, §189, 'This Court considers that a database should be established by creating a web page for tracing the disappeared children. The database should be set up with the given names and surnames, possible physical characteristics and any other existing information about the Serrano Cruz sisters and their next of kin.'

856 Ibidem, §196.

857 See L. Oette, 'Bringing Justice to Victims? Responses of Regional and International Human Rights Courts and Treaty Bodies to Mass Violations', in Ferstman, Goetz and Stephens, above note 190, at 236.

858 Annual Report of the Secretary-General on Children and Armed Conflict, above note 11.

rather scant.[859] The case law of the ACtHPR is rapidly growing, but the issue of reparations has been only incidentally addressed.

As stressed by the IACtHR the judgment is *per se* a form of reparation, nevertheless it cannot be regarded as a sufficient remedy for the victims, which clearly resort to regional human rights bodies in the hope of obtaining adequate redress for the harm suffered. The two enforcement mechanisms of the Inter-American human rights system have demonstrated great proclivity for victims' rights. The Inter-American strategy towards reparations has been built on the assumption that awards must be as comprehensive as possible, aiming at ensuring the enjoyment of the rights that were violated, addressing the consequences of these breaches and also guaranteeing their non-recurrence.[860] With regard to children both the IACHR and the IACtHR have developed and implemented an innovative approach. In the first place the Inter-American human rights bodies have promoted children's rights through the international *corpus iuris* for the protection of the child, explaining that Article 19 of the ACHR is not a stand-alone tool, but must be interpreted in line with the key principles enshrined in other relevant human rights documents. Furthermore the IACtHR has recognised the 'aggravated responsibility' of the State that has committed, or allowed the commission, of crimes against the most vulnerable segment of the population. Such recognition, which is crucial *tout court*, has, however, not always been transposed into the reparations awarded. Finally, the jurisprudence of the IACtHR had started to elaborate on the concept of victims' 'life plans' and award separate damages for this category of injuries, although this trend has ultimately been reversed on the grounds that its assessment goes beyond the financial sphere. Even though this may be true as personal fulfilment is difficult to quantify, in cases affecting children, both as direct and indirect victims, reparations, to be effective, should always take into account not only the harm suffered, but also the potentiality of the person(s) affected.

[859] See Section 6.2.1 above.

[860] Judgment of 26 September 2006 (Preliminary Objections, Merits, Reparations and Costs), (2006) IACtHR, Series C. No. 154, §136.

CHAPTER 7
CHILD VICTIMS' RIGHT TO REPARATION IN NON-JUDICIAL SETTINGS

7.1. INTRODUCTION

Quasi-judicial as well as judicial mechanisms, both at the regional and at the international level, consider reparations as a strictly legal concept subject to legal rules and procedures. Consequently, victims are necessarily identified with those who have suffered direct or indirect harm as a result of acts or omissions that amount to a violation of international law. In non-judicial settings, however, the identification of the beneficiaries of reparative measures is much more flexible and in some instances it may even coincide with the affected population as a whole. There are a number of non-judicial mechanisms which have dealt with the issue of reparations for child victims of armed conflict. These are TCs, national reparations programmes, the ICC, TFV, and DDR processes. Such mechanisms pursue the twofold aim of providing victims with wide-ranging redress measures and fostering peace, security and reconciliation 'through a heartfelt and public commitment to human rights'.[861] In many cases national reparations programmes are contingent on, or stem from, the work of TCs. As noted by de Greiff, 'there seems to be a trend towards establishing TCs in post-conflict societies and societies in transition and entrusting them with making recommendations concerning reparations'.[862] However, not all national reparations programmes rely on the findings of a TC, not all post-conflict countries have established the same mechanisms to come to terms with their past and not all mechanisms have equally taken into account child victims.

---

861 See MAGARRELL, above note 512, at 2.

862 See DE GREIFF, above note 23, at 11.

7.2. TRUTH COMMISSIONS

According to Teitel a TC can be described as 'an official body, often created by a national government, to investigate, document, and report upon human rights abuses within a country over a specified period of time'.[863] The general aim of a TC is to provide a comprehensive record and analysis of the violations committed during an armed conflict or a military dictatorship.[864] From 1974 to 2007 at least 32 TCs were established in 28 countries worldwide and, according to Heyner, by 2011 their number had increased to 40.[865] Although each TC has a different mandate, it is feasible to trace a common pattern; for instance most TCs at the end of their mandate are requested to make recommendations to the government with the purpose of helping preventing relapses and further abuses. These recommendations are often embedded in a final report, which can also contribute to the establishment of a reparation policy designed for the victims.

Truth Commissions tend to become very popular among the affected populations. In particular the relationship between a TC and the people who suffered from the violations investigated is often really strong because the TC represents the first forum where the victims have the opportunity to finally tell their stories and catch a glimpse of justice. Even if it may be difficult, sometimes impossible, to achieve the goals set in the TC's mandate and implement the actions envisaged in the subsequent report, the findings of a TC have a moral tenet and lay down the basis for future dialogue and reconciliation.[866] Over the years TCs worldwide have showed an increasing interest in children, as victims, witnesses and, in some cases, perpetrators.[867] Nevertheless, not all TCs have included children in their mandate, allowed them to actively participate in the

---

863 R.G. Teitel, 'Human Rights in Transition: Transitional Justice Genealogy', (2003) 16 *Harvard Human Rights Journal* 69, at 70–94.

864 G.G.J. Knoops, 'Truth and Reconciliation Commission Models and International Tribunals: A Comparison', Symposium on *The Right to Self-Determination in International Law*, organised by Unrepresented Nations and People Organisation (UNPO), 29 September–1 October 2006, The Hague, the Netherlands, available at: http://www.unpo.org/downloads/ProfKnoops.pdf. See also R. Rotberg, 'Truth Commissions and the Provision of Truth, Justice and Reconciliation', in R.I. Rotberg and D. Thompson (eds.), *Truth v. Justice: The Morality of Truth Commissions*, Princeton University Press, Princeton, NJ, 2000, 3, at 4–10.

865 See P.B. Hayner, *Unspeakable Truths: Transitional Justice and the Challenge of Truth Commissions*, 2nd edn. Routledge, New York, 2011. See also Amnesty International, *Commissioning Justice: Truth Commissions and Criminal Justice*, Amnesty International Publications, London, 2010.

866 M. Humphrey, 'The Individualising and Universalising Discourse of Law: Victims in Truth Commissions and Trials', in Bonacker and Safferling, above note 43, 67, at 74–77.

867 See K. Fisher, *Transitional Justice for Child Soldiers: Accountability and Social Reconstruction in Post-Conflict Contexts*, Palgrave Macmillan, New York, 2013, 147 et seq.

truth-seeking process or identified them as beneficiaries of reparations.[868] The following overview will thus focus solely on those TCs established to deal with IHRL and IHL violations committed in conjunction with an armed conflict, which have taken children's rights and needs into account.

7.2.1. CHILDREN INCLUDED IN THE TRUTH COMMISSIONS' MANDATE

Among the TCs that have dedicated part of their efforts to the enhancement of children's rights, only three have adopted a specific focus on children in their mandates. The first TC to include children in its mandate was the one established in Sierra Leone. According to the Truth Commission Act 2000 the TC's tasks included

> [working] to help restore the human dignity of victims and promote reconciliation by providing an opportunity for victims to give an account of the violations and abuses suffered and for perpetrators to relate their experiences, and by creating a climate which fosters constructive interchange between victims and perpetrators, giving special attention to the subject of sexual abuses and to the *experiences of children* within the armed conflict.[869]

In the wake of Sierra Leone's openness towards a child-friendly approach, the Timor-Leste and Liberian TCs also recognised the necessity of officially acknowledging the difficult situation of children affected by the armed conflicts, mentioning them as a particularly vulnerable group in their mandates and stressing the importance of adopting specific mechanisms and procedures to address the experiences of women, children and vulnerable groups. The TCs with children embedded in their mandates have also highlighted the need to provide opportunities for child victims to relate to their experiences and benefit from measures aimed at achieving rehabilitation and reintegration.

7.2.2. CHILDREN'S PARTICIPATION IN STATEMENT TAKING AND PUBLIC HEARINGS

Children's involvement in TCs' truth-finding activities can be limited to the initial stage of collecting statements and/or can be extended to the public

868 See D. Mazurana and K. Carlson, 'Children and Reparation: Past Lessons and New Directions', UNICEF Innocenti Research Centre, Innocenti Working Paper No. 2010-08, Florence, at 8.

869 Truth and Reconciliation Commission Act 2000 Sierra Leone, Supplement to the Sierra Leone Gazette Vol. CXXXI, No. 9, dated 10 February 2000, Part III, 6(2)(b).

hearings that take place after the information is gathered. According to a study conducted by UNICEF and the ICTJ some TCs give children the possibility to actively participate in the statement-taking phase, e.g. the ones established in Sierra Leone and Liberia.[870] Statement taking refers to meetings and interviews held between commission staff and victims, perpetrators and witnesses.[871] The average number of statements collected by each TC normally goes from 7,000 to 22,000. Including children in this process entails the adoption of specific measures; e.g. statement takers in charge of collecting children's stories need to be properly trained and require the support of child protection agencies and NGOs with a specific focus on children. In Sierra Leone a child-friendly statement-taking form was used to guide the interaction between the interviewer and the child. A similar tool was designed for the Liberian TRC, but in the end it was not adopted, resulting in statements provided by more than 300 children in 13 districts without recourse to any special measures.[872]

Children's participation in the public hearings is even more challenging than including them in the statement-taking process. The testimony, in the first place, can lead to a threat to a child's safety or to his/her stigmatisation, especially when he/she has been sexually abused; therefore it requires special efforts and precautions. In the alternative, in some cases children have been allowed to publicly share their experiences only in thematic hearings held in a child-friendly environment and without the solemnity and the pressure that allegedly characterises the official TC sessions. In particular, with regard to the TC established in South Africa, which still represents a model for many other TCs,[873] after long consultations with UNICEF and other child protection agencies, it was decided not to admit testimonies of people under the age of 18 years in the public hearings.[874] However, since South African children were directly engaged

---

870 UNICEF Innocenti Research Centre in cooperation with the International Centre for Transitional Justice, 'Children and Truth Commissions', 2010, available at: http://ictj.org/sites/default/files/ICTJ-Global-Children-Truth-2010-English.pdf.

871 See M. Freeman, *Truth Commissions and Procedural Fairness*, Cambridge University Press, Cambridge, 2006, 159–188.

872 See Aptel and Ladisch, above note 264, at 16: 'A special children's statement-taking form was prepared ... it omitted leading questions, emphasised the need for a child-friendly environment and psychosocial support, and encouraged considerations of a wider range of violations including social, economic, cultural, as well as civil and political. However, since its categories did not match the standard form and the data coding system, it was not used.'

873 See R.A. Wilson, *The Politics of Truth and Reconciliation in South Africa: Legitimising the Post-Apartheid State*, Cambridge University Press, Cambridge 2001, 19–27.

874 P. Pigou, 'Children and the South African Truth and Reconciliation Commission', in S. Parmar, M.J. Roseman, S. Siegrist and T. Sowa., *Children and Transitional Justice*, Harvard University Press, Cambridge, MA, 2009, at 126. According to the author, 'Responding to advice from many children's rights activists and professionals, the Commission decided not to take statements from children (anyone under the age of eighteen), which in turn meant that no children's testimonies would be available for the public hearing process. This automatically removed any immediate need to give special attention to the difficulties

in the struggles against apartheid and also targeted by many of the crimes that occurred, the Human Rights Violation Committee convened six special hearings exclusively focused on the experiences of children and young people. These took place in Bloemfontein, Cape Town, Durban, East London, Johannesburg and Pietersburg in May and June 1997. During the hearings, young people aged from 19 to 24 years old expressed their views and shared their stories, while children, still not allowed to bring their testimonies, were involved in workshops and in cultural and dramatic arts presentations undertaken in parallel with the truth-telling process.[875] The hearings were widely attended by children and adolescents, however concerns about the impact of these hearings on the community at large have been raised due to the scant participation of adults.

Special hearings for children on the impact of the conflict and transitional justice mechanisms were also organised in Liberia.[876] Children who participated in the hearings testified behind a screen in order to protect their identities. Furthermore, children were assisted by social workers and instructed not to divulge any detail that could result in their identification.[877] After the children had given their testimonies they were allowed to ask questions to the commissioners. This opportunity was open not only to the witnesses, but also to the members of the Children's Parliament and the children enrolled in the neighbouring community schools.[878] During one of these thematic hearings, notwithstanding the great attention devoted to the event by the national media, a representative of the Children's Parliament publicly underscored the low level of interest that Liberian society as a whole dedicated to the engagement of children.[879]

Other TCs adopted different approaches to children's participation. For example the Commission for Reception, Truth and Reconciliation in Timor-Leste ('CAVR'), which held in total 60 public hearings (a general victims' hearing in each of the 52 sub-districts and an additional eight national thematic hearings) allowed children's participation only during the final national hearing.[880]

---

associated with securing children's testimony. Under the circumstances, this may have been unavoidable, but to a certain extent it marginalised the direct participation of children and thereby children's voices.' See also D. Backer, 'Victims' Responses to Truth Commissions: Evidence from South Africa', in M. Ndulo (ed.), *Security, Reconciliation and Reconstruction: When the Wars End*, University College of London Press, London, 2006, 165, at 170–186.

875 Pigou, above note 874, at 142.

876 In 2008 the Liberian TRC has held three regional public hearings for children and two panel discussions between the commissioners and children in Zwedru, Grand Gedeh County and Tubmanburg, Bomi County. More information is available at: http://trcofliberia.org/press_releases/83.

877 See A.C. Nilsson, *Children and Youth in Armed Conflict*, Brill/Nijhoff, Leiden, 2013, 1273..

878 Ibidem.

879 See Aptel and Ladisch, above note 264, at 9. See also T. Sowa, 'Children and the Liberian Truth and Reconciliation Commission', in Parmar et al., above note 874, at 11.

880 M. Hirst and A. Linnarsson, 'Children and the Commission for Reception, Truth and Reconciliation in Timor-Leste', UNICEF Innocenti Research Centre, Innocenti Working Paper No. 2010-7, Florence, at 19.

The final hearing, held in March 2004, had the theme of 'Children and the Conflict'. As explained in the Commission's final report the hearing was intended 'not only [to highlight] the tragic plight of child victims, but also [to convey] the resilience and energy of the country's younger generation'.[881] In Peru, young people participated actively in the work of the TRC ('Comisión de la Verdad y Reconciliación', or 'CVR'), but not through thematic hearings. The Peruvian government established instead a voluntary programme named 'Promotores de la Verdad' ('PROVER', i.e. Promoters of Truth). The programme was set up to support the Commission's work and engage students and other young people. PROVER involved 1,400 youths, all of whom were children during the period of the atrocities, and it was the only formal avenue for children and adolescents to participate in the CVR.[882]

7.2.3. CHILDREN AS BENEFICIARIES OF REPARATIONS

Every TC has coped with issues related to child victims in different ways. Many of them have included children in their final reports and recognised child victims as beneficiaries of the national reparations policies. After the report is launched, or more generally after the TC's work is concluded, States are expected to translate into action the best strategy as identified by the TC to achieve accountability, reconciliation and reparation.[883] The Liberian TRC dedicated a volume of its final report to 'Children, the Conflict and the TRC Children Agenda', which also enshrined a number of recommendations concerning reparations for children. First and foremost the TRC identified investment in children as the government's top priority, stating that

> [c]hildren's rights and interests need to be approached in a holistic way for children of all origins, identities, and faiths across the country. Liberia's future hinges on its children

881 See 'Chega!' The Final Report of the Commission for Reception, Truth and Reconciliation Part 10: Acolhimento and Victim Support, §115.

882 Specifically, the volunteers participated in: organising social and cultural activities to promote participation in the CVR; training volunteers for their tasks with PROVER; disseminating information on the CVR process, objectives and activities, the CVR report and recommendations and the Campaign for the Disappeared; and providing support to people who had suffered from or witnessed violence. UNICEF Innocenti Research Centre in cooperation with the International Centre for Transitional Justice, above note 870, at 25.

883 The reception of the TC's report also varies in each country, for example in the case of Peru 'to the outrage of victim-survivors' organisations and the human rights community, President Alejandro Toledo waited several months before responding to the TC's Final Report, and then promised only a program of social development thereby sidestepping reparations'. See L.J. Laplante and K. Theidon, 'Truth with Consequences: Justice and Reparations in Post Truth Peru', (2007) 29 *Human Rights Quarterly* 228, at 228–230.

> and without affording them a prospect for educational opportunities and decent living standards, reconciliation and peace building will be hard to achieve.[884]

Furthermore, the TRC noted that responsibility for the crimes committed against children did not lie exclusively with the State and its agents. Also NSAGs involved in the Liberian wars deliberately targeted children and committed the following gross human rights violations and serious violations of IHL directed against children: extra-judicial killings and mass killings, forced recruitment, torture, rape, multiple and gang rape, sexual slavery, and forced marriage. According to the TRC, NSAGs also 'need to be brought to account to give children a sense of justice and to remedy the sense of betrayal children feel toward the adults who exploited and abused them during the war'.[885] Despite recognising the role played by NSAGs, the recommendations of the TRC only spelled out measures to be implemented by the government.

In particular the TRC distinguished between actions, i.e. access to healthcare and provisions of education, in favour of all Liberian children affected by the war; and reparations for specific categories of children, i.e. children associated with fighting forces who had not gone through the DDR process, girls who had been victims of sexual violence, rape and sexual slavery, children separated from their parents and family members, children with severe psychosocial trauma and children with social adaptation and reintegration problems.[886] These children, who suffered direct or indirect harm as a result of violations perpetrated during or in the aftermath of the armed conflict, were identified as beneficiaries of specific measures, e.g. specialised programmes of psychosocial support, post-conflict family tracing and reunification programmes and targeted assistance to victims of SGBV.

The report released by the CAVR, 'Chega!', in October 2005 also contained specific recommendations on children and youth. These included harmonisation of national legislation with the CRC, public information campaigns on positive parenting, positive role models for girls and boys,[887] allocation of resources to sporting infrastructure, reproductive health education, and universal education, and family reunions for separated children and special consideration for children who lost educational opportunities because of their clandestine work in the struggle for independence.[888] Over more than 2,500 pages 'Chega!' has analysed

---

884 Final Report of the Truth and Reconciliation Commission of Liberia, Volume Three: Appendices, Title II: Children, the Conflict and the TRC Children Agenda, June 2009, at 104.

885 Ibidem.

886 Ibidem, at 108.

887 The characters, Marta and Atoy, were used in various campaigns, including encouraging children to return to school in the aftermath of the political violence and warning them about being used for political purposes in the electoral campaign. See HIRST and. LINNARSSON, above note 880, at 31.

888 Ibidem, at 30.

both the roots and the consequences of the conflict as well as the possible ways to approach reconciliation and the measures that the government should urgently implement in order to provide redress to the victims. Timor-Leste's TC has also listed the principles which should guide any national plan aimed at achieving victims' redress. According to the CAVR, such a plan should take into account feasibility, accessibility, empowerment, gender and prioritisation based on need. The CAVR recommended the design of a reparations programme targeting the most vulnerable victims of the conflict, including also some categories of children, i.e. those suffering from disabilities or psychological damage due to gross human rights violations, those whose parents were killed or disappeared, and those born out of sexual violence whose mothers are single. However, only those who were 18 years or younger on the day the conflict ended, i.e. 25 October 1999, were eligible for reparations as children. This excluded the individuals who were children at the time of the violation but adults by the time the war ended.[889] The implementation of the reparations plan is still a work in progress, mainly because a holistic and systematic approach to put the CAVR's recommendations into practice is still lacking.[890]

In Sierra Leone the TRC determined the categories that should benefit from the reparations programme by considering those victims who were particularly vulnerable to suffering human rights violations. According to the findings of the TRC, 'most Sierra Leoneans agree that amputees, war wounded, women who suffered sexual abuse, children and war widows would constitute special categories of victims who are in dire need of urgent care'.[891] The TRC stressed that

> due to their particular vulnerability, either before or after the commission of the violation, many of the victims in each of these categories of beneficiaries suffered from multiple human rights violations. For example, a victim of sexual violence may also have been abducted, tortured, and abused or subjected to a variety of other types of inhumane acts.[892]

Whereas many of the recommendations of the Commission referred to all the children in Sierra Leone, the Commission took into account the victimhood of certain categories of children, namely those who suffered during the war or who continued to suffer from the consequences of the war, such as abducted children, forcibly conscripted children, and orphans. While most of the measures were formulated in general terms, others focused specifically on child victims. For example, the Commission recommended that children who fit in the category 'other war wounded' and child victims of sexual violence be provided with free

---

889 Chega! Part 11: Recommendations, at 41.
890 See Hirst and. Linnarsson, above note 880, at 31–32.
891 Sierra Leone TRC Report, Volume 2, Chapter 4: Reparations, §57.
892 Ibidem.

physical health care until 18 years of age, except if the injury sustained requires care past the age of 18.[893] Furthermore, the Commission asked the government to assist the organisations and bodies that provide scar removal surgery for those children who still have letters branded by the fighting forces on various parts of their body. Letters such as RUF, AFRC, and EX SLA were engraved on the forehead, chest, arms, or back of many children. According to the findings of the Commission these physical scars have affected the children psychologically and in many cases, prevented their successful reintegration with families and communities.[894]

In Sierra Leone the National Commission for Social Action ('NaCSA'), established according to the TRC's recommendations to oversee the implementation of the reparations, started the victim registration process four years after the launch of the Final report, from December 2008 to June 2009. The number of victims counted, verified and registered across the country amounted to 29,783 'including children, amputees, and others wounded in the fighting, war widows, and victims of sexual violence'.[895] The registration was part of the so-called 'Year One Program', granted by the United Nations Peacebuilding Fund and implemented by NaCSA. The project aimed at providing urgent measures to support the victims identified by the TC as most in need.[896] According to the programme, children recognised as victims, and still eligible for primary and middle education, should receive the reimbursement of school fees, uniforms and books. Although the registration process was successful in the sense that it was able to reach also children and people living in the rural areas of Sierra Leone, the implementation of the recommendations issued by the TRC has never been completed.[897]

The Peruvian TRC's mandate also included the design of a proposal for reparations, which resulted in the Comprehensive Plan for Reparations ('Plan Integral de Reparaciones', or 'PIR').[898] The PIR was based on the legal figure of

---

893 Ibidem, §127 and §135.

894 Ibidem, §156.

895 Submission to the Universal Periodic Review of the UN Human Rights Council 11th Session, May 2011 ICTJ, November 1, available at: http://ictj.org/sites/default/files/ICTJ-SierraLeone-Periodic-Review-2010-English.pdf.

896 See J. King, 'Gender and Reparations in Sierra Leone: The Wounds of War Remain Open', in Rubio-Marin above note 191, at 5. 'The TC report categorises children eligible under the reparations program as follows: children with physical injury, such as amputees or victims of sexual violence; children whose parents were killed as a consequence of any abuse or violation described in the report; children born out of an act of sexual violence and whose mothers are single; children who suffer from psychological harm; and war-wounded children'.

897 See Evans, above note 47, at 181. According to the author, 'an area where the government showed little interest in implementing recommendations was disappointingly, although not unexpectedly, that of reparations'.

898 See J. García-Godos, 'Victim Reparations in the Peruvian Truth Commission and the Challenge of Historical Interpretation', (2008) 2 *International Journal of Transitional Justice* 63, at 64–68.

'victim of violation', which referred to the violation of one or more human rights. Beneficiaries were thus identified on the basis of suffered violations. For the CVR, the term 'victims' encompassed all those people or groups of people that, due to the internal armed conflict, and living in the country between May 1980 and November 2000, suffered acts or omissions that violated norms of IHRL.[899] The status of 'victim of violation' was not dependent on whether the perpetrator had been identified or who the perpetrator might have been, in fact it applied even to guerrilla members as long as the violation did not occur during combat or confrontation.[900] The CVR singled out two types of beneficiaries for the PIR: individuals and collectives. Collective beneficiaries included peasants and native communities and settlements collectively affected by the armed conflict through scorched-earth strategies, forced displacement, destruction of local institutions and loss of local private and public infrastructures, such as land, cattle and houses, community houses and community services. With regard to children, collective reparations focused particularly on improving the quality of rural schools, prioritising inter-cultural education, improving girls' literacy, transforming authoritarian pedagogy and violence in schools, and encouraging learning for citizenship and democratic values. A curriculum based on the CVR for primary and secondary school students was developed through an NGO-university partnership, with the intention of incorporating it into Peru's national curriculum as a supplementary resource.[901] Concerning individual reparations, these mainly took the form of economic compensation, e.g. pensions or lump sums, awarded to specific groups, i.e. the relatives of the dead and disappeared; the permanently physically and/or mentally disabled, partially or totally; the unduly imprisoned; victims of sexual violation and children born as a result of sexual violation.[902]

In Chile, the TRC created in 1990 following the end of the dictatorship outlined reparations measures for the relatives of victims of forced disappearance and killing, including children. According to the report drafted by the Chilean TRC, the children of victims were eligible for a pension until the age of 25 years, and those with disabilities qualified for a pension for life; persons under the age of 35 years were also eligible for a university scholarship.[903] In 2004, a

899 Comision de la Verdad y la Reconciliacion´ (CVR), Informe Final (Lima: Comision de la Verdad y la Reconciliacio´n, 2003), vol IX, at 149.

900 Ibidem.

901 See J. Paulson, 'Truth Commissions and National Curricula', in Parmar et al. (eds.), above note 874, at 328.

902 See García-Godos, above note 898, at 77.

903 Report of the Chilean National Commission on Truth and Reconciliation, Notre Dame, Indiana: University of Notre Dame Press, 1993, vol. I/II, at 1057–1075. See also E. Salmon, 'Reflections on International Humanitarian Law and Transitional Justice: Lessons to be Learnt from the Latin American Experience' (2006) 88 *International Review of the Red Cross* 327, at 327–354.

lump-sum payment was provided to children whose age made them ineligible for the pension or who had received it only for a limited number of years before turning 25. Furthermore, boys who were victims and children of victims were exempted from military service and children of victims were included as beneficiaries in the Comprehensive Reparations Programme in Health Care.[904]

In 2003, the Chilean government established a second TC to examine the situations of victims of political imprisonment and torture, and to make recommendations for their reparations.[905] Its report revealed that 1,080 of the identified 27,255 victims were younger than 18 years old at the time of their detention and torture, and 88 were younger than 13 years. These victims came forward to claim that they had been excluded from the mandate and outreach efforts of the first TRC. According to them they had not been advised that it was necessary for every victim, including children, to provide direct testimony to the commission in order to receive reparation. The commission reviewed these testimonies and identified an additional 164 cases of victims under 18 years of age.[906] In 2005 the Chilean government decided to provide 28,459 registered victims or their relatives with lifelong governmental compensation (approximately US$200 per month) and free education, housing and health care.

The Truth, Justice and Reconciliation Commission ('TJRC') established in Kenya to make findings in respect of gross violations of IHRL inflicted on persons by the State, public institutions and holders of public office between 12 December 1963 and 28 February 2008, has also included child victims as beneficiaries of its final recommendations. The Commission found that during the mandate period, children were both direct and indirect victims of gross violations of human rights. As direct victims, they suffered atrocities including killing, maiming, torture and sexual violence. Children also witnessed atrocities, as a result of which many remain traumatised. Moreover, during the Mau Mau War, children were subjected to traumatic experiences as many of them helplessly observed the atrocious crimes committed against their parents and adults in general. The Commission also reported that NSAGs forcefully recruited children into their ranks and some of these children were subsequently involved in atrocities.[907] Likely because the TJRC's mandate was very broad and it covered different periods, the reparations for child victims have ultimately

904 See E. Lira, 'The Reparations Policy for Human Rights Violations in Chile', in De Greiff, above note 22, at 55.

905 National Commission on Political Imprisonment and Torture ('Comisión Nacional Sobre Prisón Politica y Tortura', or 'Valech Commission'). The Valech Commission was created by Supreme Decree No. 1040 (PDF-67KB), 26 September 2003.

906 UNICEF Innocenti Research Centre in cooperation with the International Centre for Transitional Justice, above note 870, at 54.

907 TJRC, Kenya, Report of the Truth, Justice and Reconciliation Commission, Vol. IV, 2013, §§194–196.

been formulated in very generic terms and encompassed 'acknowledgment and apology by the Kenyan President, psychosocial counselling for children victims of atrocities, reparation for child victims of atrocities and injustices, adequate funding of the Department of Children's Services, robust plan for integration of children with disabilities in mainstream educational facilities'.[908] Strikingly, the status of child victims has been granted only to those individuals below the age of 18 years at the time of filing the request to obtain reparations.[909]

7.3. NATIONAL REPARATIONS PROGRAMMES AND CHILD VICTIMS

National reparations programmes have been set up in several post-conflict countries to deal with the legacy stemming from widespread violations. De Greiff has described their functions and scope as follows:

> Reparations programmes are meant to (partially) redress gross and systematic human rights violations, not sporadic or exceptional ones. This has far-reaching consequences. It implies that the universe of potential beneficiaries is large and that they probably suffered various and multiple forms of abuse. It also means that a reparations programme cannot make the same contribution to strengthening the rule of law as it would if it were redressing exceptional violations of otherwise generally observed norms. Part of what needs to be redressed in the cases that are of concern here is not only a large number of individual violations, but violations that come about in systematic ways, either as a consequence of the deliberate adoption of abusive policies or as a predictable consequence of other choices. Reparations in these contexts must not only do justice to the victims, but also contribute to re-establishing essential systems of norms, including norms of justice, which are inevitably weakened during times of conflict or authoritarianism.[910]

Often national reparations programmes are established in accordance with the recommendations issued by the TCs. In other cases, for instance in the case of Colombia, reparations programmes are enacted without input from a TC. The Victims' Law adopted in 2011 has complemented the reparations plans started by the JPL in 2005 and further enhanced through Decree 1290 (2008), which provided individual reparations to those who were victims of homicide, forced disappearance, kidnapping, personal and psychological injury, recruitment of minors and forced displacement as a result of the actions of illegal armed groups at any time before 22 April 2008.[911]

---

908 Ibidem, at 65, the so-called 'implementation matrix'.

909 Ibidem, at 105.

910 De Greiff, above note 23, at10.

911 Administrative Reparations, Decree 1290 (2008).

In order to benefit from the measures envisaged by the Victims' Law, established to remedy at least some of the shortcomings of the JPL,[912] victims have to be listed in the Victims' Registry. Victims are defined as all persons who, individually or collectively, suffered harm as a result of violations of IHRL and IHL committed after 1985, during the internal armed conflict.[913] Remarkably, members of illegal armed groups can also fall within this category in cases of boys, girls or adolescents who have left the group's ranks while still underage.[914] In other words, former members of rebel or paramilitary organisations forcibly recruited as children can qualify as a victim *only if* they disassociated themselves from these groups when they were minors,[915] a distinction strongly criticised by NGOs and international organisations. In particular Article 190 establishes that until they reach the age of majority, illegally recruited girls and boys are entitled to the same reparations regime (whose enforcement has been assigned to the Colombian Institute of Welfare Service) as all the other child victims; once they turn 18 years old they can eventually be included in the process of reintegration led by the High Council for the Social and Economic Reintegration of the People and Groups meant to rehabilitate those who joined the guerrilla.[916] With regard to the kind of reparations that child victims can claim, Article 182 of the Victims' Law specifies that children are entitled to receive the whole range of reparative measures provided for adult victims.[917] As a result, any judicial authority or administrative authority which grants monetary compensation to a child victim is required to establish a trust fund, and the compensation is awarded to the victim as soon as he or she turns 18.[918] The Victims' Law instructs the National Welfare System to design and implement specific guidelines to ensure a comprehensive reparations process for child and adolescent victims.[919] Moreover, with the

912 See Chapter 3, Section 3.3.2.1above.

913 According to Art. 3(1) of the Victims' Law victims are '[T]hose persons who individually or collectively suffered harm for events occurring from 1 January 1985, as a result of violations of International Humanitarian Law or gross and flagrant violations of norms of International Human Rights law, occurring during the time of the internal armed conflict'.

914 Art.3 (2) of the Victims' Law.

915 See also Art. 190 of the Victims' Law.

916 See the Report of the Secretary-General on children and armed conflict in Colombia, UN doc. S/2012/171, 21 March 2012, §60.

917 Title VII of the Victims' Law is entirely devoted to children. The reparations envisaged by the Victims' Law include not only restitution and compensation, but also rehabilitation and satisfaction. Rehabilitation measures include the mandate to create psychological health programmes for victims and their families. Satisfaction measures include public recognition of the victim's dignity, publications, commemorative ceremonies, public monuments and more. Symbolic reparation measures include efforts to preserve historical memory (e.g. by creating an archive in respect of victims) and public acceptance of the facts and forgiveness. See Arts. 135–139 of the Victims' Law.

918 See Art. 185 of the Victims' Law.

919 See Art. 183 of the Victims' Law.

National Welfare System the Attorney General's office is requested to design a mechanism to ensure children's access to justice and reparations mechanisms[920] and the education authorities are required to ensure access to pre-school, primary and secondary-level education for all those recognised as victims under the Victims' Law.[921]

In order to obtain reparations victims have to apply at a governmental office (such as a prosecutor's office or a municipal office) to be entered into the Victims' Registry. They are expected to provide a declaration of the relevant facts and bring supporting documents. Unlike the JPL, the Victims' Law did not require victims to identify the perpetrators of the crimes. The Victims' Unit is the body in charge of reviewing the declarations provided by the victims; it verifies the facts described and decides whether to grant victim status to the applicant, independent of any judicial proceedings relating to the perpetrator.[922] With respect to determining whether an individual satisfies the definition of a victim pursuant to the Victims' Law, the State is required to treat the victim with 'good faith'. The Victims' Law establishes that it is sufficient for the victim to summarily prove the damage by any legally accepted means.[923]

The very ambitious reparations programme designed by the Colombian government suffers from a number of shortcomings. With regard to children, the most blatant limitation concerns the lack of accessibility and recognition for victims of illegal recruitment who demobilise after turning 18 years old. In contrast in the criminal proceedings established within the JPL framework, the victims who suffered from illegal recruitment and use in armed conflict were granted reparations regardless of their age when they left the armed group. The 309 former child soldiers recognised as victims in the *El Alemán* case were young adults by the time they left the group, but all of them were identified as victims and beneficiaries of reparations.[924] Another main concern with regard to the implementation of the Victims' Law relates to the situation of IDPs, asylum seekers and refugees who are at risk of being excluded from the implementation of the reparations plan.[925] Article 204 of the Victims' Law attempts to address the hurdle of reaching victims outside of Colombia by providing for the adoption of measures designed for a wide dissemination of the relevant information.

---

920 See Art. 186 of the Victims' Law.

921 See Art. 51 of the Victims' Law.

922 See the Annual Report of the UN OHCHR on the Situation of Human Rights in Colombia, UN doc. A/ HRC/19/21/Add.3, 31 January 2012, §50; Amnesty International, 'Colombia: The Victims and Land Restitution Law', June 2012, at 8.

923 See Art. 5 of the Victims' Law.

924 Judgment of 16 December 2011 (Sentencia), above note 432, see the list of the victims, at 5–45.

925 According to the UNHCR as of December 2015 in Colombia the number of IDPs amounts to 6,520,270, Colombian asylum seekers who fled the country are 6,030 and Colombian refugees, manly living in neighbouring countries, are 346,125.

In particular, it places upon the Ministry of Foreign Affairs the duty to ensure that victims outside the States are duly informed of their rights, in accordance with the provisions enshrined in Article 30, which mandates that the State shall promote mechanisms for effectively advertising the judicial and administrative routes to exercise the right to reparation.[926] Finally, the main hurdle with regard to the successful achievement of the goals set in the Colombian reparations strategy remains the absence of a stable peace to finally end over 50 years of armed conflict between the Government and NSAGs active in Colombian territory, in particular the *Fuerzas Armadas Revolucionarias de Colombia-Ejército del Pueblo* ('FARC-EP'). The transitional justice process, including the implementation of the reparations plan, has been carried out in parallel with the peace negotiations, which began officially after the signing of the 'General Agreement for the end of the conflict and the construction of a stable and lasting peace' in August 2012.[927] The talks between the FARC-EP and the Government of Colombia achieved a number of important results and ultimately led to the conclusion of the Final Peace Agreement, which also addressed the issue of victims' right to reparation.[928] The Final Peace Agreement, officially signed by the parties on 26 September 2016, was rejected one week later by the Colombian population during a historical referendum, a step recognised by the Colombian Constitutional Court as essential to legitimise the peace accord.[929]

Whereas despite the many setbacks, the Colombian government ultimately tried to set up a comprehensive reparations plan establishing links between the different initiatives and trying to add layers to the original framework, i.e. the JPL, in order to achieve a holistic approach to reparations, other countries have enacted piecemeal legislation. In Argentina, for example, each initiative for the victims stemmed from a separate legal instrument and covered a distinct category of victims. The main laws, passed between 1984 and 1985, after the National Commission on the Disappearance of Persons ('Comisiòn Nacional sobre Desapariciòn de Personas', or 'CONADEP') completed its work, dealt with disappearance, arbitrary detention and grave injuries or death while

926 See Art. 30 and Art. 204 of the Victims' Law. See also D. Cantor, UNHCR Research Paper No. 215, *Restitution, Compensation, Satisfaction: Transnational Reparations and Colombia's Victims' Law*, 2011, at 31.

927 International Crisis Group, 'Colombia: Peace at Last?', Crisis Group Latin America Report No. 45, 25 September 2012, General Agreement for the Termination of the Conflict and the Construction of a Stable And Lasting Peace, at 34. 'What is at Stake in the Colombian Peace Process?', BBC News, 15 January 2015, available at: http://www.bbc.com/news/world-latin-america-19875363. Further info is available at: http://colombiapeace.org, a blog that monitors the progress of Colombia's peace negotiations.

928 See Acuerdo Final para la Terminación del Conflicto y la Construcción de una Paz Estable y Duradera (Final Peace Agreement), at: https://www.mesadeconversaciones.com.co/sites/default/files/24_08_2016acuerdofinalfinalfinal-1472094587.pdf.

929 See Colombian Constitutional Court, Decision C-379/16, §56.

in detention.[930] A law approved almost 20 years later, in 2004, finally offered redress to categories of victims, mostly children at the time of the crimes, that had been overlooked by the initial reparations laws, i.e. persons who were born while their mothers were illegally detained, minors who remained in detention due to the detention or disappearance of their parents for political reasons or those who remained in military areas.[931] The law also tackled the delicate issue of 'identity substitution', the term used in Argentina to refer to cases of children of disappeared parents who were registered as the legitimate children of other families, often the military or security personnel, who stole them from their biological parents. The only form of reparation envisaged by Law 25,914 was monetary compensation. The Law distinguished among those who suffered identity substitution, who were entitled to receive an indemnification equivalent to 224,000 Argentinean pesos, and the victims of the other crimes, whose benefit consisted of a one-off payment equivalent to 71,288 pesos. Furthermore, in order to be eligible for reparations, the victims of identity substitution were asked to present a judicial order rectifying their identity; if they were adopted in 'good faith' they had to prove, by any possible means, the forced disappearance of their parents.[932] This last requirement appears, at the very least, questionable in light of the traumatic experience already suffered by the victims of identity substitution.

National plans in some instances have also deliberately focused on relief and assistance instead of reparations. The most known and discussed example is certainly Nepal, where the Maoist-led coalition government committed to establishing a TC and pursuing other transitional justice measures, as provided by the 2006 Comprehensive Peace Agreement ('CPA'), which formally ended an internal armed conflict lasting ten years. With regard to the establishment of a TC, the Commission on Investigation into Disappeared Persons, Truth and Reconciliation Act ('CoID-TR Act') was promulgated in May 2014 and set up two separate commissions: the TRC and a Commission of Inquiry on the Disappearances ('CoID'). The process leading to the adoption of the CoID-TR Act was very problematic, and strongly criticised, from the outset.[933]

Among the various possible transitional justice measures contemplated in the CPA, the Interim Relief Program ('IRP') administered by the government's Ministry of Peace and Reconstruction ('MoPR') has so far been the only one

930 See M.J. Guembe, 'Economic Reparations for Grave Human Rights Violations: the Argentinean Experience', in de Greiff, above note 22, at 40–42.

931 Law 25.914 of 30 August 2004.

932 See Guembe, above note 930, at 43.

933 See A. Bisset, 'Transitional Justice in Nepal: The Commission on Investigation of Disappeared Persons, Truth and Reconciliation Act 2014', Bingham Centre Working Paper 2014/07, Bingham Centre for the Rule of Law/BIICL, London, September 2014. According to the author the Commission on Investigation of Disappeared Persons, Truth and Reconciliation Act 2014 falls short of international legal standards, not least in the possibility of amnesty

implemented.[934] The IRP, which has been administered by the MoPR since 2008, is aimed at addressing victims' material needs. It does not fulfil victims' right to reparation, because it does not recognise the recipients as victims of human rights abuses nor does it acknowledge the State's responsibility for those violations. Children have been included among the beneficiaries of the IRP. In particular family members of deceased and disappeared people are entitled to receive a lump-sum compensation payment of 100,000 NPR and the children are eligible for scholarships. A child can also receive a scholarship if he/she or a parent is more than 50 per cent disabled. The scholarships are only available for children younger than 18; children who lost their schooling opportunities because of the conflict and are now older than 18 are not covered by the IRP.[935]

7.4. THE TRUST FUND FOR VICTIMS OF THE INTERNATIONAL CRIMINAL COURT

The distinction between the two mandates of the TFV has already been discussed in Chapter 4 and Chapter 5 of the present book.[936] The assistance (or humanitarian) mandate of the TFV is not decided in a Courtroom and it enables the Trust Fund to intervene on behalf of victims irrespective of the outcome of the judicial proceeding. The Executive Director of the TFV, Mr Pieter De Baan, has clarified that 'while the assistance mandate of the Trust Fund does not qualify as "reparations" in the technical sense of the Rome Statute, it does have a clear reparative purpose'.[937] Consistently with the crimes prosecuted under the Court's jurisdiction the TFV divides the target beneficiaries into six different categories: victims of SGBV, including rape, forced pregnancy, sexual slavery, and also comprising girls abducted and/or recruited into armed groups and forcefully impregnated; widows and widowers, namely those whose partners were killed; former child soldiers and abducted youth, i.e. children and youth forced and/or recruited into armed groups under the age of 15 (regardless of their particular role(s) played during abduction or conscription); orphans and vulnerable

for international crimes and gross violations of human rights. In addition, the relationship between the three mechanisms – truth seeking, amnesty and prosecution – remains unclear and safeguards for individual rights are lacking.

934 See Carranza, above note 538. See also the IOM Report 'Mapping Exercise and Preliminary Gap Analysis of the Interim Relief and Rehabilitation Programme', IOM, December 2010.

935 Ibidem, at 17–18.

936 See Chapter 4, Section 4.3 and Chapter 5, Sections 5.3.3.3.1–5.3.3.3.2 above.

937 See the Trust Fund for Victims, 'Empowering Victims and Communities towards Social Change', Summer 2012 Programme Progress Report, available at: http://www.trustfundforvictims.org/sites/default/files/imce/TFV%20PPR%20Summer%202012%20ENG%20Final_.pdf.

children, i.e. children whose parent(s) were killed or children otherwise made vulnerable by the violence; victims who suffered a physical injury and/or who were psychologically traumatised by violence; family members of victims (with the exception of widows and orphans) and others who do not fall within the above categories, but are affected by violence.[938]

Children specifically fall within three of the six categories singled out by the TFV, which distinguishes between sexually abused children, children who took part in the hostilities (not necessarily in the capacity of trained soldiers) and children who have lost one or both parents. Children who experienced different kinds of harms are included in the remaining groups and may also benefit from the initiatives established by the Trust Fund and locally implemented by its partners. If within its reparations mandate the TFV is busy drafting the reparations plan for the victims of the *Lubanga* case, within its assistance mandate the TFV implements a broad range of initiatives for the most vulnerable and marginalised survivors, through innovative projects focusing on physical rehabilitation, psychological rehabilitation, and material support. In 2008, the ICC Pre-Trial Chambers approved 34 projects for northern Uganda and the DRC and currently some of these projects have been completed or phased out.[939] Of the seven projects that ended in 2015, two specifically dealt with child victims in the DRC. The first project aimed at achieving psychological rehabilitation through peace and reconciliation activities focusing on child victims of violence associated with armed forces, child mothers, and vulnerable children affected by the conflict.[940] Through the ECOPAIX project, Missionnaires d'Afrique conducted nearly 5,000 'education for peace' sessions in targeted primary and secondary schools. The activities reached over 12,000 primary school students and 7,500 secondary school students. Using stories, games, peace-themed art, drama, poems, songs, and sharing of experiences, the sessions focused on the themes of cooperation and teamwork, peace, the importance of tolerance and respect, and (at secondary level) suffering, in particular its causes, consequences and ways to overcome it.

The second project targeted psychological rehabilitation and material support for child mothers, boys, girls, other vulnerable children and victims of armed conflict through school and socio-economic reintegration.[941] Located in Bunia town and at three other sites, the programme's beneficiaries included young mothers who were victims of rape during the conflict or who suffered mutilation,

---

938 Ibidem, at 5.

939 Since 2012 the TFV has started implementing assistance projects in the Central African Republic. See TFV, 'Healing, Empowerment and Reconciliation: Support to Victim Survivors of SGBV', PPR Winter 2014, at 33.

940 'A l'école de la paix', TFV/DRC/2007/R1/019.

941 'Réintégration Communautaires des Jeunes Victimes des Conflits Armés en Ituri pour la Lutte contre toutes Formes des Violences', TFV/DRC/2007/R2/028, 029.

forced marriage, and/or abduction into armed groups and had now returned home with their children. The programme offered psychosocial support to young mothers, access to medical care, and opportunities to reintegrate into school and learn business and professional skills. Other vulnerable children in the communities, including children born out of rape, victim survivors of sexual violence, children exploited for their labour, for example in gold mining, and those in conflict with the law, received psychological support and referrals for medical care.[942]

These two projects provide an example of the kind of support that the TFV has bestowed so far to the benefit of the 'victims' affected by situations under the Court's jurisdiction. As discussed with regard to the Appeals Chamber judgment on the appeals against the decision establishing principles and procedures to be applied to reparations in the *Lubanga* case, these forms of intervention will probably be extended to the victims of SGBV and the members of the communities excluded from the amended Order for Reparations.[943]

7.5. DISARMAMENT, DEMOBILISATION AND REINTEGRATION PROGRAMMES

The so-called disarmament,[944] demobilisation[945] and reintegration[946] process contributes to security and stability by disarming combatants, removing them from military structures, and promoting their social and economic reintegration within society.[947] Over the last 20 years DDR programmes have been set up in

942 See TFV, above note 937, at 13.

943 See Chapter 5, Section 5.3.3.3.2 above.

944 'Disarmament is the collection, documentation, control and disposal of small arms, ammunition, explosives and light and heavy weapons of combatants and often also of the civilian population. Disarmament also includes the development of responsible arms management programs.' See United Nations Note by the Secretary-General on Administrative and Budgetary Aspects of the Financing of UN Peacekeeping Operations, 24 May 2005, UN doc. A/C.5/59/31.

945 Ibidem. 'Demobilisation is the formal and controlled discharge of active combatants from armed forces or other armed groups. The first stage of demobilisation may extend from the processing of individual combatants in temporary centres to the massing of troops in camps designated for this purpose (cantonment sites, encampments, assembly areas or barracks). The second stage of demobilisation encompasses the support package provided to the demobilised, which is called reinsertion.'

946 Ibidem. 'Reintegration is the process by which ex combatants acquire civilian status and gain sustainable employment and income. Reintegration is essentially a social and economic process with an open time frame, primarily taking place in communities at the local level. It is part of the general development of a country and a national responsibility and often necessitates long-term external assistance.'

947 See P. de Greiff, Research Brief, 'Establishing Links between DDR and Reparations', ICTJ, February 2010, available at: http://ictj.org/sites/default/files/ICTJ-DDR-Reparations-ResearchBrief-2010-English.pdf. See also T. Nezam and A. Marc, 'Disarmament,

more than 30 countries[948] and some of them have included former child soldiers among the beneficiaries. DDR programmes are different from reparation programmes as the latter focus on victims affected by the conflict, while the former target ex-combatants for the purpose of triggering their reinstatement as productive members of the community. On the one hand, DDR programmes prioritise the achievement of security, stability and peace; on the other hand, reparations strive to give victims a sense of recognition and to redress the consequences of the harm suffered. If in theory the distinction between these two concepts appears quite clear, in practice it tends to be blurred, especially when it comes to former child soldiers, who, as discussed in Chapter 2, are ultimately regarded as victims rather than perpetrators.[949]

7.5.1. DISARMAMENT, DEMOBILISATION AND REINTEGRATION OF FORMER CHILD SOLDIERS

Article 39 of the CRC places upon States parties the obligation to take all the appropriate measures to promote the social reintegration of child victims of war. As discussed in the first part of this book, children associated with armed forces or groups are recognised primarily as victims,[950] also when they have actively taken part in hostilities and committed atrocities against the civilian population, their peers or their enemies. It follows that DDR programmes, which sometimes add rehabilitation to their goals ('DDRR'), as was the case in Liberia,[951] represent not only a process that contributes to security and stability, but also a means to redress the harm suffered by those children who have finally escaped from a militarised life. Unlike DDR programmes focused on adult combatants,[952] those which target children usually start prior to the conflict's end[953] and are often

---

Demobilisation and Reintegration', note commissioned by the World Bank's Department of Social Development, No. 119, February 2009.

948 Ibidem.

949 See Chapter 2, Section 2.6.3 above.

950 UNICEF, The Paris Principles, above note 200, principle 2.1.

951 On this point see Drumbl, above note 20, at 168.

952 See United Nations Department of Peacekeeping Operations (DPKO), Integrated Disarmament, Demobilisation and Reintegration Standards ('IDDRS') DPKO, New York, 2006, module 5.30, 'Children and DDR'. 'Unlike adults, children cannot legally be recruited; therefore, measures that aim to prevent their recruitment, or that attempt to reintegrate them into their communities, should not be viewed as a routine component of peace-making, but as an attempt to prevent or redress a violation of children's human rights. *This means that child DDR is not the same as that for adults.* Rather, it is a specific process with its own requirements, several of which are fundamentally different from adult demobilisation programmes' (emphasis added).

953 For example in Eastern DRC. See E. Pauletto and P. Patel, 'Challenging Child-Soldier DDR Processes and Policies in the Eastern Democratic Republic of Congo', (2010) 16 *Journal*

set up by international organisations.[954] In countries where national reparations programmes have not been established or court-ordered reparations have never been implemented,[955] DDR processes represent the only kind of relief for many children involved in armed conflict.

The transition from military to civilian life can be particularly complex for former child soldiers and while adults' DDR programmes have, especially in the past, concentrated on providing immediate transition benefits, such as compensation packages,[956] in the case of children the distribution of monetary payments has mainly been proven to be counterproductive.[957] According to the Special Representative of the Secretary-General for Children and Armed Conflict:

> In many countries, reintegration programmes provided material benefits to children formerly associated with armed groups, including cash payments (Mozambique and Liberia) or 'family kits' (El Salvador). It has now been recognised that it is not in children's best interests to offer material benefits. Such benefits can be viewed as a potential incentive for children to engage in armed conflict in the future. It can also cause tension with local communities who see those responsible for the losses and harm they had suffered being rewarded, while their children receive nothing.[958]

The distribution of material benefits through the DDR programmes, which also include waived school fees, household items and training, may exacerbate the disparities between former child soldiers, rewarded with 'blood money', and child victims, never associated with armed forces or groups, who could only rely on the creation of often inadequately resourced reparative programmes.[959] These 'privileges', as they are often perceived by the rest of the population, build on the idea that child soldiers are more damaged or more vulnerable than other children affected by war. Wessells, for example, has challenged this idea and reported that during an armed conflict

---

of Peace, Conflict and Development 35, at 35–37. See also IDDRS, above note 952, module 5.30 'Children and DDR', 'Child DDR requires that the demobilisation (or "release") and reintegration of children, especially girls, be actively carried out at all times, even during a conflict, and that actions to prevent child recruitment should be continuous'.

954 Ibidem, at 42, the authors refer to the DDR programmes set up by Caritas International and Save the Children UK in North Kivu.

955 See S. Parmar and G. Mushiata, 'Judgment Denied: The Failure to Fulfill Court-Ordered Reparations for Victims of Serious Crimes in the Democratic Republic of Congo', ICTJ Briefing, May 2012, available at: http://www.ictj.org/sites/default/files/ICTJ-DRC-Reparations-Failure-Briefing-2012-English.pdf.

956 IDDRS, above note 952, at 21.

957 Ibidem.

958 See Office of the Special Representative of the Secretary-General for Children and Armed Conflict, Working Paper No. 3, above note 152, at 46.

959 See Drumbl, above note 20, at 174.

> child soldiers often have better access to food and protection than do other children, who are subject to scourges such as attack, displacement, and HIV/AIDS, and who have no means to defend themselves. Child soldiers may also be better off because their groups meet their basic needs by looting and robbing villages.[960]

This statement of course does not take into account the exposure to violence and the trauma stemming from the experience of being associated with armed forces and groups, but it further substantiates the assumption that awarding material benefits to former child soldiers risks being understood as concentrating all the efforts on one category of victims, not necessarily the most vulnerable, and leaving all the others empty handed.

Besides the difficulties related to the identification of the best and most effective types of benefits, DDR processes are also extremely challenging when it comes to the reintegration phase. As stressed by Drumbl, many child soldiers joined the armed movements to pursue the opportunity to overthrow a life of poverty, therefore when the DDR programme fails to provide them with training, education and long-term assistance, there is a soaring possibility of being re-recruited, exploited or abducted again.[961] The success of child soldiers' reintegration is thus contingent on whether the process is tailored to the individual's needs as well as to the particular features of each conflict. There are many different types and processes of DDR, and not all of them are equally effective in each situation. At one end of the spectrum there is a minimalist approach, which aims to demobilise soldiers in order to prevent them from posing a security risk and it is not very appropriate in the case of children as it does not take into account their status as victims. At the other end of the spectrum there is a maximalist approach, which puts the accent on reintegration and may be more suitable as it aims to create opportunities for development by reintroducing children to school or providing them with vocational training.[962] Whereas for adult ex-combatants reintegration is 'the process by which ex-combatants acquire civilian status and gain sustainable employment

960 See Wessells, above note 279, at 23.

961 Drumbl reported that in the DRC, despite the existence of an official DDR programme since 2004, re-recruitment of demobilised children chronically persists. See Drumbl, above note 20, at 172. According to the author, 'child soldiers do not present a unitary narrative, many become associated with armed forces or groups through brutal abduction. Others are conscripted through threats. Significant numbers of child soldiers, however actively join armed forces or groups in an attempt to achieve various ends. In some cases, children are enlisted under false pretenses, through deception, or because of an impulsive snap-decision.'

962 R. Muggah, P. Maughan and C. Bugnion, 'The Long Shadow of War: Prospects for Disarmament Demobilisation and Reintegration in the Republic of Congo: A Joint Independent Evaluation for the European Commission', UNDP and the MDRP Secretariat, March 2003.

and income', and 'it is essentially a social and economic process with an open time-frame, primarily taking place in communities at the local level',[963] for children reintegration is the most important aspect of DDR and it is the phase that can actually enshrine a remedial component. It follows that child-specific reintegration

> shall allow a child to access education, a livelihood, life skills and a meaningful role in society. The socio-economic and psychosocial aspects of reintegration for children are central to global DDR programming and budgeting. Successful reintegration requires long-term funding of child protection agencies and programmes to ensure continuous support for education and training for children, and essential follow-up/monitoring once they return to civilian life.[964]

Several DDR processes have also included child soldiers, e.g. the DRC,[965] Nepal[966] and Colombia.[967] However, Liberia and Sierra Leone provide the most analysed and well-documented examples of DDR processes for child soldiers and deserve to be discussed in more detail.

7.5.1.1. Liberia

In Liberia there have been two different DDRR programmes in a ten-year period. The first was attempted after the signing of the Cotonou Agreement in 1993, which provided a blanket amnesty for all the fighters. Combatants were demobilised in various stages between the years 1994 and 1997. The first DDRR programme began in March 1994, but was prematurely aborted and resumed only in 1996. The process ended in July 1997, with about 24,500 of the estimated 33,000 fighters (74 per cent) disarmed and demobilised. These included 4,306 child soldiers and 250 adult female fighters. Adults and children went to the same sites and were disarmed by soldiers belonging to the Economic Community of West African States Military Observer Group ('ECOMOG').[968]

963 R. Duthie and I. Specht, 'DDR, Transitional justice, and the Reintegration of Former Child Combatants', in A. Cutter Patel, P. De Greiff and L. Waldorf (eds.), *Disarming the Past: Transitional Justice and Ex-Combatants*, Social Science Research Council, New York, 2010, 193.

964 IDDRS, above note 952, sec. 5.30, 2.

965 See Pauletto and Patel, above note 953, at 53–55.

966 T. Bleie and R. Shrestha, 'DDR in Nepal: Stakeholder Politics and the Implications for Reintegration as a Process of Disengagement', Centre for Peace Studies – University of Tromsø, 2012.

967 See Annual Report of the Secretary-General on Children and Armed Conflict, above note 11, at 36.

968 A. Adebajo, *Liberia's Civil War: Nigeria, ECOMOG, and Regional Security in West Africa*, Lynne Rienner, Boulder, CO, and London, 2002, 208–209.

Some of the children gave their weapons to their commanders to hand in because they were afraid to give them to the ECOMOG soldiers whom they considered to be their enemies. One of the major weaknesses of this first DDRR attempt was in fact its emphasis and focus on 'gun-carrying combatants', which predictably downsized the participation of both women and children. In general the low turnout of child soldiers to the DDRR programme was ascribed to three interrelated factors: some children voluntarily and independently returned to their homes and communities after the end of the conflict; others were reluctant to register with ECOMOG soldiers, i.e. the enemies they fought during the war; and others believed that registering meant they would be returned to the front line to fight.[969] The children who took part in the DDRR process could choose to stay in the so-called 'transit centres' that would attempt to trace and reunite them with their families; directly stay with parents or family; live on their own or with friends; or work on plantations, company camps or mining areas. Those who decided to stay at the transit centres benefitted from the programme led by UNICEF for war-affected youth, which included vocational and literacy training and trauma counselling.[970]

Almost ten years later, in December 2003, after the negotiation of the Comprehensive Peace Agreement, the second DDRR process was initiated. The most recent DDRR process officially ended on 30 October 2004, although rehabilitation and reintegration programmes for ex-combatants continued for many years afterwards.[971] Children unlawfully recruited by armed groups were included among the beneficiaries of the DDRR programme set up at the end of 2003 by the UN Mission in Liberia ('UNMIL') and the Liberian National Commission on DDRR.[972] According to the Liberian TRC:

> A significant number of children were part of the DDRR process. At the final count, out of the total of 103,019 individuals demobilised, 11,780 were children (11.4%), including 9,042 boys and 2,738 girls. Children associated with fighting forces ['CAFF'] were disarmed, taken to cantonment sites together with adult combatants, but then

---

969 T. Jaye, 'Transitional Justice and DDR: The Case of Liberia', ICTJ, June 2009, at 7, available at: https://www.ictj.org/sites/default/files/ICTJ-DDR-Liberia-CaseStudy-2009-English.pdf.

970 K. Peters, 'When Children Affected by War Go Home: Lessons Learned from Liberia', Save the Children, London, 2003, at 22–23.

971 See Jaye, above note 969, at 6.

972 See UNICEF, 'The impact on Women and Girls in West and Central Africa and the UNICEF Response', 2005, at 15, available at: http://www.unicef.org/publications/files/Impact_final.pdf. See also UN FOCUS, 'Seven Years of Peace', Vol. 7 No. 1, September–November 2010; 'The National Commission on Disarmament, Demobilization, Rehabilitation and Reintegration disarmed and reintegrated more than 101 000 former fighters, of which there were 22 000 women and 11 000 children. The ex-fighters were supported in schools, colleges and vocational training centres and given monthly allowances. Some were given business start-up capital and logistical support to engage in self-employed business.'

> transferred to child-focused Interim Care Centres, from where their families or existing relatives were traced, counselled on and prepared for reunification, which in most cases happened within a few weeks. The Interim Care Centres, as well as community-based Drop-in Centres catering to ex-children associated with the fighting forces who had spontaneously disarmed and did not go through the official process, also assisted children and their families through psycho-social counselling to help them break their relationships with commanders and armed groups and prepare them for reintegration into civilian life.[973]

Children, just like adult combatants, received a US$300 Transition Support Allowance for officially disarming and demobilising.[974] The allowance was meant to assist the children in the transition to civilian life and to provide an added incentive for reunification with their families and reintegration in home communities. However, the cash payments to children represented one of the most controversial aspects of the Liberian DDRR process. UNMIL, overwhelmed by the large number of combatants demanding DDRR benefits during the attempted disarmament in December 2003, tried to appease the crowds by handing out the first payment of the expected US$300 total payment to all combatants, thus making no distinction between children, youth and adults. Child protection agencies initially fought the policy of payments to children but realised that they were going to take place whether or not child protection agencies were involved. In order to ensure that children were not further victimised, protection agencies found themselves having to negotiate with the military structure of UNMIL to be included in the process.[975] When the DDRR process was resumed in April 2004, UNMIL continued to give cash payments to child combatants. This was done out of fear that withholding the allowance would be a disincentive for children associated with fighting forces to enter the process.[976] Moreover, facilitated by the unclear criteria set for entry into the DDRR programme and by the existence of a strong hierarchical structure still enforced in many areas, former commanders took advantage of the cash payments and started to send not only former child soldiers but also their own children and other children in their communities to collect money.[977]

After the disarmament and demobilisation phases, the programme encompassed also rehabilitation and reintegration as separate components.

---

973 Final Report of the Truth and Reconciliation Commission of Liberia, Volume Three: Appendices, Title II: Children, the Conflict and the TRC Children Agenda, June 2009, at 71.

974 P. Vinck, P.N. Pham and T. Kreutzer, 'Talking Peace: A Population-Based Survey on Attitudes about Security, Dispute Resolution, and Post-Conflict Reconstruction in Liberia', Human Rights Centre, University of California, Berkeley, 2011.

975 S. Martin and F. Lumeya, 'Liberia: Payments to Disarmed Child Soldiers Create Protection Problems', Refugees International Bulletin, 26 January 2005.

976 Ibidem.

977 See JAYE, above note 969, at 15.

The former was meant to focus on psychosocial and trauma counselling as well as vocational and formal educational training with the objective of preparing the ex-fighters to rejoin society. Reintegration was aimed at achieving the actual reinsertion of ex-combatants into their families and within their communities. The rehabilitation encompassed training opportunities that were subdivided into three principal categories, namely formal education at primary, secondary and university levels; vocational training; and apprenticeship. The ex-fighters were given an opportunity to choose or identify their training preferences; 40 per cent chose formal education, whereas the remaining 60 per cent chose other training activities. Children could also opt for schooling or a nine-month skills training programme.[978] With regard to female fighters, UNMIL reported that 22,370 women and 2,440 girls were disarmed and demobilised. Women were treated separately from the rest of the ex-fighters. Taking into account also the age and maternity status of women, female child ex-combatants and pregnant and lactating mothers were registered separately from other adult women. In terms of rehabilitation, care was provided, including pre- and antenatal care, as well as provision of education.

Even though during the DDRR process serious attempts were made to actively involve female soldiers, the prospect of participating in the programme was still considered traumatic for many women and girls. Most of them in fact were afraid to be identified as combatants, and feared repercussions and prosecution as well as going to cantonment sites and facing the men who had exploited them when they were members of the same armed group.[979] Ultimately the most significant problem with the DDRR process was the widespread late delivery of the reintegration assistance. According to UNICEF, reintegration assistance was under-resourced in comparison to the previous phases and delayed throughout the country. In the gap between demobilisation and the delivery of reintegration assistance, girls and boys were left on the streets with nothing to do. This put boys at high risk of becoming involved in military or criminal activities and girls at high risk of being exploited as prostitutes. In 2005 Human Rights Watch reported extensive efforts to recruit youths in West Africa for the war in Ivory Coast. Young demobilised ex-combatants were being asked to become mercenaries in neighbouring countries and the delay in the reintegration programme was one of the main reasons why several former child soldiers decided to take up the offer.[980]

---

978 Schools that accepted children formerly associated with armed groups received significant support through a UNICEF-funded Community Education and Investment Programme ('CEIP').

979 See I. Specht, *Red Shoes: Experiences of Girl-Combatants in Liberia*, ILO, 2006, 87.

980 Ibidem, at 97. See also Human Rights Watch, 'Recruitment of Ex-Child Soldiers in Cote d'Ivoire: Background, Accounts, and Recommendations', Background Briefing, 31 March 2005.

Despite the attempt to implement the DDRR process in a diffuse way, the Liberian TRC found that a significant number of children formerly associated with the armed forces did not have the chance to benefit from the programme and became particularly vulnerable to exploitation and homelessness.[981] As a result, former CAFF who had not gone through the DDRR process were identified by the TRC as beneficiaries of the reparations outlined in its final recommendations.[982] The underlying scope of this strategy is clearly to avoid the risk of doubly rewarding child soldiers, to the detriment of other categories of child victims who could not benefit from the DDRR process.

7.5.1.2. Sierra Leone

Like the armed conflicts that took place in Liberia, the Sierra Leonean war was also characterised by an unprecedented use of children recruited to participate in hostilities or to perform support roles. More than 48,000 child soldiers were recruited by both sides of the conflict and roughly 12,000 of them were girls.[983] The DDR process in Sierra Leone was interrupted and resumed several times due to the fighting flaring up. Overall there have been three phases: the first two were disrupted by outbreaks of violence and the third one has been completed.[984] The Lomè Agreement provided a separate DDR process for children and adults. With regard to the latter, the disarmament and demobilisation stage involved the establishment of reception centres in which officials collected and destroyed weapons, and ex-combatants demobilised. In order to qualify for DDR, adult combatants had to be 18 years of age and be able to assemble and disassemble a gun. At the reintegration stage, adult combatants received reinsertion packages and registered for reintegration assistance. A total of US$150 in cash was offered to ex-combatants as the reinsertion package. The reinsertion package, which was exclusive to participants of the Reintegration Opportunity Programme ('ROP'), was supposed to be an incentive for former fighters to return to their towns of

---

981 Final Report of the Truth and Reconciliation Commission of Liberia, Volume Three: Appendices, Title II: Children, the Conflict and the TRC Children Agenda, June 2009, at 97.

982 See Section 7.2.3 above.

983 See Wessells, above note 279, at 165.

984 M. Gibril Sesay and M. Suma, 'Transitional Justice and DDR: The Case of Sierra Leone', ICTJ, 2009, at 12. Phase One began just after the reinstatement of the Kabbah government in 1998, when the government of Sierra Leone and its supporters were in a stronger position militarily, given that the AFRC and RUF were in retreat. Phase Two of the DDR process was a result of the LPA. Its design and implementation this time reflected the weak military position of the government at the time of the LPA. As opposed to Phase One, which had no RUF involvement, Phase Two of the DDR included RUF representatives. Phase Three started after the signing of the Abuja agreements and it proceeded without interruption from further outbreaks of violence.

origin. The reintegration assistance included skills training and other educational programmes provided in the recipient communities where the ex-combatants went or returned to after demobilisation.[985]

Child soldiers instead participated in a different DDR programme.[986] Children who met the following criteria were eligible for entry into the demobilisation programme, including reintegration assistance. Between the ages of 12 and 17 children had to be able to handle a weapon and they needed to be presented by a commander as a 'combatant'. Predictably, the criterion requiring that children be presented by a commander resulted in many children not entering the DDR process. Children between the ages of 7 and 11 were eligible for entry into the demobilisation programme if any of the following criteria applied: the child must have learned to cock and load a weapon, he/she should have been trained in the use of arms, he/she must have spent more than six months with the fighting forces, held a rank, been used as a spy or in raiding missions.[987] Depending on the United Nation Mission in Sierra Leone ('UNAMSIL') personnel involved in the screening process, some children had to demonstrate their ability to lock and load a weapon; others had to pass the more demanding test of disassembling and reassembling a weapon.

As a result of the criteria adopted, thousands of children who were not involved in the fighting, but who played multiple other roles, were excluded from the process. Interviews conducted by Betancourt and her team proved that during their time with the RUF, children faced many physical difficulties and risks, but very few of them actually took part in combat.[988] The vast majority of former child soldiers of both genders said that their main duties were to carry heavy loads and to help with other camp-related jobs such as cooking and laundry; in other words children often acted as domestic slaves for specific RUF officers or their wives. The children reported that they were 'seriously working' to an exhausting degree and were beaten if they failed to accomplish their tasks quickly enough. Girls faced frequent rape at the hands of male RUF members, sometimes resulting in physical injury or unwanted pregnancy.[989]

---

985 By December 2002, 56,700 ex-combatants had registered for reintegration support. A total of 51,122 ex-fighters had participated in different programmes within the ROP categorised as vocational/apprenticeship, formal education, agriculture and job placement. See IDDRS, above note 952, module 4.30 'Reintegration'.

986 Over 6,774 children entered the DDR programme: 3,710 had been with the RUF, 2,026 with the CDF, 471 with the Sierra Leone Army and 427 with the AFRC; 144 were with other factions or non-affiliated.

987 J. Williamson and L. Cripe, 'Assessment of DCOF-Supported Child Demobilization and Reintegration Activities in Sierra Leone', UNICEF, June 2002, at 8.

988 T.S. Betancourt, 'High Hopes, Grim Reality: Reintegration and the Education of Former Child Soldiers in Sierra Leone', (2008) 52 *Comparative Education Review* 565, at 566–587.

989 Ibidem, at 572.

After disarmament and initial screening in demobilisation transit centres, some of the children who fought with the Civil Defence Forces ('CDF') and almost all of those who had been with the RUF, were sent to Interim Care Centres ('ICCs') while family tracing took place. Significantly, most CDF children were living with their families during military conscription, so they simply returned home, whereas the majority of children associated with the RUF had been abducted and therefore remained alone.[990] As a matter of policy, the period of stay in ICCs was no more than six weeks and the vast majority of children transited through ICCs within this time limit. The children who could not be reunited within six weeks were either placed in foster care, or, if old enough, allowed to live in small groups with limited adult supervision. Although relatively brief, this period of transition was crucial as activities focused on a return to normal life were implemented on a daily basis, such as a regular schedule, chores, classes, play, art work, singing, and learning culturally appropriate behaviour.[991]

After the time spent in the ICCs, former child soldiers went through the reintegration phase. In terms of social acceptance, this phase was easiest for the children who were part of the CDF as most of them remained in their communities or close by and were even considered protectors of their villages. Children who had been abducted by the RUF, instead, were not welcomed home with open arms and in many cases community members expressed hatred and fear of these children and never wanted to see them again.[992]

Despite the fact that girls represented approximately 30 per cent of child soldiers, only 8 per cent of them entered the programme.[993] The criteria set for entering the DDR process prevented the inclusion of the girls associated with armed forces or groups, who, instead of fighting, were used to perform different tasks. Girls who did not attend DDR programmes missed out on not only school fees and training assistance but also psychosocial treatment, assistance in locating family members, and medical care. In order to overcome, at least to some extent, the discriminatory policy which hampered girls' access to the DDR programme, in 2004 UNICEF established a special project to reach more than 1,000 young women who, as children, were associated with fighting forces.[994] The Girls Left Behind ('GLB') project provided girls with different services, from family tracing and reunification to school and counselling. However, according to the results shared by UNICEF, at least half of the girls who joined GLB, after

990 See Williamson and Cripe, above note 987, at 27.

991 J. Williamson, 'The Disarmament, Demobilisation, and Reintegration of Child Soldiers: Social and Psychological Transformation in Sierra Leone', (2006) 4 *International Journal of Mental Health, Psychosocial Work, and Counselling in Areas of Armed* Conflict 185, at 190–205.

992 Ibidem.

993 See Williamson and Cripe, above note 987, at 32.

994 See S. Whittington, 'The Impact of Conflict on Women and Girls in West and Central Africa and the UNICEF Response', UNICEF, 2005.

completing the programme, which lasted only a few months, decided to return to former male ex-combatant partners or to a same-sex peer group, instead of staying with their re-found families.[995] This happened mainly because many girls who had been abducted remained under the control of their 'commanders' or 'bush husbands'.

Generally speaking, the ambition to remove former child soldiers from a context of violence and place them in a safe place often collides with the reality, especially in the case of girls who suffered sexual violence and face a higher risk of being stigmatised and even rejected by their communities.[996] However, it is worth noting that in some instances rather than DDR processes, communities and families employed 'rituals of welcome' to incorporate returned girl soldiers into acceptable social positions.[997] Various organisations involved with the reintegration process in Sierra Leone stressed the importance of traditional cleansing ceremonies. These ceremonies seemed to have been important in facilitating family and community reintegration, apparently making the girls feel accepted and acceptable to their family members and others in the community. Despite their potential benefits, it should be borne in mind that when the scope is solely to disempower girls and subjugate them in a patriarchal microsystem, the advocacy of traditional practices can have the inadvertent outcome of reinforcing stigma and marginalisation rather than fostering psychosocial well-being for children.[998]

As in Liberia, in Sierra Leone former child soldiers who have not been included in the DDR process have also been recognised as victims entitled to the measures enshrined in the reparations recommended by the TRC.[999] This approach, correct in principle, is very problematic in practice as while the DDR process has actually been implemented, the same cannot be said with regard to the reparations programme. Therefore, child victims of unlawful recruitment and use in hostilities have received some form of redress, whereas child victims of other crimes, including those perpetrated by child soldiers, got nothing or very little.

---

995 Ibidem, at 17.

996 See Pauletto and Patel, above note 953, at 38.

997 S. McKay and D. Mazurana, *Where Are the Girls? Girls in Fighting Forces in Northern Uganda, Sierra Leone and Mozambique: Their Lives during and after War*, Rights & Democracy, Montreal, 2004. See also S. Shepler, 'The Rites of the Child: Global Discourses of Youth and Reintegrating Child Soldiers in Sierra Leone', (2005) 4 *Journal of Human Rights* 197, at 198–205.

998 See W.A. Tol, M.J.D. Jordans, B.A. Kohrt, T.S. Betancourt and I.H. Komproe., 'Promoting Mental Health and Psychosocial Well-Being in Children Affected by Political Violence: Part I – Current Evidence for an Ecological Resilience Approach', in Fernando and Ferrari, above note 180, 11, at 13–29.

999 Duthie and Specht, above note 963, at 206.

7.6. CONCLUSIONS

Truth Commissions, national reparations programmes, the TFV and, in the case of child soldiers, DDR processes, depart from quasi-judicial and judicial mechanisms in a number of aspects, e.g. degree of victim participation, scope, reach of the measures awarded and so on. Even though not all of them can be regarded as able to provide 'reparations' in the legal meaning of the term, non-judicial mechanisms certainly offer some form of redress to victims of armed conflict, including children.

The goal to repair the harm to victims in non-judicial settings is set off against the need to achieve wider outcomes, such as long-lasting peace, security and reconciliation. To this end, non-judicial mechanisms are designed and implemented taking into account the broader context rather than the situation of the individuals affected. When the harm is not only personal, but is deeply rooted in the community, the establishment of measures that seek to achieve social justice, dialogue, truth and reintegration is a crucial step towards healing. Putting in place far-reaching initiatives and tools does not automatically infer that the most vulnerable victims are taken into account. With the exception of the TFV, which due to its assistance nature is by default prone to help those most in need, in particular women and children, the other non-judicial mechanisms have only paid attention to child victims to a limited extent. Some TCs in their recommendations have highlighted the need to redress a broken social fabric that disproportionately affects children and makes them over-exposed to victimisation in situations of insecurity or armed conflict. However, TCs' recommendations have not been well implemented in most countries[1000] and national reparations programmes have also failed to fully address child victims' needs. Most of the TCs' reports and the national reparations programmes considered in this chapter have identified as the legitimate beneficiaries of reparations those victims under the age of 18 years who could still be regarded as 'children'.[1001] Given the large number of victims and the limited resources available, it does not come as a surprise that decision makers had to draw a line and prioritise those perceived as most vulnerable. However, this approach overlooks the consequences of the traumas experienced by adult victims when they were children.

1000 See Evans, above note 47, at 181.

1001 See Section 7.2.3 above. The CAVR, for example, established that only those who were 18 years or younger on the day the conflict ended, i.e. 25 October 1999, were eligible for reparations as 'children'. Instead, within the Chilean framework the 'children' of the direct victims identified by the TRC were eligible for a pension until the age of 25 years, and those with disabilities qualified for a pension for life; persons under the age of 35 years were also eligible for a university scholarship.

With regard to the DDR process, this 'discriminatory' approach covers both age and gender. Only individuals under the age of 18 years can enter the DDR programmes envisaged for children, but no distinction is made within the adult DDR process between those who joined an armed group after turning 18 and those who were instead conscripted or abducted as minors. Moreover, the criteria adopted to determine who is entitled to participate in the DDR process leads to the exclusion of girls and exacerbates their marginalisation and stigmatisation, thus hampering, instead of fostering, their reintegration. It is important to highlight also that there is a tension, rather than a constructive interaction, between DDR programmes and reparations plans. The former usually include reinsertion and/or reintegration benefits for ex-combatants, which can encompass cash payments, travel allowances, or vocational training and employment opportunities. Such payments can cause resentment among victims and the broader public, especially given the frequent absence of reparations.[1002] As noted by some authors,[1003] in countries that seek to implement both a DDR process and a reparation plan, the international community often invests much in the former and very little in the latter. The result is that it is very difficult to strike a balance between DDR and reparations, which, especially in the case of children, should be complementary and not antithetic. In fact, in the absence of addressing the needs of other vulnerable children or groups, reintegration of former child soldiers may be resisted and fuel discontent and hatred among the affected communities.

1002 See E. Witte, 'Beyond "Peace vs. Justice": Understanding the Relationship between DDR Programmes and the Prosecution of International Crimes', in Cutter Patel, De Greiff and Waldorf above note 963, at 96.

1003 See Evans, above note 47, at 182. See also Y. Sooka, 'Dealing with the Past and Transitional Justice: Building Peace through Accountability', (2006) *88 International Review of the Red Cross* 311, at 320–327.

CHAPTER 8
FINAL REMARKS

8.1. INTRODUCTION

This book represents a, hopefully significant, step in clarifying an under-researched topic in the field of reparations. The right to reparation has been steadily gaining momentum and it is well rooted in the international law framework. Nonetheless, shifting the attention from the inter-State to the individual dimension of reparations has triggered several questions and raised a large number of important issues. The abundance of armed conflicts worldwide and the emergence of new methods of warfare have resulted in high numbers of persons affected, individually or collectively, by violations of IHRL and IHL. Children are among those who suffer the most in connection with an armed conflict, be it international or internal. Recent global trends regarding the impact of armed conflict on children show that lately children have been affected 'to a degree which is an affront to our common humanity'.[1004] Almost 20 years ago Ms Machel reported to the General Assembly that

> [m]illions of children are caught up in conflicts in which they are not merely bystanders, but targets. Some fall victim to a general onslaught against civilians; others die as part of a calculated genocide. Still other children suffer the effects of sexual violence or the multiple deprivations of armed conflict that expose them to hunger or disease. Just as shocking, thousands of young people are cynically exploited as combatants.[1005]

Since then, despite the mechanisms set up by the UN and the efforts made by specialised NGOs and other local and international actors, very little has changed and atrocities committed against children show no sign of abating, although these violations are, at last, recognised as a stand-alone category that requires the adoption of specific measures for prevention and intervention. Armed conflicts, especially protracted ones, 'have a significant impact on health and well-being across almost all domains of children's lives, due to

1004 See Annual Report of the Secretary-General on Children and Armed Conflict, above note 11, at 46.

1005 See 'Impact of Armed Conflict on Children: Note by the Secretary-General', above note 36, at 5.

exposure to violence, pervasive poverty, ongoing insecurity, strained family relations, disrupted networks of social support, curtailed education and poor health'.[1006] Thus, in comparison to other members of the society, all children are disproportionately affected by war. However, some children suffer harm, direct or indirect, as a result of violations of IHRL and IHL and therefore they are entitled to be recognised as victims and obtain not only assistance and aid, which should be provided to everyone dealing with a situation of emergency or distress, but also reparations in the legal definition of the term. Child victims' vulnerability has been thoroughly discussed in light of their dependent status and the likely exposure to multiple forms of victimisation. The characteristics attached to their fragility are crucial, but represent only one side of the coin. The other side, i.e. children's resilience, is equally important and deserves to be taken into account while designing and implementing reparations for this category of victims. As stressed throughout this study, not all child victims of armed conflict suffer in the same way and to the same degree and not all the violations trigger the same reaction. Over recent years, for example, a lot of attention has been devoted to the issue of child soldiering, which is one of the most discussed and widely observed aspects of the impact of war on children. The growing interest in this phenomenon is reflected also in the case law of the ICC, the SCSL and domestic courts. Thanks to the relevant work of outstanding authors such as Wessells and Drumbl, the main problems connected to the recruitment and use of children in armed conflict have been widely discussed and better understood. Even though the results of the critical studies undertaken with regard to child soldiers have revealed that the image of the helpless, poor and frightened child is not always the most realistic or correct,[1007] for the purpose of this book the issue of child soldiering has been presented through a victimological perspective, without contributing to the important and timely discussion concerning possible accountability modalities. Therefore the phenomenon of child soldiers has only been discussed in light of their victimhood, stressing that most of them are still facing the consequences of the harm suffered during the time spent in the ranks of armed forces or groups.

The analysis carried out in this book has ultimately shown that reparations awarded through judicial and non-judicial mechanisms have focused mainly on child soldiers, even though they represent only one of the different categories of children victimised in conjunction with an armed conflict. Far less attention has been placed on children who suffered as a result of any of the other grave violations identified by the UN and who are equally entitled to claim and receive adequate, effective and prompt reparations. And yet, despite the fact that child

[1006] P. Ventevogel, 'Child Mental Health, Psychosocial Well-Being and Resilience in Afghanistan: A Review and Future Directions', in Fernando and Ferrari, above note 180, 51, at 55.

[1007] See Chapter 2, Section 2.6.3 above.

soldiers have been extensively placed under the spotlight in comparison to other categories such as refugees and internally displaced children, children sexually abused or exploited and children injured by landmines and unexploded ordnance, the critical issues flagged throughout the present book still apply to the whole group of child victims of armed conflict. How is this possible? Why has greater attention and extensive research not led to more effective reparations?

The many problems identified by this study both at the normative and at the empirical level, e.g. lack of NSAGs' engagement, absence of enforcement mechanisms for IHL violations, dearth of child-friendly procedures, and inadequate response to the long-term consequences of children's victimhood and to the causes that exacerbate their vulnerability, are at the core of child victims' marginal role in the reparations discourse and cannot be overcome unless multi-layered and coordinated efforts are put in place by all the relevant stakeholders. States, in particular, bear the primary responsibility to award and implement reparations in the aftermath of IHRL and IHL violations. These multi-layered and coordinated efforts are especially warranted in three areas, i.e. the normative framework governing reparations for child victims; the existing mechanisms, judicial and otherwise; and the substantive forms of the reparations awarded.

8.2. OVERCOMING THE LACUNAE OF THE CURRENT LEGAL FRAMEWORK

Adequate, effective and prompt reparation is intended to promote justice by redressing gross violations of IHRL or serious violations of IHL.[1008] Achieving this outcome requires in the first place the existence of a solid and sufficiently developed legal framework. As discussed in Chapters 2 and 3 of this book, while the right to reparation is constantly evolving and adjusting to an idea of international law more inclined to include individuals in the equation, there are several issues that still hinder the realisation of this goal, especially in relation to child victims. In particular it is worth stressing again that the CRC incorporates only one, very general, provision that makes explicit reference to States' obligation to promote children's physical and psychological recovery and social reintegration.[1009] In comparison to the CRC, the other IHRL treaties have all placed more emphasis on victims' right to access remedies and reparation for violations of the rights enshrined therein.[1010] Children as human beings are of course entitled to the enjoyment of all human rights promoted by the core legal instruments and they also benefit from special protection during armed

[1008] UNBPG, above note 2, §15.

[1009] Art. 39 of the CRC.

[1010] See Chapter 3, Section 3.2.1 above.

conflict,[1011] but this does not necessarily entail that the existing IHRL framework is sufficiently developed and that child victims are provided with enough means to obtain reparations.

Under IHL the recognition of an individual's right to reparation is still a recent achievement that has not been coupled with the establishment of enforcement mechanisms able to give effect to this right. As stressed by the ILA Committee on reparations for victims of armed conflict, 'looking at the situation in its entirety, one can hardly avoid concluding that, as of today, only very few possibilities exist where individual war victims can claim reparations for their suffering. The most complicated situation arises, when the individual victim tries to sue a foreign State directly.'[1012] This statement was corroborated by the judgment of the ICJ in the *Jurisdictional Immunities of the State* case.[1013] Remarkably, few months after the ICJ judgment the Tel Aviv District Court ruled in favour of a group of 217 Holocaust survivors, children at the time of the Nazi persecution, who claimed to have been neglected during Israel's distribution of the reparations received from Germany. The judgment set an important precedent as it recognised State accountability for a previously unchallenged, and to some extent taboo, issue, i.e. how inter-State reparations are actually implemented *by* the recipient State. The hope is that this case will pave the way for further claims and will encourage more victims to seek justice for the unfair administration of reparations awards.

ICL has also contributed to addressing some of the limitations related to the scant opportunities to obtain redress for the victims of IHL violations. Through the establishment of the ICC the international community has at last acknowledged the importance of promoting victims' participation in the proceedings and enabling them to request reparations. The latest developments in the *Lubanga* case suggest that the reparations phase of a judgment can potentially be just as significant and important for the development of ICL as the judgment itself.[1014] However, the process to achieve meaningful and effective inclusion of victims is still far from being complete and the *Lubanga* case has been a lengthy and challenging test for the ICC. Even though the Appeals Chamber judgment, which reversed the decision of Trial Chamber I and amended the reparations order, has shed light on some crucial points, *inter alia* the five core elements that must be part of every reparations order pursuant to Article 75 of the Rome Statute and the interplay between the Court and the TFV, the approach of the Court with regard to reparations is still not fully delineated. For example, it is not

---

1011 Given the particular vulnerability of children, the Geneva Conventions of 1949 and their Additional Protocols of 1977 lay down a series of rules according them special protection. Fourth Geneva Convention, Arts. 23–24, 38, 50, 76 and 89; Protocol I, Art. 77(1); and Protocol II, Art. 4(3).

1012 See HOFMANN and RIEMANN, above note 14, at 48.

1013 See Chapter 3, Section 3.3.1 above.

1014 See SWART, above note 704, at 188.

yet clear whether the ICC will ever be able to implement individual reparations or if in the future reparations hearings will be held before an *ad hoc* 'Reparations Chamber'.[1015]

The shortcomings of the existing normative framework culminate in the lack of engagement of non-State actors, in particular NSAGs, which are responsible for many of the violations committed against children in armed conflict. During the past ten years, the UN has achieved important results in terms of enhancing children's protection in war. To this end six grave violations have been identified and monitored to gather credible information, subsequently channelled into tangible attempts to strengthen NSAGs' compliance with IHRL and IHL.[1016] Nonetheless, the actions plans and the UN MRM in general do not yet contemplate the possibility of imposing secondary obligations upon the NSAGs that violate children's rights. The most interesting 'push' in this sense stems from the work of bodies like the Commission of Inquiry on Syria, which has boldly called on all the parties involved to redress the harm caused. Nevertheless, it should be noted that a positive response to such a request would still appear as a voluntary commitment and it would not stem from a binding obligation.[1017] In fact, apart from soft law instruments like the UNBPG, which also spells out the subsidiary role that States should play in the case of violations committed by non-State actors,[1018] there is no binding document imposing an actual obligation to provide reparations. Thus, how can reparations be adequate, effective and prompt if those responsible for the violations are not held accountable?

Also, given the dearth of legal provisions as well as mechanisms to enforce them, some authors have underlined that NSAGs may only be capable and willing to award symbolic reparations, such as acknowledgement of the truth and apologies.[1019] If on the one hand this approach stems from both practical and legal considerations, at least *de lege lata*, on the other hand such a compromise does overshadow victims' needs and downsizes the scope of reparations. Reasoning in terms of *lege ferenda* instead, it would be possible to overcome many of the existing limitations that hinder child victims' right to reparation, including the exclusion of non-State actors from the reparations discourse, through the adoption of a binding instrument aimed at crystallising the principles already enshrined in the UNBPG. A treaty on the right to reparation for victims of IHRL and IHL violations should build on the existing international law and incorporate the most recent developments which have emerged in relation to several important aspects, including the transformative potential of reparations.

1015 See Stahn, above note 727, at 811.

1016 See Chapter 3, Section 3.3.2.2 above.

1017 In Colombia through the JPL NSAGs have 'voluntarily' provided reparations to victims in order to avail themselves of reduced sentences.

1018 UNBPG, above note 2, §15.

1019 See Dudai, above note 438.

Such an instrument should necessarily include specific articles focusing on child victims' needs and peculiar status, in the wake of the Colombian Victims' Law, which enshrines a number of provisions on children.[1020]

8.3. IMPROVING THE EXISTING MECHANISMS

Reparations for child victims should always be the result of child-friendly proceedings, in both judicial and non-judicial settings. With regard to the former, according to the Council of Europe child-friendly justice is an umbrella term that

> means creating a justice system which guarantees the respect and the effective implementation of all children's rights, giving due consideration to the child's level of maturity and understanding and to the circumstances of the case. It is, in particular, justice that is accessible, age appropriate, speedy, diligent, adapted to and focused on the needs and rights of the child, respecting the rights of the child including the rights to due process, to participate in and to understand the proceedings, to respect for private and family life and to integrity and dignity.[1021]

This definition and the characteristics enshrined therein already appear difficult to pursue in normal contexts and even more so in international judicial settings or post-conflict and fragile situations, where the rule of law and human rights standards are particularly precarious and difficult to enforce.

A child-friendly approach is needed also when implementing programmes and strategies aimed at providing redress for the victims of IHRL and IHL violations as well as contributing to achieving reconciliation and long-lasting peace. Reparations, in fact, are not awarded in a vacuum, but they are normally part of wider efforts and plans: if children's rights are strengthened in every step of the transition towards stability then they are likely to be respected also when reparations are designed and put in place. The Special Rapporteur on the promotion of truth, justice, reparation and guarantees of non-recurrence has expressed alarm at the failure of a number of programmes, which fell significantly short of providing adequate, effective and prompt reparations, as requested under the UNBPG.[1022] As demonstrated in this book, reparations programmes as well as other non-judicial processes have paid little attention to the implementation of the key CRC principles, resulting, for instance, in

1020 See Arts. 181–190 of the Victims' Law.

1021 Guidelines of the Committee of Ministers of the Council of Europe on Child-friendly Justice, Art. II(c).

1022 Report of the Special Rapporteur on the promotion of truth, justice, reparation and guarantees of non-recurrence, UN doc. A/69/518, 14 October 2014, §87.

limited involvement of children in truth-seeking mechanisms, few consultations with child protection agencies and specialised NGOs, and rare consideration of the child's bests interests, all of which have ultimately led to the adoption of inadequate redress measures.

It is striking to note that also quasi-judicial bodies devoted in principle to strengthening children's rights to the maximum extent possible, i.e. the Committee on the Rights of the Child and the African Committee of Experts on the Rights and Welfare of the Child, present significant shortcomings that hamper children's access to remedies.[1023] If these specialised Committees 'fail' to duly address children's quest for justice and reparations, is it logical or fair to expect otherwise from mechanisms established to pursue different objectives? The source of the Committees' limitations is ultimately found in States' unaltered reluctance to recognise children as victims entitled to exercise all the relevant rights attached to this status. The CRC-OP3, for example, is a watered-down version of the draft originally discussed and it significantly downsizes the potential impact that the Optional Protocol could have had on child victims' lives. Furthermore, the version that entered into force does not allow the Committee to play a crucial role with regard to widespread and systematic violations of children's rights. In the first place this is because the CRC-OP3 does not envisage the possibility to hear collective or anonymous complaints and secondly because it does not provide the Committee with the opportunity to transfer to the ICC information concerning grave violations against children, where the communication enshrines facts relevant to determine an individual's liability. With regard to the African Committee of Experts on the Rights and Welfare of the Child, it is important to stress that it monitors States parties' compliance with a convention that does not contain any provision concerning the right to a remedy.[1024] Its power to recommend reparations, although exercised through non-binding instruments, has, in theory, the potential to fill a significant gap in the African human rights system. Despite its undeniable potential, the Committee is still developing its position in relation to reparations and in practice its contribution to this field has been very limited.

Quasi-judicial bodies, as well as regional and international courts and tribunals, in any case will benefit only an exiguous number of victims. Their main scope is thus to set a benchmark for reparations that can raise awareness and commitment at the domestic level, where most victims, including children, seek redress.[1025] This is the reason why it is so important to strengthen, at the regional and international levels, the design and implementation of child-friendly procedures able to incorporate to the maximum degree possible the key principles enshrined in the CRC.

1023 See Chapter 5, Section 5.2. Chapter 6, Section 6.2.1 above.

1024 See Chapter 3, Section 3.2.1 above.

1025 On this point see Evans, above note 47, at 235.

8.4. AWARDING AND IMPLEMENTING MEANINGFUL REPARATIONS FOR CHILD VICTIMS OF ARMED CONFLICT

In addition to the requirement of a sound normative framework coupled with the enhancement of the existing mechanisms, meaningful redress measures for child victims of armed conflict must also be designed and implemented effectively and in a prompt way. Ideally this infers that reparations should be awarded quickly enough to allow the victims to recover and resume their lives. Of course the cases reported in this book have shown a different reality, common to both judicial and non-judicial mechanisms. The ECCC is probably one of the most shocking examples of justice delayed,[1026] but the *Lubanga* case itself, despite all the unprecedented pressure placed on the ICC, has demonstrated that victims always wait a considerable amount of time before having their claims heard, not to mention satisfied. This certainly calls for a more efficient use of time and resources when dealing with reparations, but it also highlights the importance of not limiting reparations for child victims to those who are under the age of 18 years at the time the claim is brought forward or the programme is implemented, which unfortunately is the common approach followed by national reparations programmes, DDR processes for children and TCs.[1027] Also the CRC-OP3 provides only persons under 18 years with the possibility to submit a complaint to the Committee, without taking into account the long-term and profound consequences of *having been* a child victim.[1028] Children's victimhood has far-reaching repercussions on their adult lives. This is true in peace time and even more so in situations of insecurity and armed conflict when vulnerable children are likely to be exposed to multiple forms of violence. As stressed by UNICEF in its submission on the principles and procedures to be applied to reparations in the *Lubanga* case, the fact the victims *were* children when the offences were committed should be given great weight by the Court in assessing the harm they endured because of their vulnerability as children.[1029] The IACtHR has relied on the age and vulnerability of the victims to affirm that States violating children's rights face an 'aggravated responsibility'.[1030] The particular seriousness attached to violations perpetrated against children has been stressed by the

1026 See Chapter 3, Section 3.2.3 above.

1027 See Chapter 7 above. Particularly remarkable is the case of Colombia where the Victims' Law established that child victims of unlawful recruitment are entitled to reparations only if they leave the armed group before turning 18 years.

1028 On children's vulnerability in armed conflict, see M. Wessells, 'Children, Armed Conflict and Peace', (1998) 35 *Journal of Peace Research* 635, at 640–646.

1029 See UNICEF, Submission on the Principles to be Applied and the Procedures to be followed by the Chamber with regard to Reparations, ICC-01/04–01/06-2878 11-05-2012, §2.

1030 See Nilsson, above note 877, at 404; see also Feria Tinta, above note 6, at 419.

IACtHR on several occasions and, in some cases, it has also been reflected in the reparations awarded.[1031] Despite not being a crystallised legal principle, the notion of aggravated responsibility should be taken into account not only with regard to reparations that look backwards, such as compensation for pecuniary and moral damages, but also in relation to measures that look forwards, such as rehabilitation and guarantees of non-repetition.

The identification of the forms of reparations represents another important aspect that can significantly impact on the effectiveness of the award. The ECOSOC Guidelines strongly stress that 'child victims should, wherever possible, receive reparation in order to achieve *full* redress, reintegration and recovery'.[1032] These results would preferably be accomplished combining restitution with other forms of reparations, awarded through individual as well as collective measures whenever the number of victims, the type of harm suffered or the violation itself so requires. If in theory this proposal appears both logical and desirable, in practice imagining restitution as a viable option for victims of armed conflict, including children, is very difficult, if not unrealistic. Thus the goal must shift towards the achievement, to the maximum extent possible, of reparations that, in whatever forms and modalities, are capable of providing child victims with recognition for the harm suffered, either as individuals or as members of a larger group; the potential to transform the situation of vulnerability that triggered their victimisation; and opportunities to build as much as possible on any existing resilience factors.

8.5. CONCLUSIONS

In the field of transitional justice, reading about 'bridging the gap between theory and practice' is rather common and the main concern seems to be the alignment of the theoretical framework with its implementation.[1033] With regard to the specific topic addressed in this book, more than bridging a gap the goal should be to lay down the foundations to reach a common understanding as 'to what extent' child victims' needs differ from those of other victims and what can be done to provide them with adequate, effective and prompt reparations. Children's capability, according to their personal development and evolving capacities,[1034] to be actively engaged in transitional justice processes can no

1031 See Chapter 6, Section 6.3.2.2 above.

1032 See Chapter 1, Section 1.4 above.

1033 See, for instance, Stover and Weinstein, above note 61, at 21. See also R. Mani, 'Restoring Justice in the Aftermath of Conflict: Bridging the Gap between Theory and Practice', in T. Coates (ed.), *International Justice*, Ashgate Publishing, Burlington, VT, 2000, 264.

1034 G. Lansdown, Innocenti Insight, 'The Evolving Capacities of the Children', UNICEF and Save the Children, Florence, 2005, at 9-13.

longer be questioned and significant illustrations can be found, for instance, in Tunisia,[1035] Colombia,[1036] and South Africa.[1037] Yet this capability has not been duly taken into account by those in charge of awarding, designing and implementing reparations.

Ms Malala Yousafzai, the youngest winner of the Nobel Peace Prize, is perhaps the best-known example of a child participating in society as an active stakeholder. In her powerful speech on the right to education at the UN Headquarters, Ms Yousafzai explained that her goal was not to speak for herself, but for those without a voice, so that they could finally be heard.[1038] Given her undisputed role as a champion of girls' access to education, many overlook the fact that Ms Yousafzai was the victim of a terrorist attack and that, in principle, she is entitled to receive redress for the harm suffered.[1039] The questions are, then, *who* is responsible? *How* could she claim for reparations? *What kind* of measures should be awarded? This book has tried to answer these questions, for Ms Yousafzai and for the thousands of children around the world who have been victimised by different actors in situations of armed conflict.

1035 A. Khalil, 'Tunisia's Women: Partners in Revolution', in L. Sadiki (ed.), *Handbook of the Arab Spring: Rethinking Democratisation*, Routledge, Abingdon, 2015, 285, at 288–289.

1036 Colombia has a long history of initiatives aimed at including children in the transition to peace. After Graca Machel's visit to Colombia, in 1996, the Children's Peace Movement organised an unprecedented vote on children's rights. As the most important rights the majority of children voted for the right to live, the right to peace as well as the right to love and to have a family. Further information is available at: http://www.korubo.com/Colombia/mouvement.htm. Significantly, during the peace process between the Colombian government and the FARC, 60 victims have been invited in person to the negotiating table, representing geographic, ethnic, gender, age and sexual orientation diversity. See Annual report of the United Nations High Commissioner for Human Rights Addendum, Report of the United Nations High Commissioner for Human Rights on the situation of human rights in Colombia, 23 January 2015, UN doc. A/HRC/28/3/Add.3, at §7.

1037 See Pigou, above note 874, at 117.

1038 Making a Wish for Action on Global Education, Malala Yousafzai addresses Youth Assembly at UN on her 16th Birthday, 12 July 2013, available at: http://webtv.un.org/watch/malala-yousafzai-addresses-united-nations-youth-assembly/2542094251001/.

1039 Malala Yousafzai was attacked on her way home from school in Mingora, the Swat region's main town on 9 October 2012.

BIBLIOGRAPHY

ABDULLAH I., 'Bush Path to Destruction: the Origin and Character of the Revolutionary United Front/Sierra Leone', (1998) 36 *Journal of Modern African Studies*.

ADEBAJO A., *Liberia's Civil War: Nigeria, ECOMOG, and Regional Security in West Africa*, Lynne Rienner, Boulder, CO, and London, 2002.

ALFREDSON L., 'Child Soldiers, Displacement and Human Security', Disarmament Forum: Children and Security. UNIDIR No. 3, 2002.

AMBOS K. and NJIKAM O., 'Charles Taylor's Criminal Responsibility', (2013) 11 *Journal of International Criminal Justice*.

AMNESTY INTERNATIONAL, *Commissioning Justice: Truth Commissions and Criminal Justice*, Amnesty International Publications, London, 2010.

AMOROSO D., 'Armed Opposition Groups' (and Foreign Fighters') Abidance by International Human Rights Law: The Issue of Compliance in Syria and Iraq', in A. DE GUTTRY, F. CAPONE and C. PAULUSSEN (eds.), *Foreign Fighters under International Law and Beyond*, Springer/Asser Press, The Hague, 2016.

ANTKOWIAK M., 'Remedial Approaches to Human Rights Violations: The Inter-American Court of Human Rights and Beyond', (2008) 46 *Colombia Journal of Transnational Law*.

APTEL C. and V. LADISCH, 'Through a New Lens: A Child-Sensitive Approach to Transitional Justice', ICTJ, August 2011, available at: http://ictj.org/sites/default/files/ICTJ-Children-Through-New-Lens-Aptel-Ladisch-2011-English.pdf.

ARCHARD D., *Children, Rights and Childhood*, Routledge, London, 2004.

ARIÈS P., *Centuries of Childhood*, Jonathan Cape, London, 1962.

ATTANAYAKE V., R. MCKAY, M. JOFFRES, S. SINGH, F. Jr BURKLE and E. MILLS, 'Prevalence of Mental Disorders among Children Exposed to War: A Systematic Review of 7,920 Children', (2009) 25 *Medicine Conflict and Survival*.

BACKER D., 'Victims' Responses to Truth Commissions: Evidence from South Africa', in M. NDULO (ed.), *Security, Reconciliation and Reconstruction: When the Wars End*, University College of London Press, London, 2006.

BAKKER C., 'Prosecuting International Crimes against Children: the Legal Framework', UNICEF Innocenti Research Centre, Innocenti Working Paper no. 2010-13, Florence.

BALABKINS N., *West German Reparations to Israel*, Rutgers University Press, New Brunswick, NJ, 1971.

BANTEKAS I. and L. OETTE, *International Human Rights Law and Practice*, Cambridge University Press, Cambridge, 2013.

BARENBAUM J., V. RUCHKIN and M.C. SCHWAB-STONE, 'The Psychosocial Aspects of Children Exposed to War: Practice and Policy Initiatives', (2004) 45 *Journal of Child Psychology and Psychiatry*.

BARNETT K. and A. JEFFERYS, 'Full of Promise: How the UN's Monitoring and Reporting Mechanism Can Better Protect Children', Humanitarian Practice Network at ODI Network Paper 62, 2008.

Barria L.A. and S.D. Roper, 'How Effective are International Criminal Tribunals? An Analysis of the ICTY and the ICTR', (2005) 9 *The International Journal of Human Rights.*

Bassiouni M.C., 'Universal Jurisdiction for International Crimes: Historical Perspectives and Contemporary Practice', (2001) 42 *Virginia Journal of International Law.*

Bassiouni M.C., 'Facing Atrocity: The Importance of Guiding Principles on Post-conflict Justice', *Introduction to the Chicago Principles on Post-conflict Justice*, International Human Rights Institute, Chicago, 2007.

Bassiouni M.C. (ed.), *International Criminal Law* 3rd edn., Martinus Nijhoff Publishers, Leiden, 2008.

Bassiouni M.C., 'The New Wars and the Crisis of Compliance with the Law of Armed Conflict by Non-State Actors', (2008) 98 *Journal of Criminal Law and Criminology.*

Bellal A., G. Giacca and S. Casey-Maslen, 'International Law and Armed Actors in Afghanistan', (2011) 93 *International Review of the Red Cross.*

Belser E.M., K. Hanson and A. Hirt, *Sourcebook of International Children's Rights*, Staempfli Publishers, Berne, 2009.

Beresford S., 'Child Witnesses and the International Criminal Justice System: Does the International Criminal Court Protect the Most Vulnerable?', (2005) 3 *Journal of International Criminal Justice.*

Bergsmo M., C. Rodriguez-Garavito, P. Kalmanovitz and M. P. Saffon (eds.) *Distributive Justice in Transitions*, Torkel Opsahl Academic EPublisher (TOAEP), 2010.

Bertolini G., Riparazione per Violazione dei Diritti Umani e Ordinamento Internazionale, Jovene, Naples, 2009.

Betancourt T.S., 'High Hopes, Grim Reality: Reintegration and the Education of Former Child Soldiers in Sierra Leone', (2008) 52 *Comparative Education Review.*

Betancourt T.S. and K.T. Khan, 'The Mental Health of Children Affected by Armed Conflict: Protective Processes and Pathways to Resilience', (2008) 20 *International Review of Psychiatry.*

Bisset A., 'Transitional Justice in Nepal: The Commission on Investigation of Disappeared Persons, Truth and Reconciliation Act 2014', Bingham Centre Working Paper 2014/07, Bingham Centre for the Rule of Law/BIICL, London, September 2014.

Boyden J. and G. Mann, 'Children's Risk, Resilience, and Coping in Extreme Situations', in M. Ungar (ed.), *Handbook for Working with Children and Youth: Pathways to Resilience Across Cultures and Contexts*, Sage Publications, Thousand Oaks, CA, 2005.

Bradley R.H. and R.F. Corwyn, 'Socioeconomic Status and Child Development', (2002) 53 *Annual Review of Psychology.*

Brinton Lykes M. and M. Mersky, 'Reparations and Mental Health: Psychosocial Interventions towards Healing, Human Agency and Rethreading Social Realities', in P. De Greiff (ed.), *The Handbook of Reparations*, Oxford University Press, New York, 2006.

Brownlie I., *Principles of Public International Law*, 7th edn., Oxford University Press, Oxford, 2008.

Buergenthal T., 'The UN Human Rights Committee', (2001) 5 *Max Planck Yearbook of United Nations Law.*

Burgorgue-Larsen L. and A. Ubeda De Torres, *The Inter American Court of Human Rights: Case Law and Commentary*, Oxford University Press, Oxford, 2011.

Buss D., J. Lebert, B. Rutherford, D. Sharkey and O. Aginam (eds.), *Sexual Violence in Conflict and Post-Conflict Societies: International Agendas and African Contexts*, Routledge, London, 2014.

Buxbaum R.M., 'A Legal History of International Reparations', (2005) 23 *Berkeley Journal of International Law.*

Cançado Trindade A.A., *Évolution du droit international au droit des gens. L'accès des individus à la justice internationale: Le regard d'un juge*, Pédone, Paris, 2008.

Cançado Trindade A.A., *The Access of Individuals to International Justice*, Oxford University Press, Oxford, 2011.

Cantor D., UNHCR Research Paper No. 215, *Restitution, Compensation, Satisfaction: Transnational Reparations and Colombia's Victims' Law*, 2011.

Capone F., '*Remedies*', in R. Wolfrum (ed.), *Max Planck Encyclopedia of Public International Law*, Oxford University Press, Oxford, 2012.

Capone F., K. Hausler, D. Fairgrieve and C. McCarthy, *Education and the Law of Reparations in Insecurity and Armed Conflict*, BIICL/PEIC, London, 2013.

Capone F., 'Comparing and Discussing the Different Approach to Remedies for Child Victims before the European Court of Human Rights and the Inter-American Court of Human Rights', in D.M. Vicente (ed.), *Towards a Universal Justice? Putting International Courts and Jurisdictions into Perspective*, Brill, Leiden, 2016.

Carranza R., 'Relief, Reparations and the Root Causes of Conflict in Nepal', ICTJ 2012, footnote no. 5 Available at: http://www.ictj.org/sites/default/files/ICTJ-Nepal-Reparations-2012-English.pdf.

Carrillo A.J., 'The Relevance of the Inter-American Human Rights Law', in P. de Greiff (ed.), *The Handbook of Reparations*, Oxford University Press, New York, 2006.

Cassel D., 'The Expanding Scope and Impact of the Inter-American Court of Human Rights', in K. De Feyter, S. Parmentier, M. Bossuyt and P. Lemmens (eds.), *Out of the Ashes: Reparations for Victims of gross and Systematic Human Rights Violations*, Intersentia, Antwerp, 2005.

Cassel D., 'The Inter-American Court of Human Rights', in Due Process of Law Foundation, *Victims Un-silenced: The Inter-American Human Rights System and Transitional Justice in Latin America*, July 2007, available at: http://www.dplf.org/uploads/1190403828.pdf.

Cassese A., P. Gaeta and J.R.W.D. Jones (eds.), *The Rome Statute of the International Criminal Court: A Commentary*, Vol. I, Oxford University Press, Oxford, 2002.

Cassese A., *International Criminal Law* 3rd edn., Oxford University Press, Oxford, 2013.

Chamberlain C., *Children and the International Criminal Court, Analysis of the Rome Statute through a Children's Rights Perspective*, Intersentia, Antwerp, 2015.

Charli Carpenter R. (ed.), *Born of War: Protecting Children of Sexual Violence Survivors in Conflict Zones*, Kumarian Press, Bloomfield, 2007.

Chernor Jalloh C. (ed.), *The Sierra Leone Special Court and its Legacy: The Impact for Africa and International Criminal Law*, Cambridge University Press, Cambridge, 2015.

Chirwa D., 'The Merits and Demerits of the African Charter', (2002) 10 *International Journal of Children's Rights.*

Chung C.H., 'Victims' Participation at the International Criminal Court: Are Concessions of the Court Clouding the Promise?' (2008) 6 *Northwestern Journal of International Human Rights.*

Cipriani D., *Children's Rights and the Minimum Age of Criminal Responsibility: A Global Perspective*, Ashgate, Farnham, 2009.

Clapham A., *Human Rights Obligations of Non-State Actors*, Oxford University Press, Oxford, 2006.

Clapham A., 'Extending International Criminal Law beyond the Individual to Corporations and Armed Opposition Groups', (2008) 6 *Journal of International Criminal Justice*.

Clapham A., 'Focusing on Armed Non-State Actors', in A. Clapham and P. Gaeta (eds.), *The Oxford Handbook of International Law in Armed Conflict*, Oxford University Press, Oxford, 2014.

Clapham A., 'Non-State Actors', in D. Moeckli, S. Shah and S. Sivakumaran (eds.), *International Human Rights Law*, Oxford University Press, Oxford, 2014.

Clark R.S. and O. Triffterer, 'Article 26: Exclusion of Jurisdiction over Persons under Eighteen', in O. Triffterer (ed.), *Commentary on the Rome Statute of the International Criminal Court: Observers' Notes, Article by Article*, Nomos, Baden-Baden, 1999.

Clark T., 'Assessing the Special Court's Contribution to Achieving Transitional Justice', in C. Chernor Jalloh (ed.), *The Sierra Leone Special Court and its Legacy: The Impact for Africa and International Criminal Law*, Cambridge University Press, Cambridge, 2015.

Cole B., M. Maxwell and A. Chipaca, 'Surviving in the Shadows of War: Polyvictimised Children in Post-conflict Angola', (2014) 16 *Crime Prevention and Community Safety*.

Colonomos A. and A. Armstrong, 'German Reparations to the Jews after World War II', in K. De Feyter, S. Parmentier, M. Bossuyt and P. Lemmens (eds.), *Out of the Ashes: Reparations for Victims of Gross and Systematic Human Rights Violations*, Intersentia, Antwerp, 2005.

Connors J. and M. Schmidt, 'United Nations', in D. Moeckli, S. Shah and S. Sivakumaran (eds.), *International Human Rights Law*, Oxford University Press, Oxford, 2014.

Contreras-Garduño D., 'Defining Beneficiaries of Collective Reparations: The Experience of the Inter-American Court of Human Rights', (2012) 4 *Amsterdam Law Forum*.

Contreras-Garduño D. and J. Fraser, 'The Identification of Victims Before the Inter-American Court of Human Rights and the International Criminal Court and its Impact on Participation and Reparations: A Domino Effect?', (2015) 7 *Inter-American and European Human Rights Journal*.

Contreras-Garduño D. and S. Rombouts, 'Collective Reparations for Indigenous Communities Before the Inter-American Court of Human Rights', (2010) 27 *Utrecht Journal of International and European Law*.

Couillard V., 'The Nairobi Declaration: Redefining Reparations for Women Victims of Sexual Violence', (2007) 1 *International Journal of Transitional Justice*,

Crane D.M., 'Back to the Future. Reflections on the Beginning: International Criminal Law in the Twenty-first Century', (2008) 32 *Fordham International Law Journal*.

Crawford J., *The International Law Commission's Articles on State Responsibility: Introduction, Text and Commentaries*, Cambridge University Press, Cambridge, 2002,

Cunningham H., *Children and Childhood in Western Society since 1500*, Addison Wesley, London, 2005.

Cyr K., C. Chamberlandb, M. E. Clément, G. Lessard, J. Wemmers, D. Collin-Vézina, M. H. Gagné and D. Damant, 'Polyvictimization and Victimization of Children and Youth: Results from a Population Survey', (2013) 37 *Child Abuse and Neglect*.

Danieli Y., *The International Handbook of Multigenerational Trauma*, Springer, New York, 1998.

Danieli Y., 'Reappraising the Nuremberg Trials and their Legacy: The Role of Victims in International Law', (2006) 27 *Cardozo Law Review*.

D'Argent P., 'Reparations after WWII', in R. Wolfrum (ed.), *Max Planck Encyclopedia of International Law*, Oxford University Press, Oxford, 2012.

David E., *Principes de Droit des Conflits Armés*, 3rd edn., Bruylant, Brussels, 2002.

Davidson S., 'Remedies for Violations of the American Convention on Human Rights', (1995) 44 *International and Comparative Law Quarterly*.

De Brouwer A.M., *Supranational Criminal Prosecution of Sexual Violence*, Intersentia, Antwerp, 2006.

De Brouwer A.M., 'Reparation to Victims of Sexual Violence: Possibilities at the International Criminal Court and at the Trust Fund for Victims and Their Families', (2007) 20 *Leiden Journal of International Law*.

De Greiff P., *The UN Rule of Law Tools for Post-Conflict States*, OHCHR, 2008.

De Mause L., *The History of Childhood*, Souvenir Press, London, 1974.

Denov M.S., 'Wartime Sexual Violence: Assessing a Human Security Response to War-Affected Girls in Sierra Leone', (2006) 37 *Security Dialogue*.

Detrick S. (ed.), *The United Nations Convention on the Rights of the Child: A Guide to the Travaux Préparatoires*, Martinus Nijhoff Publishers, Dordrecht, 1992.

Doswald-Beck L., *Human Rights in Times of Armed Conflict and Terrorism*, Oxford University Press, Oxford, 2011.

Dolzer R., 'The Settlement of War-Related Claims: Does International Law Recognise a Victim's Private Right of Action? Lessons after 1945', (2002) 20 *Berkeley Journal of International Law*.

Drumbl M.A., 'Punishment Post-Genocide: From Guilt to Shame to Civis in Rwanda', (2000) 75 *New York University Law Review*.

Drumbl M., 'International Criminal Law: Taking Stock of a Busy Decade', (2009) 4 *Melbourne Journal of International Law*.

Drumbl M., *Reimagining Child Soldiers in International Law and Policy*, Oxford University Press, Oxford, 2012.

Drumbl M.A., 'The Effects of the Lubanga Case on Understanding and Preventing Child Soldiering', in T. Gill R. Geiß, R. Heinsch, T. McCormack and C. Paulussen (eds.), *Yearbook of International Humanitarian Law*, TMC Asser Press, The Hague, 2013.

Dudai R., 'Closing the Gap: Symbolic Reparations and Armed Groups', (2011) 93 *International Review of the Red Cross*.

Duggan C. and R. Jacobson, 'Reparations of Sexual and Reproductive Violence: Moving from Codification to Implementation', in Rubio-Marin R. (ed.), *The Gender of Reparations Unsettling Sexual Hierarchies while Redressing Human Rights Violations*, Cambridge University Press, Cambridge, 2011.

Duthie R. and I. Specht, 'DDR, Transitional justice, and the Reintegration of Former Child Combatants', in A. Cutter Patel, P. De Greiff and L. Waldorf (eds.), *Disarming the Past: Transitional Justice and Ex-Combatants*, Social Science Research Council, New York, 2010.

Ellis M.S., 'International Justice and the Rule of Law: Strengthening the ICC through Domestic Prosecutions', (2009) 1 *Hague Journal on the Rule of Law*.

El Zeidy M.M., 'From Primacy to Complementarity and Backwards: (Re)-Visiting Rule 11 *Bis* of the *Ad Hoc* Tribunals' (2008) 57, *International and Comparative Law Quarterly*.

Evans C., *The Right to Reparation in International Law for Victims of Armed Conflict*, Cambridge University Press, Cambridge, 2012.

EVANS M. and K. STRATOS (eds.), *Remedies in International Law: The Institutional Dilemma*, Hart Publishing, Oxford, 1998.

FALK R., 'Reparations, International Law, and Global Justice: A New Frontier', in P. de GREIFF (ed.), *The Handbook of Reparations*, Oxford University Press, New York, 2006.

FARRALL J.M., *United Nations Sanctions and the Rule of Law*, Cambridge University Press, Cambridge, 2007.

FERIA TINTA M., *The Landmark Rulings of the Inter American Court of Human Rights on the Rights of the Child*, Martinus Nijhoff Publishers, Leiden, 2008.

FERNÁNDEZ de CASADEVANTE ROMANI C., 'International Law of Victims', in A. VON BOGDANDY and R. WOLFRUM (eds.), (2010) 14 *Max Planck Yearbook of United Nations Law*.

FERSTMAN C., M. GOETZ and A. STEPHENS, 'Introduction', in FERSTMAN C., M. GOETZ and A. STEPHENS (eds.), *Reparations for Victims of Genocide, War Crimes and Crimes against Humanity*, Martinus Nijhoff Publishers, Leiden, 2009.

FINKELHOR D., *Childhood Victimisation: Violence, Crime, and Abuse in the Lives of Young People*, Oxford University Press, New York, 2008.

FINKELHOR D. and J. DZIUBA-LEATHERMAN, 'Children as Victims of Violence: A National Survey', (1994) 4 *Pediatrics*.

FINKELHOR D., R.K. OMROD and H.A. TURNER, 'Poly-victimization. A Neglected Component in Child Victimisation', (2007) 31 *Child Abuse and Neglect*.

FIRESTONE S., *The Dialectic of Sex: The Case for Feminist Revolution*, Farrar, Strauss and Giroux, New York, 2003.

FISHER K., *Transitional Justice for Child Soldiers: Accountability and Social Reconstruction in Post-Conflict Contexts*, Palgrave Macmillan, New York, 2013.

FLECK D. (ed.), *The Handbook of International Humanitarian Law*, Oxford University Press, Oxford, 2013.

FORD J.D., D.J. GRASSO, J. HAWKE and J.F. CHAPMAN, 'Poly-victimization among Juvenile Justice-Involved Youths', (2013) 37 *Child Abuse and Neglect*.

FREEMAN M., *The Rights and Wrongs of Children*, F. Pinter Publishers, Dover, 1983.

FREEMAN M., *Truth Commissions and Procedural Fairness*, Cambridge University Press, Cambridge, 2006.

FREEMAN M., 'Why It Remains Important to Take Children's Rights Seriously?', (2007) 15 *International Journal of Children's Rights*.

FRULLI M., *Immunità e crimini internazionali. L'esercizio della giurisidizione penale e civile nei confronti degli organi statali sospettati di gravi crimini internazionali*, G. Giappichelli editore, Turin, 2007.

FRULLI M., 'Piercing the Veil of Head-of-State Immunity: the Taylor Trial and beyond', in C. CHERNOR JALLOH (ed.), *The Sierra Leone Special Court and its Legacy: The Impact for Africa and International Criminal Law*, Cambridge University Press, Cambridge, 2015.

GARCÍA-GODOS J., 'Victim Reparations in the Peruvian Truth Commission and the Challenge of Historical Interpretation', (2008) 2 *International Journal of Transitional Justice*.

GARCÍA-GODOS J. and K.A. O. LID, 'Transitional Justice and Victims' Rights before the End of a Conflict: The Unusual Case of Colombia', (2010) 42 *Journal of Latin American Studies*.

GATTINI A., 'The UN Compensation Commission: Old Rules, New Procedures on War Reparations', (2002) 13 *European Journal of International Law*.

GATTINI A., 'To What Extent are State Immunity and Non-Justiciability Major Hurdles to Individuals' Claims for War Damages?', (2003) 1 *Journal of International Criminal Justice*.

GILLARD, E.C., 'Reparations for Violations of International Humanitarian Law', (2003) 85 *International Review of the Red Cross*.

GLASIUS M. and T. MEIJERS, 'Constructions of Legitimacy: The Charles Taylor Trial', (2012) 6 *International Journal of Transitional Justice*.

GOLDBLATT B., 'Evaluating the Gender Content of Reparations: Lessons from South Africa', in R. RUBIO-MARIN (ed.), *What Happened to the Women? Gender and Reparations for Human Rights Violations*, Social Science Research Council, New York, 2006.

GOLDMAN R.K., 'History and Action: The Inter-American Human Rights System and the Role of the Inter-American Commission on Human Rights', (2009) 31 *Human Rights Quarterly*.

GOZZI M.H. and J.P. LABORDE, 'Les Nations Unies et le Droit des Victimes du Terrorisme', (2005) 76 *Revue Internationale de Droit Pénal*.

GRAF R., 'The International Criminal Court and Child Soldiers: An Appraisal of the Lubanga Judgment', (2012) 10 *Journal of International Criminal Justice*.

GRAHAM K., *Contemporary Political Philosophy: Radical Studies*, Cambridge University Press, Cambridge, 1982.

GRAY C., *Judicial Remedies in International Law*, Clarendon Press, Oxford, 1987.

GREENWOOD C., 'International Humanitarian Law', in F. KALSHOVEN (ed.), *The Centennial of the First International Peace Conference: Reports and Conclusions*, Kluwer Law International, The Hague, 2000.

GROSSMANN K.R., *Germany and Israel: Six Years Luxemburg Agreement*, Herzl Press, New York, 1958.

GROVER S.C., *Child Soldier Victims of Genocidal Forcible Transfer*, Springer, Heidelberg, 2012.

GROVER S.C., *Children Defending their Human Rights Under the CRC Communications Procedure: On Strengthening the Convention on the Rights of the Child Complaints Mechanism*, Springer-Verlag, Berlin-Heidelberg, 2015.

GUEMBE M.J., 'Economic Reparations for Grave Human Rights Violations: the Argentinean Experience', in P. de GREIFF (ed.), *The Handbook of Reparations*, Oxford University Press, New York, 2006.

GUPTA L., UNICEF, 'Rwanda: Follow-up Survey of Rwandan Children's Reactions to War Related Violence from the 1994 Genocide', 1998, available at: http://www.unicef.org/evaldatabase/index_14242.html.

HAMBER B., 'Narrowing the Micro and Macro: A Psychological Perspective on Reparations in Societies in Transition', in P. DE GREIFF (ed.), *The Handbook of Reparations*, Oxford University Press, New York, 2006.

HAMMARBERG T., 'The UN Convention on the Rights of the Child and How to Make it Work', (1990) 25 *Human Rights Quarterly*.

HAMZEI H., 'Child Victims before the International Criminal Court: Avenue to Justice for the Most Vulnerable?', in L. HOPKINS, M. MACLEOD and W.C. TURGEON (eds.) *Negotiating Childhoods* Inter-Disciplinary Press, Oxford, 2011.

HAPPOLD M., 'The Age of Criminal Responsibility in International Criminal Law', in K. ARTS and V. POPOVSKI (eds.), *International Criminal Accountability and the Rights of Children*, TMC Asser Press, The Hague, 2006.

Harbom L., E. Melander and P. Wallensteen, 'Dyadic Dimensions of Armed Conflict, 1946–2007', (2008) 45 *Journal of Peace Research*.

Harris J., 'The Political Status of Children' in K. Graham (ed.), *Contemporary Political Philosophy: Radical Studies*, Cambridge University Press, Cambridge, 1982.

Hart J., 'Children's Participation and International Development: Attending to the Political', (2008) 16 *International Journal of Children's Rights*.

Hausler K., N. Urban and R. McCorquodale, *Protecting Education in Insecurity and Armed Conflict: an International Law Handbook*, BIICL/PEIC, London, 2012.

Hayner P.B., *Unspeakable Truths: Transitional Justice and the Challenge of Truth Commissions*, 2nd edn. Routledge, New York, 2011.

Henckaerts J.M. and L. Doswald-Beck (eds.), *Customary International Humanitarian Law*, Cambridge University Press, Cambridge, 2006.

Heyns C. and M. Killander, 'Africa' in D. Moeckli, S. Shah and S. Sivakumaran (eds.), *International Human Rights Law*, Oxford University Press, Oxford, 2014.

Hirst M. and A. Linnarsson, 'Children and the Commission for Reception, Truth and Reconciliation in Timor-Leste', UNICEF Innocenti Research Centre, Innocenti Working Paper no. 2010-7, Florence.

Hoegen E. and M. Brienen, *Victims of Crime in 22 European Criminal Justice Systems: The Implementation of Recommendation (85) 11 of the Council of Europe on the Position of the Victim in the Framework of Criminal Law and Procedure*, Wolf Legal Publishers, Eindhoven, 2003.

Hoogeveen J., E. Tesliuc and R. Vakis, *A Guide to the Analysis of Risk, Vulnerability and Vulnerable Groups*, World Bank, 2005, available at: http://siteresources.worldbank.org/INTSRM/Publications/20316319/RVA.pdf.

Horn R., S. Vahidy and S. Charters, 'Testifying in the Special Court for Sierra Leone: Witness Perceptions of Safety and Emotional Welfare', (2011) 17 *Psychology, Crime & Law*.

Humphrey M., 'The Individualising and Universalising Discourse of Law: Victims in Truth Commissions and Trials', in T. Bonacker and C. Safferling (eds.), *Victims of International Crimes: An Interdisciplinary Discourse*, TMC Asser Press, The Hague, 2013.

Ibanez A.M. and J.C. Munoz, 'The Persistence of Land Concentration in Colombia: What Happened between 2000 and 2010?', in M. Bergsmo, C. Rodriguez-Garavito, P. Kalmanovitz and M.P. Saffon (eds.), *Distributive Justice in Transitions*, Torkel Opsahl Academic EPublisher, 2010.

Ingadottir T., F. Ngendahayo and P. Sellers, 'The Victims and Witnesses Unit', in T. Ingadottir (ed.), *The International Criminal Court: Recommendations on Policy and Practice*. Transnational Publishers, New York, 2003.

Iovane M., La Riparazione nella Teoria e nella Prassi dell'Illecito Internazionale, Giuffrè Editore, Milano, 1990.

Iovane M., 'The Italian Constitutional Court Judgment No. 238 and the Myth of the 'Constitutionalization' of International Law', (2016) 14 *Journal of International Criminal Justice*.

Jacobs D., 'The Unique Rules and Procedures of the STL', in A. Alamuddin, N.N. Jurdi and D. Tolbert (eds.), *The Special Tribunal for Lebanon: Law and Practice*, Oxford University Press, Oxford, 2014.

JAYE T., 'Transitional Justice and DDR: The Case of Liberia', ICTJ, June 2009, at 7, available at: https://www.ictj.org/sites/default/files/ICTJ-DDR-Liberia-CaseStudy-2009-English.pdf.

JOSEPH S., K. MITCHELL and L. GYORKI, *Seeking Remedies for Torture Victims: A Handbook on the Individual Complaints Procedures of the UN Treaty Bodies*, OMCT Series, Volume 4, Geneva, 2006.

KALDOR M., *New and Old Wars: Organised Violence in a Global Era*, Polity Press, Cambridge, 2006.

KALSHOVEN F., 'State Responsibility for Warlike Acts of the Armed Forces: From Article 3 of the Hague Convention IV of 1907 to Article 91 of Additional Protocol I and Beyond', (1991) 40 *International and Comparative Law Quarterly*.

KALSHOVEN F., 'Article 3 of the Convention (IV), Respecting the Laws and Customs of War on Land', in H. FUIJTA, I. SUZUKI and K. NAGANO (eds.), *War and Rights of Individuals*, Nippon Hyoronsha Co Ltd. Publishers, Tokyo, 1999.

KALSHOVEN F. and L. ZEGVELD, *Constraints on the Waging of War: An Introduction to International Humanitarian Law*, 4th edn., Cambridge University Press, Cambridge, 2011.

KARIMOVA T., G. GIACCA and S. CASEY-MASLEN, *United Nations Human Rights Mechanisms and the Right to Education in Insecurity and Armed Conflict*, Geneva Academy of International Humanitarian Law and Human Rights/Protect Education in Insecurity and Conflict, 2013.

KELLEY M.J. and T.L.H. MCCORMACK, 'The Nuremberg Trial and the Subsequent Development of International Law', in D. BLUMENTHAL and T.L.H. MCCORMACK (eds.), *The Legacy of Nuremberg: Civilising Influence or Institutionalised Vengeance?*, Martinus Nijhoff Publishers, Leiden, 2008.

KHALIL A., 'Tunisia's Women: Partners in Revolution', in L. SADIKI (ed.), *Handbook of the Arab Spring: Rethinking Democratisation*. Routledge, Abingdon, 2015.

KING J., 'Gender and Reparations in Sierra Leone: The Wounds of War remain Open', in R. RUBIO-MARIN (ed.), *What Happened to the Women? Gender and Reparations for Human Rights Violations*, Social Science Research Council, New York, 2006.

KLEFFNER J.K., 'The Applicability of International Humanitarian Law to Organised Armed Groups', (2011) 93 *International Review of the Red Cross*.

KRACKE K. and H. HAHN, 'The Nature and Extent of Childhood Exposure to Violence: What We Know, Why We Don't Know More, and Why it Matters', (2008) 8 *Journal of Emotional Abuse*.

KRAJEWSKI M. and C. SINGER, 'Should Judges be Front-Runners? The ICJ, State Immunity and the Protection of Fundamental Human Rights', in A. VON BOGDANDY and R. WOLFRUM (eds.), *Max Planck UNYB*, Martinus Nijhoff Publishers, Leiden, 2012, vol. 16.

KUKLICK B., 'The Division of Germany and American Policy on Reparations', (1970) 23 *The Western Political Quarterly*.

LANGFORD M. and S. CLARK, 'The New Kid on the Block: A Complaints Procedure for the Convention on the Rights of the Child', Working Paper no. 1. Socio-Economic Rights Programme, Norwegian Centre for Human Rights, University of Oslo, 2010, available at: http://www.jus.uio.no/smr/english/people/aca/malcolml/new-kid-on-the-block-langford-clark.pdf.

LANSDOWN G., Innocenti Insight, 'The Evolving Capacities of the Children', UNICEF and Save the Children, Florence, 2005.

LAPLANTE L.J. and K. THEIDON, 'Truth with Consequences: Justice and Reparations in Post Truth Peru', (2007) 29 *Human Rights Quarterly*.

LARA C.E., 'Child Soldier Testimony Used in Prosecuting War Crimes in the International Criminal Court: Preventing Further Victimisation', (2011) 17 *Southwestern Journal of International Law*.

LEBLANC L.J., *The Convention on the Rights of the Child: UN Law-making on Human Rights*, University of Nebraska Press, Lincoln, NE, 1995.

LETSCHERT R.M. and T. van BOVEN, 'Providing Reparation in Situations of Mass Victimization: Key Challenges Involved', in R. M. LETSCHERT, R. HAVEMAN, A. M. DE BROUWER and A. PEMBERTON (eds.), *Victimological Approaches of International Crimes*, Intersentia, Antwerp, 2011.

LIRA E., 'The Reparations Policy for Human Rights Violations in Chile', in P. DE GREIFF (ed.), *The Handbook of Reparations*, Oxford University Press, New York, 2006.

LIVY T., *The Early History of Rome: Books I–V of the Ab Urbe Condita*, Penguin, London, 2002.

LUDI R., *Reparations for Nazi Victims in Postwar Europe*, Cambridge University Press, Cambridge, 2012.

MACHEL G., *The Impact of War on Children: A Review of Progress Since the 1996 United Nations Report on the Impact of Armed Conflict on Children*, Palgrave MacMillan, Basingstoke, 2001.

MAGARRELL L., 'Reparations in Theory and Practice', ICTJ, 2007, available at: http://ictj.org/sites/default/files/ICTJ-Global-Reparations-Practice-2007-English.pdf.

MANI R., 'Restoring Justice in the Aftermath of Conflict: Bridging the Gap between Theory and Practice', in T. COATES (ed.), *International Justice*, Ashgate Publishing, Burlington, VT, 2000.

MASTEN A.S., 'Resilience in Children Threatened by Extreme Adversity: Frameworks for Research, Practice, and Translational Synergy', (2001) 23 *Development and Psychopathology*.

MASTEN A.S., K.M. BEST and N. GARMEZY, 'Resilience and Development: Contributions from the Study of Children who Overcome Adversity', (1990) 2 *Development and Psychopathology*.

MASTEN A.S. and A.J. NARAYAN, 'Child Development in the Context of Disaster, War, and Terrorism: Pathways of Risk and Resilience', (2012) 63 *Annual Review of Psychology*.

MAZURANA D. and K. CARLSON, 'Children and Reparation: Past Lessons and New Directions', UNICEF Innocenti Research Centre, Innocenti Working Paper No. 2010-08, Florence.

MCBRIDE J., *The War Crime of Child Soldier Recruitment*, TMC Asser Press, The Hague, 2014.

MCCARTHY C., 'Victim Redress and International Criminal Justice: Competing Paradigms, or Compatible Forms of Justice?', (2012) 10 *Journal of International Criminal Justice*.

MCCARTHY C., *Reparations and Victim Support in the International Criminal Court*, Cambridge University Press, Cambridge, 2013.

MCCORQUODALE R., 'An Inclusive International Legal System', (2004) 17 *Leiden Journal of International Law*.

McCorquodale R., 'Non-State Actors and International Human Rights Law', in S. Joseph and A. McBeth (eds.), *Research Handbook on International Human Rights Law*, Edward Elgar, Cheltenham, 2010.

McDiarmid C., 'An Age of Complexity: Children and Criminal Responsibility in Law', (2013) 13 *Youth Justice*.

McDonald A., 'Correspondents' Report', *Yearbook of International Humanitarian Law*, TMC Asser Press, The Hague, 2002.

McDougall C., *The Crime of Aggression under the Rome Statute of the International Criminal Court*, Cambridge University Press, Cambridge, 2013.

McEvoy K. and K. McConnachie, 'Victims and Transitional Justice: Voice, Agency and Blame', (2013) 22 *Social & Legal Studies*.

McKay S. and D. Mazurana, *Where Are The Girls? Girls in Fighting Forces in Northern Uganda, Sierra Leone and Mozambique: Their Lives during and after War*, Rights & Democracy, Montreal, 2004.

Melzer N., 'Interpretive Guidance on the Notion of Direct Participation in Hostilities under International Humanitarian Law', February 2009, available at: https://www.icrc.org/eng/assets/files/other/icrc-002-0990.pdf.

Meron T., 'The Ad Hoc International Tribunals and the Proposed International Criminal Court', (1995) 9 *ASIL Bulletin* 5.

Meron T., *The Humanization of International Law*, The Hague Academy of International Law Monographs, Martinus Nijhoff Publishers, Leiden, 2006.

Moffett L., 'Beyond Attribution: Responsibility of Armed Non-State Actors for Reparations in Northern Ireland, Colombia and Uganda', (2013) 20 *Queen's University Belfast School of Law: Research Paper*.

Moffett L., *Justice for Victims before the International Criminal Court*, Routledge, Abingdon, 2014.

Moffett L., 'Beyond Attribution: Responsibility of Armed Non-State Actors for Reparations in Northern Ireland, Colombia and Uganda', in N. Gal-Or, C. Ryngaert and M. Noortmann (eds.), *Responsibilities of the Non-State Actor in Armed Conflict and the Market Place: Theoretical Considerations and Empirical Findings*, Brill, Leiden, 2015.

Moffett L., 'Transitional Justice and Reparations: Remedying the Past', in D. Jacobs (ed.), *Research Handbook on Transitional Justice*, Edward Elgar, Cheltenham, forthcoming 2016.

Murray D., 'How International Humanitarian Law Treaties Bind Non-State Armed Groups', (2014) 20 *Journal of Conflict and Security Law*.

Neugebauer R., P.W. Fisher, J. B. Turner, S. Yamabe, J.A. Sarsfield and T. Stehling-Ariza, 'Post-traumatic Stress Reactions among Rwandan Children and Adolescents in the Early Aftermath of Genocide', (2009) 38 *International Journal of Epidemiology*.

Newell P., 'Expert Briefing to the First Session of the Working Group to Explore the Possibility of Elaborating an Optional Protocol to the Convention on the Rights of the Child', September 2010.

Ni Aolàin F., N. Cahn and D. Haynes, 'Masculinities and Child Soldiers in Post-Conflict Societies', in F.R. Cooper and A.C. McGinley (eds.), *Masculinities and the Law: A Mutual Approach*, New York University Press, New York, 2012.

Nilsson A.C., *Children and Youth in Armed Conflict*, Brill/Nijhoff, Leiden, 2013.

Njikam O., *The Contribution of the Special Court for Sierra Leone to the Development of International Humanitarian Law*, Duncker & Humblot, Berlin, 2013.

Oette L., 'Bringing Justice to Victims? Responses of Regional and International Human Rights Courts and Treaty Bodies to Mass Violations', in C. Ferstman, M. Goetz and A. Stephens (eds.), '*Reparations for Victims of Genocide, War Crimes and Crimes against Humanity*, Martinus Nijhoff Publishers, Leiden, 2009.

Oosterveld V., 'The Special Court for Sierra Leone's Consideration of Gender-based Violence: Contributing to Transitional Justice?', (2009) 10 *Human Rights Review*.

Oppenheim L., *International Law: a Treatise*, Longmans, Green and Co, London, 1905.

Palombino F. M., 'Italy's Compliance with ICJ Decisions vs. Constitutional Guarantees: does the "Counter-limits" Doctrine Matter?', *Italian Yearbook of International Law*, (2013) XXII.

Parmar S. and G. Mushiata, 'Judgment Denied: The Failure to Fulfill Court-Ordered Reparations for Victims of Serious Crimes in the Democratic Republic of Congo', ICTJ Briefing, May 2012, available at: http://www.ictj.org/sites/default/files/ICTJ-DRC-Reparations-Failure-Briefing-2012-English.pdf.

Pasqualucci J.M., *The Practice and Procedure of the Inter-American Court of Human Rights*, 2nd edn., Cambridge University Press, Cambridge, 2013.

Pasqualucci J., 'The Americas', in D. Moeckli, S. Shah and S. Sivakumaran (eds.), *International Human Rights Law*, Oxford University Press, Oxford, 2014.

Pauletto E. and P. Patel, 'Challenging Child-Soldier DDR Processes and Policies in the Eastern Democratic Republic of Congo', (2010) 16 *Journal of Peace, Conflict and Development*.

Paulson J., 'Truth Commissions and National Curricula', in S. Parmar M.J. Roseman, S. Siegrist and T. Sowa (eds.), *Children and Transitional Justice*, Harvard University Press, Cambridge, MA, 2009.

Pavoni R., 'How Broad is the Principle Upheld by the Italian Constitutional Court in Judgment No. 238?', (2016) 14 *Journal of International Criminal Justice*.

Peschke K., 'The Role and Mandates of the ICC Trust Fund for Victims', in T. Bonacker and C. Safferling (eds.), *Victims of International Crimes: An Interdisciplinary Discourse*, TMC Asser Press, The Hague, 2013.

Peters K., *When Children Affected by War Go Home: Lessons Learned from Liberia*, Save the Children, London, 2003.

Pigou P., 'Children and the South African Truth and Reconciliation Commission', in S. Parmar, M.J. Roseman, S. Siegrist and T. Sowa (eds.), *Children and Transitional Justice*, Harvard University Press, Cambridge MA, 2009.

Pinto M., 'The Role of the Inter-American Commission and Court of Human Rights in the Protection of Human Rights: Achievements and Contemporary Challenges', (2013) 20 *Human Rights Brief*.

Pisillo Mazzeschi R., 'Reparations Claims by Individuals for State Breaches of International Humanitarian Law and Human Rights: an Overview', (2003) 1 *Journal of International Criminal Justice*.

Politi M., 'The ICC and the Crime of Aggression A Dream that Came Through and the Reality Ahead', (2012) 10 *Journal of International Criminal Justice*.

Pross C., *Paying for the Past: The Struggle Over Reparations for the Surviving Victims of the Nazi Terror*, Johns Hopkins University Press, Baltimore, MD, 1998.

REDRESS, 'A Sourcebook for Victims of Torture and Other Violations of Human Rights and International Humanitarian Law', 2003, available at: http://www.redress.org/downloads/publications/SourceBook.pdf.

REDRESS, 'Victims, Perpetrators or Heroes: Child Soldiers before the International Criminal Court', September 2006, available at: http://www.redress.org/downloads/publications/childsoldiers.pdf.

RODHAM H., 'Children under the Law', (1973) 43 *Harvard Education Review*.

RODHAM H., 'Children's Policies: Abandonment and Neglect', (1977) 86 *Yale Law Journal*.

RODLEY N.S., 'Can Armed Opposition Groups Violate Human Rights?', in K.E. MAHONEY and P. MAHONEY (eds.), *Human Rights in the Twenty-first Century*, Martinus Nijhoff Publishers, Dordrecht, 1993.

ROHT-ARRIAZA N., 'Reparations in the Aftermath of Repression and Mass Violence', in E. STOVER and H.M. WEINSTEIN (eds.), *My Neighbor, My Enemy: Justice and Community in the Aftermath of Mass Atrocity*, Cambridge University Press, Cambridge, 2004.

ROHT-ARRIAZA N. and K. ORLOVSKY, 'A Complementary Relationship: Development and Reparations', ICTJ Research Briefing, July 2009, available at http://ictj.org/sites/default/files/ICTJ-Development-Reparations-ResearchBrief-2009-English.pdf.

ROMBOUTS H., P. SARDARO and S. VANDEGINSTE, 'The Right to Reparation for Victims of Gross and Systematic Violations of Human Rights', in K. DE FEYTER, S. PARMENTIER, M. BOSSUYT and P. LEMMENS (eds.), *Out of the Ashes: Reparations for Victims of Gross and Systematic Human Rights Violations*, Intersentia, Antwerp, 2005.

ROMBOUTS H. and S. PARMENTIER, 'The International Criminal Court and its Trust Fund Are Coming of Age: Towards a Process Approach for the Reparation of Victims', (2009) 8 *International Review of Victimology*.

ROSE C., 'An Emerging Norm: The Duty of States to Provide Reparations for Human Rights Violations by Non-State Actors', (2010) 32 *Hastings International Comparative Law Review*.

ROSEN D.M., *Armies of the Young: Child Soldiers in War and Terrorism*, Rutgers University Press, New Brunswick, NJ, 2005.

ROSENFELD F., 'Collective Reparations for Victims of Armed Conflicts', (2010) 92 *International Review of the Red Cross*.

ROTBERG R., 'Truth Commissions and the Provision of Truth, Justice and Reconciliation', in R.I. ROTBERG and D. THOMPSON (eds.), *Truth v. Justice: The Morality of Truth Commissions*, Princeton University Press, Princeton, NJ, 2000.

RUBIO-MARIN R. (ed.), *What Happened to the Women? Gender and Reparations for Human Rights Violations*, Social Science Research Council, New York, 2006.

RUBIO-MARIN R. (ed.), *The Gender of Reparations: Unsettling Sexual Hierarchies While Redressing Human Rights Violations*, Cambridge University Press, Cambridge, 2011.

RUBIO-MARIN R. and C. SANDOVAL, 'Engendering the Reparations Jurisprudence of the Inter-American Court of Human Rights: The Promise of the Cotton Field Judgment', (2011) 33 *Human Rights Quarterly*.

RYNGAERT C., 'Non-State Actors and International Humanitarian Law', University of Leuven, Working Paper no. 1, 2008.

RYNGAERT C. and J. D'ASPREMONT, 3rd Report of the ILA Non-State Actors Committee, 2014, available at: http://www.ila-hq.org/en/committees/index.cfm/cid/1023.

Sabates-Wheeler R., S. Devereux and A. Hodges, 'Taking the Long View: What Does a Child Focus Add to Social Protection?', (2009) 40 *IDS Bulletin*.

Sack W.H., C. Him and D. Dickson, 'Twelve-year Follow-up Study of Khmer Youths who Suffered Massive War Trauma as Children', (1999) 38 *Journal of the American Academy of Child & Adolescent Psychiatry*.

Salmon E., 'Reflections on International Humanitarian Law and Transitional Justice: Lessons to be Learnt from the Latin American Experience', (2006) 88 *International Review of the Red Cross*.

Salzman T.A., 'Rape Camps as a Means of Ethnic Cleansing: Religious, Cultural, and Ethical Responses to Rape Victims in the Former Yugoslavia', (1998) 20 *Human Rights Quarterly*.

Sandoz Y., C. Swinarski, and B. Zimmermann (eds.), *Commentary to the Additional Protocols to the Geneva Conventions*, Martinus Nijhoff Publishers, The Hague, 1987.

Sanfilippo M., C. de Neubourg and B. Martorano, 'The Impact of Social Protection on Children: A Review of the Literature', Working Paper 2012-06, UNICEF Office of Research, Florence, 2012.

Sanin K. and A. Stirneman, *Child Witnesses at the Special Court for Sierra Leone*, War Crimes Study Centre University of Berkeley, March 2006, available at: http://wcsc.berkeley.edu/wp-content/uploads/documents/ChildWitnessReport_000.pdf.

Sarkin J., 'Reparations for Gross Human Rights Violations as an Outcome of Criminal versus Civil Court Proceedings', in K. De Feyter, S. Parmentier, M. Bossuyt and P. Lemmens (eds.), *Out of the Ashes: Reparations for Victims of Gross and Systematic Human Rights Violations*, Intersentia, Antwerp, 2005.

Sarkin J., 'The Role of Regional Systems in Enforcing State Human Rights Compliance: Evaluating the African Commission on Human and Peoples' Rights and the New African Court of Justice and Human Rights with Comparative Lessons from the Council of Europe and the Organisation of American States', (2008) 2 *Inter-American and European Human Rights Journal*.

Sassòli M., 'The Implementation of International Humanitarian Law: Current and Inherent Challenges', (2007) 10 *Yearbook of International Humanitarian Law*.

Sassòli M., 'Taking Armed Groups Seriously: Ways to Improve their Compliance with International Humanitarian Law', (2010) 1 *International Humanitarian Legal Studies*.

Saul B., 'Compensation for Unlawful Death in International Law: A Focus on the Inter-American Court of Human Rights', (2004) 19 *The American University International Law Review*.

Schabas W., 'Reparation Practice in Sierra Leone and the Truth and Reconciliation Commission', in K. de Feyter, S. Parmentier, M. Bossuyt and P. Lemmens (eds.), *Out of the Ashes: Reparations for Victims of Gross and Systematic Human Rights Violations*, Intersentia, Antwerp, 2005.

Shany Y., *The Competing Jurisdiction of International Courts and Tribunals*, Oxford University Press, Oxford, 2003.

Shelton D., 'The UN Principles and Guidelines on Reparation: Contest and Contents', in K. De Feyter, S. Parmentier, M. Bossuyt and P. Lemmens (eds.), *Out of the Ashes: Reparations for Victims of Gross and Systematic Human Rights Violations*, Intersentia, Antwerp, 2005.

SHEPLER S., 'The Rites of the Child: Global Discourses of Youth and Reintegrating Child Soldiers in Sierra Leone', (2005) 4 *Journal of Human Rights*.

SIVAKUMARAN S., 'Binding Armed Opposition Groups', (2006) 55 *International and Comparative Law Quarterly*.

SIVAKUMARAN S., 'Re-envisaging the International Law of Internal Armed Conflict', (2011) 22 *European Journal of International Law*.

SOOKA Y., 'Dealing with the Past and Transitional Justice: Building Peace through Accountability', (2006) 88 *International Review of the Red Cross*.

SOWA T., 'Children and the Liberian Truth and Reconciliation Commission', in S. PARMAR M.J. ROSEMAN, S. SIEGRIST and T. SOWA (eds.) *Children and Transitional Justice*, Harvard University Press, Cambridge, MA, 2009.

SPECHT I., *Red Shoes: Experiences of Girl-Combatants in Liberia*, ILO, 2006.

STAHN C., 'Reparative Justice after the Lubanga Appeals Judgment: New Prospects for Expressivism and Participatory Justice or "Juridified Victimhood" by Other Means?', (2015) 13 *Journal of International Criminal Justice*.

STARK L. and M. WESSELLS, 'The Fallacy of the Ticking Time Bomb: Resilience of Children Formerly Recruited into Armed Forces and Groups', in C. FERNANDO and M. FERRARI (eds.), *Handbook of Resilience in Children of War*, Springer-Verlag, New York, 2013.

Stockholm International Peace Research Institute, 'Trends in Armed Conflicts', *SIPRI Yearbook 2008*, SIPRI, Stockholm, 2008.

SUMMERS N., 'Colombia's Victims' Law: Transitional Justice in a Time of Violent Conflict?', (2012) 25 *Harvard Human Rights Journal*.

SWART M., 'The Lubanga Reparations Decision: A Missed Opportunity?', (2013) 32 *Polish Yearbook of International Law*.

TAMS C.J., *Enforcing Obligations Erga Omnes in International Law*, Cambridge University Press, Cambridge, 2005.

TEITEL R.G., 'Human Rights in Transition: Transitional Justice Genealogy', (2003) 16 *Harvard Human Rights Journal*.

TOL W.A., M.J.D. JORDANS, B.A. KOHRT, T.S. BETANCOURT and I.H. KOMPROE, 'Promoting Mental Health and Psychosocial Well-Being in Children Affected by Political Violence: Part I – Current Evidence for an Ecological Resilience Approach', in C. FERNANDO and M. FERRARI (eds.), *Handbook of Resilience in Children of War*, Springer-Verlag, New York, 2013.

TOMUSCHAT C., 'Reparation for Victims of Grave Human Rights Violations', (2002) 10 *Tulane Journal of International and Comparative Law*.

TOMUSCHAT C., 'The Legacy of Nuremberg', (2006) 4 *Journal of International Criminal Justice*.

TOMUSCHAT C., 'Human Rights and International Humanitarian Law', (2010) 21 *The European Journal of International Law*.

TRACHTENBERG M., *Reparation in World Politics*, Columbia University Press, New York, 1980.

TRUMBULL C.P. IV, 'The Victims' Participation in International Criminal Proceedings', (2008) 29 *Michigan Journal of International Law*.

TURNER H.A., D. FINKELHOR and R. OMROD, 'Poly-victimisation in a National Sample of Children and Youth', (2010) 38 *American Journal of Preventative Medicine*.

Van Boven T., 'Victim-Oriented Perspectives: Rights and Realities', in T. Bonacker and C. Safferling (eds.), *Victims of International Crimes: An Interdisciplinary Discourse*, TMC Asser Press, The Hague, 2013.

Van de Voorde C. and R. Barberet, 'Children and International Criminal Justice', in M. Natarajan (ed.), *International Crime and Justice*, Cambridge University Press, Cambridge, 2011.

Van Sliedregt E., *The Criminal Responsibility of Individuals for Violations of International Humanitarian Law*, TMC Asser Press, The Hague, 2003.

Van bueren G., *International Documents on Children*, Martinus Nijhoff Publishers, The Hague, 1993.

Van Bueren G., *The International Law on the Rights of the Child*, Martinus Nijhoff Publishers, The Hague, 1998.

Ventevogel P., 'Child Mental Health, Psychosocial Well-Being and Resilience in Afghanistan: a Review and Future Directions', in C. Fernando and M. Ferrari (eds.), *Handbook of Resilience in Children of War*, Springer-Verlag, New York, 2013.

Wagner N., 'A Critical Assessment of Using Children to Participate Actively in Hostilities in Lubanga: Child Soldiers and Direct Participation', (2013) 24 *Criminal Law Forum*.

Wemmers J.O., 'Where Do They Belong? Giving Victims a Place in the Criminal Justice Process', (2009) 20 *Criminal Law Forum*.

Werle G., 'Individual Criminal Responsibility in Article 25 ICC Statute', (2007) 5 *Journal of International Criminal Justice*.

Werner E.E., 'Children and War: Risk, Resilience, and Recovery', (2012) 24 *Development and Psychopathology*.

Wessells M., 'Children, Armed Conflict and Peace', (1998) 35 *Journal of Peace Research*.

Wessells M., *Child Soldiers: From Violence to Protection*, Harvard University Press, Cambridge, MA, 2006.

Wiersing A., 'Lubanga and its Implications for Victims Seeking Reparations at the International Criminal Court', (2012) 4 *Amsterdam Law Forum*.

Williamson J., 'The Disarmament, Demobilisation, and Reintegration of Child Soldiers: Social and Psychological Transformation in Sierra Leone', (2006) 4 *International Journal of Mental Health, Psychosocial Work, and Counselling in Areas of Armed Conflict*.

Wilson R.A., *The Politics of Truth and Reconciliation in South Africa: Legitimising the Post-Apartheid State*, Cambridge University Press, Cambridge, 2001.

Witte E., 'Beyond "Peace vs. Justice": Understanding the Relationship between DDR Programmes and the Prosecution of International Crimes', in A. Cutter Patel, P. de Greiff and L. Waldorf (eds.), *Disarming the Past: Transitional Justice and Ex-Combatants*, Social Science Research Council, New York, 2010

Wooldridge F. and O. Elias, 'Humanitarian Considerations in the Work of the United Nations Compensation Commission', (2003) 85 *International Review of the Red Cross*.

Wouters J. E. Brems, S. Smis and P. Schmitt, 'Accountability for Human Rights Violations by International Organisations: Introductory Remarks', in Wouters J., E. Brems, S. Smis and P. Schmitt (eds.), *Accountability for Human Rights Violations by International Organisations*, Intersentia, Antwerp, 2010.

Yehuda R., S.L. Halligan and L.M. Bierer, 'Relationship of Parental Trauma Exposure and PTSD to PTSD, Depressive and Anxiety Disorders in Offspring', (2001) 35 *Journal of Psychiatric Research*.

YEPES UPRIMNY R., 'Between Corrective and Distributive Justice: Reparations of Gross Human Rights Violations in Times of Transition', Inaugural Address of the UNESCO Chair in Education for Peace, Human Rights and Democracy, available at: http://www.uu.nl/university/research/EN/international_collaboration/latinamerica/Documents/OratieRodrigoUprimny.pdf.

ZACK-WILLIAMS T., 'When Children Become Killers: Child Soldiers in the Civil War in Sierra Leone', in C. FERNANDO and M. FERRARI (eds.), *Handbook of Resilience in Children of War*, Springer-Verlag, New York, 2013.

ZAMMIT BORDA A., 'The Role of Victims in the First Trial of the International Criminal Court', (2010) 9 *Trinity College Dublin Journal of Postgraduate Studies*.

ZEGVELD L., *The Accountability of Armed Opposition Groups in International Law*, Cambridge University Press, Cambridge, 2002.

ZEGVELD L., 'Remedies for Victims of Violations of International Humanitarian Law', (2003) 85 *International Review of the Red Cross*

ZEGVELD L., 'Victims' Reparations Claims and International Courts', (2010) 8 *Journal of International Criminal Justice*.

INDEX

H

I

Lightning Source UK Ltd.
Milton Keynes UK
UKOW05n0606081117
312354UK00001B/10/P

9 781780 684383